Expenses: A Civil Practitioner's Handbook

Expenses: A Civil Practitioner's Handbook

Iain W Nicol and James S Flett

EDINBURGH
University Press

Edinburgh University Press is one of the leading university presses in the UK. We publish academic books and journals in our selected subject areas across the humanities and social sciences, combining cutting-edge scholarship with high editorial and production values to produce academic works of lasting importance. For more information visit our website: edinburghuniversitypress.com

Edinburgh University Press Ltd
The Tun – Holyrood Road
12(2f) Jackson's Entry
Edinburgh EH8 8PJ

Typeset in 10/11 Plantin by
Cheshire Typesetting Ltd, Cuddington, Cheshire, and
printed and bound in Great Britain

A CIP record for this book is available from the British Library

ISBN 978 1 4744 8365 0 (hardback)
ISBN 978 1 4744 7739 0 (paperback)
ISBN 978 1 4744 7741 3 (webready PDF)
ISBN 978 1 4744 7740 6 (epub)

Contents

Foreword

I welcome this opportunity to provide the foreword to Iain Nicol and James Flett's book. I regard it as an honour to be asked to do so.

Iain is a well-respected legal practitioner in Scotland and is regarded as an expert in civil litigation in our jurisdiction, particularly in the field of personal injury law, where he and I have viewed our respective clients' interests, and prospects, from rather opposite ends of the telescope! Iain is a part-time sheriff and Fellow of the Association of Personal Injury Lawyers, he is accredited by the Law Society of Scotland as a specialist in personal injury law, and is convenor of their Civil Justice Committee, on which I have served with him for a number of years. He is a past member of the Scottish Civil Justice Council's Costs and Funding Committee. Most importantly of all, he has been and remains a hugely experienced and successful personal injury lawyer. He has had to grapple with the intricacies and details of our system in Scotland that governs the way in which parties to a civil litigation both pay for their own legal representation, and reclaim that from their opponent when, and if, successful.

James, as chairman of one of Scotland's largest and most respected firms of law accountants, has extensive knowledge and experience of all aspects of the taxation process, from the preparation of judicial accounts, negotiation of the accounts, to the conduct of lengthy and complex taxations.

So, I cannot think of a better qualified duo to author *Expenses: A Civil Practitioners Handbook*.

I was trained and mentored early on in my own career by a senior partner in my firm who carried around in his head more knowledge about the dark art of expenses than anyone else at that time, and subsequently became a hugely respected auditor of the Court of Session. One of the complaints I had at that time was that that knowledge and experience was inaccessible other than by mind-reading or, in his case, excellent training. Iain and James's book provides a much needed and welcome guide for a busy practitioner who does not have the time to trawl through the relevant legislation, which is, of course, available but often seemingly impenetrable. This book provides the ideal ready and easy reckoner and pulls together the relevant legislation in each chapter in the commentary sections. It is over thirty years since a similar update has been produced and it is very welcome indeed. The chapters dealing with qualified one-way cost shifting, success fee agreements and pursuers' offers, in particular, demonstrate how bang up-to-date this reference book is, and the comprehensive coverage of every aspect of the rules and law relating to the subject of expenses in civil litigation in Scotland makes this, in my view, a publication that should feature in every civil practitioner's library, physically or virtually.

I wholeheartedly welcome this new treatise on the essential law and practice relating to expenses, judicial or otherwise, governing civil litigation in Scotland. This book, I believe, will be of great assistance to the many civil practitioners in our jurisdiction, and as one of them I have no hesitation in commending it to them.

Gordon S Keyden
Clyde & Co (Scotland) LLP
Edinburgh
February 2022

Preface

If you have taken the trolley bus through Stanley Park in Vancouver, you may have noticed a statue that looks pretty much like a mermaid sitting by the waterside. To ensure his small band of tourists did not jump to the wrong conclusions, the friendly trolley driver/tour guide was quick to observe 'They think it's a mermaid, but it's no' a mermaid'.

Whilst somewhat similar to the Little Mermaid in Copenhagen, he explained it was a statue of a girl in a wet suit. The guide kept repeating the fact that it wasn't what it appeared to be and somehow managed to hold the interest of his patrons, even though, in the overall scheme of things, no one on the trolley could have cared less if it was a mermaid or not.

By the same token, and to avoid any misunderstandings, this is not a textbook. It does not seek to emulate the styles of the weighty tome that is McLaren from 1912 or the more recent offering from Hastings in 1989. Others will doubtless produce more academic and authoritative works. This is simply, and unashamedly, a handbook written by practitioners for practitioners. We would also be delighted if law students could, as part of their studies, be introduced to some of the topics to give them a head start. All too often, our experience is that junior lawyers have little or no understanding of expenses issues and have no idea where to turn to find out the answers.

We want to provide a readily accessible source of information on what is an ever-changing area of civil practice. We felt there was a need for something that could bring together the old and the new, include extracts from legislation, court rules and judgments where it might be useful to see those set out in the body of the book rather than go hunting for them elsewhere. We wanted to create something that is user friendly. We cannot offer all the answers, not least because the jurisprudence in some areas (such as qualified one-way cost shifting) is so new, there is no precedent, in Scotland. In that situation we have attempted to set out some of the issues that may be relevant to the arguments to be adopted in court. Unfortunately, Amazon do not yet have a crystal ball that predicts outcomes in the civil courts so we have to make do with our professional judgement and experience. Practitioners will come up with their own arguments but hopefully this is a helpful start.

The book is an outline of the expenses position as at November 2021. The new court rules on mode of attendance will no doubt be published before this book sees the light of day. The impact of COVID-19 on civil business has not been resolved. Who knows what the future holds. Amazon need to hurry up with a crystal ball. It seems likely that there will continue to be extensive change in work practices in the civil courts that brings an urgent need to develop new parts to the tables of fees to ensure the work that is required as part of adapting to the COVID-19 crisis is appropriately remunerated. To highlight a couple of examples, courts are insisting more and more on lodging written submissions. There is no provision in the tables for solicitors' fees for that work.

Also, the extra work that is generated for agents in arranging and conducting fully virtual or hybrid proofs needs to be considered and the tables of fees altered to reflect that. Various experienced solicitors have anecdotally recounted to us that additional personnel are required to ensure that everything is in place from an IT perspective, that contact is maintained with witnesses to let them know when they will be needed, that good communication links are in place between agent and counsel and the client if they are in different locations. There is a minutiae of detail that is not yet adequately reflected in the fee tables.

It is all a moveable feast and the concern is that the pace of change results in important aspects of costs and funding matters being overlooked. At the moment all there has been is a consultation on mode of attendance that has been conducted prior to the civil courts reopening to any real extent for in-person hearings. There is therefore a lack of empirical data to justify medium to long-term change. We simply hope that the appropriate time is taken to reflect on what has worked well, what has not and what the consequences of changes will be. Take stock. There is no rush to force permanent change through and it should only be done if the evidence from court users clearly indicates that the new system will be better than the old.

Finally, we wish to extend our deepest gratitude to those who have contributed to this book namely John West, who at the time was a family law solicitor at SKO, Gordon Bathgate, partner at Allan McDougall & Co and Simon Nolan, partner at Nolans, Solicitors who wrote the chapters on family law, employment and simple procedure respectively. And to Peter Nicholson, the editor of the Journal of the Law Society of Scotland who provided his invaluable editing skills and useful suggestions for revisions. Thank you for all your help in putting this handbook together.

Iain Nicol, Thorntons Law LLP
James Flett, Alex Quinn & Partners Ltd
February 2022

Table of Statutes

Table entries relating to the text are given by paragraph number; those relating to appendices have the prefix 'App' followed by page number.

Table of Orders, Rules and Regulations

Table entries relating to the text are given by paragraph number; those relating to appendices have the prefix 'App' followed by page number.

Table of Cases

Chapter 1

Law Society of Scotland Rules and Guidance on Fees

Notwithstanding any rule of court or legislative requirement in relation to **1.01** solicitors' fee charging, a solicitor has a professional obligation to issue a client with a letter of engagement in terms of the client communications section of the Law Society of Scotland's practice rules and guidance 2011,[1] s. B4 of which provides:

4.1 In this r. 4, unless the context otherwise requires, terms listed in the first column of r. 4.1 shall have the meanings respectively ascribed to them in the second column of that rule:

Term	Definition
advice and assistance	advice and assistance as defined in section 6(1) of the 1986 Act to which Part II of the *1986 Act* applies
client	a person who instructs a *regulated person* or to whom a *regulated person* tenders for business
legal aid	the meaning given to it in section 41 of the *1986 Act*
special urgency work	the meaning given to it in Regulation 18 of the Civil Legal Aid (Scotland) Regulations 2002 (SSI 2002 No.494)

4.2 When tendering for business or at the earliest practical opportunity upon receiving instructions to undertake any work on behalf of a client, you shall provide the following information to the client in writing:

(a) an outline of the work to be carried out on behalf of the client;

(b) save where the client is being provided with legal aid or advice and assistance, details of either—

(i) an estimate of the total fee to be charged for the work, including VAT and outlays which may be incurred in the course of the work; or

(ii) the basis upon which a fee will be charged for the work, including VAT and outlays which may be incurred in the course of the work;

(c) if the client is being provided with advice and assistance or legal aid—

(i) where advice and assistance is being provided, details of the level of contribution required from the client, and

(ii) where civil legal aid, special urgency work or advice and assistance is being provided, an indication of the factors which may affect any contribution which may be required from the client or any payment which may be required from property recovered or preserved;

(d) the identity of the person or persons who will principally carry out the work on behalf of the client the identity of the person whom the client should contact if the client becomes concerned in any way with the manner in which the work is being carried out; and

---

1 Law Society of Scotland, *https://www.lawscot.org.uk/members/rules-and-guidance/rules-and-guidance/*.

(f) confirmation that if that person is unable to resolve any such concerns to the satisfaction of the client, the client may make a complaint to the Scottish Legal Complaints Commission (setting out its current contact details) about the manner in which the work is being or has been carried out, or the conduct of the person or persons carrying out the work.

4.3 Where a client regularly instructs you in the same type of work, he need not be provided with the information set out in rule 4.2 in relation to a new instruction to do that type of work, provided that he has previously been supplied with that information in relation to a previous instruction to do that type of work and is informed of any differences between that information and the information which, if this rule 4.3 did not apply, would have been required to be provided to him in terms of rule 4.2.

4.4 Where there is no practical opportunity for you to provide the information set out in rule 4.2 to a client before the conclusion of the relevant work for that client then that information need not be provided to that client.

4.5 Where a client is a child under the age of 12 years then the information set out in rule 4.2 need not be provided to that client.

1.02   Failure to issue a letter of engagement, or to do so timeously, can give rise to a finding of professional misconduct.

In addition, a solicitor should heed the guidance issued by the Law Society in relation to the preparation of their business accounts and taxation of such accounts.

FEEING

1.03   Section E, Division C of the Law Society of Scotland's rules and guidance provides as follows:

Fees:

NOTE:
*This guidance does **not** apply to the taxation of solicitors' accounts remitted to the Auditor of the Court of Session in terms of Rule 42.7 of the Rules of the Court of Session or to a Sheriff Court Auditor in terms of the Act of Sederunt (Solicitor and Client Accounts in the Sheriff Court) 1992 (SI 1992 No 1434);*

1. Business Accounts – preparation and presentation

(a) The form in which a solicitor presents a business account is a matter for the solicitor's personal preference but if the person liable to pay requires details, the solicitor must give a narrative or summary sufficient to indicate the nature and the extent of the work done. If a breakdown is requested the solicitor should give such information as can readily be derived from the records, such as the total recorded time spent, the number and length of meetings, the number of letters and of telephone calls. No charge may be made for preparing the note of fee or for the provision of such information. However if having been given such information the party paying insists on a fully itemised account, the cost of preparing that may be charged to them.

(b) A solicitor may submit his file to a law accountant or auditor for assessment of the fee either before or after the note of fee is issued, but it is stressed that a unilateral reference of this kind does not constitute a taxation. Such an assessment of a fee must never be represented as a taxation; as having any official status; or as being final and binding. The fee for such a reference is not chargeable to the party paying unless that has been included in the terms of business intimated to the client at the outset. If a note of fee which has been assessed in this way requires to be taxed (see 2 below), it should be taxed by an Auditor of Court.

Where a solicitor acts:

- as an administrator of a client's funds under a power of attorney where the granter is incapable; or
- in a representative capacity, e.g. a sole executor

he should consider having a fee note prepared by an Auditor of Court.

2. Joint Remit for Taxation

A solicitor and client may agree that the solicitor's fee should be taxed by an Auditor of Court in advance of a note of fee being issued. Only a small number of court auditors are permitted to carry out such a taxation.

The solicitor and client should sign a joint remit to the Auditor in terms similar to the following:

> *(place) (date). I, AB (client) and we, Messrs E & F, Solicitors, hereby request the Auditor of the (Sheriff Court of .... /Court of Session) to tax the remuneration due and payable to the Solicitors for their whole work and responsibility in connection with (matter) and agree that the Auditor's decision on matters of taxation will be final and binding. [In executry add – The Auditor's fee for carrying out the taxation will be payable out of the estate before distribution to residuary beneficiaries]*
>
> *Signed: AB, E & F*

This precise wording however is not essential. All the Auditor requires is to be satisfied that both parties accept that the taxation will be binding. Any reasonable written record of such an agreement will be sufficient for the Auditor.

A formal diet of taxation will not usually be required in these cases.

3. Taxation of disputed business accounts

(a) If an account continues to be disputed after the provision of the information set out in 1(a) above, the solicitor must inform the paying party of the availability of taxation by an Auditor of Court, and of the procedure involved. If the payer has not requested a fully itemised account, the solicitor may have such an account prepared at his own expense. That full account may be submitted for taxation even if it is for a greater amount than the original note of fee.

(b) A solicitor who is a co-executor with an unqualified person must not make a unilateral reference for taxation. Such a reference needs the concurrence of the other executor.

(c) The solicitor cannot refuse to agree to taxation unless the client is to pay the account and the solicitor and client have entered into a written fee charging agreement in which the actual fee has been agreed, as opposed to the basis on which the fee is to be charged. Refusal to submit the account for taxation may lead to a conduct complaint.

(d) The solicitor and client should agree which Auditor will tax the account, failing which the account should be taxed by the Auditor of the Court of Session.

(e) The solicitor must then forthwith submit the file and all relevant information including the note of fee or detailed account to the chosen Auditor who will decide whether to proceed by way of oral or written representations. If there is to be an oral hearing this will be intimated to the client and the solicitor. There will be no appeal against the decision on whether to have an oral hearing or to proceed by written representations. If it is to proceed by way of written submissions, each party will be made fully aware of the other's representations.

(f) The decision of an Auditor on matters of taxation of business accounts will be final and binding. However the client or party paying is entitled to refer a complaint of inadequate service by the solicitor to the Scottish Legal Complaints Commission irrespective of the outcome of the taxation.

4. Charge for taxation

If the taxation is by an Auditor a fee, usually of 5% of the amount of the account as presented for taxation, will be charged, and may attract VAT.

In the case of disputed business accounts, any award of expenses of a taxation - not only the Auditor's fee (which may be apportioned between the solicitor and the client) but also the time and expenses of parties attending – is wholly within the discretion of the Auditor. If the matter is settled within the seven days preceding the arranged oral hearing, the Auditor may still charge a proportion of his fee, not exceeding 50%, at his discretion.

1.04   Whilst the foregoing represents guidance as opposed to a professional practice rule, such guidance, if breached, can give rise to a basis of complaints to the Scottish Legal Complaints Commission.

1.05   Whilst a solicitor can delegate work to other solicitors in the practice, they cannot delegate responsibility for compliance with professional practice rules. A principal solicitor has the duty to supervise all aspects of their practice, including such fees as are rendered and transferred.[2]

1.06   Submitting a fee note for grossly excessive fees, whether knowingly or recklessly, is prohibited.[3]

1.07   It is fundamentally important to comply with the solicitors' accounts rules.[4] In the case of Discipline Tribunal Decision 723/97 a firm, to assist with its poor cash flow, had rendered fees in executry cases at a level that was necessary to meet the firm's financial requirements each week regardless of the amount of work done in the executry. The fees generated were grossly excessive for the work carried out. The Solicitors' Discipline Tribunal held that whilst interim feeing was permitted, the fees had to be commensurate with the work actually undertaken and in this case the solicitor was indirectly using client money to fund his practice when the level of the interim fees were not justified. This resulted in a lengthy suspension from practice.

1.08   Several other examples of grossly excessive fee charging have resulted in fines, suspensions of practising certificates or striking off the roll of solicitors.[5]

The gravity of the offence is heightened where the client is vulnerable, e.g. where the solicitor is acting under a power of attorney in relation to the client's affairs. If the solicitor is acting as sole executor in an executry estate great care should be taken to ensure no excessive fee is charged and consideration should be given to having the file assessed by the Auditor of Court as per the Law Society of Scotland guidance.

REFERRAL FEES AND PROHIBITION ON FEE SHARING

1.09   In England, referral fees were banned with effect from 1 April 2013 by the Legal Aid, Sentencing and Punishment of Offenders Act 2012. However, the Taylor Report recommended the retention of referral fees in Scotland as it was likely to prove too difficult to enforce a ban and too difficult to distinguish referral fees from other forms of marketing expenditure.

---

2 *MacColl v Council of the Law Society of Scotland* 1987 SLT 524.
3 Solicitors (Scotland) Act 1980 s. 39A, which applies whether or not the fees have been paid by the client.
4 The Scottish solicitors' accounts rules are to be found on the Law Society of Scotland's website: *http://www.lawscot.org.uk* (last accessed 11 February 2022).
5 Discipline Tribunal Decision McQuitty (11/08/02); Discipline Tribunal Decision McCormick (11/01/06); Discipline Tribunal Decision Sykes (19/12/07); Discipline Tribunal Decision Pirie 930/96.

The position in relation to solicitors in Scotland is covered by rule B.3.5(a) **1.10**
and the guidance thereto (advertising fees), together with rule D9 and the guidance thereto (multi-disciplinary practices), of the Law Society of Scotland's
practice rules and guidance 2011, which provide:

Rule B3.5(a) Any advertisement or promotional material issued by you or on your
behalf or any promotional activity by you or on your behalf shall be decent and shall
not:

(a) contain any inaccuracy or misleading statement;

B.3 Guidance:
Where your fees for your services are advertised either by you or by a third party
and whether or not you are named in such an advertisement the advertisement must
include mention of outlays and VAT with no less prominence than the fees. Where
"legal fees" or similar expressions are used, the fees quoted should be the fees to be
charged by you and the figure quoted should not conceal a commission or referral
fee to be paid to a third party. Any such commission or referral fee should be shown
separately.

Failure to mention outlays and VAT with no less prominence than the fees may be
regarded as misleading and inaccurate and therefore in breach of rule B3.5. In terms
of rule A4, such a breach may be treated as professional misconduct.

Systems should be put in place to ensure that any outsourced provider of your
services complies with this Rule'.

Rule D9.2.1
In this rule 9.2, unless the context otherwise requires, terms listed in the first column
of rule 9.2.1 shall have the meanings respectively ascribed to them in the second
column of that rule:

Term	Definition
citizens advice body	as defined in s65(1) of the *1980 Act*
law centre	as defined in s65(1) of the *1980 Act*
lawyer	an *advocate,* a law centre, a citizens advice body, a *licensed provider* (or a member, director or employee of, or partner or investor in, a *licensed provider*) or a legal practitioner offering legal services to the public who is qualified and licensed to practise in accordance with the law of a legal jurisdiction other than that of Scotland, and includes a firm of lawyers, a European Economic Interest Group the membership of which is exclusively lawyers, an incorporated practice of lawyers and any association (whether corporate or unincorporate) consisting exclusively of lawyers or exclusively of lawyers and *regulated person*s
overheads	costs and expenses incurred by a *practice unit* in the running of its business which may include the costs of services provided to the *practice unit* (including services in relation to the advertisement and promotion of the *practice unit*) but shall exclude any payment purely for the introduction or referral of clients or business to the *practice unit* or any of its directors, members or employees save for any fee paid by the *practice unit* for its inclusion on a panel of legal advisers to whom referrals of business may be made provided that such fee is not expressed as a proportion of the fees generated from the business so referred
unqualified person	as defined in s65(1) of the *1980 Act*

9.2.2 You shall not share with any unqualified person any profits or fees or fee derived from any business transacted by you of a kind which is commonly carried on by *regulated person*s in Scotland in the course of or in connection with their practice; provided always that:
(a) a *practice unit* may pay its overheads out of income from fees; and
(b) the provisions of this rule shall not apply to the sharing of profits or fees where:
  (i)   a person who has ceased to practise as a *regulated person* shall receive from any *regulated person* a share of the profits or fees of the latter, as a price or value of the business which he has transferred to the latter or shall receive a share of such profits as a voluntary or other allowance out of the profits or fees of a business in which he had been a *manager*; or
  (ii) the widow, widower, civil partner, heirs, executors, representatives, next of kin or dependants of any deceased *regulated person* receive from any *regulated person* who has purchased or succeeded to the business of such deceased *regulated person* or from any *practice unit* of which such deceased *regulated person* was a *manager* at his death any share of the profits of such business; or
  (iii) the salary of any employee of a *regulated person* is partly or wholly paid in the form of a percentage on the profits of such *regulated person*'s business or any part thereof; or
  (iv) such profits or fees are received by any public officer in respect of work done in the course of his duty; or
  (v)   an agreement for sharing such profits or fees is made between a *regulated person* and a lawyer; or
  (vi) such profits or fees are received by an officer of a public body who is a *regulated person* or by the public body and are dealt with in accordance with statutory provisions.

Rule 9.2 Guidance:

Rule D9.2 prohibits solicitors and others from sharing "with any unqualified person any profits or fees or fee derived from any business transacted by you of a kind which is commonly carried on by regulated persons in Scotland in the course of or in connection with their practice"; with certain limited exceptions. Those exceptions are, broadly, (a) payment of overheads (as defined in the rule) and (b) retired partners ("managers" in the rule) and their executors, heirs or representatives; employees who are wholly employed in the practice unit; public officers in respect of work done in the course of their duty; and other lawyers – including lawyers in other jurisdictions – and law centres, citizens advice bodies and licensed legal services providers and those within them.

The Professional Practice Committee take the view that the principal type of arrangement which the rule prohibits is an arrangement to pay commission for the introduction of business on a case by case basis. Solicitors are entitled to pay for the cost of marketing or promoting the practice unit as part of their overheads. They are entitled to pay a fee to be included on a panel to whom referrals will be made provided that that fee is not expressed as a specific sum per referral or as a percentage of the fees chargeable for referred business. A flat fee is not in breach of the rules and that may be a fee which is reviewed periodically.

You are entitled to pay for the provision of services to the practice unit as part of overheads. Even if the service is provided by the person who introduces the client, you are entitled to pay for the service. However the service must be a real service and not merely the introduction of the client. The Committee has also decided that the carrying out of a money laundering check by the introducer would not, however, be a service for which payment could be made as that is an obligation on solicitors themselves in terms of the Accounts Rules (Rule B6). Services which have been accepted as not breaching the rules have included carrying out hearing tests; taking statements of witnesses; obtaining photographs of a locus; and completing a detailed client questionnaire relating to the particular matter in which the solicitor is instructed. The introduction of capital in return for a percentage of fees would be regarded as breaching the practice rules, but the provision of loan funds with a variable rate of interest expressed as a percentage of the funds advanced would not.

The inclusion of a commission paid to an introducer as an outlay in a solicitor's fee note – and not a hidden part of the fee – would not be in breach of the rules however the position would have to be made clear to the client at the outset in the terms of business.

Finally solicitors and others are of course entitled to receive commission from third parties for the introduction of business, but the existence of such arrangements should be disclosed to the client although the actual amount of commission does not need to be disclosed unless the client specifically seeks that information. Such commission received must relate to any work undertaken by the solicitors in connection with the business referred. If no work has been undertaken, unless the commission is of a nominal amount it should be accounted for to the client.

COMMENTARY

- There is a ban on a solicitor or practice unit sharing its profits with an **1.11** unqualified person where the fee arises from work that is commonly carried out by a regulated person.
- 'Unqualified person' includes claims management companies and lead generators.
- Advertising costs are allowed as an overhead but any fee paid purely for the introduction or referral of a client is prohibited unless:
  (a) a block fee is paid for a tranche of business as opposed to paying for referrals on a case-by-case basis; or
  (b) the solicitor is paying for a meaningful service that is provided by the referrer, e.g. supplying a precognition or completed questionnaire; or
  (c) the fee is paid to be a member of a panel; and the fee is not expressed as a percentage of the fee that the referral work will generate.
- As fiduciary agents, solicitors may not retain commissions or payments from third parties without disclosure of the arrangement to the client. The amount of the commission does not require to be disclosed unless the client requests details but the commission can only be retained if it relates to work performed by the client, otherwise, leaving aside nominal sums, commission needs to be paid to the client.
- The Law Society of Scotland have recently become the regulator for Alternative Business Structures although no date has been set, at the time of publication, as to when ABS structures will be permitted. As and when ABSs are permitted, the rules and guidance on fee sharing will have to be altered. For further information see the section on the Law Society's website under licensed legal services providers.

Chapter 2

Pre-Action Protocols

VOLUNTARY PRE-ACTION PROTOCOL FOR PERSONAL INJURY CLAIMS (VPAP)

2.01 Prior to 1 January 2006, there was no suggested structure for the handling of personal injury claims in Scotland. There was no protocol to give an outline of what should be done and when. Any claims that settled pre-litigation generally followed the pattern of intimating a claim and waiting for a decision from the insurer (which could take an inordinate length of time). Agents took as long as they wanted to ingather the quantum information and disclosed what they wanted to the insurer in the hope an acceptable offer would be received. There may then have followed some negotiation and hopefully, settlement, failing which litigation would ensue at some point. The timescales for resolution of a claim varied enormously depending on which insurer was involved and how efficient parties were in carrying out the claims handling process.

2.02 If a claim did settle, costs in accordance with Ch. 10 of the Law Society of Scotland's General Table of Fees were generally paid by insurers in addition to the compensation, but it was by no means compulsory for the insurers to make any payment of pre-litigation costs.

2.03 In 2005, Ch. 10 was abolished. Around the same time, the Law Society of Scotland and the Forum of Scottish Claims Managers devised a pre-action protocol for personal injury claims. This voluntary protocol – commonly referred to as VPAP – applies to personal injury claims, valued at £10,000 or less, that settle on or after 1 January 2006 with the exception of clinical negligence, disease and illness cases.

2.04 With the advent of the Compulsory Pre-Action Protocol (CPAP) in 2016, the applicability of VPAP is fast diminishing for claims made by adults but it will, subject to the terms of VPAP, continue to apply to any accident claim that occurred prior to 28 November 2016. Claims for children arising from accidents prior to that date can therefore still be subject to VPAP, since a child's claim will not usually time bar until their nineteenth birthday.

2.05 The aims of VPAP are:

- to put parties in a position where they may be able to settle cases fairly and without litigation;
- to ensure the early provision of reliable information reasonably required to enter into meaningful discussions on liability and quantum; and
- to enable appropriate offers to be made either before or after litigation commences.

VPAP is reproduced in full in Appendix 1 and it sets out a structure of reason-   **2.06**
able timescales for obtaining a decision, not only on liability after intimation
of a claim but also on obtaining and disclosing medical and other quantum
evidence, together with timescales for negotiation and settlement. It also sets
out a new fee scale that applies to any claim that settles after 1 January 2006
where there is agreement that VPAP applies. In essence, the fee scale creates
an additional element to the former Ch. 10 scale by adding an investigation
fee.

A fee of £370 is added for claims that settle for £1,500 or less, whereas   **2.07**
£810 is added for claims that settle for more than £1,500. In addition, a
completion fee is payable based on the old Ch. 10 scale:

- 25 per cent of the first £2,500 of damages.
- 15 per cent of the next £2,500.
- 7.5 per cent of the next £5,000.
- 5 per cent of the next £10,000.
- 2.5 per cent of the excess.

Examples
For a settlement of £1,400 the fee is:

- Investigation fee: £370.
- Completion fee: £350.
- Total fee: £720.

For a settlement of £30,000 the fee is:

- Investigation fee: £810.
- Completion fee: £2,125 (£625 + £375 + £375 + £500 + £250).
- Total fee: £2,935.

To the total fees are added VAT and any reasonably incurred outlays. It would   **2.08**
be unusual, but not unheard of, for counsel's fees and VAT to be claimed
as an outlay. Whether or not an outlay is justified depends on the specific
circumstances of each case.

Style letters for intimating and responding to claims and instructing medical   **2.09**
experts form part of VPAP, as does an extensive list of 'standard disclosure'
documents for different types of claim.

VPAP is not without its limitations. As the name suggests, it is voluntary.   **2.10**
Appendix 1 also lists approximately thirty-five insurers or brokers who are
signatories to it, but even as signatories, it was always open to them to decline
to agree to the protocol on a case-by-case basis. Furthermore, a number of
insurers and self-insured organisations simply refused to agree to work to the
protocol. That may have been due to a reluctance to be bound by a set method
of claims handling, or an unwillingness to be bound by the applicable fee scale,
usually opting instead to pay costs under the old Ch. 10 scale.

VPAP was intended to apply to claims worth up to £10,000. Parties were   **2.11**
always at liberty to agree to it applying in higher value cases and, indeed, the
fee scale makes provision for fees to be calculated based on settlements of
more than £10,000. However, an admission of liability issued by an insurer
in response to a claim is only binding on the insurer if the value of the claim
is £10,000 or less. If parties had agreed to VPAP applying at the outset and
it then becomes clear that the claim is going to be worth more than £10,000,

the insurer is not bound by any admission of liability, unless made as part of a bilateral agreement concluded between the parties, or as a unilateral obligation by the defender with the intention of being bound by the admission. This is discussed in more detail below.

DEVELOPMENTS SINCE 2006

2.12   Within a relatively short space of time after the introduction of VPAP, the question of the use of pre-action protocols was looked at in detail. The then Lord Justice Clerk, the Rt Hon Lord Gill, published his *Report on the Scottish Civil Courts Review* in September 2009. Section 8 of that report deals with pre-action protocols (Vol. 1, pp. 175–195). The review quotes anecdotal evidence from personal injury practitioners which suggested that VPAP was not being adopted across the board and, where it was being used, the insurers regularly failed to comply with the time limits set down for issuing decisions on liability or making settlement offers. There was a tendency from some insurers to offer 'below value' settlements using computer programs designed for that purpose. Further, some insurers would deliberately refrain from making pre-litigation offers because it was less expensive for them to wait until the case was litigated and immediately lodge a tender rather than pay the protocol fees.

2.13   A consultation exercise into the use of pre-action protocols led to the following recommendations:

- the creation of a Scottish Civil Justice Council that would be tasked, amongst other things, with the development, extension and adaptation of pre-action protocols;
- the personal injury protocol should be compulsory;
- the compulsory protocol should apply to all types of personal injury claim, albeit a separate medical negligence protocol ought to be devised;
- a higher limit should apply to the value of claims to be dealt with under the protocol – £50,000 was suggested; and
- there should be sanctions for non-compliance.

COMPULSORY PRE-ACTION PROTOCOL FOR PERSONAL INJURY (CPAP)

2.14   The Scottish Civil Justice Council was duly constituted on 28 May 2013 and, through its Personal Injury and Costs and Funding committees, set about the task of creating a CPAP for personal injury.

2.15   CPAP was introduced by Act of Sederunt,[1] which added a new Ch. 3A and Appendix 4 to the Act of Sederunt (Sheriff Court Ordinary Cause Rules) 1993[2] (Ordinary Cause Rules) and a new Ch. 4A and Appendix 1A to the Act of Sederunt (Summary Cause Rules) 2002.[3] It came into force on 28 November 2016. A copy of the amending Act of Sederunt can be found in Appendix 1.

---

1 Act of Sederunt (Sheriff Court Rules Amendment) (Personal Injury Pre-Action Protocol) 2016 (SSI 2016/215).
2 Act of Sederunt (Sheriff Court Ordinary Cause Rules) 1993 (SI 1993/1956) (OCR).
3 Act of Sederunt (Summary Cause Rules) 2002 (SI 2002/132).

In cases where CPAP applies, the court normally expects parties to have complied with it prior to proceedings being commenced.

If a sheriff considers that a party either failed without just cause to comply **2.16** with the requirements of CPAP, or unreasonably failed to accept an offer made in accordance with it, or lodged as a tender prior to the lodging of defences, they can:

- sist the action to allow any party to comply with the requirements of the protocol;
- make an award of expenses against the non-compliant party;
- modify an award of expenses; or
- make an award regarding the interest payable on any award of damages.[4]

The sheriff is required to consider the nature of the breach and the conduct of the parties during the protocol.[5] The wide discretionary powers that a court has in relation to expenses are not restricted by these new provisions.

Schedules 1 and 2 to the Act of Sederunt contain the new Appendices 4 and **2.17** 1A setting out the terms of CPAP. The protocol applies to all personal injury damages claims unless:

- the claimant reasonably estimates that the total liability value of the claim exclusive of interest exceeds £25,000;
- the accident or circumstances giving rise to the claim occurred before 28 November 2016;
- the claimant is not represented by a solicitor during the stages of the protocol; or
- the injuries arise from alleged clinical negligence, professional negligence or take the form of a disease.

It should be noted that the claimant, and only the claimant, is the one to **2.18** make a reasonable assessment of the likely value to determine whether the protocol applies. But the use of the word 'reasonably' leaves that assessment open to objective assessment by a court in any dispute that may arise as to the protocol's applicability. This may be important in any argument over non-compliance and whether sanctions should apply.

Further, the protocol still applies if the defender is not represented or if the defender is uninsured – the disapplication of the protocol only applies where the claimant is not represented by a solicitor.

The whole ethos of the protocol is to assist parties in resolving their dispute **2.19** without the need for litigation. It specifically seeks to encourage the fair, just and timely settlement of disputes prior to litigation. It promotes good practice regarding early and full disclosure of information, the investigation of the circumstances and the narrowing of the issues should a case have to be litigated.

If it becomes clear to the claimant that the value of the claim is going to **2.20** exceed £25,000, the onus is on the claimant to draw that to the attention of the opponent. In that event, there is no compulsion to continue following the protocol but parties can, if they wish, choose to do so.

The recommended method of intimation of any CPAP document is by **2.21** email, failing which it should be sent by recorded delivery post.

---

4 OCR r. 3A.3(2).
5 OCR r. 3A.3(4).

CPAP states that proceedings should only be commenced if:

- all stages of the protocol have been completed without reaching settlement;
- the defender fails to complete a stage of the protocol within the prescribed period;
- the defender refuses to admit liability, or does so by making it clear they do not intend to be bound by the admission;
- contributory negligence, or the extent thereof, is disputed;
- settlement is not implemented within five weeks of the date settlement terms were agreed; or
- it is necessary to do so for time bar reasons.

2.23 Paragraphs 11–35 of the protocol set out a nine-stage process for compliance:

- Stage 1: Issuing of claim form.
- Stage 2: The defender's acknowledgment of the claim.
- Stage 3: The defender's investigation of the claim and response thereto.
- Stage 4: Disclosure of documents and reports following admission of liability.
- Stage 5: Issuing of statement of valuation.
- Stage 6: Offer of settlement.
- Stage 7: Claimant's response to offer of settlement, including the fee scale applicable if the case settles.
- Stage 8: Stocktaking period.
- Stage 9: Payment.

2.24 The full protocol is reproduced in Appendix 1 and the terms are largely self-explanatory. However, it should be borne in mind that the conduct of the parties may well be subject to scrutiny by the court if a dispute on compliance arises. Agents would be wise to regularly self-evaluate their conduct when making decisions as to how to handle protocol compliance issues and bear in mind that the court may well expect not only the letter of the protocol to be complied with but also the spirit of the protocol.

2.25 The main aspects to be alert to are:

(1) A suggested style of claim form is included in Annex A of the protocol, depending on whether or not the insurers of the defender are known. Sufficient information should be contained in the intimation form to give the opponent fair notice of the issues to enable them to carry out an investigation and reach a view on liability.

(2) The claim should be acknowledged by the defender (or their insurer) within twenty-one days of receipt – if intimated by email the twenty-one days runs from the day the email was sent or, in the case of recorded delivery, the day after the letter was sent.

(3) A decision on liability must be issued within three months of receipt of the claim. Contrast that with VPAP where the three-month period runs from the date the insurers acknowledge receipt of the claim, which they are obliged to do within twenty-one days of the claim being intimated.

(4) The insurers are required to state whether any admission is intended to be binding. If they fail to admit liability or fail to confirm they intend to be bound by the admission, it is open to the pursuer to raise proceedings. Denials of liability should be accompanied by relevant documentation to

justify the decision, where such documents would otherwise be recoverable. There is no compulsion on the part of the opponent to disclose documentation that would otherwise be privileged.

(5) Contributory negligence issues, if relevant, need to be canvassed before proceedings are raised.

(6) Medical evidence should be disclosed at the earliest opportunity and in any event no more than five weeks after the admission unless there is a good reason to depart from that time scale.

(7) A valuation in the form PI6 of the Ordinary Cause Rules should be sent as soon as the quantum information is available and the defenders have five weeks to make an offer or ask for any additional information needed to make an offer. Such information should be supplied by the claimant within fourteen days.

(8) Only in cases where the injuries are minor and no medical treatment is sought can an offer be made to settle without a medical report. Otherwise, medical evidence has to be obtained.

(9) Offers in settlement have to be accompanied by an offer to pay expenses; see para. 2.26 below.

(10) Fourteen days are allowed to accept an offer or ask for additional information to consider an offer, which must be responded to by the opponent within twenty-one days. Reasons must be given if an offer is rejected or a counter-offer made.

(11) No proceedings should be raised for a period of at least fourteen days after the reasoned response is issued to enable the parties to reflect on their positions and negotiate further if desired.

(12) Payment of both the damages and expenses have to be made within five weeks of settlement terms being agreed, failing which interest at the judicial rate is payable on whatever amount of damages and expenses is outstanding.

(13) Annex B to the protocol contains a list of documents that would constitute standard disclosure depending on the type of case.

The Costs and Funding Committee of the Scottish Civil Justice Council set up **2.26** a working group to devise an appropriate fee scale. The fee scale that applies under CPAP differs in some material respects to the scale under VPAP.

It was recognised that each claim has a core element of work that requires to be undertaken regardless of the value so a fixed fee element of £546, equating to 3.5 hours of work at £156 per hour is included in the new scale.

In addition to that, and to try to make the new table inflation-proof, the **2.27** second element of the new scale prescribes a charge of 3.5 per cent of the value of the claim, capped at damages of £25,000. In practice, some insurers do not insist on the cap in higher value claims and will simply pay the 3.5 per cent on the full value. The third element of the new scale is similar to the method of charging the completion fee under VPAP but with different bands:

• 25 per cent of the agreed damages up to £3,000.
• 15 per cent of damages between £3,000 and £6,000.
• 7.5 per cent of damages between £6,000 and £12,000.
• 5 per cent of damages between £12,000 and £18,000.
• 2.5 per cent of damages over £18,000.

In addition, VAT and reasonably incurred outlays are chargeable.

For example, a claim that settles for £30,000, where the parties have agreed to the application of CPAP, results in a fee of:

- Part 1: £546 plus.
- Part 2: £875 (3.5 per cent of the capped maximum of £25,000).
- Part 3: £2,250 (£750 + £450 + £450 + £300 + £300).
- Total fee: £3,671.
- Plus VAT and outlays.

Consideration of some of the judicial decisions on expenses that have arisen in relation to conduct of agents or parties can be found in Chapter 6.

PRE-LITIGATION ADMISSIONS OF LIABILITY

2.28   It was a common feature under VPAP that insurers or claims handlers would fail to formally admit liability. Often, decisions on liability would be couched in terms such as, 'we are prepared to deal with your client's claim subject to production of satisfactory evidence of losses. We reserve our rights in relation to causation'. This presented the pursuer's agents with a dilemma. Do they take at face value an apparent willingness to explore the possibility of settlement or, given the absence of a clear and binding admission, do they litigate? The latter course could have adverse implications for expenses on the basis that an action is raised prematurely as illustrated in *McIlvaney v A Gordon & Co Ltd*.[6]

2.29   *McIlvaney v A Gordon & Co Ltd* was an action for damages arising out of an accident at work. The pursuer's agent sought to have the claim conducted under the protocol, which the defenders' insurers refused. There was, however, a pre-litigation offer of £6,000 made to the pursuer, which was rejected. Proceedings were raised in the Court of Session. The defenders lodged a minute of tender in the sum of £6,000, which was formally accepted by the pursuer. The Lord Ordinary acceded to the defenders' motion to modify the pursuer's expenses to nil.

2.30   However, consider the approach taken by Lord Boyd in *Brown v Sabre Insurance*.[7] In this case the defenders, pre-litigation, 'confirmed that liability was not an issue'. They otherwise refused to agree to the protocol applying. They indicated a willingness to negotiate on receipt of a medical report and any vouching. None was produced. The pursuer raised proceedings. A minute of tender in the sum of £3,500 was lodged. The pursuer enrolled a motion, *inter alia*, for decree in terms of the tender, seeking expenses on the summary cause scale. The defenders sought modification of the pursuer's expenses to nil on the basis that the litigation was premature and unnecessary as no medical evidence had been produced pre-litigation.

2.31   Lord Boyd recognised the benefits of VPAP. He was alert to the fact that there may be access to justice problems in smaller value claims if a pursuer cannot recover a proper and reasonable amount of expenses. Solicitors may not be inclined to take on such cases, or the value of the work done compared

6   *McIlvaney v A Gordon & Co Ltd* [2010] CSOH 118.
7   *Brown v Sabre Insurance* [2013] CSOH 51.

to the expenses recovered may mean the pursuer has to bear a shortfall in expenses out of their compensation and end up receiving substantially less. Lord Boyd held that the pursuer was 'entitled to raise the action in the absence of agreement to negotiate under the protocol' (para. 19). He found the pursuer entitled to expenses on the summary cause scale but modified those expenses by 15 per cent to reflect the fact that medical evidence should have been disclosed at an earlier stage.

WITHDRAWALS OF ADMISSIONS OF LIABILITY

Situations often arise in practice where pursuers have been assuming that **2.32** liability is not in dispute only for an apparent admission to be withdrawn. They may well have ceased carrying out any liability investigations reliant on a perceived willingness of insurers to settle. They may have reached the stage of submitting their valuation to the insurers in good faith with full disclosure of all quantum information and then receive the dreaded letter saying 'we are withdrawing our admission of liability'. The pursuer would then have to revisit the issue of liability potentially many months, if not years, after the accident and face insurmountable difficulties in carrying out investigations at that stage. Liability investigations may well have been minimal at the time a claim was intimated with the pursuer's agent simply relying on the pursuer's own account. Witnesses would not necessarily be interviewed at length at the outset pending a decision on liability. When an admission is withdrawn any witnesses may, by that stage, be untraceable, uncooperative or even deceased. Reports from skilled witnesses on liability issues would not be ordered at the outset until the defender's stance on liability becomes clear. All of which is arguably justifiable as part of efficient case management and to avoid incurring potentially needless costs. But it is an approach not without risk.

The problem was highlighted in the case of *Van Klaveren v Servisair UK Ltd*[8] **2.33** where the defender's insurers had issued a letter to the pursuer's agents at the pre-litigation stage stating:

> 'We accept that our insured is liable for the purposes of this claim, and will pay damages, to be assessed when we receive details of the claim. We will also be paying your costs in accordance with the Civil Procedure Rules.'

The judge at first instance held that the defenders were bound by that admis- **2.34** sion and granted summary decree, repelling the defence on liability. The decision was reclaimed. The Inner House stated at para. [5]:

> 'The critical question is the proper analysis of the defender's insurer's letter ... read in the context of the correspondence between the insurers' and the pursuer's representatives. In theory the letter may be categorised in three different ways: first, as a letter setting out the terms of a bilateral agreement concluded between the parties' representatives to the effect that the defenders would accept liability; secondly, as a letter containing a unilateral obligation on the part of the defenders to accept liability; and thirdly, as a mere extrajudicial admission of liability. The distinction between the third of these categories and the first two is important.'

---

8 *Van Klaveren v Servisair UK Ltd* [2009] CSIH 37.

2.35 The court went on to analyse the position in terms of *Walker and Walker, The Law of Evidence in Scotland*[9]:

> 'An extrajudicial admission, when proved, does not preclude the party making it from stating a case which contradicts it. It's probative effect depends upon its terms and its importance in relation to the facts in issue in the cause, and to some extent on whether the cause is civil or criminal. In a civil cause, the party who made the admission is entitled to establish that it was made for some secondary reason and was not true, and the whole circumstances in which it was made are relevant to qualify or explain its terms ... '

2.36 In *Liquid Gas Tankers Ltd v The Forth Ports Authority*,[10] Lord Kincraig approved of the statement of the law in *Walker and Walker* and stated, '[s]uch an admission is merely part, albeit an important part, of the proof of negligence against the defenders in a case which is based on negligence, but cannot per se found a claim for damages'.

2.37 The issue was also looked at in the case of *Gordon v East Kilbride Development Corporation*.[11] There, an admission of liability was issued pre-litigation and a payment of interim damages was made. However, liability was denied in the defences. Lord Caplin (at p. 64), held that a measure of confidentiality is accorded to admissions or concessions made by parties in the course of abortive negotiations that precede litigation, albeit he held in the circumstances of that case no privilege attached to the relevant correspondence. He recognised, however, that the pursuer had not even quantified his case at the time the admission was made and, even if the admission had been made in the defences, it could have been removed by adjustment prior to closure of the record. He recognised that circumstances can change, that a claim may become much more valuable than first thought or an important witness may come forward that alters views on liability. For those reasons he held that the admission in that case was no more than a representation of the defender's position and was not conclusive of the liability position in the subsequent litigation.

2.38 The Inner House in *Van Klaveren* followed the position adopted in *Walker and Walker, Liquid Gas Tankers* and *Gordon*. At para. 7b of their judgment the court stated that '[i]f an extrajudicial admission does not have contractual force, it may be withdrawn at any time prior to the closing of the record', recognising that legal advice or expert opinion can change over time. The letter issued by the insurers in *Van Klaveren* did not contain any clear words that indicated a binding undertaking to pay damages; any admission of liability made before the parties' positions are finally set out must normally be provisional, open to modification if new material emerges. Nothing had been said by the pursuer's agents that could reasonably be construed as an acceptance of any offer contained in the insurer's letter and the letter left open the assessment of damages, causation and expenses. The court granted the reclaiming motion although one issue that remained unresolved was the pursuer's averments that the defender was personally barred from denying liability.

2.39 What can be deduced from all of the foregoing? It seems clear that where there has been an admission of liability made in a case where both parties

---

9 *Walker and Walker, The Law of Evidence in Scotland*, 1st edn (Edinburgh: W. Hodge, 1964), pp. 28–29.
10 *Liquid Gas Tankers Ltd v The Forth Ports Authority* 1974 SLT (Notes) 35.
11 *Gordon v East Kilbride Development Corporation* 1995 SLT 62.

have agreed that the VPAP applies and the claim is worth no more than £10,000, the admission is deemed to be binding (VPAP, para. 3.6) assuming the claim has not been made fraudulently. Similarly, in a case that is subject to the CPAP, worth no more than £25,000 and the defender confirms that the admission is intended to be binding, the parties will be bound by that admission, absent any fraud.

Otherwise, there is a requirement to have a bilateral agreement between the parties or a unilateral undertaking by the defender with the intention of being bound by the admission before the parties will be bound by it. All of which means that careful consideration has to be given to whether an 'admission' of liability is in fact binding on the defender and whether further investigations on liability require to be undertaken to avoid potential pitfalls further down the line.   **2.40**

Chapter 3

Qualified One-Way Cost Shifting

3.01 Unlike most other chapters in this book, some time will be devoted to the historical background and to understanding the reasons why qualified one-way cost shifting (QOCS) has been introduced into Scottish personal injury litigation. QOCS is the concept that a pursuer in a personal injury claim should not be found liable for their opponent's legal costs if they are unsuccessful with their claim. The fact that the name includes the word 'qualified' means that the rule is not absolute. Exceptions apply. At the time of publication of this book, jurisprudence on the application of QOCS has not developed. Section 8 of the Civil Litigation (Expenses and Group Proceedings) (Scotland) Act 2018 (the 2018 Act) and the Act of Sederunt (Rules of the Court of Session 1994) 1994, Sheriff Appeal Court Rules and Sheriff Court Rules Amendment) (Qualified One-Way Costs Shifting) 2021 introducing the relevant new court rules only took effect on 30 June 2021. The application of the new rules will only start to have practical implications as the courts inevitably have to grapple with arguments over the loss of QOCS protection. By looking at the reasons for its introduction, what mischief it is designed to cure and the situations that were contemplated to justify losing QOCS when the Taylor report, *Review of Expenses and Funding of Civil Litigation in Scotland*, was published, personal injury practitioners may find it easier to shape the arguments for and against the general proposition that QOCS applies in any personal injury action raised on or after 30 June 2021.

3.02 The 2018 Act and 2021 regulations are produced at Appendix 1. The commencement order for s. 8 of the 2018 Act is the Civil Litigation (Expenses and Group Proceedings) (Scotland) Act 2018 (Commencement No. 4 and Transitional Provision) Regulations 2021.[1]

The fundamental reason for its introduction was to promote access to justice. As the Taylor report recognised,[2] the possibility of being found liable for their opponent's judicial expenses was often a disincentive to claimants from bringing a claim to court, especially, as is often the case, affordable 'after the event' (ATE) legal expenses insurance is unavailable. It follows that for access to justice to be improved through the introduction of QOCS there must be certainty for a claimant. If there are too many exceptions to the general rule or the exceptions are interpreted by the courts too widely, the whole ethos underpinning the legislation will be defeated.

---

1 Civil Litigation (Expenses and Group Proceedings) (Scotland) Act 2018 (Commencement No. 4 and Transitional Provision) Regulations 2021 (SSI 2021/125).
2 The Taylor report, Ch. 8.

There are, of course, several existing methods of protection available to a **3.03** claimant that may help them avoid having to personally pay an opponent's costs, such as civil legal aid, 'before the event' (BTE) insurance (often built in to household contents insurance policies), trade union membership, costs protection orders and ATE insurance but, whilst each of these funding methods will continue to exist, each has its drawbacks and limitations. All but civil legal aid provide a level of indemnity that is available to meet an adverse costs award. Even opponents who do not have legal aid can apply to the Legal Aid Board in limited circumstances to recover costs where they have been successful against an assisted person.[3]

Legal aid thresholds are seen by many as being so low as to prevent all but **3.04** those of very modest means from availing themselves of the legal aid system. Not to mention that very few personal injury practitioners in Scotland, especially those dealing with volume business, still offer a legal aid service because the rates of remuneration are so poor and the bureaucracy associated with legal aid is so cumbersome that it is of no interest to many. It is true that some practitioners still undertake personal injury claims, particularly medical negligence, on legal aid as they see it: (a) as an insurance policy to at least provide a means of recovering outlays and some level of fees if the case is unsuccessful; and (b) as a way of progressing cases that would otherwise never be pursued due to the associated expense of making the claim. But the practitioner is prevented from charging the client a success fee if the case is won, having to settle for whatever judicial recovery can be made. A client in possession of a legal aid certificate does at least have the ability to move the court to modify their liability for an opponent's costs if they lose and such motions are frequently granted. Some would argue that QOCS therefore already existed for those less able to afford the financial consequences of losing a court action.

BTE Insurance is only built in to some household policies, often because **3.05** the client has paid an additional premium for that protection. Many clients do not even know they have the cover until asked by their solicitor to check, assuming that the solicitor actually asks the client whether BTE insurance is available to them. There will inevitably be a limit on indemnity that can rapidly be exhausted and can lead to difficulties for a claimant if the indemnity is exhausted part-way through a court action. Top up cover would have to be purchased, often at significant cost, if the client was to remain fully indemnified.

Trade union membership schemes vary enormously in the nature and extent **3.06** of the legal services that they offer. Some are merely a signposting service where the union will have an arrangement with a solicitors' firm to refer their members, on the understanding the client is not charged any fees or outlays for the representation provided. This leaves the client exposed to adverse costs awards if no other protection is put in place. Other schemes will pay the solicitor for the representation and indemnify the client for any adverse cost awards. Again, indemnity limits may not be sufficient for some complex and protracted claims where judicial expenses can be substantial.

ATE insurance policies, designed to protect a claimant from having to **3.07** pay their own outlays and also to cover any adverse costs exposure to their

3 Legal Aid (Scotland) Act 1986 s. 19(1) and Act of Sederunt (Civil Legal Aid Rules) 1987 r. 6.

opponent, are not without difficulty. Some firms with volume business can negotiate excellent premiums with ATE insurers on the understanding they take out policies for all clients and do not cherry-pick cases by only taking out policies where prospects are lower. But some firms who only deal with low volume personal injury work are unable to secure affordable premiums for their clients.

Furthermore, there are usually stringent reporting requirements obliging the insured's solicitor to periodically report any developments and changes in views on prospects, which can lead to indemnity being refused if there is a failure to follow the reporting requirements.

In certain types of cases, such as clinical negligence and industrial disease claims, the premiums charged by ATE insurers are simply prohibitive, especially if top up cover is required beyond the initial level of indemnity.

3.08   If none of the foregoing expenses protections are available to a claimant, they invariably have to embark upon litigation with an open-ended exposure to paying for their own outlays, their opponent's expenses if they are ultimately unsuccessful and possibly also the fees for their own solicitor and counsel. It's therefore easy to understand why many such claimants are put off accessing the courts in an attempt to vindicate their rights. Even with the introduction of success fee agreements under Part 1 of the 2018 Act and the 2021 Regulations, whilst a pursuer cannot be charged full fees and VAT or any outlays by their own solicitor if a success fee agreement is in place, the client will still be liable to pay their opponent's costs if no financial protection is arranged. The introduction of QOCS goes some way to alleviating these issues.

ENGLAND AND WALES

3.09   In 1999 civil legal aid was withdrawn in England and Wales for many types of civil litigation, including all personal injury actions except clinical negligence. The Access to Justice Act 1999 sought to alleviate the impact of that change by allowing for the recovery of ATE premiums from the opponent. Ten years later, *Jackson LJ* in his Review of *Civil Litigation Costs* concluded that the recovery of ATE premiums was indefensible and proposed the introduction of QOCS for personal injury claims.

3.10   He stated: '[i]t would be substantially cheaper for defendants to bear their own costs in every case, whether won or lost, than to pay out ATE insurance premiums in the cases which they lost'.[4]

3.11   This meant that the defendant would pay the claimant's costs if the claim succeeded, but each side would pay their own costs if the claim was unsuccessful. He formed the view:

'It seems to me inevitable that provided the costs rules are drafted so as to a) deter frivolous or fraudulent claims and b) to encourage acceptance of reasonable offers, the introduction of one way costs shifting will materially reduce the costs of personal injuries litigation.'[5]

---

4 Jackson LJ, *Review of Civil Litigation Costs: Final Report* (London: The Stationary Office, 2009) Ch. 9 para. 4.1.
5 *Review of Civil Litigation Costs: Final Report*, Ch. 19, para. 4.6.

The Legal Aid, Sentencing and Punishment of Offenders Act 2012 imple- **3.12**
mented some, but not all, of Jackson LJ's recommendations and the Civil
Procedure Rules in England and Wales were altered on 1 April 2013 to introduce QOCS. In essence the English position, which is more than eight years
ahead of the position in Scotland, is:

(1) QOCS applies to claims for personal injury or death.
(2) Costs orders are unenforceable except in special circumstances.
(3) Claimants will lose the protection of QOCS if:
    (3.1) the claim is found to be fundamentally dishonest on the balance of
        probabilities;
    (3.2) the claimant has not bettered a Part 36 offer (the English equivalent
        of a tender) made by the defendant during the claim. The claimant
        will, however, only be ordered to pay the defendant's costs up to
        the amount of damages actually awarded);
    (3.3) The case has been struck out on the grounds that: (1) the claimant
        has disclosed no reasonable grounds for bringing the proceedings;
        or (2) the proceedings are an abuse of the court's process; or (3) the
        conduct of the claimant, or person acting on the claimant's behalf
        and with the claimant's knowledge of such conduct, is likely to
        obstruct the just disposal of the proceedings.

        Interestingly, the English position is that the claimant will not
        lose QOCS protection on discontinuance (abandonment) of the
        claim post-issue of proceedings, unless one of the exceptions (3.1)
        to (3.3) above applies. The theory behind that is that to do other-
        wise could lead to a claimant progressing an unmeritorious claim
        simply to retain QOCS protection. As we will see below this is in
        direct contrast to the Scottish position.

A substantial body of satellite litigation has arisen south of the border. Some **3.13**
recent Court of Appeal decisions are worth considering to compare the
approach taken in various scenarios.

In terms of loss of QOCS for fundamental dishonesty see *Howlett v Davies
and Ageas Insurance Ltd*,[6] where the court took the view that a defendant
does not require to plead fraud – the trial judge can form a view based on the
evidence that the claim is fraudulent.

The definition of fundamental dishonesty was also considered, with Newey **3.14**
LJ stating:

16. ... one-way costs shifting can be displaced if a claim is found to be "fundamentally dishonest". The meaning of this expression was considered by His Honour
Judge Moloney QC, sitting in the County Court at Cambridge, in **Gosling v Hailo**
(29 April 2014). He said this in his judgment:
    "44. It appears to me that this phrase in the rules has to be interpreted purposively
and contextually in the light of the context. This is, of course, the determination
of whether the claimant is 'deserving', as Jackson LJ put it, of the protection (from
the costs liability that would otherwise fall on him) extended, for reasons of social
policy, by the QOCS rules. It appears to me that when one looks at the matter in
that way, one sees that what the rules are doing is distinguishing between two levels
of dishonesty: dishonesty in relation to the claim which is not fundamental so as to

6 *Howlett v Davies and Ageas Insurance Ltd* [2017] EWCA Civ 1696.

expose such a claimant to costs liability, and dishonesty which is fundamental, so as to give rise to costs liability.

45. The corollary term to 'fundamental' would be a word with some such meaning as 'incidental' or 'collateral'. Thus, a claimant should not be exposed to costs liability merely because he is shown to have been dishonest as to some collateral matter or perhaps as to some minor, self-contained head of damage. If, on the other hand, the dishonesty went to the root of either the whole of his claim or a substantial part of his claim, then it appears to me that it would be a fundamentally dishonest claim: a claim which depended as to a substantial or important part of itself upon dishonesty.'"

3.15   The court in *Howlett* followed this approach, unchallenged by any of the parties appearing in the case.

3.16   *Andrea Brown v The Commissioner of Police of the Metropolis & the Chief Constable of the Greater Manchester Police & the Equality and Human Rights Commission (Intervener)*[7] was a 'mixed' claim where the litigation was based not only on damages for personal injury but also breaches of data protection and human rights legislation, breach of contract, misfeasance in public office and misuse of private information. The breach of contract claim was not pursued. Liability was admitted under the Data Protection Act 2018 and Human Rights Act 1998. The claim for misfeasance and misuse of private information went to trial where the claimant lost on the former but won on the latter. The court held that the claimant had not suffered personal injury and the damages she was awarded were general compensatory awards for the causes of action that she had succeeded with. She failed to beat the Part 36 offers that had been lodged. As this was a 'mixed' claim including damages for matters unconnected with personal injury, one of the express exceptions to the QOCS regime – Civil Procedure Rules r. 44.16(2) – was triggered and automatic costs protection was lost, though the court retained a discretion as to how to deal fairly with the issue of costs. In this case the claimant was found liable for the defendants' costs.

3.17   In essence, a claim for personal injury that can include ancillary claims for the likes of loss of earnings, services and loss in value of a pension fund would benefit from QOCS protection. However, under the civil procedure rules, where there were elements of the claim that did not relate to personal injury such as property damage or breaches for statutory duty under the Data Protection Act 2018, QOCS did not automatically apply. If an action could be described as a personal injury claim 'in the round' then a minor non-personal injury element should not prevent QOCS from applying. Conversely, it was considered that if a personal injury claim was merely included in a mainly non-personal injury claim with the purpose of attracting QOCS, the costs protection would not necessarily apply.

3.18   *Summers v Fairclough Homes Ltd*,[8] a case that pre-dated the introduction of QOCS in England, sets out useful considerations for how exaggerated claims should be considered.

3.19   Quoting from the decision of the Court of Appeal in *Widlake v BAA*[9] and in particular from paras 36–44 of the judgment of Ward LJ, with whom Smith

---

7 *Andrea Brown v The Commissioner of Police of the Metropolis & the Chief Constable of the Greater Manchester Police & the Equality and Human Rights Commission (Intervener)* [2019] EWCA Civ 1724.

8 *Summers v Fairclough Homes Ltd* [2012] UKSC 26.

9 *Widlake v BAA* EWCA Civ 1256.

and Wilson LJJ agreed, the judges identified these five propositions as relevant to this case:

(1) If, as here, the conduct of the claimant is unreasonable the court must take it into account.
(2) As regards such conduct, the court should principally enquire into its causative effect. To what extent did the claimant's lies and gross exaggeration cause costs to be incurred or wasted?
(3) In addition, the court is entitled in an appropriate case to say that the conduct is so egregious that a costs penalty should be imposed on the offending party. There is, however, a considerable difference between a concocted claim and an exaggerated claim and the court must be astute to measure how reprehensible the conduct is.
(4) Defendants have the means of defending themselves against false or exaggerated claims by making a Part 36 offer.
(5) Where the facts are well enough known for the defendant to make a Part 36 offer, failure to make a sufficiently high offer counts against the defendant.

Further, the judgment of the Supreme Court in *Summers v Fairclough* is authority for the proposition that the courts in England have the power under the CPR, as well as their inherent jurisdiction, to strike out cases for an abuse of process at any stage in the proceedings, including at the end of a trial, and that to deliberately make a false claim and to adduce false evidence is an abuse of process. However, such power should only be exercised in exceptional circumstances[10] (the default position being that after trial the judge would simply issue a judgment dismissing the claim if they felt the claimant had failed for whatever reason to prove their case) and exaggeration is unlikely to be sufficient for a finding of fundamental dishonesty or indeed justification for a strike out.   **3.20**

In terms of sanctions, the Supreme Court considered a number of options: **3.21**

> 'As to costs, in the ordinary way one would expect the judge to penalise the dishonest and fraudulent claimant in costs. It is entirely appropriate in a case of this kind to order the claimant to pay the costs of **any part of the process** which have been caused by his fraud or dishonesty and moreover to do so by making orders for costs on an indemnity basis. Such cost orders may often be in substantial sums perhaps leaving the claimant out of pocket. It seems to the Court that the prospect of such orders is likely to be a real deterrent.'[11]

It was also noted that the court can reduce interest that would otherwise be awarded and confirmed that a finding of contempt was open to the court.[12]   **3.22**

The test in every case is what is just and proportionate[13] but the court made it clear that whilst a strike out was not appropriate in this case after the trial evidence had been heard, nothing in the judgment should be construed so as to prevent applications for strike out being made at an earlier stage in the proceedings if the circumstances justified it.[14]   **3.23**

---

10 *Summers v Fairclough Homes Ltd*, Lord Clarke at para. 33.
11 *Summers v Fairclough Homes Ltd*, Lord Clarke at para. 53.
12 *Summers v Fairclough Homes Ltd*, Lord Clarke at para. 55.
13 *Summers v Fairclough Homes Ltd*, Lord Clarke at para. 61.
14 *Summers v Fairclough Homes Ltd*, Lord Clarke at para. 62.

3.24   *Alpha Insurance A/S v Roche & Roche*[15] confirms that whilst a claimant will
normally be entitled to retain QOCS protection if a claim is discontinued
(or abandoned) with a reasonable explanation, it remains open to a defendant to argue that the claim was fraudulent and adduce evidence of that at a
post-discontinuance hearing to determine whether QOCS protection should
be lost.

3.25   On the day before the first instance trial, a notice of discontinuance was
filed but no explanation was offered. The defences, filed a year previously,
had made it clear that allegations of fundamental dishonesty were being made.

3.26   Ordinarily, under CPR 38.6(1), the default burden on costs is shifted
post-discontinuance, such that claimants are made liable for the defendant's
costs up to the date of discontinuance. However, this was a case where QOCS
applied. As a result, the defendant required leave of the court to enforce such
an order.

3.27   The defendant's case on fundamental dishonesty was encapsulated within
CPR Practice Direction 44 r. 12.4:

> In a case to which r. 44.16(1) applies (fundamentally dishonest claims)—
> (a) the court will normally direct that issues arising out of an allegation that the
>   claim is fundamentally dishonest be determined at the trial;
> (b) where the proceedings have been settled, the court will not, save in exceptional
>   circumstances, order that issues arising out of an allegation that the claim was
>   fundamentally dishonest be determined in those proceedings;
> (c) where the claimant has served a notice of discontinuance, the court may direct
>   that issues arising out of an allegation that the claim was fundamentally dis-
>   honest be determined notwithstanding that the notice has not been set aside
>   pursuant to rule 38.4;
> (d) the court may, as it thinks fair and just, determine the costs attributable to the
>   claim having been found to be fundamentally dishonest.

3.28   Mrs Justice Yip, who gave judgment on appeal, held that 'the very late stage at
which the claim was discontinued and the complete absence of an explanation
from the claimants were factors to consider. She believed that an explanation
for discontinuing should be reasonably expected of claimants, given that there
are many reasons for discontinuing. Also, she saw that the expense, inconvenience and use of court resources was an important consideration.

In allowing a hearing to permit the defendants to adduce evidence of fundamental dishonesty the judge stated: '[f]or my part, any reasonable explanation
for the late discontinuance may well have tipped the balance the other way'.[16]

QOCS IN SCOTLAND

3.29   Scotland lags eight years behind England and Wales in the introduction of
QOCS not least of all because England introduced QOCS within four years
of the Jackson review whereas it took five years before the primary legislation
required to start implementing the Taylor recommendations even reached
the statute books, and a further three years for the necessary statutory instrument setting out the rules of court to be delivered. The Scottish rules and

---

15 *Alpha Insurance A/S v Roche & Roche* [2018] EWHC 1342 (QB).
16 *Alpha Insurance A/S v Roche & Roche*, Mrs Justice Yip at para. 31.

regulations are, in some respects, similar, but by no means identical, to those that apply south of the border. As these new rules are likely to play an important part in any personal injury solicitor's practice in the months and years ahead, they are reproduced fully here with a subsequent commentary on the salient provisions:

Section 8 of the 2018 Act states: **3.30**

Restriction on pursuer's liability for expenses in personal injury claims
(1) This section applies in civil proceedings where—
    (a) the person bringing the proceedings makes a claim for damages for—
        (i)   personal injuries, or
        (ii)   the death of a person from personal injuries, and
    (b) the person conducts the proceedings in an appropriate manner.
(2) The court must not make an award of expenses against the person in respect of any expenses which relate to—
    (a) the claim, or
    (b) any appeal in respect of the claim.
(3) Subsection (2) does not prevent the court from making an award in respect of expenses which relate to any other type of claim in the proceedings.
(4) For the purposes of subsection (1)(b), a person conducts civil proceedings in an appropriate manner unless the person or the person's legal representative—
    (a) makes a fraudulent representation or otherwise acts fraudulently in connection with the claim or proceedings,
    (b) behaves in a manner which is manifestly unreasonable in connection with the claim or proceedings, or
    (c) otherwise, conducts the proceedings in a manner that the court considers amounts to an abuse of process.
(5) For the purpose of subsection (4)(a), the standard of proof is the balance of probabilities.
(6) Subsection (2) is subject to any exceptions that may be specified in an act of sederunt under section 103(1) or 104(1) of the Courts Reform (Scotland) Act 2014.
(7) In subsection (1)(a), 'personal injuries' include any disease and any impairment of a person's physical or mental condition.

Detailed court rules governing QOCS, introduced on the back of the 2018   **3.31**
Act, are contained in Act of Sederunt (Rules of the Court of Session 1995, Sheriff Appeal Court Rules and Sheriff Court Rules Amendment) (Qualified One-Way Costs Shifting) 2021.[17] This introduced, from 30 June 2021, new chapters to the Rules of the Court of Session (RCS) (Ch. 41B), Sheriff Appeal Court Rules (Ch. 19A), Ordinary Cause Rules (Ch. 31A) and Summary Cause Rules (Ch. 23A). As personal injury claims cannot be dealt with under simple procedure, there is no change to the Simple Procedure Rules. As the various chapters are in broadly similar terms, only RCS Ch. 41B is reproduced below but the whole statutory instrument setting out the other chapters can be found in Appendix 1.

CHAPTER 41B QUALIFIED ONE-WAY COSTS SHIFTING
Application and interpretation of this Chapter
41B.1—(1) This Chapter applies in civil proceedings, where either or both
    (a) an application for an award of expenses is made to the court;
    (b) such an award is made by the court.

---

17 Act of Sederunt (Rules of the Court of Session 1995, Sheriff Appeal Court Rules and Sheriff Court Rules Amendment) (Qualified One-Way Costs Shifting) 2021 (SSI 2021/226).

(2) Where this Chapter applies
    (a) rules 29.1(2) and (3) (abandonment of actions), 40.15(6) (appeals deemed abandoned) and 41.17(3)(b) (procedure on abandonment); and
    (b) any common law rule entitling a pursuer to abandon an action or an appeal, to the extent that it concerns expenses, are disapplied.

(3) In this Chapter:
'the Act' means the Civil Litigation (Expenses and Group Proceedings) (Scotland) Act 2018;
'the applicant' has the meaning given in rule 41B.2(1), and 'applicants' is construed accordingly;
'civil proceedings' means civil proceedings to which section 8 of the Act (restriction on pursuer's liability for expenses in personal injury claims) applies.

Application for an award of expenses

41B.2—(1) Where civil proceedings have been brought by a pursuer, another party to the action ('the applicant') may make an application to the court for an award of expenses to be made against the pursuer, on one or more of the grounds specified in either or both:
    (a) section 8(4)(a) to (c) of the Act;
    (b) paragraph (2) of this rule.

(2) The grounds specified in this paragraph, which are exceptions to section 8(2) of the Act, are as follows:
    (a) failure by the pursuer to obtain an award of damages equal to, or greater than, the sum offered by way of a tender lodged in process;
    (b) unreasonable delay on the part of the pursuer in accepting a sum offered by way of a tender lodged in process;
    (c) abandonment of the action or the appeal by the pursuer in terms of rules 29.1(1), 40.15(1) or 41.15(1), or at common law.

Award of expenses

41B.3—(1) The determination of an application made under rule 41B.2(1) is at the discretion of the court, subject to paragraph (2).

(2) Where, having determined an application made under rule 41B.2(1), the court makes an award of expenses against the pursuer on the ground specified in rule 41B.2(2)(a) or (b) *[failure to beat a tender or failure to timeously accept a tender]*—
    (a) the pursuer's liability is not to exceed the amount of expenses the applicant has incurred after the date of the tender;
    (b) the liability of the pursuer to the applicant, or applicants, who lodged the tender is to be limited to an aggregate sum, payable to all applicants (if more than one) of 75% of the amount of damages awarded to the pursuer, and that sum is to be calculated without offsetting against those expenses any expenses due to the pursuer by the applicant, or applicants, before the date of the tender;
    (c) the court must order that the pursuer's liability is not to exceed the sum referred to in sub-paragraph (b), notwithstanding that any sum assessed by the Auditor of Court as payable under the tender procedure may be greater or, if modifying the expenses in terms of rule 42.5 (modification or disallowance of expenses) or 42.6(1) (modification of expenses awarded against assisted persons), that such modification does not exceed that referred to in sub-paragraph (b);
    (d) where the award of expenses is in favour of more than one applicant the court, failing agreement between the applicants, is to apportion the award of expenses recoverable under the tender procedure between them.

(3) Where, having determined an application made under rule 41B.2(1), the court makes an award of expenses against the pursuer on the ground specified in rule

41B.2(2)(c), the court may make such orders in respect of expenses, as it considers appropriate, including—

(a) making an award of decree of dismissal dependant on payment of expenses by the pursuer within a specified period of time;

(b) provision for the consequences of failure to comply with any conditions applied by the court.

Procedure

41B.4—(1) An application under rule 41B.2(1)—

(a) must be made by motion, in writing, and Chapter 23 (motions) otherwise applies to motions made under this Chapter;

(b) may be made at any stage in the case prior to the pronouncing of an interlocutor disposing of the expenses of the action or, as the case may be, the appeal.

(2) Where an application under rule 41B.2(1) is made, the court may make such orders as it thinks fit for dealing with the application, including an order—

(a) requiring the applicant to intimate the application to any other person;

(b) requiring any party to lodge a written response;

(c) requiring the lodging of any document;

(d) fixing a hearing.

Award against legal representatives

41B.5 Section 8(2) of the Act does not prevent the court from making an award of expenses against a pursuer's legal representative in terms of section 11[18] (awards of expenses against legal representatives) of the Act.'

COMMENTARY

The application of QOCS is limited to proceedings for damages for: (i) personal injuries; and (ii) the death of a person from personal injuries. This includes disease and any physical or mental impairment. Medical negligence claims involving injury or death fall within the definition. **3.32**

The rules apply to first instance proceedings and appeals initiated on or after 30 June 2021.[19] Subject to the important caveat mentioned in the next paragraph, this has the effect that QOCS will not apply in relation to an accident that occurred in, say, 2019 and is litigated in 2020 but will apply to a case where the accident occurred in 2019 but is not litigated until on or after 30 June 2021. In other words, the date of the accident is largely irrelevant to the application of QOCS, it's the date of raising the proceedings that determines whether QOCS applies. **3.33**

However, the terms of the commencement order makes an important, but easily overlooked, transitional provision that qualifies that position: **3.34**

Transitional provision

—[...]

(2) Where a claim has commenced prior to 30 June 2021, the provisions listed in regulation 2 [which refers to s. 8 of the 2018 Act]—

(a) apply to proceedings commenced on or after that date,

(b) do not apply to action taken by the person bringing the claim or their legal representative in connection with the claim before that date.

18 As at the date of publication, s. 11 of the 2018 Act is not yet in force.

19 Act of Sederunt (Rules of the Court of Session 1995, Sheriff Appeal Court Rules and Sheriff Court Rules Amendment) (Qualified One-Way Costs Shifting) 2021 reg. 1.

In other words, the pre-litigation work undertaken prior to 30th June 2021 in a court action that is commenced on or after 30 June 2021 is not covered by the QOCS rules and can be the subject of an award of expenses in favour of the opponent.[20]

3.35   Prudent personal injury practitioners, knowing of the impending introduction of QOCS, would have considered refraining from raising proceedings until the Act of Sederunt came into force so their clients would obtain QOCS protection. It remains to be seen whether unsuccessful pursuers, whose actions were raised prior to QOCS coming into effect, and who end up with a personal liability for their opponent's expenses, would have the basis for a professional negligence claim against their solicitor if they were not given the option of deferring the raising of proceedings until they could benefit from QOCS.

3.36   Subject to the exceptions listed in the 2018 Act and the Act of Sederunt, QOCS applies if the person bringing the proceedings conducts the proceedings in an appropriate manner.[21] This creates the presumption that the proceedings have been conducted appropriately unless a challenge is made by the opponent and upheld by the court in relation to one or more of the scenarios listed in s. 8(4) of the 2018 Act, outlined below, or the court *ex proprio motu* rules that the proceedings have not been conducted in an appropriate manner due to s. 8(4)(a),(b) or (c) being established. Section (8)4 lists the only three scenarios that, if established, allow the court to conclude that the proceedings have not been conducted appropriately. Such a finding would mean the court is not bound by s. 8(2), thus permitting it to make any award of expenses it deemed appropriate.

3.37   The basic position now, contrary to the previous normal rule that expenses follow success, is that the court must not make an award of expenses against the person bringing the claim, which relate to the claim or any associated appeal,[22] but awards of expenses can still be made for claims of a non-personal injury nature.[23] The new rules apply equally to expenses for individual procedures, such as amendment, as they do to final awards at the conclusion of the case.

3.38   The proceedings are conducted in an appropriate manner unless the person or their legal representative:

(a) makes a fraudulent representation or otherwise acts fraudulently in connection with the claim or proceedings.[24] This is judged on the balance of probabilities, notwithstanding the 'offence' may be tantamount to criminal conduct.[25] This exception differs from the English equivalent, which, as we have seen above, refers to fundamental dishonesty; although like in England, it is not anticipated that mere exaggeration would be viewed as a fraudulent misrepresentation or an act of fraud;

(b) behaves in a manner that is manifestly unreasonable in connection with the claim or proceedings.[26] It is implicit in this exception that the standard

---

20 Civil Litigation (Expenses and Group Proceedings) (Scotland) Act 2018 (Commencement No. 4 and Transitional Provision) Regulations 2021 reg. 3.
21 2018 Act s. 8(4).
22 2018 Act s. 8(2).
23 2018 Act s. 8(3).
24 2018 Act s. 8(4)(a).
25 2018 Act s. 8(5).
26 2018 Act s. 8(4)(b).

to be reached to justify loss of QOCS protection is as per *Wednesbury* principles and should therefore be a rare basis for loss of QOCS. Merely acting unreasonably is insufficient; and

(c) otherwise conducts the proceedings in a manner that the court considers amounts to an abuse of process.[27] The court, of course, already has an inherent discretion to make a finding of expenses against a party where an abuse of process is established. The 2018 Act simply includes 'abuse of process' as a basis for a finding of inappropriate conduct that in turn can lead to the loss of some or all of QOCS protection.

It is within the court's discretion to determine whether and to what extent **3.39** QOCS protection should be lost. It does not necessarily follow that if an abuse of process, or indeed any of the other grounds under s. (8)(4), is established that QOCS protection is fully lost. If the position as per the English authorities above is followed, it is anticipated that the court's discretion will be exercised proportionately to reflect the nature and extent of the abuse. The exercise of this discretion should be used sparingly, even in cases where a defender succeeds with a summary decree motion.

The 2018 Act permitted additional exceptions to QOCS to be introduced **3.40** and these appear in the Act of Sederunt:

These are broadly the same for all courts and relate to:

(a) failure by the pursuer to obtain an award of damages equal to or greater than the sum offered by way of a tender lodged in process;

(b) unreasonable delay on the part of the pursuer in accepting a sum offered by way of a tender lodged in process; and

(c) abandonment of the action or the appeal by the pursuer in terms of the relevant court rules or at common law.

It should be noted that there is a subtle but important difference between:

(1) s. 8(4) of the 2018 Act, which outlines the three situations that are deemed to constitute grounds for holding 'inappropriate conduct'; and

(2) the additional exceptions to the rule listed in the Act of Sederunt.
     The latter are not dependent on any finding of 'inappropriate conduct'.

It was readily anticipated that the additional exceptions would cover the sit- **3.41** uations in relation to failure to beat, or failure to timeously accept, tenders.

If there are multiple parties making the application for loss of QOCS, **3.42** the court shall, in the absence of agreement between them, apportion the recoverable expenses between those parties in whatever proportions it deems appropriate.

The third exception in the Act of Sederunt, namely abandonment, came **3.43** as a complete surprise to many personal injury practitioners. It was not a recommended exception under the Taylor report and it is not an exception that is necessarily based on adverse conduct of the claimant or their legal representatives. If the rationale for loss of QOCS is to penalise inappropriate behaviour, the loss of QOCS must surely be limited to situations where the conduct of the claimant or their agent is so reprehensible that the removal of QOCS protection is justified. The other exceptions all have a clear conduct

27 2018 Act s. 8(4)(c).

element built in. But abandonment can arise in a multitude of ways that are out with the control of the claimant or their representative. A skilled person can alter their opinion after considering the reports of an opponent's skilled witness. An essential witness may die making it much more difficult to prove the case. A solicitor may, in a finely balanced case, change their mind about whether sufficient prospects of success exist and terminate a success fee agreement leaving a claimant in the invidious position of having to secure alternative representation part way through a litigation. That is often difficult and sometimes impossible, especially if the pursuer needs the new agent to operate under a success fee agreement.

3.44   Is the lesser evil not to abandon a case that, for whatever reason, no longer enjoys sufficiently high prospects than persist with a claim with limited prospects simply to retain QOCS protection? It is likely to be very difficult for a defender, who has made no attempt to obtain, and been successful with a motion for, summary decree, to argue that a weak but stateable case should not benefit from QOCS protection. And even harder for the defender to argue for loss of QOCS protection if a summary decree motion is attempted but refused.

3.45   It is true to say that, apart from the tender exceptions, the court retains complete discretion on whether to make an award of expenses against a pursuer, whether due to abandonment or indeed any other ground under s. 8(4),[28] and one would expect that any decisions to remove QOCS will only arise in the context of inappropriate conduct. But the fact that the abandonment exception exists at all leads to greater uncertainty and may lead to difficult discussions between a claimant and their representative, and potentially a conflict between the two. There are unlikely to be many situations that arise that would justify loss of QOCS in an abandonment context that could not have been successfully argued under one of the grounds in s. 8(4) of the 2018 Act. Which begs the question, why include abandonment as an exception? If there does indeed need to be adverse conduct of some description on the part of the claimant, it can be anticipated that the English position on discontinuance will be followed and QOCS protection will be retained if a reasonable explanation is advanced.

AWARD OF EXPENSES

3.46   In relation to the exceptions involving tenders, if the court makes an award of expenses against a pursuer due to a failure to beat a tender or where there was unreasonable delay in accepting a tender, the liability of the pursuer extends only to expenses incurred after the date of the tender.[29]

3.47   Further, 25 per cent of the pursuer's damages is protected as the award of expenses is capped at 75 per cent of the damages award.[30]

3.48   If there is more than one applicant seeking an award of expenses against the pursuer, in the absence of agreement between the parties it is incumbent on the court to apportion the award between the applicants.[31]

---

28 For example, RCS r. 41B.3(1).
29 RCS r. 41B.3(2)(a).
30 RCS r. 41B.3(2)(b) and (c).
31 RCS r. 41B.3(2)(d).

RCS r. 41B.3(2)(b) makes specific provision that any award of expenses **3.49** made against a pursuer for failing to beat a tender or failing to timeously accept a tender cannot be offset against the pre-tender expenses award in favour of the pursuer. However, no similar provision is made for the situation that may arise if there is a partial loss of QOCS under the other exceptions, or where an award is made against the pursuer in respect of a part of the proceedings that did not attract QOCS protection. The recent Supreme Court decision of *Ho v Adelekun*,[32] which deals with the interpretation of English civil procedure rules on QOCS, makes it clear no set-off can arise:

> '[44] Any apparent unfairness in an individual case such as this … is part and parcel of the overall QOCS scheme devised to protect claimants against liability for costs and to lift from defendants' insurers the burden of paying success fees and ATE premiums in the many cases in which a claimant succeeds in her claim without incurring any cost liability towards the defendant.'

Where the award of expenses is made in the context of abandonment, the **3.50** court can make such order as it considers appropriate, including the granting of decree of dismissal being dependent on payment of expenses by the pursuer within a specified period. The court can also provide for the consequences of failure to comply with any order it makes.[33] For example, failure to pay the expenses within the time period specified by the court would probably result in the opponent being assoilzied as opposed to the action simply being dismissed.

PROCEDURE FOR APPLYING FOR QOCS REMOVAL

The procedure for determining an application for loss of QOCS protection is **3.51** set out in the Act of Sederunt, e.g. RCS r. 41B.3(4) and the corresponding provisions for other courts. The application is made by written motion.

The application must be made prior to the court pronouncing an inter- **3.52** locutor finding a party entitled to the expenses of the action, i.e. the final interlocutor disposing of the expenses of the action or any appeal as opposed to any incidental findings of expenses as the case progresses.

Whilst the rules clearly state that the court may make such orders as it thinks **3.53** fit for dealing with the application, it is considered unlikely to be appropriate in applications involving allegations of fraudulent representation, acts of fraud, manifestly unreasonable conduct or abuse of process to deal with them based on *ex parte* statements alone unless the court has had the benefit of hearing evidence at proof.

Included within its general powers, is the ability to make orders: **3.54**

(a) requiring the applicant to intimate the application to any other person;
(b) requiring any party to lodge a written response;
(c) requiring the lodging of any document; and
(d) fixing a hearing.

The normal procedure in England and Wales, where a defendant seeks to **3.55** argue that QOCS protection should be lost, is for a post-discontinuance

---

32 *Ho v Adelekun* [2021] UKSC 43.
33 RCS R. 41B.3(3)(a) and (b).

hearing to be fixed. Leave of the court is required for such a hearing. Given the significant implications for claimants in losing QOCS protection, and the fact that loss of QOCS should very much be the exception rather than the rule, it would be just and equitable to afford a claimant the opportunity of leading evidence to respond to any allegations made against them, unless the parties dispense with such an approach by agreement. This is especially so where fraudulent conduct or manifestly unreasonable behaviour is alleged and would allow the court to take an informed view and issue a proportionate response.

3.56   Finally, agents will require to bear in mind that even though the general rule under s. 8(2) of the 2018 Act prevents awards of expenses being made against the claimant unless s. 8(4) or one of the exceptions applies, there continues to be no prohibition against awards of expenses being made against the legal representative. This will, in due course, be governed by s. 11 of the 2018 Act if the circumstances warrant it but in any event is something that the court has an inherent discretion to order.

3.57   When the 2018 Act came into force, provision was made for a review of how the Act and its associated regulations were working in practice. The 2018 Act provided for a review after five years of its inception. Unfortunately, given that it has taken three years to implement the QOCS rules following the 2018 Act coming into force, the review will need to take place after only two years of the rules operating.

Chapter 4

Success Fee Agreements

SPECULATIVE AGREEMENTS PRE-27 APRIL 2020

There has never been any prohibition on a solicitor entering into an agreement with a client whereby the solicitor will only charge a fee if the piece of work they are instructed to do is successful (or partly successful) and charge no fee if it is not. That applies to all types of business, not simply litigation, and the fee can be a fixed fee (as opposed to an hourly rate), only payable on success. **4.01**

Since 1992,[1] a solicitor and client may agree, in relation to a litigation undertaken on a speculative basis, that, in the event of the litigation being successful, the solicitor's fee shall be increased by such a percentage as may be agreed.[2] The maximum percentage increase is prescribed by Act of Sederunt at 100 per cent.[3] **4.02**

This means that there are now three ways of entering into a speculative (known in England as a 'conditional') fee agreement: **4.03**

(1) The solicitor can accept the judicial expenses that they get from the opponent and at the same time charge their client a success fee that should be no more than 100 per cent of the judicial fees. The success fee calculation is not based on the total of the judicial account, i.e. it ignores those parts relating to copying and the part of the process fee and posts and incidents exigible thereon as well as any additional fee/charge and outlays.[4] Nothing is charged to the client if the action is unsuccessful.

(2) Alternatively, the solicitor can charge their client on an agent/client basis and can, if they wish, set the charge out rates at a higher level than they normally would to reflect the speculative nature of the work. However, if the client's fees are based on an agent/client account, no success fee can be charged. The recovered judicial expenses require to be offset against the agent/client account. Nothing would be charged to the client if the action is unsuccessful.

1 Law Reform (Miscellaneous Provisions) (Scotland) Act 1990 s. 36 (effective from 20 April 1992).
2 Solicitors' (Scotland) Act 1980 s. 61A(3).
3 Sheriff Court: Act of Sederunt (Fees of Solicitors in Speculative Actions) 1992 (SI 1992/1879) and Court of Session: Act of Sederunt (Rules of the Court of Session Amendment No. 8) (Fees of Solicitors in Speculative Actions) 1992 (SI 1992/1898).
4 Act of Sederunt (Fees of Solicitors in Speculative Actions) 1992 and Act of Sederunt (Rules of the Court of Session Amendment No. 8) (Fees of Solicitors in Speculative Actions) 1992 reg. 2(4).

(3) The third option is for the solicitor and client to enter into a written fee-charging agreement setting out the level of fee recoverable if the case is successful. This can be a fixed fee. No additional success fee can be charged.

COUNSEL AND SPECULATIVE FEES

4.04 An advocate and the person instructing them may agree, in relation to a litigation undertaken on a speculative basis, that, in the event of the litigation being successful, the advocate's fee shall be increased by such percentage as may be agreed.[5] The percentage increase that may be agreed shall not exceed such limit as the court may, after consultation with the Dean of the Faculty of Advocates, prescribe by Act of Sederunt.[6]

4.05 However, in August 2020, the Faculty Scheme for Accounting of Counsels' fees, reproduced at Appendix 3, was updated with new provisions in relation to the instruction of counsel in speculative cases. Many agents until then had arrangements with counsel who they regularly instructed whereby the advocate would be paid only what was judicially recovered. A situation arose where sanction for the employment of counsel was refused in a sheriff court case and whilst the case was successful, and the pursuer's agent recovered judicial expenses, the advocate was told he was going to be paid nothing. As a result, the scheme now states:

> 6.3. Subject to para 6.5 below, counsel may accept instructions on the basis that counsel will receive only such fees as are recovered by way of judicial expenses from another party to the litigation (the judicial recovery basis) but is not bound to do so.
>
> 6.4 If an instructing person wishes to instruct counsel on the basis set out in paragraph 6.3 this must be stated explicitly in every letter of instruction in the case. In the absence of an explicit statement to that effect counsel shall be entitled to be paid a fee regardless of whether or not any fee has been recovered by way of expenses from another party to the litigation where successful.
>
> 6.5. Counsel may not accept instructions on the basis specified in paragraph 6.3 where the client has entered into a success fee agreement within the meaning of sec. 1 of the Civil Litigation (Expenses and Group Proceedings) (Scotland) Act 2018 (asp. 10) with any provider relevant to the instruction (whether or not the provider is the instructing person or another person). In any such case, counsel shall be entitled to be paid a fee, on success, regardless of whether or not any fee has been recovered by way of expenses from another party to the litigation where successful.

4.06 There is therefore now a prohibition on counsel from acting speculatively if the client whose case they are being instructed in has entered into a success fee agreement. In that event, the advocate must be paid if the case is successful regardless of whether those fees are recoverable from the opponent. The terms of the scheme were subsequently clarified by the Dean as still permitting counsel to negotiate with the instructing agent on the level of fee that counsel would be paid where the case is successful but sanction in the sheriff court is refused. A fixed sum or a substantially discounted rate could be agreed.

---

5 Law Reform (Miscellaneous Provisions) (Scotland) Act 1990 s. 36(1).
6 Law Reform (Miscellaneous Provisions) (Scotland) Act 1990 s. 36(2).

TAXATION IN SPECULATIVE CASES

Where a solicitor and their client have reached an agreement in writing as to **4.07**
the solicitor's fees in respect of any work done or to be done by them for their
client, it shall not be competent, in any litigation arising out of any dispute
as to the amount due to be paid under any such agreement, for the court to
remit the solicitor's account for taxation.[7] If there is no written fee-charging
agreement, it is competent for the court to remit for taxation.[8] The key phrase
is 'any dispute as to the amount due to be paid'. It has been argued[9] that the
written agreement must specify the actual fee to be charged. If it does not, but
specifies merely the hourly rate, then it will be open to the client to request
taxation over the number of hours charged even if they are personally barred
from challenging the hourly rate. We would respectfully disagree with that
analysis. A client who seeks to dispute the number of hours charged is creating
a dispute as to the amount due to be paid under the written fee-charging
agreement. The wording of the Solicitors (Scotland) Act 1980 s. 61A(2)
clearly renders it incompetent for a court to remit the solicitor's account for
taxation in such circumstances.

THE CIVIL LITIGATION (EXPENSES AND GROUP PROCEEDINGS) (SCOTLAND) ACT 2018

Until the commencement of Part 1 of the Civil Litigation (Expenses and **4.08**
Group Proceedings) (Scotland) Act 2018 on 27 April 2020,[10] a solicitor was
prevented from enforcing *pacta de quota litis* (agreements for the share of a
litigation). We know them as damages based (or contingency) agreements.
Such agreements are not *pacta illicita* (unlawful agreements). There is no
legal prohibition on a solicitor entering into such an agreement with a client
but a solicitor, until now, has not been able to enforce such an agreement if
challenged by a client.

No such enforceability issues affected claims management companies **4.09**
(CMC),[11] even if those CMCs were owned and operated by solicitors, and
even if they were not subject to any regulatory scrutiny. Many of the larger
firms of solicitors, dealing with volume personal injury work, circumvented
the issue of enforceability by setting up their own CMC, which were able to
charge a percentage of the client's damages. The directors of the CMC were
often the equity partners of the firm of solicitors who were acting for the claimant. The CMC would be paid the success fee at the end of a case whilst the
instructed firm of solicitors was able to retain the recovered judicial expenses.
Whether these were truly CMC, or merely companies providing a method of
indemnity to the client from having to pay anything towards their own outlays
or their opponent's judicial expenses, will be looked at in more detail below.

---

7 Solicitors (Scotland) Act 1980 s. 61A(1).
8 Solicitors (Scotland) Act 1980 s. 61A(2).
9 Paterson & Ritchie, *Law, Practice and Conduct for Solicitors*, 2nd edn (Edinburgh: W. Green, 2014) para. 10.04.08.
10 The Civil Litigation (Expenses and Group Proceedings) (Scotland) Act 2018 (Success Fee Agreements) Regulations 2020 (SSI 2020/110).
11 *Quantum Claims Compensation Specialists Ltd v Powell* 1998 SLT 228.

4.10　The Taylor report in Chs 7 (speculative fee agreements) and 9 (damages based agreements) analysed the pros and cons of these funding methods and concluded that they provide a method of promoting access to justice, particularly given the limited availability of legal aid. The Taylor report made various recommendations to allow solicitors to enter into damages based agreements. It further recommended that caps are set on the level of success fee that can be charged; that a written agreement, dealing with a variety of specific issues, is entered into at the outset; and that any unrecoverable costs, including counsel's fees, require to be borne by the solicitor out of the success fee and, if that is exhausted, out of the solicitor's own pocket.

4.11　Much of what the Taylor report recommended appears in the 2018 Act and the implementing regulations,[12] which are both reproduced in full in Appendix 1.

4.12　The 2018 Act regulates success fee agreements (SFA), which are defined as an agreement between a person providing relevant services (the provider) and the recipient of those services (the recipient) where the recipient pays a success fee to the provider if the recipient obtains a financial benefit 'in connection with a matter in relation to which the services are provided'[13] but 'is not to make any payment, or is to make a payment of a lower amount than the success fee, in respect of those services if no such benefit is obtained'.[14]

4.13　The definition covers both speculative (conditional) and damages (contingency) based agreements. Therefore, subject to what is said below, any SFA, whether based on a percentage uplift of the fees in the judicial account, an agent/client or fixed fee only payable in the event of success or a success fee based on a percentage of damages are subject to the requirements of the 2018 Act and the 2020 Regulations, if entered into on or after 27 April 2020.

4.14　Relevant services is defined as legal services or claims management services provided in connection with a matter:

(a)　which is the subject of civil proceedings to which the recipient is a party before a Scottish court or tribunal; or

(b)　in relation to which such proceedings are in contemplation.[15]

4.15　When a solicitor or CMC accepts instructions to deal with a claim, absent any time bar issues, they would not have proceedings before a court or tribunal in contemplation. The focus would be to achieve a pre-litigation settlement. That would certainly be the case in personal injury claims that are subject to the compulsory pre-action protocol. No proceedings should be issued in the normal course of events unless the protocol stages have been exhausted and no settlement has been reached or one party has breached the terms of the protocol to give the other party a basis for litigating.

It must logically follow that the terms of the 2018 Act do not apply until the solicitor or CMC contemplates litigation. Which, in turn, means that solicitors would be free to enter into speculative (but not damages based) fee agreements with clients to cover pre-litigation work, free of any incumbrance

---

12　The Civil Litigation (Expenses and Group Proceedings) (Scotland) Act 2018 (Success Fee Agreements) Regulations 2020.

13　Civil Litigation (Expenses and Group Proceedings) (Scotland) Act 2018 s. 1(1)(a).

14　Civil Litigation (Expenses and Group Proceedings) (Scotland) Act 2018 s. 1(1)(b).

15　Civil Litigation (Expenses and Group Proceedings) (Scotland) Act 2018 s. 1(2).

imposed by the 2018 Act or 2020 Regulations. Similarly, CMC can put clients on damages based agreements, charging higher percentages than the caps imposed by the 2018 Act, until such times as 'litigation is contemplated'.

Legal services means services consisting of the provision of legal advice, **4.16** assistance or representation.[16]

The definition of claims management services is services consisting of the **4.17** provision of advice or services, other than legal services, in connection with the making of a claim for damages or other financial benefit including:

(a) advice or services in relation to:
    (i) legal representation;
    (ii) the payment or funding of costs associated with making the claim.
(b) referring or introducing one person to another; and
(c) making inquiries.[17]

But compare that to what constitutes a CMC under the Financial Guidance **4.18** and Claims Act 2018 and the Financial Services and Markets Act 2000 (Claims Management Activity) Order 2018, which makes the Financial Conduct Authority (FCA) the regulator of CMC. A CMC requires permission to trade if it carries out any of the following activities:

- Seeking out, referring and identifying claims.
- Advising, investigating and representing in relation to personal injury claims.
- Advising, investigating and representing in relation to financial services and product claims.
- Advising, investigating and representing in relation to employment claims.
- Advising, investigating and representing in relation to criminal injury claims.
- Advising, investigating and representing in relation to industrial injury disablement benefit claims.
- Advising, investigating and representing in relation to housing disrepair claims.

If permission has not been granted to a CMC for the foregoing purposes and an SFA is entered into for an activity where permission has not been given, it is highly likely that the SFA would be unenforceable.

The FCA regulates all CMC in England, Wales and Scotland whereas the **4.19** previous regulator, the Claims Management Regulation Unit, only had jurisdiction over English and Welsh CMC.

Whilst an SFA is not unenforceable merely because it is a *pacta de quota* **4.20** *litis*, i.e. an agreement for a share of the litigation, that does not affect any other basis for rendering an SFA unenforceable. As we will see, if terms of a written agreement are materially at odds with the requirements of the 2020 Regulations, the offending provisions will be deemed unenforceable.

If the recipient of legal services is successful with their claim and is awarded **4.21** expenses, or becomes entitled to expenses as part of the settlement agreement, the provider of the services is entitled to recover and retain the judicial expenses as well as the success fee. The recovered expenses do not have to

16 Civil Litigation (Expenses and Group Proceedings) (Scotland) Act 2018 s. 1(2).
17 Civil Litigation (Expenses and Group Proceedings) (Scotland) Act 2018 s. 1(2).

be set off against the success fee unless the agreement between provider and recipient provides otherwise.[18]

4.22   A success fee is not recoverable from the opponent under any circumstances, even where the successful party has been awarded expenses on a agent/client, client paying basis.[19]

4.23   If the recipient, either before or after entering into an SFA, has been in receipt of civil legal aid, any expenses recovered from an opponent must be paid by the provider into the hands of the Scottish Legal Aid Board.[20] The provider would provide the Scottish Legal Aid Board with the account synopsis form and breakdown of fees, VAT, non-faculty outlays and faculty outlays in the normal way.

SUCCESS FEE CAPS

4.24   The 2018 Act allowed for the introduction of caps on the level of success fees that can be charged in different types of cases. An SFA is unenforceable to the extent that it provides for a success fee of an amount that is higher than the cap. The 2018 Act did not include the caps. However, Sheriff Principal Taylor had made recommendations in his report as to what he thought the caps should be.[21] Following a consultation exercise by the Scottish Government, the recommended caps were adopted and introduced by the Civil Litigation (Expenses and Group Proceedings) (Scotland) Act 2018 (Success Fee Agreements) Regulations 2020,[22] which came into force on 27 April 2020. The Regulations are reproduced in Appendix 1.

4.25   In short, an SFA must not require a recipient to pay a higher success fee, inclusive of VAT, than the caps set out in reg. 2. The calculation of the success fee is based on the financial benefit derived by the recipient.[23] Different caps apply to different types of civil claims.

Personal injury caps

4.26   In a matter that is or could become a claim for damages for personal injuries or the death of a person from personal injuries, the maximum caps are:

- 20 per cent of the first £100,000 of financial benefit.
- 10 per cent of the financial benefit between £100,000 and £500,000, i.e. 10 per cent of the next £400,000 of financial benefit.
- 2.5 per cent of the financial benefit over £500,000 (subject to the conditions mentioned below in relation to future damages).

---

18 Civil Litigation (Expenses and Group Proceedings) (Scotland) Act 2018 s. 3(1) and (2).
19 *Cabot Financial UK Ltd v Weir* [2021] SAC (Civ) 2.
20 Civil Litigation (Expenses and Group Proceedings) (Scotland) Act 2018 s. 3(3) and Legal Aid (Scotland) Act 1986 s.17(2).
21 The Taylor report, Ch. 9, pp. 88–90.
22 Civil Litigation (Expenses and Group Proceedings) (Scotland) Act 2018 (Success Fee Agreements) Regulations 2020.
23 Civil Litigation (Expenses and Group Proceedings) (Scotland) Act 2018 (Success Fee Agreements) Regulations 2020 reg. 2(2).

For example, a personal injury claim settles for £650,000. The maximum **4.27** success fee chargeable by the provider is £63,750 (£20,000 plus £40,000 plus £3,750) inclusive of VAT and unrecoverable outlays.

Employment tribunal caps

In a matter that is or could become the subject of proceedings before an **4.28** employment tribunal, the success fee cap is 35 per cent of the financial benefit.[24]

Caps in all other cases

In any other matter to which the regulations apply, the success fee cap is **4.29** 50 per cent of the financial benefit.[25]

The caps are, of course, maximums. A provider and recipient can agree **4.30** that lower percentages will be charged. For those recipients who shop around, providers will have to take a view on how far they are prepared to reduce the success fee percentages having regard to the risk and anticipated level of work that the claim presents. Too many unsuccessful claims with no return, taken on initially to simply undercut a competitor, presents significant problems to the profitability and the long-term business model of providers.

Only one success fee can be charged.[26] If a recipient enters into more than **4.31** one agreement, e.g. with their initial provider and there is then a change of agency, the providers will require to agree amongst themselves as to how any success fee is to be apportioned between them. Normally law accountants would be asked for advice on a fair allocation of the success fee between the different providers, having regard to the extent of the work done by each. A solicitor, as a matter of professional practice, is not entitled to exercise a lien over the files where to do so would cause prejudice to the client. What constitutes prejudice in any given case depends on the case circumstances, but mere inconvenience is insufficient to cause prejudice. Issues in relation to who is entitled to the success fee and in what proportions are discussed below.

Family proceedings (as defined by s. 135 of the Courts Reform (Scotland) **4.32** Act 2014) cannot be the subject of a damages based agreement, i.e. one where the success fee is determined by the amount of financial benefit derived by the recipient.[27] They can, however, be the subject of a speculative fee agreement.[28]

The 2018 Act allows regulations to be introduced to exclude additional **4.33** categories of civil proceedings from being dealt with under a success fee agreement, whether a damages based or conditional fee agreement, but at the time of implementation of the regulations, the only specified exclusion is for family proceedings.

---

24 Civil Litigation (Expenses and Group Proceedings) (Scotland) Act 2018 (Success Fee Agreements) Regulations 2020 reg. 2(4).
25 Civil Litigation (Expenses and Group Proceedings) (Scotland) Act 2018 (Success Fee Agreements) Regulations 2020 reg. 2(5).
26 Civil Litigation (Expenses and Group Proceedings) (Scotland) Act 2018 (Success Fee Agreements) Regulations 2020 reg. 2(6).
27 Civil Litigation (Expenses and Group Proceedings) (Scotland) Act 2018 (Success Fee Agreements) Regulations 2020 reg. 3.
28 Solicitors (Scotland) Act 1980 s. 61A.

Form and content of a success fee agreement

4.34 An SFA must be in writing.[29] It must also specify the basis upon which the success fee is to be determined.[30] Beyond that, the 2020 Regulations prescribe eleven additional requirements in relation to the content of SFAs.

4.35 An SFA must:

(a) include details of the matter, claim or proceedings, or parts thereof, to which the SFA relates;

(b) specify the type of civil remedy that the recipient seeks;

(c) include a description of the work to be carried out by the provider;

(d) provide that in the event of a conflict with the provider's standard terms of engagement, the terms of the SFA take precedence;

(e) specify the basis on which the amount of any fee potentially payable under the SFA is to be determined;

(f) oblige the provider to consult with the recipient on any significant development including, but not limited to, the receipt of an offer of settlement;

(g) specify whether or not the provider intends to retain any expenses that are awarded to the recipient in civil proceedings or that it is agreed with another person that the recipient is entitled to recover;

(h) explain how to access the relevant procedure for dealing with complaints about the provider or providers;

(i) set out the circumstances in which the provider may, as a consequence of the recipient's conduct, terminate the agreement prior to the resolution of the matter to which it relates and require payment from the recipient for services provided prior to termination;

(j) provide that where the recipient terminates the SFA prior to the resolution of the matter to which it relates, the recipient will normally be liable to pay for services provided prior to termination; and

(k) provide details of the fee that would be charged by the provider and any other sums that would be payable by the recipient to the provider, in the event that the provider or recipient terminates the agreement prior to the resolution of the matter to which it relates.

4.36 Some of these requirements, such as scope of work and complaints procedures are also requirements of the Law Society of Scotland in relation to what a solicitor should have in their letters of engagement. The regulations, of course, are not limited to contracts with solicitors and in any event it is clear from the Regulations that the SFA takes precedence over any other business terms if there is a conflict between the two.

Template agreement

4.37 The Law Society of Scotland set up a working group to draft an SFA that would be compliant with the Act and Regulations, and therefore enforceable. The agreement can be found in Appendix 2. It is not mandatory for providers to use the style, it has simply been published as a suggested version that is believed to be compliant with the legislation.

---

29 2018 Act s. 7(1).
30 2018 Act s. 7(2).

The requirements for the content of the agreement are to ensure clarity as   **4.38**
to what will happen if certain situations arise and to ensure that the recipient,
who is often a consumer with little or no experience of the legal system, has
a succinct and easily understandable contract regulating their dealings with
a provider. To protect the recipient, the regulations provide that an SFA is
unenforceable to the extent that it makes provision that is materially contrary
to s. 7(1) and (2) of the 2018 Act and the 2020 Regulations. That does not
mean the whole agreement is unenforceable, only the offending provisions.

Personal injury cases

Special rules apply only to personal injury actions or damages for the death of   **4.39**
a person due to personal injuries. These rules create additional requirements
in relation to the content of the agreement and how future damages require
to be dealt with.

The agreement must provide that the recipient is not liable to make any   **4.40**
payment, including outlays incurred, to the provider apart from the success
fee. Outlays do not include any sum paid in respect of insurance premiums[31]
in connection with the claim to which the agreement relates.[32] So, any premium for an 'after the event' (ATE) insurance policy can be deducted from
the recipient's damages.

The implication of s. 6(2) is that the provider cannot charge the recipient for   **4.41**
any unrecoverable outlays. If a provider fails to obtain certification of a skilled
person, the costs associated with the instruction of that skilled person cannot
be charged by the provider to the recipient. The provider has to pay those
costs out of their own pocket. Similarly, if a provider is unable to obtain sanction for the employment of counsel in sheriff court proceedings, the recipient
cannot be charged for counsel's fees. Any outlays disallowed by the auditor of
court cannot be charged to the recipient.

BREACHES OF SFA OBLIGATIONS

However, there is one very important exception to not charging the recipient   **4.42**
beyond the terms of the success fee and ATE premium and that is where the
recipient breaches the terms of the SFA. The Taylor report makes no specific
recommendation for how breaches of an SFA should be dealt with, but it
is inconceivable that s. 6(2) applies in a situation where: (a) the provider is
entitled to terminate the SFA due to a recipient's breach; or (b) the recipient
ends the agreement prior to the conclusion of the case. Such eventualities
would leave the provider with no right of recourse to be paid for the work that
has been carried out and that they are prevented from successfully concluding
due to the recipient failing to comply with one or more of their obligations
under the SFA.

Regulations 4(i) and 4(j) of the 2020 Regulations specifically require the   **4.43**
agreement to stipulate the type of conduct on the part of the recipient that
justifies the provider charging the recipient for some or all of the services that

31 2018 Act s. 6(2).
32 2018 Act s. 6(3).

have been provided due to early termination. Regulation 4(k) requires the agreement to set out the charging arrangements that apply in those scenarios. It can therefore be inferred that s. 6(2) prohibiting the recipient being charged anything other than the success fee or ATE insurance premium only applies where the agreement is not breached or terminated prematurely by the recipient.

4.44   The Law Society of Scotland template in Appendix 2 was devised after much debate between the members of the working group as to how to deal with breaches. The group consisted of a cross-section of those with an interest in SFAs, whether pursuers' agents, defenders' agents, academics or, most importantly, lay persons representing the client interest. All accepted that the legislation had to be interpreted so as to permit the provider to render fees if the recipient breached the agreement.

The template sets out the recipient's obligations in cl. 2 as follows:

(a) Give instructions that allow the provider to do their work properly.
(b) Not ask the provider to work in an improper or unreasonable way.
(c) Not deliberately mislead the provider.
(d) Co-operate with the provider when asked.
(e) Go to any medical or expert examination when asked to do so by the provider or the opponents.
(f) Subject to cl. 3(a), accept the provider's professional opinion, given in good faith, if they believe objectively that you are unlikely to win.
(g) Subject to cl. 3(a), accept the provider's professional opinion, given in good faith, about making a settlement with the opponents.

4.45   However, the template in clause 5 provides for different consequences depending on why the agreement is terminated.

(5) (1) The Recipient can end the Agreement at any time. If the Recipient ends the Agreement prior to the final resolution of the claim, whether litigated or not or prior to the Provider receiving payment of judicial or extra judicial fees, VAT and outlays from the opponent or their insurers on settlement of the Recipient's claim, the Provider has the right to charge for all work done on the Recipient's behalf up to that date. The charge out rates as at [insert date] are:

Partner   £A per hour
Associate Solicitor   £B per hour
Assistant Solicitor   £C per hour
Administrative Assistant   £D per hour

The Provider is entitled to add VAT to the foregoing rates at the prevailing rate from time to time in force and be paid for any outlays incurred or which the Provider has committed to incur on the Recipient's behalf.

These rates are reviewed on [specify] each year and are available from the Provider on request. These charges will be notified by the Provider to the Recipient in writing as soon as reasonably practicable after they take effect.

(2) The Provider can end the Agreement at any time:
    a. if the Recipient does not fulfil their responsibilities as outlined in Clauses 2(a), (b), (c), (d) or (e) above. The Provider then has the right to decide whether the Recipient must pay fees, VAT and any outlays incurred for the work done on their behalf up to that date. If the Provider decides to charge said fees VAT and outlays, the Provider will charge for the work using the rates mentioned in 5(1) above. The Provider shall be entitled to

exercise a lien over all documents / files relating to the Recipient's claim pending payment of said fees, VAT and outlays.

b. if they form the opinion acting objectively and in good faith that the Recipient is unlikely to win and the Recipient rejects that advice. Provided the Recipient has complied with all of their other obligations under Clause 2, the Recipient will only be responsible to the Provider for payment of expenses recovered, relative to the period up to the date this agreement is terminated. Further, the Provider may only claim a share of expenses, if the Recipient goes on to derive a financial benefit from the claim. The Provider will be entitled to a share of expenses (including VAT and outlays) recovered on behalf of the Recipient, to be determined on an equitable basis having regard to the relevant services provided by the Provider and any new Provider who is subsequently instructed. In the event of disagreement with any new Provider or other person as to relative share or shares, the matter will be referred at the expense of the Providers to the Auditor at Edinburgh Sheriff Court, who will determine an equitable apportionment of expenses on the basis of the relevant services provided by each Provider in relation to the whole expenses recovered. In these circumstances no success fee shall be chargeable by the Provider first instructed.

c. if the Recipient rejects the Provider's opinion, arrived at objectively and in good faith about making a settlement with their opponent:

1. In the event the recipient goes on to derive a financial benefit, the Provider is entitled to charge for the expenses (consisting of the fees, VAT and outlays) which have been incurred on the Recipient's behalf up to the date this agreement is terminated. The expenses payable by the Recipient to the Provider under this subclause are confined to those recoverable judicially from the opponent(s), and are recoverable by the Provider in addition to the success fee mentioned above. The amount of the success fee payable shall be calculated by reference to the financial benefit actually obtained but shall not exceed the level of the success fee which would have been chargeable if the Provider's advice had been accepted by the Recipient. The success fee under this agreement becomes payable as soon as the financial benefit is obtained, whether as a result of extra judicial agreement or judicial determination.

Where expenses have been recovered in the claim, a share of the recovered expenses is payable to the Provider on the receipt of those expenses from the opponent. The Provider's share of expenses shall be determined on the same basis and in the same manner as set out in clause 5(2)(b).

The Recipient hereby undertakes to:

a. Notify the Provider of the identity of any new Provider who is instructed to provide relevant services in connection with the claim and

b. Instruct the new Provider to account to the Provider under this agreement for all sums due under this clause.

If the Recipient does not instruct a new provider but represents him or herself and derives a financial benefit, the Recipient shall make payment to the Provider under this agreement in accordance with the same timescales as if a new Provider had been instructed.

2. In the event that the Recipient does not go on to derive a financial benefit, having rejected the Provider's advice to settle, the Recipient shall be liable to pay to the Provider all outlays which the Provider incurred or is liable to incur on the Recipient's behalf.

(3) In any scenario in clause 5 where the Recipient pays the Provider a fee charged at the hourly rates referred to clause 5(1) above, the total paid by the Recipient to the Provider shall be fair and reasonable in the circumstances.

(4) In the event that the Recipient dies or becomes incapax prior to the final resolution of the claim, whether litigated or not, or prior to the Provider receiving payment

of judicial or extra judicial fees, VAT and outlays from the opponent or their insurers on settlement of the Recipient's claim, and the Recipient's executor, guardian or other representative, as the case may be, do not choose to continue instructing the Provider to provide ongoing advice with the claim, the Provider has the right to charge for all work done on the Recipient's behalf up to the date when the Provider becomes aware of the death or incapacity. The applicable charge out rates are those set out in clause 5(1) above, as amended by any annual increases.

4.46   The view taken by the Law Society of Scotland's working group was that cl. 2(a) to (e) inclusive are 'conduct' breaches where the recipient's conduct justifies time and line charging. However, it was considered a potential bar to accessing a second opinion where a genuine difference of opinion arises between provider and client on the issues of prospects of success or acceptance of a settlement offer if clients faced time and line charging in those scenarios.

The SFA template is worded in such a way that:

(1) If advice about prospects is rejected but the client goes on to win, the original provider is not entitled to a share of the success fee, only a fair share of recovered judicial expenses.

(2) If advice about settlement is rejected and the client goes on to win, the original provider is entitled to charge a success fee calculated by reference to the value of the financial benefit that the recipient actually obtains, capped at what the success fee would have been if the settlement advice had been accepted.

(3) If advice about settlement is rejected and the client goes on to lose, they only have to pay the original provider for the outlays that they incurred, or were committed to incur, prior to the agreement being terminated.

4.47   It remains open to all providers to adapt the wording of the template on a case-by-case basis to suit the needs of specific clients provided the terms are compliant with the 2018 Act and 2020 Regulations.

FUTURE DAMAGES

4.48   The question of whether future damages should be included in the calculation of a success fee was a contentious issue at the time of the Taylor report. Some were of the view that damages for future loss should be excluded altogether from the calculation, as to do otherwise would deprive an accident victim of a portion of compensation that they know they will need in future life, whether to make up for loss of earnings or to pay for care, etc. Others argued that future loss can often be the most time-consuming aspect of a claim that requires the most work and often gives rise to the most complex issues. To exclude future damages would deprive the provider from proper remuneration for a labour-intensive part of the service provision.

4.49   The 2018 Act permits the inclusion of future damages in the success fee calculation provided certain conditions are met.

For the provider to be able to include future damages in the success fee calculation, reference has to be made in the agreement itself to the terms of s. 6(5) of the 2018 Act. If it does not make reference to the terms of s. 6(5), the agreement must provide that any future damages will not be included in the value of damages that is used for calculating the success fee.

Section 6(5) provides that the future element is within this subsection if it is **4.50** to be paid in a lump sum and:

(a)   does not exceed £1 million; or
(b)   exceeds £1 million and:
    (i)   the provider had not advised the recipient to accept that the future element be paid in periodical instalments; and
    (ii)   the condition in subs. 6 is met.

The subs. 6 condition is that: **4.51**

(a)   In the case where the damages are awarded by a court or tribunal, the court or tribunal in awarding the future element has stated that it is satisfied that it is in the recipient's best interests that the future element be paid as a lump sum rather than in periodical payments,
(b)   In the case where the damages are obtained by agreement, that an independent actuary has, after having consulted the recipient personally in the absence of the provider, certified that in the actuary's view it is in the recipient's best interests that the future element be paid as a lump sum rather than in periodical instalments.

COMMENTARY

There is no requirement for any independent scrutiny of a decision to pay **4.52** future damages as a lump sum if the value of the future damages is £1million or less. It is worth emphasising that the £1million figure is for the future element and not the overall value of the compensation award. A success fee on a £2,000,000 settlement could be charged on the full amount of damages if the future element is no more than £1,000,000.

Failure to clearly set out in the SFA how future damages are to be dealt with **4.53** when calculating the success fee will result in the provider not being able to charge a success fee on the future element.

No procedure is set out for the court to follow in satisfying itself as to whether **4.54** it is in the recipient's best interests to award future loss as a lump sum. The fact that subs. 6a does not mirror subs. 6b, i.e. the court does not *have* to consider a report from an actuary, suggests that the court has a wide discretion as to how to handle such situations. But if the provider wants to be in a position to include future damages in any success fee, it would be prudent for an actuarial report to be commissioned and evidence from the actuary agreed or led at proof if a lump sum is the recipient's preferred option. Failure to do so runs the risk of the court forming the view that it has not been persuaded to order a lump sum. The opponent's preferred option normally would be to seek a periodical payment order as opposed to make an expensive lump sum settlement and they can of course lead their own evidence on why it is appropriate to make a periodical payment order. There would be nothing precluding the court from ordaining the recipient's agents to obtain an actuarial report if it was felt appropriate and the attitude of the court would be best canvassed by both parties in their statements of proposals and, if necessary, at the case management hearing.

4.55   Neither the 2018 Act nor the 2020 Regulations make any reference to the commonly encountered situation where the settlement is paid partly as a lump sum and partly as periodical payments. There may be a portion of the future loss element required straight away to allow for the purchase of accommodation, house adaptations or other immediate capital expenditure needs, but the rest of the future loss is to be paid as periodical payments. In that situation, the question arises as to whether the portion of future damages paid as a lump sum falls to be included in the value of the financial benefit for the purposes of calculating the success fee. There is no logical reason why it should not, provided all the other requirements for dealing with future loss damages are met. The element of future loss to be included in the success fee calculation would have to be restricted to £1,000,000. The portion of future loss payable in periodical instalments cannot be included in the success fee calculation.

4.56   Who pays for the actuarial report or any other evidence ordered by the court to satisfy s. 6? The Taylor report recommended that liability for the actuary's fee should fall upon the solicitor should the solicitor advise that a lump sum award be made, regardless of the actuarial recommendation.

That recommendation does not specifically appear in the 2018 Act or 2020 Regulations, which is undoubtedly deliberate on the part of the Government drafters who would have been well aware of the Taylor proposal but have chosen to ignore it. That is not surprising. The requirement for actuarial scrutiny is a legal requirement for the resolution of a litigation. Expenses necessarily incurred as part of a litigation would, in the normal course of events, be payable by the unsuccessful party on the 'expenses follow success' principle. Imposing a personal liability on a pursuer's solicitor has only ever been seen in the context of adverse conduct of that agent.

Chapter 5

Certification of Skilled Persons

Many court actions will involve the instruction of skilled persons to investigate   **5.01**
and report on matters pertaining to the dispute. Ultimately, the purpose is
to assist the court in determining issues with which it is not familiar. Such
evidence may, of course, assist parties prior to or during the conduct of a
litigation to achieve an extra-judicial resolution.

There is no definition of 'skilled' laid down in the rules. According to   **5.02**
MacPhail,[1] there is no rigid rule that the person must possess some technical
qualification.[2] It is thought that they 'must however possess either a theoret-
ical acquaintance with matters of scientific knowledge or practical experience
of the rules of any trade, manufacture or business with which men of ordinary
intelligence are not likely to be familiar'.[3]

Before the costs payable to a skilled person are recoverable by the entitled   **5.03**
party from the opponent, the skilled person requires to be certified by the
court as a skilled person. If that is done then it is the auditor's job to assess the
reasonableness of the charges that the skilled person has levied.

Such witnesses in the past have been referred to as expert witnesses or   **5.04**
skilled witnesses. The correct terminology is skilled person to reflect the phra-
seology in the court rules.

RELEVANT COURT RULES RE CERTIFICATION
OF SKILLED PERSONS

For actions commenced prior to 29 April 2019, the rule in relation to the cer-   **5.05**
tification of skilled persons is found in the Act of Sederunt (Fees of Solicitors
and Witnesses in the Sheriff Court) (Amendment) 2011,[4] which states:

> 1. (1) If at any time before the Diet of Taxation the Sheriff has granted a motion for
> the certification of a person as skilled, charges shall be allowed for any work done
> or expenses reasonably incurred by that person that were reasonably required for a
> purpose in connection with the cause or in contemplation of the cause.
> (2) A motion under paragraph 1 may be granted only if the Sheriff is satisfied
> that (a) the person was a skilled person and (b) it was reasonable to employ the
> person ...

---

1 Macphail, *Sheriff Court Practice*, 3rd edn (Edinburgh: W. Green, 2006) para. 19.62.
2 *Hopes and Lavery v HMA* 1960 JC 104 per Lord Sorn at 113–114.
3 *Allison v Chief Constable of Strathclyde Police* 2004 SLT 340.
4 Act of Sederunt (Fees of Solicitors and Witnesses in the Sheriff Court) (Amendment) 2011
(SSI 2011/403).

(3) The charges which shall be allowed under paragraph 1 shall be such as the Auditor of Court determines are fair and reasonable ...

5.06 The motion for certification can be presented at any time before the diet of taxation. There is no requirement to obtain certification prospectively. The court determines the certification motion by considering whether the witness was 'skilled' and whether it was reasonable to employ them.

5.07 The rules for certification of skilled persons in actions raised on or after 29 April 2019 are found in the Act of Sederunt (Taxation of Judicial Expenses Rules) 2019 (the 2019 Rules)[5]:

4.5.—(1) No charge incurred to a person who has been engaged for the purposes of the application of that person's skill is to be allowed as an outlay unless—
> (a) the person has been certified as a skilled person in accordance with rule 5.3 (certification of skilled persons); and
> (b) except where paragraph (4) applies, the charge relates to work done, or expenses incurred, after the date of certification.

(2) Where a person has been so certified, the Auditor is to allow charges for work done or expenses reasonably incurred by that person which were reasonably required for a purpose in connection with the proceedings, or in contemplation of the proceedings.

(3) The charges to be allowed under paragraph (2) are such charges as the Auditor determines to be fair and reasonable.

(4) This paragraph applies where—
> (a) the account relates to—
>> (i) proceedings subject to Chapter 43 of the Rules of the Court of Session 1994;
>> (ii) proceedings subject to Chapter 36 of the Ordinary Cause Rules 1993; or
>> (iii) a simple procedure case; or
> (b) the sheriff has determined in accordance with rule 5.3(5) that the certification has effect for the purposes of work done, or expenses incurred, before the date of certification.

5.3.—(1) On the application of a party the court may certify a person as a skilled person for the purpose of rule 4.5 (skilled persons).

(2) The court may only grant such an application if satisfied that—
> (a) the person is a skilled person; and
> (b) it is, or was, reasonable and proportionate that the person should be employed.

(3) The refusal of an application under this rule does not preclude the making of a further application on a change of circumstances.

(4) Where the application is made in proceedings other than—
> (a) proceedings subject to Chapter 43 of the Rules of the Court of Session 1994;
> (b) proceedings subject to Chapter 36 of the Ordinary Cause Rules 1993; or
> (c) a simple procedure case,

paragraph (5) applies.

(5) Where this paragraph applies, the court may only determine that the certification has effect for the purposes of work already done by the person where the court is satisfied that the party applying has shown cause for not having applied for certification before the work was done.

---

5 Act of Sederunt (Taxation of Judicial Expenses Rules) 2019 (SSI 2019/75).

PRE-29 APRIL 2019 CASE LAW

The following cases remain relevant to the position post-29 April 2019 as they **5.08**
deal with the court's application of the applicable test for certification, the
fundamentals of which remain the same.

* *Boyle v CIS Ltd*, ASPIC 7/6/17 (Sheriff McGowan).
* *Delaney v* Jet2.com *Ltd*, ASPIC 12/2/19 (Sheriff Braid).

Boyle v CIS Ltd[6] is a decision relating to the certification of Professor Alan **5.09**
Carson, a skilled person for the pursuer.

Up until this case was decided, it seemed to be ASPIC's preference that **5.10**
motions for certification of skilled witnesses would simply include details of
what the skilled person had done in the case, for example, prepare a report or
attend a consultation, etc. It wasn't normally the case that the motion would
narrate anything about why the witness was skilled or why it was reasonable
to employ them.

In the *Boyle* case, the pursuer had instructed reports from a neurosurgeon, **5.11**
a psychologist and, in addition, a report from Professor Carson, an eminent
consultant neuropsychiatrist who has a special interest in chronic pain management and somatoform disorders. His report had been obtained but never
disclosed to the opponents.

The defenders did not take any issue with the fact that Professor **5.12**
Carson was a skilled person. The issue was whether it was reasonable to
employ him.

There was a suggestion that the psychiatrist who had prepared a report had **5.13**
commented on somatoform disorder and the court would therefore have to
be satisfied that there was no overlap between the reports and that a separate
report from Professor Carson was required. The pursuer's agent did not
supply the court with copies of Professor Carson's report nor the psychiatrist's
report to allow the court to satisfy itself on the reasonableness issue. Not
surprisingly, the pursuer failed to satisfy the court that it was reasonable to
instruct Professor Carson and his certification was refused.

The decision effectively required a change of practice for the certification **5.14**
of skilled persons in ASPIC where e-motion procedure is used so that the
motions that are presented, at least the motions that are marked as opposed
and are then enrolled for calling, require to fully set out the basis for saying
that a particular witness is a skilled person and why it was reasonable to
instruct them.

Where traditional paper-based motion procedure is used (at the time of **5.15**
publication e-motion procedure has not been rolled out across all sheriff
courts) it is suggested that a sufficiently clear basis on 'skill' and 'reasonableness' is set out in the main body of the motion to enable a sheriff to grant any
unopposed motion without further inquiry. Paper-based notices of opposition
do not require grounds of opposition to be set out but normal and reasonable
practice would involve parties' agents having a dialogue to be clear on the
grounds of opposition to at least focus the specific points for argument at a
hearing.

---

6 *Boyle v CIS Ltd* [2017] SC EDIN 36.

5.16   The case of *Delaney v Jet2.com Ltd*[7] is a decision of Sheriff Braid in a case where there was opposition to a motion to certify Dr Martin Livingston, consultant psychiatrist, as a skilled person.

5.17   Reference was made to the case of *Webster v McLeod*[8] where the Sheriff Appeal Court stated at para. 20:

> 'Reasonableness falls to be determined objectively: it falls to be assessed at the time of instruction. That requires consideration of the state of affairs at the point of instruction. Implicit in the concept of reasonableness is proportionality: proportionality between the decision to instruct that skilled person at that particular time and the matters in issue or likely to be in issue.'

5.18   There is no dispute that Dr Livingston was a skilled person, the issue was whether it was reasonable to instruct him. The orthopaedic report that was available recommended a psychiatric opinion and the general practitioner records contained reference to some psychiatric injury.

5.19   The issue in the case related to the competency of the psychiatric claim that proceeded under the Montreal Convention because the pursuer had sustained an accident whilst disembarking an aircraft. The Convention stated that the carrier is liable for damage sustained in the case of death or bodily injury of a passenger only where the accident that caused the death or injury took place onboard the aircraft or in the course of any of the operations of embarking or disembarking. It was argued that psychiatric injury is not included in that definition.

5.20   The court held that the tender proposed in the case was made in the knowledge that there was at least a risk of the pursuer being found entitled to damages for psychiatric injury. Having the tender accepted bought off that risk.

5.21   The law was clear that if there was only psychiatric injury there was no claim but it was much less clear where there was both physical and psychiatric injury. With the tender accepted, the legal issue of whether psychiatric damages could be recovered was left uncertain.

5.22   The court held that regardless, no claim would have been presented without a psychiatric report. The law must be given the opportunity to develop and the sheriff concluded that it was reasonable for the pursuer to have instructed Dr Livingston for a report.

Certification of skilled persons under the 2019 Rules

5.23   *Finlay v Borders Health Board*[9] is a useful exposition of how motions for certification, and indeed sanction for counsel, are to be handled under the 2019 Rules.

5.24   The court was concerned with an unopposed motion for the pursuer in the following terms:

    i.   remit the action to Chapter 36A with reference to Rule 36.1(2);

    ii. in terms of sections 4.3 and 5.1(c) of the Act of Sederunt (Taxation of Judicial Expenses) Rules 2019 to: 1) grant sanction for the employment of junior

---

7 *Delaney v Jet2.com Ltd* [2019] SC EDIN13.
8 *Webster v McLeod* 2018 SLT (Sheriff Court) 429.
9 *Finlay v Borders Health Board* [2019] SC EDIN 99.

counsel to assist with the conduct of the entire cause as a whole; and 2) in respect that junior counsel has already drafted the initial writ necessary to allow these proceedings to be raised, to retrospectively sanction the employment of junior counsel for the work already undertaken;

iii. in terms of sections 4.5 and 5.1(b) of the Act of Sederunt (Taxation of Judicial Expenses) Rules 2019 to: 1) certify the following persons as skilled persons for the entire conduct of these proceedings: a) Mr Patrick Foster, Consultant Orthopaedic Surgeon ...; and b) Dr Naida Forbes, Consultant Psychiatrist ...; 2) in respect that Mr Patrick Foster has already undertaken work necessary to allow these proceedings to be raised, to retrospectively certify this person as a skilled person in respect of work already done; iv. thereafter, to sist the cause ...'

Sheriff McGowan recapped on the relevant parts of the 2019 Rules and made **5.25** the following observations:

- Rule 4.5 contains a general prohibition on the auditor allowing charges to skilled persons predating certification as a recoverable outlay. In other words, certification of a skilled persons does not ordinarily have retrospective effect.
- That prohibition does not apply to certification in two situations. The first is if certification is granted in one of the three types specified, namely proceedings under Ch. 43 in the Court of Session, Ch. 36 of the Ordinary Cause Rules 1993 in the sheriff court; or simple procedure cases.[10] The second is if the sheriff has determined in accordance with r. 5.3(5) that the certification has effect for the purposes of work done, or expenses incurred, before the date of certification.[11]
- Applications for certification are regulated by r. 5.3. Before a person can be certified as skilled for the purpose of r. 4.5, the court must be satisfied that they are a skilled person and that it is, or was, reasonable and proportionate that they should be employed.[12]
- Where a motion for certification is made in cases other than Ch. 36, Ch. 43 of the Rules of the Court of Session 1994 or simple procedure cases r. 5.3(5) applies in requiring cause to be shown as to why certification was not applied for sooner, i.e. an application for certification with retrospective effect has to be justified.

The sheriff analysed the particular motion: **5.26**

[46] I have already noted that where an application is made to the court under legislation or rules, the language used should follow closely the wording of the law or rule under which the application is made.

[47] Applications for sanction are properly made not under rules 4.5 and 5.1(b) (sic) but under Rule 5.3(1) and (2) – and, where necessary, Rule 5.3(5).

[48] Phrases like " ... for the entire conduct of these proceedings ... " are unnecessary and inaccurate. The order made by the court is that a person is certified as skilled (with or without retrospective effect – see above). It is then a matter for the Auditor to decide to what extent charges for work done or expenses incurred by the skilled person are recoverable: Rule 4.5(2).

[49] Retrospective certification sanction is also sought for work already done by Mr Foster.

---

10 Act of Sederunt (Taxation of Judicial Expenses Rules) 2019 r. 4.5(4)(a).
11 Act of Sederunt (Taxation of Judicial Expenses Rules) 2019 r. 4.5(4)(b).
12 Act of Sederunt (Taxation of Judicial Expenses Rules) 2019 r. 5.3(1) and (2).

[50] In my view, this part of the motion is unnecessary ... In short, this case is presently proceeding under Chapter 36. Thus, if I grant the motion for certification in respect of Mr Foster, that has retrospective effect.

[51] I shall sanction the proceedings as suitable for the employment of junior counsel; certify Mr Patrick Foster, Consultant Orthopaedic Surgeon and Dr Naida Forbes, Consultant Psychiatrist as skilled persons; refuse as unnecessary the motion for retrospective sanction (under Rule 5.4(6)) for particular work already carried out and retrospective certification under Rule 5.3(5) for work already done; remit the action to Chapter 36A; and sist the cause."

COMMENTARY

5.27 The first point to make is that the motion in question was being considered at a time when the case was still proceeding under Ch. 36 of the Ordinary Cause Rules 1993. It had not yet been remitted to Ch. 36A of the Ordinary Cause Rules 1993 procedure and therefore certifying a skilled person automatically meant, in terms of r. 4.5(4)(a)(i), that retrospective certification was not required. Providing the certification is granted prior to the remit to Ch. 36A, it will subsist throughout the case and cover work done both before and after the certification.

5.28 Secondly, the mere fact that a skilled person is certified does not mean that the cost of all the work they do in the case is recoverable as part of a judicial account. It is for the auditor to decide what is a reasonable charge to allow.

5.29 Thirdly, in all cases it is for the party seeking certification to satisfy the court on two issues, namely:

(1) that the person to be certified is a skilled person; and
(2) that it is or was reasonable and proportionate that they should be employed. This should be adequately set out in the body of the motion.

5.30 Fourthly, if the case is not one proceeding: (1) under Ch. 36 of the Ordinary Cause Rules 1993; (2) Ch. 43 of the Rules of the Court of Session 1994; or (3) as a simple procedure case, retrospective certification is required for any work done by the skilled person prior to the motion being granted. In terms of r. 5.3(5) this can only be granted by the court where it is 'satisfied that the party applying has shown cause for not having applied for certification before the work was done'.

5.31 One obvious example is the work done by a skilled person prior to the action being raised. There is nothing in the rules that prescribes the appropriate stage in procedure for lodging a motion for retrospective certification of pre-litigation work after an action is raised, but it is suggested that this should be done as soon as a notice of intention to defend is lodged. The longer the gap between raising the action and presenting the motion, the harder it may become to show cause for not having applied earlier. That said, the wording of the rule simply requires the applying party to have 'shown cause'. It does not set a high bar. It does not require exceptional reasons or impose on the court a duty to only grant such motions in exceptional circumstances. Oversight or administrative error may be sufficient reasons. The court has a wide discretion in how to decide such motions, including the making of appropriate orders in relation to variation of timetables and/or expenses orders to deal with any prejudice that may arise if the motion is granted.

Chapter 6

Conduct and Expenses

The court possesses an inherent power to make awards of expenses as it sees **6.01** fit, in accordance with the principles of fairness and reasonableness and provided that in doing so it does not breach any statutory provision, such as the rules on Qualified One-Way Cost Shifting.

To that end, the court has always had the power to reflect its displeasure **6.02** at the way a litigation is conducted through an award of expenses. This can be against a party to the action or against a legal representative. The power to make an award against a legal representative tends to arise relatively infrequently and only in the context of reprehensible conduct that has needlessly wasted time and expense.

At the time of publication, s. 11 of the Civil Litigation (Expenses and Group **6.03** Proceedings) (Scotland) Act 2018 has yet to come into force. Section 11 is in the following terms:

Awards of expenses against legal representatives
11.—(1) This section applies in civil proceedings where the court considers that a legal representative of a party to the proceedings has committed a serious breach of that representative's duties to the court.
(2) The court may make an award of expenses against the legal representative.
(3) This section is subject to any limitations that may be specified in an act of sederunt under section 103(1) or 104(1) of the Courts Reform (Scotland) Act 2014.

An Act of Sederunt has been in draft form since 2019[1] but never completed. It is anticipated that it will amend the rules of the Court of Session, Ordinary Cause Rules, Sheriff Appeal Court Rules, Simple Procedure Rules and Summary Cause Rules by:

(1) permitting the court to find a legal representative liable for expenses incurred by a party where the representative is guilty of a serious breach of their duties to the court and the expenses are attributable to that breach;
(2) restricting the amount to the level of expenses incurred by a party who has suffered the loss attributable to that breach of duty;
(3) permitting the court to make an order for expenses: (a) on its own account; or (b) on the motion of a party for whom the representative does not act, and never has acted;

---

1 Provisionally entitled: Act of Sederunt (Rules of the Court of Session, Sheriff Appeal Court Rules, Ordinary Cause Rules, Summary Cause Rules and Simple Procedure Rules Amendment) (Awards of Expenses against Legal Representatives).

(4) providing for a hearing to be fixed to allow the representative, and any party, to be heard on the matter, with written submissions being lodged in advance.

6.04 Therefore, whilst there is an existing common law discretionary power permitting the court to make awards against legal representatives, the new legislation is likely to regulate the procedure to be followed before such an award is made. There is likely to be a requirement for the court to be satisfied that the breach of duty is serious and that a loss, in the form of legal fees, VAT and/or outlays, has been caused by that breach.

6.05 In the meantime, the case law is the best guide to the attitude of the courts in making expenses awards based on 'adverse' conduct of a party or their representative. The following are a selection of cases relating to conduct:

- *Steven Devine v Ian Laurie*, 10 October 2016 (decision of Sheriff McGowan).
- *Robertson v Edinburgh City Council*, 4 July 2017 (decision of Sheriff McGowan).
- *Tomczak v Reid*, 19 September 2017 (decision of Sheriff McGowan).
- *Graham v Farrell*, October 2017 (decision of Sheriff McGowan).
- *Russell v Russell*, 24 October 2017 (decision of Lord Boyd in the Court of Session).
- *Zdrzalka v Sabre Insurance* [2018] SC EDIN57 (decision of Sheriff McGowan).

6.06 *Devine v Laurie*[2] was one that led to the pursuer's account of expenses being modified by 20 per cent for failing to timeously disclose medical evidence. At para. 61 of his judgment, Sheriff McGowan said that solicitors are officers of court and have obligations to the court and to their opponents. So, if the circumstances reasonably required the disclosure of the medical reports, the fact that the pursuer themselves did not want to is not a sound reason for failing to do so. Secondly, agents have a responsibility to ensure, so far as is possible, that the court is asked to adjudicate only on matters in respect of which there is a live dispute between parties. Part of that duty entails the obligation to identify or facilitate the identification of matters that are not truly in dispute. The disclosure of the medical reports would have allowed the adjusters to say whether they were prepared to accept them and discuss valuation of the claim based on them and if that had happened an agreement on quantum might have been reached either before or very soon after the action was raised.

6.07 *Robertson v Edinburgh City Council*[3] outlines what is expected of agents during the conduct of a litigation, not just to the court but in dealing with their opponent. The sheriff stated that:

> 'the procedure in this court (ASPIC) is built around the timetable. Once proceedings are commenced, parties are supposed to act in such a way as to enable them to comply with the timetable but there is another aspect to this: parties are also expected to co-operate with their opposite numbers so that as far as possible the action can move forward smoothly. In virtually every action in this court, the pursuer's agent must know that at some stage in the case, defender's agents will wish to access

---

2 *Devine v Laurie* [2016] SC EDIN 83.
3 *Robertson v Edinburgh City Council* [2017] SC EDIN 63.

some or all of the pursuer's medical records usually with a view to commissioning a medico-legal report. If records have been recovered under Specification, in my view the principles enunciated above mean that on request these documents should be disclosed to other parties.'

The Act of Sederunt (Ordinary Cause Rules) 1993[4] require the party recovering documents to tell the other side that they have got them and lodge the recovered documents in process or give the other party the opportunity to borrow, inspect or copy them.   **6.08**

The sheriff took the view that the same principles apply, broadly speaking, to any records recovered by mandate and to make those available if requested to do so.   **6.09**

The sheriff held that both parties were at fault – the defenders could have been much more proactive and the pursuer's agents had simply not disclosed records when they ought to have. Some records were disclosed but they were incomplete so in the context of the case a motion by the pursuer for the expenses of an amendment procedure and the discharge of a proof diet was refused and the court made a finding of no expenses due to or by.   **6.10**

Tomczak v Reid[5] was a case that had proceeded under the voluntary pre-action protocol, where an offer in settlement had been made along with reasonable expenses. The offer for the principal sum was agreed in principle but no agreement could be reached in relation to expenses and, in particular, the reasonableness of two outlays. The first was a police abstract accident report where the defenders argued that there was no need to obtain it and the second a psychiatric report because there was an issue over whether the psychiatrist's fee was rendered through an agency.   **6.11**

The pursuer's agent took the view that because there was no agreement on expenses, he required to litigate the issue. However, Sheriff McGowan took the view that what the pursuer's agents should have done was propose to the defender's agent that the issue of the reasonableness of the outlays be remitted to the auditor of court to rule upon and only if the defender's agent had refused should there be any litigation before ASPIC.   **6.12**

What, in effect, happened here was that the action was raised, a tender for the same amount that had been offered pre-litigation was lodged and accepted and then the expenses arguments ensued. The court took the view that the pursuer had failed to beat the pre-litigation offer, the basis for the action was highly questionable, the motion for expenses was refused so all that the court did was make an order for payment of the principal sum with no expenses due to or by either party. It is not clear whether the defenders got off 'scot free' in avoiding having to pay what they would have had to have paid under the voluntary pre-action protocol for fees, VAT and non-disputed outlays or whether the non-disputed costs had been paid prior to the motion calling.   **6.13**

Graham v Farrell[6] contains a highly significant decision. This was a simple procedure case where the defender had tendered and the pursuer had accepted the tender. Given the level of settlement, which was £3,000, the Simple Procedure Rules state that expenses should be restricted to 10 per cent of the sum decerned for, meaning expenses would be limited to £300.   **6.14**

4 Act of Sederunt (Ordinary Cause Rules) 1993 r. 28.3(4)(a) and (5).
5 *Tomczak v Reid* [2017] SC EDIN 63.
6 *Graham v Farrell* [2017] SC EDIN 75.

6.15   An argument was presented that where the defender effectively withdraws a defence prior to the evidence hearing in a simple procedure case, the pursuer should be entitled to claim expenses without that restriction applying.

6.16   The old Small Claims Rules allowed a party to claim summary cause expenses against the opponent if the opponent had stated a defence and had not proceeded with it through an evidential hearing.

6.17   Sheriff McGowan took the view that it did not matter whether the case settled by way of tender and acceptance or whether it was simply an offer made in correspondence duly accepted by the pursuer. The crucial point is the meaning of the phrase 'has not proceeded with the defence stated'. This, in the court's view, meant that the defender had not proceeded with the hearing on evidence and obtained a decision or judgment of the court. It follows, therefore, that if a defender either abandons their defence or settles a simple procedure case by negotiation prior to the evidential hearing, they will have to pay the full expenses of process as assessed. See, however, Chapter 25 on simple procedure, which highlights some conflicting authorities.

6.18   *Russell v Russell*[7] contains a sobering decision for solicitors. The pursuer's agent had actively sought to resolve the dispute from the outset. Medical records had been recovered and provided to the defender's agent. There were a number of criticisms made of the defender's agent and the pursuer was seeking an order for expenses against him personally. The court recognised that a number of issues could have been handled better in relation to his failure to respond to correspondence, failure to question witnesses as to how they reached conclusions, failure to properly precognosce witnesses and the leisurely conduct of the litigation. However, the court held that none of those particular issues justified an allegation of fault on the part of the solicitor, which, individually or cumulatively, would render him liable to pay costs. Where fault did arise, which led to a finding of expenses against the solicitor, was in respect of his failure to properly instruct a medical expert and ensure that that expert had all the relevant medical records. The expert's final advice was not received until thirteen days before the proof as a result of the solicitor's failures to deal with matters properly.

6.19   The court did not consider that the award of expenses against the solicitor should be on an agent and client basis but did find him liable to pay the expenses of process on a party/party basis. See Chapter 21 for details of the different basis of charging.

6.20   *Zdrzalka v Sabra Insurance*[8] was a case that should have been subject to the compulsory pre-action protocol but the defenders issued an admission of liability that they did not intend to be binding. On that basis, the pursuer raised court proceedings and once the notice of intention to defend was lodged, they disclosed their medical evidence and the case rapidly settled. The defenders tried to argue that they should not be found liable for the expenses of the litigation because the pursuer: (1) should not have raised the court action in the circumstances; and (2) had failed to timeously disclose their medical evidence.

6.21   The court held that by failing to issue a binding admission of liability, the defender had failed to comply with the compulsory pre-action protocol and the pursuer was entitled forthwith to raise proceedings. The terms of the

7   *Russell v Russell* [2017] CSOH 137.
8   *Zdrzalka v Sabra Insurance* [2018] SC EDIN 57.

protocol thereafter were of no relevance. However, common law principles then apply as to whether or not expenses should be awarded, refused or modified.

The writ was warranted on 11 July and served on 18 July. The medical **6.22** evidence was not disclosed until 26 July when a copy of it was intimated to the defenders' solicitor who had by that stage lodged their notice of intention to defend three days earlier.

Sheriff McGowan stated that as a matter of generality, medical reports that **6.23** are to be relied on should be disclosed within a reasonable period of having been obtained. In his view, in that case the medical report should have been disclosed no later than the date upon which the writ was served. The pursuer's agent had stated to the court that it was their policy not to disclose medical reports until the action was defended although they could not put forward any explanation to justify that position.

The court took the view that had the report been disclosed at the time the **6.24** writ was warranted there was every chance that the action would have settled prior to the expiry of the period of notice and would not have become defended. To reflect its displeasure at the pursuer's agent's conduct, the court awarded expenses of process as taxed, but modified the award by 50 per cent up to the date of the tender and then awarded the defenders judicial expenses from the date of the tender onwards, also modified by 50 per cent.

It is submitted that this is a harsh decision. No reason appears to have been advanced as to why the defender failed to comply with the terms of the compulsory protocol and issue a binding admission of liability. Had such an admission been issued it seems, on the face of things, no litigation would have been necessary. Can an agent justifiably be criticised in those circumstances for only disclosing their medical evidence at the time the notice of intention to defend is lodged?

Basically, the lesson to be learned here is if a pursuer fails to 'timeously' **6.25** disclose their medical evidence, they may face an argument that they should not recover all of their costs. The court has an almost unfettered discretion to come up with any expenses order that it considers to be fair and reasonable in the circumstances.

Chapter 7

Sanction for Counsel in the Sheriff Court

7.01   There is no automatic right of recovery for a successful party in relation to the costs of employing counsel in sheriff court or Sheriff Appeal Court proceedings. Sanction for counsel is not required for Court of Session proceedings.

7.02   The starting point for all applications to sanction counsel's involvement is s. 108 of the Courts Reform (Scotland) Act 2014 (the 2014 Act), whether made before or after 29 April 2019. The Act provides:

> **108.**—(1) This section applies in civil proceedings in the Sheriff Court or the Sheriff Appeal Court where the court is deciding, for the purposes of any relevant expenses rule, whether to sanction the employment of counsel by a party for the purposes of the proceedings.
> (2) The court must sanction the employment of counsel if the court considers, in all the circumstances of the case, that it is reasonable to do so.
> (3) In considering that matter, the court must have regard to—
>   (a) whether the proceedings are such as to merit the employment of counsel, having particular regard to—
>   (i) the difficulty or complexity, or likely difficulty or complexity, of the proceedings,
>   (ii) the importance or value of any claim in the proceedings, and
>   (b) the desirability of ensuring that no party gains an unfair advantage by virtue of the employment of counsel.
> (4) The court may have regard to such other matters as it considers appropriate.
> (5) References in this section to proceedings include references to any part or aspect of the proceedings.
> (6) In this section—
>   • "counsel" means—
>   a.   an advocate,
>   b.   a solicitor having a right of audience in the Court of Session under section 25A of the Solicitors (Scotland) Act 1980,
>   • "court", in relation to proceedings in the sheriff court, means the sheriff,
>   • "relevant expenses rule" means, in relation to any proceedings mentioned in subsection (1), any provision of an act of sederunt requiring, or having the effect of requiring, that the employment of counsel by a party for the purposes of the proceedings be sanctioned by the court before the fees of counsel are allowable as expenses that may be awarded to the party.
> (7) This section is subject to an act of sederunt under section 104(1) or 106(1).

7.03   The 2014 Act therefore requires that the court must sanction the employment of counsel if the court considers in all the circumstances of the case that it is reasonable to do so. In considering whether it is reasonable, the court must have regard to whether the proceedings are difficult or complex and the importance or value of any claim. It must also have regard to the desirability to ensure that no party gains an unfair advantage by virtue of the employment of counsel – the level playing field argument – and there is the catch-all provision that the court can have regard to 'such other matters as it considers appropriate'. The fact that difficulty, complexity, importance, value and equality of arms are specifically mentioned as factors in applying the test would suggest that the court's main focus should be on these areas in determining the application. However, as we will see below, situations arise where sanction will still be granted having regard to 'such other matters as [the court] considers appropriate', emphasising that the court retains a wide discretion.

PRE-29 APRIL 2019

Also relevant to the position prior to the introduction of the 2019 taxation[1] rules was the Act of Sederunt (Sanction for the Employment of Counsel in the Sheriff Court) 2011.[2] **7.04**

The 2011 Act of Sederunt provided that the sheriff can sanction the employment of counsel in relation to appearance at any hearing in the proceedings or preparation of any document to be lodged in relation to the proceedings. It goes on to say that the motion for sanction can be made at any time prior to the disposal of the proceedings. This Act of Sederunt has now been revoked with effect from 29 April 2019 for actions raised on or after this date.[3] For the avoidance of doubt, there was/is no requirement in any type of proceedings raised prior to 29 April 2019 to prospectively apply for sanction. **7.05**

Prior to the introduction of the 2019 Rules, there were a number of cases in the All-Scotland Sheriff Personal Injury Court (ASPIC) and the Sheriff Appeal Court on motions to sanction counsel: **7.06**

- *Dow v M&D Crolla*, 14 March 2016 (decision of Sheriff Reith).
- *V v M&D Leisure Ltd*, 17 March 2016 (decision of Sheriff Braid).
- *Cumming v SSE Plc*, 4 May 2016 (decision of Sheriff Reith).
- *Harrison v Compass Group*, 5 June 2017 (decision of Sheriff Reith).
- *Burns v Hamilton & Forbes Ltd*, 26 October 2017 (decision of Sheriff Braid).
- *McKenzie v McCormack*, September 2017 (decision of Sheriff Mackie).
- *Brown v Aviva Insurance Ltd*, 25 October 2017 (decision of Appeal Sheriff Andrew Cubie).
- *Cullen v Scan Building Services Ltd*, 21 February 2018 ASPIC (decision of Sheriff McGowan).
- *Patrick Burns v Lord Keen of Elie QC* [2019] SC EDIN49 (decision of Sheriff Braid).

In *Dow v Crolla*,[4] a limited sanction request was made to cover the cost of a consultation. The decision was reached based on the court accepting that there was a degree of difficulty or complexity and importance to the party. **7.07**

---

1 Act of Sederunt (Taxation of Judicial Expenses Rules) 2019 (SSI 2019/75).
2 Act of Sederunt (Sanction for the Employment of Counsel in the Sheriff Court) 2011 (SSI 2011/404).
3 Act of Sederunt (Rules of the Court of Session, Sheriff Appeal Court Rules and Ordinary Cause Rules Amendment) (Taxation of Judicial Expenses) 2019 (SSI 2019/74).
4 *Dow v Crolla* [2016] SC EDIN 21.

There had been significant orthopaedic injuries in the accident and Counsel had been brought in to consult with the orthopaedic expert so that causation and quantum issues could be explored. There were issues in relation to the pursuer's job security and she was concerned if she accepted a much lower offer than the claim was potentially worth, she could go back to work and be made redundant. As in all sanction applications, the decision will turn on the specific facts of the case and, in this instance, the court held that the test under s. 108 was met.

7.08   In *V v M&D Leisure*,[5] a 10 year old boy had an accident in a theme park. Sheriff Braid indicated that he was interpreting s. 108 as imposing an objective reasonableness test having regard to the interests of both parties. He took the view that the proceedings were not especially difficult or complex – the child had simply slipped on a wet surface whilst holding a golf club with a sharp end. The complexity issues were insufficient of themselves to justify sanction.

7.09   The value of the claim was not particularly high and he did not consider that the case had any greater importance for that pursuer than any other pursuer. There was no issue submitted in relation to counsel being required to provide a level playing field.

7.10   The motion depended upon the 'other factors' test. It was argued that because of the child's age and the difficulty in taking his evidence in the context of a case where liability was disputed, assumptions had to be made that the case would require to go through to proof on both liability and quantum. There was a permanent and obvious injury that the child might have difficulty speaking about. The defenders concluded that had the case gone through to proof, it may well have been appropriate for the proof to be conducted by counsel. The court took the view that it would have been unreasonable to expect the child to have coped with the introduction into the case at a late stage of an advocate whom he had not previously met. It was reasonable, therefore, that counsel was instructed at a fairly early stage in the action and the motion was granted.

7.11   *Cumming v SSE Plc*[6] was a case that settled by minute of tender and acceptance but there was a dispute about sanction for counsel. It was a pleural plaques case. The court was satisfied on the facts of the case that it was complex and important enough to justify counsel's involvement because the pursuer had a fairly complex work history. Liability was denied. There were various detailed calls made in the defences. There were potential evidential complications involving different types of exposure to asbestos and the pursuer's agents were entitled to assume that the case would not settle. There was also an issue as to whether provisional damages required to be sought. Sheriff Reith made a comment that if it was deemed to have been previously reasonable to have litigated such cases in the Court of Session and the only reason that they are now being litigated in the sheriff court is because of the increased privative jurisdiction of the sheriff court, she considered that to be a relevant consideration in granting sanction to employ counsel. Counsel's full involvement was sanctioned. It should not, however, be assumed that just because a case has a value of over £5,000 (the former privative jurisdiction limit for the sheriff court) that strengthens an argument for sanction, as it could never be said that every case worth over £5,000 should have been previously litigated

5   *V v M&D Leisure* [2016] SC EDIN 22.
6   *Cumming v SSE Plc* [2016] SC EDIN 35.

in the Court of Session simply because it was possible to do so. It would, however, be expected that where a case is worth over £100,000 and, under the current privative jurisdiction rules, the pursuer chooses to litigate in ASPIC or the local sheriff court, an application for sanction would have a high chance of success.

Harrison v Compass Group[7] was a case where settlement terms had been agreed and there was a motion to dispose of the action in terms of a joint minute with sanction for counsel. The motion was opposed in relation to the sanction of counsel as the defenders argued that the action had been unnecessary. Indeed, they tried to get the court to modify the defenders' liability for expenses for that reason. It was an action that settled by way of an offer of £45,000 net of benefits. The defenders' criticism mainly stemmed from the fact that a supplementary medical report had not been ordered early enough by the pursuer's agents and had it been, there was a high likelihood of the action settling without the need for litigation. However, the court was satisfied by the explanations given by the pursuer's agents as to the timing of ordering their medical evidence and, in any event, the defenders introduced a contributory negligence argument after the action was raised that had not been advanced pre-litigation. Therefore, the court rejected any suggestion of modifying the defenders' liability and took the view that it was reasonable on the grounds of complexity, importance and value that counsel's work be sanctioned.

7.12

Robert Burns v Hamilton & Forbes Ltd[8] is another case where settlement terms had been agreed and the action was to be disposed of by way of a joint minute but the motion for sanction to employ senior counsel, in addition to a junior, was opposed. It was a pleural plaques case where the pursuer had a 35 per cent chance of developing asbestos-related lung cancer, so full and final damages were sought or, failing that, provisional damages. Liability was disputed. There was a four-day proof assigned. Junior counsel was initially instructed up to the time of the pre-trial meeting and the failure to achieve settlement at the pre-trial meeting resulted in the pursuer instructing senior counsel to prepare for the proof. Five days before the proof a tender was lodged and ultimately there was a settlement the day before the proof.

7.13

Sheriff Braid considered the specific circumstances as requiring him to grant sanction for the employment of senior counsel. He made the point that does not mean to say that every pleural plaques case is suitable for the employment of senior counsel. Junior counsel's involvement had already been agreed between the parties.

7.14

McKenzie v McCormack[9] involved a bicycle accident where it was alleged that the cyclist had been intoxicated and simply fallen off their bike into the path of a car. The defenders' allegations could be inferred as meaning that the pursuer had fabricated the claim. However, Sheriff Mackie took the view that the accident circumstances were not complex. There was a dispute about whether a particular injury pre-dated the accident but that was not beyond the scope of a competent solicitor to deal with. Indeed, the claim settled for £4,500 albeit it was probably worth significantly more on a full liability/full

7.15

---

7   *Harrison v Compass Group* [2017] SC EDIN 42.
8   *Robert Burns v Hamilton & Forbes Ltd* [2017] SC EDIN 72.
9   *McKenzie v McCormack* [2017] SC EDIN 67.

valuation basis. Sheriff Mackie was not satisfied that it was reasonable to employ counsel in that case and refused the motion.

7.16   *Brown v Aviva*[10] is a rare case as it relates to an appeal on an issue of expenses. It is as interesting for the analysis of the circumstances in which appeals on expenses will be entertained as it is for the actual decision to overturn the local sheriff's refusal to sanction the employment of counsel.

7.17   It was an uncontested appeal. Aviva had already paid the pursuer's expenses, including counsel's fees, before the appeal was even heard. But the appeal court still had to be satisfied that the sheriff had erred in law. The sheriff had said in his decision, 'The trouble for the Pursuer is ... that the importance of the claim was not the reason why the Pursuer or his agents chose to instruct counsel'.

7.18   Counsel had been instructed by the pursuer to achieve equality of arms. The appeal court ruled that it did not matter what the reason was – importance was a relevant factor in the reasonableness of the decision to instruct counsel even though it had not been the trigger for doing so. The appeal was granted.

7.19   *Cullen v Scan Building Services Ltd*[11] is an example of where the court, applying the test of 'objective reasonableness' refused the pursuer's motion to sanction the instruction of counsel due to lack of complexity.

7.20   *Burns v Lord Keen of Elie*[12] is another decision by Sheriff Braid. In this case, a pursuer's motion sought correction of what they referred to as an incidental error within a previous interlocutor. The interlocutor in question had granted sanction for the instruction of senior and junior counsel for specific elements of work undertaken. However, it emerged that the pursuer had intended to seek blanket sanction for all work done by senior and junior counsel throughout the case. The significance of the wording of the interlocutor had not been immediately appreciated.

7.21   The court was informed that prior to the motion being enrolled, it had been agreed by senior counsel for the defenders that sanction for counsel would not be opposed. There was no argument before the court that sanction for counsel was inappropriate and the issue that Sheriff Braid had to rule on was whether it was competent for the court, at this stage, to grant sanction as regards all other work undertaken by senior and junior counsel beyond that specified in the previous interlocutor. Counsel for the pursuer referred to MacPhail at para. 12(24), which says that sanction can be granted at any time up to taxation. The defenders argued that it was not competent to grant further sanction at this stage, sanction for specific items of work having previously been granted and all matters concerning expenses should be dealt with at the same time.

7.22   The court disagreed with the defenders' position. Certification of skilled persons can be dealt with at any time prior to taxation by virtue of the Act of Sederunt (Fees of Witnesses and Shorthand Writers in the Sheriff Court) 1992 Sch. 1(1) and whilst the position regarding sanction for counsel is not expressly dealt with by that Act of Sederunt, nonetheless on the basis of the authorities relied on by the pursuer, sanction for counsel may likewise be sought at any time prior to taxation.

10 *Brown v Aviva* [2017] SAC (CIV) 34.
11 *Cullen v Scan Building Services Ltd* [2018] SC EDIN 15.
12 *Burns v Lord Keen of Elie* [2019] SC EDIN 49.

The court did make a parting shot that agents are reminded of the need to take care both when drafting motions and when checking interlocutors. That should be done upon receipt, not some six months later and to ensure that the actual motion clearly sets out what the court is being asked to do rather than expect the court to pick through the submissions section of a motion to work out what is intended. **7.23**

APPLICATIONS FOR SANCTION FOR COUNSEL UNDER THE 2019 RULES

For actions raised on or after 29 April 2019 the 2019 Rules include provision for how matters relating to counsel's employment in the sheriff court and Sheriff Appeal Court require to be dealt with, including the need to apply for sanction prospectively in certain cases. **7.24**

There are advantages associated with the need to apply prospectively. It means a party will know whether sanction is granted prior to incurring the costs associated with counsel's work and will therefore avoid the possibility of running a case where counsel has been involved only for sanction to be ultimately refused. Predictability in costs recovery is thus enhanced, albeit full recovery is not guaranteed as the reasonableness of counsel's fees is still subject to the scrutiny of the auditor. The requirement also gives an opponent advance notice of counsel's involvement and allows the opponent to factor that into the economics of how to proceed and to take a view on whether they consider it necessary to also instruct counsel to achieve equality of arms. The requirement to apply prospectively is something that care should be taken not to overlook as the oversight could be extremely costly. On the downside, additional cost requires to be borne by a party, possibly on a one-off basis or possibly on multiple occasions throughout an action, depending on the extent of the sanction applied for, in relation to paying court dues and presenting motions for sanction that previously would normally have been dealt with in the motion disposing of an action. **7.25**

The relevant provisions of the 2019 Rules are: **7.26**

Instructing and attending with counsel
3.8.—(1) Subject to paragraph (2), where fees of counsel are allowed as an outlay in the sheriff court or Sheriff Appeal Court, the Auditor is also to allow the applicable charge for instructing counsel.
(2) Where the fees allowed are those of a solicitor advocate, paragraph (1) does not apply unless the solicitor advocate is acting on the instructions of another solicitor.
(3) Paragraph (4) applies where—
    (a) a solicitor advocate exercises a right of audience in the Court of Session; or
    (b) fees of a solicitor advocate are allowed as an outlay in the sheriff court or Sheriff Appeal Court in accordance with rule 4.3 (fees of counsel in the sheriff court or Sheriff Appeal Court).
(4) Where the solicitor advocate is assisted by another solicitor or a clerk the Auditor may allow the applicable attendance charge.

Fees of counsel in the sheriff court or Sheriff Appeal Court
4.3.—(1) This rule applies to the taxation of accounts of expenses relating to proceedings in the sheriff court or Sheriff Appeal Court.

(2) No fees are to be allowed for the work of counsel unless the proceedings, or particular work involved in the conduct of the proceedings, have been sanctioned as suitable for the employment of counsel in accordance with rule 5.4 (sanction for the employment of counsel in the sheriff court and Sheriff Appeal Court).

(3) Where particular work has been sanctioned as suitable for the employment of counsel the Auditor is to allow the reasonable fees of counsel for—

    (a) doing that work, and

    (b) subject to paragraph (6), consultations reasonably required in relation to that work.

(4) Where the proceedings have been sanctioned as suitable for the employment of counsel—

    (a) it is for the Auditor to determine the work in relation to which it was reasonable for counsel to be instructed;

    (b) subject to sub-paragraph (c), the Auditor is to allow the reasonable fees of counsel for carrying out that work;

    (c) subject to paragraph (3), no fees are to be allowed for work carried out before the date on which sanction was granted unless the proceedings are—

        (i) proceedings subject to Chapter 36 of the Ordinary Cause Rules 1993;

        (ii) a simple procedure case; or

        (iii) proceedings in the Sheriff Appeal Court.

(5) In the determination of reasonable fees for the purposes of paragraphs (3) and (4) the Auditor must disregard the fact that counsel who carried out the work was senior counsel unless the proceedings, or the particular work, have been sanctioned as suitable for the employment of senior counsel.

(6) Except on cause shown, the Auditor is to allow fees for only two consultations in the course of proceedings.

(7) In this rule, references to fees of counsel for carrying out work include, where appropriate in the case of proofs, trials or other hearings that do not proceed, fees reflecting counsel's inability to accept alternative commitments.

Sanction for the employment of counsel in the sheriff court and Sheriff Appeal Court

5.4.—(1) This rule applies to proceedings in the sheriff court and Sheriff Appeal Court.

(2) On the application of a party the court may, subject to paragraphs (4) to (6), sanction—

    (a) the proceedings;

    (b) any part of the proceedings;

    (c) particular work involved in the conduct of the proceedings; or

    (d) any combination of (a), (b) and (c),

as suitable for the employment of counsel by that party.

(3) Where proceedings or work are sanctioned as suitable for the employment of senior counsel, or as suitable for the employment of more than one counsel, the interlocutor must record that.

(4) Paragraphs (5) and (6) apply where the application is made in proceedings other than—

    (a) proceedings subject to Chapter 36 of the Ordinary Cause Rules 1993;

    (b) a simple procedure case; or

    (c) proceedings in the Sheriff Appeal Court.

(5) An interlocutor sanctioning proceedings, or a part of proceedings, as suitable for the employment of counsel has no effect as regards work carried out by counsel before the date of the interlocutor.

(6) The court may only sanction particular work already carried out as suitable for the employment of counsel when satisfied that the party applying has shown cause for not having applied for sanction before the work was carried out.

(7) The refusal of an application under this rule does not preclude the making of a further application on a change of circumstances.

The *Finlay* case,[13] mentioned in Chapter 5 on Certification of Skilled Persons **7.27** (para 5.23) also deals with sanction for counsel under the 2019 Rules. The court started with a general overview of the rules pertaining to sanction for counsel in the sheriff court and noted:

' … as a matter of generality, Rule 4.3(4)(c) prohibits the Auditor from allowing as a recoverable outlay any fee to counsel pre-dating the sanctioning of the proceedings as suitable for the employment of counsel, unless the proceedings are one of the three types specified [Chapter 36, Simple Procedure or Sheriff Appeal Court cases]'.[14]

The court considered the application process regulated by r. 5.4, drawing **7.28** a distinction between that rule and r. 4.3. The following is paras 12–23 of Sheriff McGowan's judgment:

[12] Rule 5.4(2) provides: "(2) On the application of a party the court may, subject to paragraphs (4) to (6), sanction— (a) the proceedings; (b) any part of the proceedings; (c) particular work involved in the conduct of the proceedings; or (d) any combination of (a), (b) and (c), as suitable for the employment of counsel by that party."

[13] I observe in passing that the terminology in this rule is different to that in Rule 4.3. Rule 4.3 contains two categories for which sanction may be sought, namely "the proceedings" and "particular work involved in the conduct of the proceedings", whereas Rule 5.5(2) contains three, namely "the proceedings"; "any part of the proceedings"; and "particular work involved in the conduct of the proceedings". It is not immediately clear to me what the difference is between "any part of the proceedings" and "particular work involved in the conduct of the proceedings", but it may be that the distinction is made for the purposes of making the meaning and effect of rules 5.4(5) and 5.4(6) clearer – see below.

[14] Rule 5.4(4) provides that: "Paragraphs (5) and (6) apply where the application is made in proceedings other than— (a) proceedings subject to Chapter 36 of the Ordinary Cause Rules 1993; (b) a simple procedure case; or (c) proceedings in the Sheriff Appeal Court."

[15] This mirrors the distinction drawn between different types of proceedings in Rule 4.3(4)(c). Pausing there, and reading Rule 5.4(2) and 5.4(4) together, means that sanction of "the proceedings", "any part of the proceedings", "particular work involved in the conduct of the proceedings" or any combination thereof may be sought at any time in proceedings subject to Chapter 36 of the Ordinary Cause Rules 1993; simple procedure cases; or proceedings in the Sheriff Appeal Court ("SAC"); and if and when granted in these categories of cases, may have prospective and/or retrospective effect, as appropriate.

[16] In attempt to express that in concrete terms, I give the following hypothetical examples. A motion in a case brought under Chapter 36 to sanction the proceedings as suitable for the employment of counsel may be made at any time and will have effect for work done both before and after the date is granted (i.e. for the whole proceedings); a motion to sanction a simple procedure proof as suitable for the employment of counsel may be made before or after the proof and if granted will

---

13 *Finlay v Borders Health Board* [2019] SC EDIN 99.
14 *Finlay v Borders Health Board*, para. 10.

have effect for that part of the proceedings; and a motion to sanction the drafting of grounds of appeal as suitable for the employment of counsel in appeal proceedings before the SAC may be made before or after the grounds are drafted and has effect for that particular work.

[17] Turning then to Rule 5.4(5), it provides: "An interlocutor sanctioning proceedings, or a part of proceedings, as suitable for the employment of counsel has no effect as regards work carried out by counsel before the date of the interlocutor."

[18] Rule 5.4(6) provides: "The court may only sanction particular work already carried out as suitable for the employment of counsel when satisfied that the party applying has shown cause for not having applied for sanction before the work was carried out."

[19] There are several points to be made about these rules.

[20] First, they apply to all types of proceedings in the sheriff court except proceedings under Chapter 36 OCR; simple procedure cases; or proceedings in the Sheriff Appeal Court.

[21] Second, given the use of the phrases "proceedings, or a part of the proceedings" in Rule 5.4(5) on the one hand and "particular work" in Rule 5.4(6) on the other, these rules read together must mean that applications for sanction with retrospective effect cannot ever competently be made for proceedings or a part of them. Instead, sanction with retrospective effect can only be sought and obtained in relation to "particular work involved in the conduct of the proceedings" which has already been carried out.

[22] Third, it is implicit in the foregoing that the particular work must be specified.

[23] Fourth, where an application to retrospectively sanction particular work involved in the conduct of the proceedings already carried out is made as suitable for the employment of counsel, cause must be shown for that not being done before the work was carried out.

COMMENTARY

7.29   The position can be summarised as follows:

(1) Counsel's fees can only be allowed by the auditor if sanction has been obtained from the court.

(2) The court does not sanction the employment of counsel – it sanctions the proceedings or particular parts of the proceedings or particular work as being suitable for the employment of counsel.

(3) Where particular work is sanctioned, the auditor assesses what is a reasonable fee for counsel to charge. Only two consultations are allowed unless cause is shown to justify more than two. This, however, does not require a separate motion for sanction for more than two consultations – it is a matter of reasonableness for the auditor to determine.

(4) There is now a specific requirement to have senior counsel's involvement sanctioned and for that to be stated in the interlocutor. This also applies where more than one counsel is employed.

(5) There is now specific provision to permit the auditor to allow counsel to charge a fee even where a hearing does not proceed. The level of the 'cancellation' or 'disappointment' fee is within the discretion of the auditor and will be assessed having regard, in the main, to the period of notice given to counsel that the hearing was not going to proceed, and the number of days that the hearing had been set down for.

(6) If the proceedings have been sanctioned, the auditor has to assess what work it was reasonable for counsel to undertake in the proceedings as well as the reasonableness of counsel's charges.

(7) Retrospective sanction is not required in cases that are: (a) proceeding under Ch. 36 of the Act of Sederunt (Sheriff Court Ordinary Cause Rules) 1993; (b) simple procedure cases; or (c) cases proceeding in the Sheriff Appeal Court. In these types of cases, sanction for the proceedings, a particular part of the proceedings or particular work to be undertaken by counsel may be made at any time (up to the time of taxation) and, if granted, will have both prospective and retrospective effect.

(8) Retrospective sanction can only be sought for particular work carried out as suitable for the employment of counsel. It cannot competently be sought for 'the proceedings' or 'part of the proceedings' and any interlocutor purporting to grant such sanction would have no effect.

(9) A retrospective application must clearly specify the nature of the particular work that is the subject of the application and the court can only grant retrospective sanction if the applying party has shown cause for not having applied earlier. Therefore, the applying party's motion must not only address the requirements of s. 108 of the 2014 Act in satisfying the court of why particular work should be sanctioned for the employment of counsel, it also needs to justify the request for retrospective sanction under r. 5.4(6) of the 2019 Rules.

Chapter 8

Party Litigants

8.01 In general terms any person has the right to conduct their own cause in court. There is no requirement on the part of a natural person to instruct a solicitor or advocate to appear on the party's behalf.

Non-natural persons

8.02 The general rule has exceptions. Prior to 28 November 2016, a party to an action who was a 'non-natural person' such as a company, limited liability partnership, other type of partnership or unincorporated association required to be legally represented. It was commonplace for company directors to try to appear in court to represent their company only to be met with a refusal on the part of the court to hear them.

8.03 The Courts Reform (Scotland) Act 2014[1] makes provision whereby a lay representative can, in certain circumstances, conduct proceedings on behalf of a non-natural person. Specific rules apply to simple procedure cases.[2] Provided the court is satisfied that the conditions set out in s. 96 of the 2014 Act are complied with, no formal application process is required in a simple procedure case.

8.04 For all types of case other than simple procedure, ss. 97 and 98 set out the criteria that require to be fulfilled before permission will be granted by the court to allow the lay person to represent the non-natural person. In essence there must be an inability on the part of the non-natural person to be able to pay for legal representation, the lay representative must be a suitable person and it must be in the interests of justice to grant permission.

8.05 A prescribed form, with authorisation document, requires to be lodged with the court, which, if granted, will allow lay representation as follows:

Table 8.1

Type of non-natural person	Relevant position
A company	A director or secretary of the company
Limited liability partnership	A member of the LLP
Any other partnership	A partner in the partnership
An unincorporated association	Association member or office holder

1 Courts Reform (Scotland) Act 2014 ss. 95–98.
2 Courts Reform (Scotland) Act 2014 s. 96.

The judge or sheriff may determine the application in chambers[3] and can **8.06** impose such conditions on the exercise of functions by the lay representative where necessary to do so in the interests of justice.[4]

In any type of cause, including simple procedure, if the lay representa- **8.07** tive acts unreasonably in the conduct of the proceedings and an award of expenses is made against the non-natural person, the court may find the lay representative and the non-natural person jointly and severally liable for those expenses.[5]

Lay representatives for natural persons

In the Court of Session a party who is not legally represented can apply to the **8.08** court for lay support[6] or to be represented by a lay person.[7]

Lay support in the Court of Session

Lay support includes providing moral support, helping to manage the court **8.09** documents and other papers, taking notes of the proceedings and quietly advising on points of procedure, issues that the litigant might wish to raise with the court and questions that the litigant might wish to ask a witness. It does not permit the person providing lay support to speak on behalf of the litigant.

Permission is required and the Act of Sederunt (Rules of the Court of **8.10** Session 1994) 1994 (RCS) r. 12.A.1 sets out the procedure that, in the Court of Session, involves making a motion (written or oral) accompanied by Form 12.A-A.[8]

The application can be made at any time during the proceedings[9] and can **8.11** only be refused if the named individual is unsuitable to act in the capacity of 'lay supporter' or the court takes the view that it would be contrary to the efficient administration of justice to grant it.[10]

It is a condition of such permission that the named individual does not **8.12** receive from the litigant, whether directly or indirectly, any remuneration for his or their assistance.[11] Any expenses incurred by the litigant as a result of the support are not recoverable in the expenses of the proceedings.[12]

Lay representation in the Court of Session

If a litigant requires more than support and wishes a non-legally qualified **8.13** person to speak on their behalf in court, they may apply to the court for permission for a named individual (a lay representative) to appear, along with

---

3 Act of Sederunt (Lay Representation for Non-Natural Persons) 2016 (SSI 2016/243) r. 3.
4 Act of Sederunt (Lay Representation for Non-Natural Persons) 2016 r. 4.
5 Act of Sederunt (Lay Representation for Non-Natural Persons) 2016 r. 5.
6 Act of Sederunt (Rules of the Court of Session 1994) 1994 (RCS) r. 12.A.1.
7 RCS r. 12.B.
8 RCS r. 12.A.1(4).
9 RCS r. 12.A.1.(1).
10 RCS r. 12.A.1(3).
11 RCS r. 12.A.1(2).
12 RCS r. 12.A.1(8).

the applicant, at a specified hearing for the purpose of representing the litigant at the hearing.[13]

8.14   The application requires to be made by motion prior to the day of the hearing, accompanied by Form 12B.2[14] and can only be granted on the day of the hearing itself if exceptional reasons exist to justify why it was not made earlier.[15]

8.15   The application can only be granted by the court if it is in the interests of justice to grant it.[16] Therefore, unlike 'lay support' where the court must grant an application unless certain criteria apply, there is a positive requirement to satisfy the court that it should be granted because the interests of justice require it.

8.16   It is a condition of permission granted by the court that the lay representative does not receive, directly or indirectly, from the litigant any remuneration or other reward for their assistance.[17]

8.17   The granting of the application permits the lay representative to do whatever the litigant is entitled to do,[18] but again, any expenses incurred by the litigant in connection with lay representation under the rule are not recoverable expenses in the proceedings.[19]

Sheriff court lay representation

8.18   There is no equivalent to RCS r. 12.A.1 (lay support) in the sheriff court. The sheriff court rules refer only to lay representation. Whilst they are in broadly similar terms to RCS r. 12B there are two main differences:

(1)   The rule specifically requires the application for permission to be made orally.

(2)   It requires to be made on the date of the first hearing. There is no rule specifically allowing the court to consider an application on a later date although the dispensing power could be exercised if there was justification for so doing.

8.19   Otherwise, the same provisions as set out in RCS r. 12.B apply, including the prohibition on the lay representative receiving, directly or indirectly, from the litigant any remuneration or reward for their assistance and the fact that expenses incurred by the litigant in connection with lay representation are not recoverable expenses in the proceedings.

Citation of witnesses by a party litigant in the Court of Session

8.20   A party litigant to a cause, not later than twelve weeks before the diet of proof, requires to apply to the court by motion to fix caution for the expenses of witnesses in answering a citation in such sum as the court considers reasonable

---

13 RCS r. 12B.2(1).
14 RCS r. 12B.2(2).
15 RCS r. 12B.2(3).
16 RCS r. 12B.2(4).
17 RCS r. 12B.2(7).
18 RCS r. 12B.2(7).
19 RCS r. 12B.2(9).

having regard to the number of witnesses they propose to cite and the period for which they may be required to attend court.[20]

Before instructing a messenger-at-arms to cite a witness, a party litigant **8.21** must find the caution that has been fixed.[21]

A party litigant who does not intend to cite all the witnesses referred to in **8.22** their application may apply by motion for variation of the amount of caution.[22]

Citation of witnesses by a party litigant in the sheriff court

A party litigant to a cause, not later than four weeks before the diet of proof, **8.23** requires to apply to the sheriff by motion to fix caution in such sum as the sheriff considers reasonable having regard to the number of witnesses they propose to cite and the period for which they may be required to attend court.[23]

Before instructing a sheriff officer to cite a witness, the party litigant shall **8.24** find caution for such expenses as can reasonably be anticipated to be incurred by the witness in answering the citation.[24]

A party litigant who does not intend to cite all the witnesses referred to in **8.25** their application may apply by motion for variation of the amount of caution.[25]

EXPENSES AWARDS IN FAVOUR OF PARTY LITIGANTS (ACTIONS COMMENCED PRE-29 APRIL 2019)

Act of Sederunt (Sheriff Court Ordinary Cause Rules) 1993 r. 30.10 provides: **8.26**

> A party who—
> (a) is or has been represented by a person authorised under any enactment to conduct proceedings in the sheriff court; and
> (b) would have been found entitled to expenses if he had been represented by a solicitor or an advocate,
> may be awarded any expenses or outlays to which a party litigant may be found entitled under the Litigants in Person (Costs and Expenses) Act 1975 or any enactment under that Act.

Section 1(2) of the Litigants in Person (Costs and Expenses) Act 1975 **8.27** provides:

> Where, in any proceedings to which this subsection applies, any costs or expenses of a party litigant are ordered to be paid by any other party to the proceedings or in any other way, there may, subject to rules of court, be allowed on the taxation or other determination of those costs or expenses sums in respect of any work done, and any outlays and losses incurred, by the litigant in or in connection with the proceedings to which the order relates. This subsection applies to civil proceedings
> (a) in the sheriff court, the Scottish Land Court, the Court of Session or the Supreme Court on appeal from the Court of Session,
> (b) before the Lands Tribunal for Scotland,
> (ba) before the First-tier Tribunal or the Upper Tribunal, or

---

20 RCS r. 36.2(5)(a).
21 RCS r. 36.2(5)(b).
22 RCS r. 36.2(6).
23 Act of Sederunt (Sheriff Court Ordinary Cause Rules) 1993 (OCR) r. 29.8(1).
24 OCR r. 29.8(2).
25 OCR r. 29.8(3).

(c)   in or before any other court or tribunal specified in an order made under this subsection by the Lord Advocate.

8.28 The expenses allowable by the auditor to party litigants under the pre-2019 taxation rules are such sums as appear to the auditor to be reasonable having regard to all the circumstances in respect of:

(a) Work done that was reasonably required in connection with the cause up to the maximum of two-thirds of the sums allowable to a solicitor; and

(b) outlays reasonably incurred for the proper conduct of the cause.[26]

8.29 The two-thirds ceiling on the sum recoverable by a party litigant based on what a solicitor can recover by way of expenses is not incompatible with arts 6 and 14 of the European Convention on Human Rights 1950.[27]

8.30 The matters that the auditor requires to consider are:

(a) The nature of the work.

(b) The time taken and the time reasonably required to do the work.

(c) The amount of time spent in respect of which there is no loss of earnings.

(d) The amount of any earnings lost during the time required to do the work.

(e) The importance of the cause to the party litigant.

(f) The complexity of the issues involved in the cause.[28]

8.31 Whilst the provisions setting out what the auditor has to consider have been revoked with effect from 29 April 2019, they are still relevant to the determination of party litigant expenses for actions commenced prior to that date.

EXPENSES AWARDS IN FAVOUR OF PARTY LITIGANTS (ACTIONS COMMENCED ON OR AFTER 29 APRIL 2019)

8.32 The position now is broadly similar to that which existed pre-29 April 2019. The Act of Sederunt (Taxation of Judicial Expenses Rules) 2019 provides:

3.10. (1) Where the entitled party was not represented by a solicitor the Auditor may, subject to paragraph (3), allow a reasonable sum in respect of work done by the entitled party which was reasonably required in connection with the proceedings. (2) In determining what would be a reasonable sum the Auditor is to have regard to all the circumstances, including—

(a) the nature of the work;

(b) the time required to do the work;

(c) the amount of any earnings lost during that time;

(d) the importance of the proceedings to the entitled party; and

(e) the complexity of the issues involved in the proceedings.

(3) Any sum allowed under this rule must not exceed two thirds of the charges that would be allowed under this Chapter if the same work had been done by a solicitor.

---

26 Act of Sederunt (Expenses of Party Litigants) 1976 (SI 1976/1606) as amended by Act of Sederunt (Expenses of Party Litigants) 1983 (SI 1983/130) r. 2(1) and Act of Sederunt (Rules of the Court of Session, Sheriff Appeal Court Rules and Sheriff Court Rules Amendment) (Sheriff Appeal Court) 2015 (SSI 2015/419). N.B. SI 1976/1606 has been revoked by Act of Sederunt (Rules of the Court of Session, Sheriff Appeal Court Rules and Ordinary Cause Rules Amendment) (Taxation of Judicial Expenses) 2019 (SSI 2019/74) with effect from 29 April 2019.

27 *Bank of Scotland Plc v Forbes* [2012] CSIH 76.

28 Act of Sederunt (Expenses of Party Litigants) 1976 r. 2(2).

SOLICITORS AS PARTY LITIGANTS

A solicitor who has been awarded expenses having acted in their own cause is **8.33**
entitled to charge for work done on exactly the same basis as a solicitor who
had been instructed by a solicitor of another firm, subject to the qualification
that they are not entitled to charge for the likes of consulting with themselves
or taking instructions from themselves.[29]

29 *Edward v Porter* 2012 SLT (Sh Ct) 225.

Chapter 9

Amendment of Pleadings

9.01   The procedure governing amendment of pleadings is set out in the Act of Sederunt (Rules of the Court of Session 1994) 1994 (RCS) r. 24, the Act of Sederunt (Sheriff Court Ordinary Cause Rules) 1993 (OCR) r. 18 and, in relation to alteration of a summons, etc. in a summary cause, the Act of Sederunt (Summary Cause Rules) 2002 (SCR) r. 13.

RCS r. 24.4 provides that:

> The court shall find the party making an amendment liable in the expenses occasioned by the amendment unless it is shown that it is just and equitable that the expenses occasioned by the amendment should be otherwise dealt with, and may attach such other conditions as it thinks fit.'

OCR r. 18.6 is in similar terms but SCR r. 13 makes no mention of expenses in relation to alteration of a summons, etc. in a summary cause, thus leaving it to the inherent discretion of the sheriff to make such expenses order as is appropriate.

9.02   The default position in the Court of Session and under the Sheriff Court ordinary cause rules is that the party making the amendment will automatically be found liable for the expenses occasioned by the amendment unless the motion to amend seeks an alternative expenses order and the court is satisfied that it would be just and equitable not to find the party undertaking the amendment liable. If the motion that is presented to the court is silent on the issue of expenses the default position will be, or at least should be, reflected in the court's interlocutor.

9.03   Unless the amendment is formal in nature and does not require a period for answers, adjustment and a procedural hearing, the expenses occasioned by amendment procedure can be significant. It is all too often the case that insufficient regard is had by agents and counsel to the adverse costs award that an amendment procedure will ultimately give rise to. Often lack of early preparation or the timeous ingathering of skilled person reports leads to the record being closed before the pleadings are adequately developed and the attitude adopted is that 'we can sort it out by lodging a minute of amendment'. But an amendment can frequently give rise to a contra account totalling thousands of pounds. It is seldom the fault of the amending party but they end up bearing the costs of not only the opponent's contra-account but the fees, VAT and outlays incurred by their own solicitor and counsel for something that may have been completely avoidable.

Situations may arise where the court finds the party making the amendment liable for not only the expenses occasioned by the amendment but also in other expenses. This is to reflect the need to protect the party who has to answer an amendment from having to incur unnecessary and improper charges[1] or where that party is put to extensive additional investigations, such as instructing skilled persons.

An amendment made at a debate or appeal that renders the hearing abortive **9.04** may result in the amending party being held liable for the expenses of the debate or appeal.[2]

As specifically mentioned in the court rules, the court can impose such **9.05** conditions as it thinks fit. The conditions must be appropriate to the action. For example, an interim decree was pronounced and payment of the sum and interest decerned for was made a condition precedent of an amendment that necessitated an additional proof.[3]

The position now is mitigated somewhat if the case is being handled under **9.06** a success fee agreement, in which case there is a prohibition on the provider of legal services charging the recipient anything other than a success fee and an 'after the event' insurance premium. See Chapter 4. It is mitigated further in personal injury cases raised on or after 30 June 2021 where qualified one-way cost shifting (QOCS) applies as the court cannot make an order for expenses against a pursuer who amends their pleadings unless one of the exceptions to QOCS applies. See Chapter 3. But for those actions where QOCS does not apply, in what circumstances might a court be persuaded not to find the party making the amendment liable for the expenses occasioned by the amendment procedure?

It was previously the case that the auditor of court would exercise their **9.07** discretion to allow the amending party, who is ultimately successful in the action, to recover the cost of amendments that could not be foreseen when the summons or other pleadings were drawn and where the amendment was necessary for the proper conduct of the case. Hastings[4] cites the example of a pursuer's condition deteriorating unexpectedly requiring the sum sued for to be increased.

Care should be taken to avoid the situation where the court does not make **9.08** a specific order for expenses. Nowadays this will be unusual given the terms of RCS r. 24.4 and OCR r. 18.6. It would arise, for example, if expenses of an amendment procedure are, for whatever reason, reserved and then overlooked with the effect that the amendment expenses are covered by the final interlocutor in the case disposing of all expenses not previously dealt with.[5]

The auditor's discretion is confined to what level of expenses are reasonable **9.09** in the circumstances. It does not follow that just because counsel has been sanctioned in a sheriff court case for the 'proceedings' that counsel's fees in framing a minute of amendment or adjustments to the answers will be recoverable. Much will depend on the complexity of the amendment. An amendment simply to increase the sum sued for, or some straightforward updating of the medical position, would be viewed as being within the capabilities of a competent solicitor and there would be no justification for counsel to be involved in

---

1 *Mackenzie v Mackenzie* 1951 SC 163 at 165–166.
2 *Murdison v Scottish Football Union* (1896) 23 R 449; *Mackenzie* 1951 SC 163; *Calbron v United Glass Ltd* 1965 SLT 366.
3 *Castlehill Ltd v Scott* (unreported) Sh. Pr. Reid, Glasgow Sh Ct 2 October 1979.
4 Hastings, *Expenses in the Supreme and Sheriff Courts of Scotland* (Edinburgh: W. Green, 1989), p. 15, para. 9.
5 *Bank of Scotland v Morrison* 1911 S.C. 593.

the amendment. But receipt of a complex skilled person report that requires pleadings to be substantially changed, for example, by adding a further ground of fault in a medical negligence case, or changing/extending the pleadings on causation, may well be viewed by the auditor as providing a reasonable basis for the involvement of counsel. Of course, if the court has specifically sanctioned counsel for the particular work associated with the amendment of the pleadings, or a particular part of the proceedings that includes the amendment procedure, the only discretion the auditor would have is in relation to assessing the reasonableness of counsel's fee. In Court of Session cases where no sanction is required for counsel's involvement, the framing of a minute of amendment by counsel will be allowed by the auditor who will simply assess the reasonableness of counsel's fees.

9.10   If little or no further expense is occasioned by the amendment procedure, the equitable course would be to either make the expenses in the cause, make an order for no expenses due to or by,[6] make a nominal award[7] or make a modified award[8] depending on the specific circumstances of what is just and equitable.

9.11   An example of where amendment expenses were made expenses in the cause was in relation to a pursuer's unopposed motion to amend the closed record to reflect the appointment of a *curator ad litem*.[9]

---

6   *Murdison* (1896) 23 R 449 per Lord McLaren at pp. 460–461; *Gillespie v Duncan* (1933) 50 Sh.Ct.Rep. 60.
7   *Macdonald v Forsyth* (1898) 25 R 870.
8   *Woodbury v Sutherland's Trs* 1939 SLT 218.
9   *Walker v Armadale Group Practice* (unreported) COS A212/19 interlocutor 24 March 2021.

Chapter 10

Caution, Consignation and Other Security

Orders for caution (pron. kay-shun) or consignation may be made by a court **10.01** in two distinct situations:

(1) A pursuer may obtain security requiring the defender to find caution for the whole or part of the sum sued for, or to consign in the hands of the court the whole or part of the sum sued for pending the final determination of the action. This may be appropriate where, *ex facie*, the debt is due but the defender claims deductions that are disputed or there is a dispute in relation to the pursuer's title to sue and, therefore, caution or consignation is more appropriate than interim decree. This type of caution or consignation is not relevant to a book on costs and funding and is fully considered elsewhere.[1]

(2) Caution for expenses. Where a party is concerned about the other side's ability to pay expenses in the event they are unsuccessful in proceedings, an order for caution or security can be sought. This requires the party against whom the order is made to lodge a bond of caution (or other form of security as ordered by the court) before they can proceed with the action. Caution for expenses can be sought under common law or, in the case of companies, under s. 726 of the Companies Act 1985.

The procedure regulating orders for caution or other security for expenses **10.02** is to be found in Act of Sederunt (Rules of the Court of Session 1994) 1994 (RCS) r. 33 and Act of Sederunt (Sheriff Court Ordinary Cause Rules) 1993 (OCR) r. 27. An application requires to be made by motion setting out why the order is sought.

The court has a wide discretion on whether to order a party to find caution **10.03** and will not make such an order unless the interests of justice appear to require it.[2] There is no prescribed list of circumstances when such an order is appropriate, but some examples are outlined below. It is competent for any party to an action to seek an order for caution at any stage in the proceedings.

Orders to find caution against a pursuer will not normally be made unless **10.04** special circumstances exist or the pursuer is an undischarged bankrupt or is a nominal pursuer. Poverty or impecuniosity alone are insufficient to justify an order for caution against a natural person – to hold otherwise would deprive the poor pursuer access to justice and it would be 'clearly wrong that a litigant with a stateable case should in effect be excluded from the court by an order for caution with which he could not comply, unless in exceptional

---

1 MacPhail, *Sheriff Court Practice*, 3rd edn (Edinburgh: W. Green, 2006) pp. 392–395.
2 *Thom v Andrew* (1888) 15 R 780 per Lord Young at 782; *Cooney v Kirkpatrick* 1989 SLT 457.

circumstances'.[3] However, where the impecunious party does not have a relevant case and therefore does not have probable cause, the court is likely to order caution as 'it would be grossly unfair to oblige defenders to carry on defending an obviously irrelevant action without any hope of recovering expenses if successful'.[4]

10.05 In the full bench decision of *McCue v Scottish Daily Record*,[5] where absolvitor was granted following a failure to find caution, it was open to the party to argue that the requirement to find caution was itself granted in error.

ORDERS AGAINST PURSUERS

10.06 If a pursuer is an undischarged bankrupt or becomes bankrupt during the currency of the proceedings, an order for caution will normally be granted.[6] An undischarged bankrupt would generally require the consent and concurrence of their trustee to initiate or continue proceedings. A discharged bankrupt is unlikely to have an order for caution made against them, including the situation where they are suing for sums that their trustee had failed to ingather.[7]

10.07 A pursuer/reclaimer was ordered to find caution in the sum of £10,000 in respect of the anticipated costs of an appeal to the Inner House where he had failed to meet previous awards of expenses, had, subsequent to the raising of the proceedings, been declared a vexatious litigant and had been sequestrated. The pursuer accepted that he would probably be unable to meet the expenses associated with the reclaiming motion if he was unsuccessful.[8]

10.08 If the pursuer is not the true *dominis litis* in the action, i.e. they are not the person controlling the action, the court will normally order caution.[9]

10.09 It is competent to recall or modify an order to find caution if there has been a material change of circumstances.[10] A grant of civil legal aid to a pursuer after an order for caution was made against her was sufficient, in the circumstances of the case, to lead the court to recall an order for caution.[11]

ORDERS AGAINST DEFENDERS

10.10 It is highly unusual for a defender to be ordered to find caution since they (a) have not initiated the proceedings; and (b) require to defend themselves.[12] One example of where a defender was found liable to find caution is the case

---

3 *Stevenson v Midlothian DC* 1983 (HL) 50 per Lord Fraser of Tullybelton at 58; *McTear's Executors v Imperial Tobacco Ltd* 1997 SLT 530.
4 *Rush v Fife Regional Council* 1985 SLT 451 per LJC Wheatley at 453.
5 *McCue v Scottish Daily Record* 1998 SC 811.
6 *Ritchie v McIntosh* (1881) 8 R 747; *Neil v South-East Lanarkshire Insurance Co* 1930 SC 629.
7 *Cooper v Frame & Co* (1893) 20 R 920; *Cunningham v Skinner* (1902) 4 F 1124.
8 *Duff, Petitioner* [2013] CSIH 112.
9 *Porteous v Pearl Assurance Co Ltd* (1901) 8 SLT 430.
10 *Whyte v City of Perth Co-operative Society* 1932 SC 482, Lord Anderson at 484 followed in *Forrest v Fleming Builders Ltd* [2013] CSOH 105.
11 *Forrest* [2013] CSOH 105.
12 *Balfour Beatty Ltd v Brinmoor Ltd* 1997 SLT 888; *Matheson v Marsh* 1996 SC 25.

of *Robertson v McCaw*.[13] In that case the defender husband was disposing of matrimonial property to the prejudice of the pursuer and was therefore ordained to find caution for the expenses of the action.

An undischarged bankrupt defender will not normally be expected to find caution.[14] An order may be granted if the defence is lacking any real substance although consideration would no doubt be given in that situation to a motion for summary decree; or, where the defender has divested themselves of their estate, after the action is raised.[15]

COMPANIES

An order for caution against a pursuer company under s. 726 of the Companies Act 1985 (company being defined as per s. 735 of the 1985 Act, which does not include foreign companies) can be granted merely on the basis of impecuniosity. The section states the order can be granted 'if it appears by credible testimony that there is reason to believe that the company will be unable to pay the defender's expenses if successful in his defence'. There is no mention of the need to show the pursuer's case is irrelevant.

10.11

Notwithstanding that foreign companies do not fall within the terms of s. 726, the same test applies to them as per *Total Containment Engineering Ltd v Total Waste Management Alliance Ltd*.[16] Therefore mere impecuniosity of the pursuer foreign company may be sufficient to justify an order for caution.

10.12

Normal practice would be for the action to be sisted until caution is found. There is conflicting authority as to whether a time limit should be imposed for caution to be found. If no such time limit is imposed the finding of caution should be within a reasonable period, failing which the sist can be recalled and decree of absolvitor sought.[17]

10.13

SISTING A MANDATARY

The court has the discretion to order that a person from Scotland is sisted as a mandatary if a party to the proceedings is resident abroad. The nationality of the party is irrelevant, the relevant issue is where they reside. If a mandatary is sisted to the proceedings the court can order that they are liable for any expenses in place of the actual party.[18] It is unusual for a mandatary to be sisted for a defender for the same reasons as it is unusual for an order for caution to be made against a defender.[19]

10.14

---

13 *Robertson v McCaw* 1911 SC 650.
14 *Crichton Bros v Crichton* (1902) 5 F 178.
15 *Stevenson v Lee* (1886) 13 R 913.
16 *Total Containment Engineering Ltd v Total Waste Management Alliance Ltd* [2012] CSOH 163.
17 *Pioneer Seafoods Ltd v The Braer Corporation* 1999 SCLR 1126; *Augustinus Ltd v Anglia Building Society* 1990 SLT 298.
18 *Renfrew and Brown v Magistrates of Glasgow* (1861) 23 D 1003; *D'Ernesti v D'Ernesti* (1882) 9 R 655.
19 *Taylor v Taylor* 1919 1 SLT 169.

OTHER FORMS OF SECURITY

10.15   It is a requirement that a bond of caution or other security shall be given only by a person who is an 'authorised person' within the meaning of s. 31 of the Financial Services and Markets Act 2000.[20] It is becoming very difficult for a party who is ordained to find caution to actually find a caution provider who issues anything other than bonds of caution in guardianship or executry matters. Historically, the likes of RSA and Zurich would routinely issue bonds of caution. However, both have closed their book on issuing bonds to parties who have been ordained to find caution for expenses. If, in practical terms, it is impossible to source a bond of caution provider, that should be drawn to the attention of the court and alternative methods of finding security should be considered.

CONSIGNATION OF A SUM OF MONEY

10.16   As an alternative to a party being ordained to find caution, the court can make an order that a sum of money is consigned to court in terms of the Court of Session Consignations (Scotland) Act 1895 or the Sheriff Court Consignations (Scotland) Act 1893. Where a consignation order is made the amount of money specified in the order must be paid into court before the action can proceed. Clearly, such an order deprives the party against whom the order is made of the use of that money until the action is determined.

RCS R. 33.4 AND OCR R. 27.4

10.17   The court may approve a method of security other than caution or consignation including a combination of two or more methods of security. One example that may be acceptable to the court is a joint deposit receipt in the names of the parties.

---

20 RCS r. 33.5 and OCR r. 27.5.

Chapter 11

Expenses of Commissions

The procedure relating to the two forms of commission, namely a commission **11.01** and diligence for recovery of documents and a commission for examination of a witness, is set out in the Act of Sederunt (Rules of the Court of Session 1994) 1994 (RCS) r. 35, Act of Sederunt (Sheriff Court Ordinary Cause Rules) 1993 (OCR) r. 28 and Summary Cause Rule r. 18.

The general rule is that where a proof or evidential hearing is allowed, the **11.02** successful party will be entitled to recover costs that they incurred relative to commission procedure on a party/party basis.

A commissioner, unless appointed as part of their proper judicial function as **11.03** a Lord Ordinary or sheriff, is entitled to a fee.[1] If there is a disagreement as to the amount this shall be determined by the auditor.[2] The courts are reluctant to interfere with the auditor's assessment.[3]

The fees of the commissioner and clerk require to be paid at the time they **11.04** are incurred.[4]

If the commissioner's fee is not paid timeously a motion may be enrolled by **11.05** the commissioner in the action for payment of their fee and that of the clerk to the commission, or the commissioner may sue for payment in a separate action.[5]

The commissioner's fee is personal to them as they are acting in the capacity **11.06** of judicial appointee. It should therefore not be paid to their firm if a solicitor, or faculty services if an advocate. Normal practice is to appoint an advocate as commissioner in Court of Session proceedings and a solicitor in sheriff court proceedings.

Shorthand writer's fees are the responsibility of the party executing the **11.07** commission in the first instance.[6]

Historically, the auditor was likely to disallow the fees of counsel in relation **11.08** to a commission for the recovery of documents even in Court of Session proceedings.[7] The instruction of counsel in the execution of any commission in modern day practice is subject to any sanction requirements that exist and where sanction in the sheriff court is granted for the proceedings, counsel's involvement in a commission will remain subject to the scrutiny of the

---

1 Maclaren, *Expenses in the Supreme and Sheriff Court* (Edinburgh, 1912) p. 1,044.
2 *Menzies v Baird* 1912 1 SLT 84.
3 *Owners of Hilda v Owners of Australia* (1885) 12 R 547 per Lord Young at p. 548.
4 MacPhail, *Sheriff Court Practice*, 3rd edn (Edinburgh: W. Green, 2006) para. 15.36.
5 *McLauchlan v Flower Due* (1851) 13 D 1345.
6 RCS r. 35.4(1)(d) and OCR r. 28.4(1)(c).
7 Hastings, *Expenses in the Supreme and Sheriff Courts of Scotland* (Edinburgh: W. Green, 1989) p. 14.

auditor on the grounds of reasonableness. The auditor's discretion is limited to assessing the reasonableness of the counsel's fee if sanction is granted to employ counsel for the commission or a part of the proceedings that includes the commission. Further, in Court of Session proceedings it is seldom the case that objection is taken when negotiating a judicial account that a commission was conducted by counsel.

11.09   Havers' fees and outlays:

There are three elements that can constitute a haver's fee. The haver is permitted to charge for:

(1) the time spent searching for the documents and sending them to the commissioner;
(2) copying the documents if asked to do by the party who is responsible for their fee; and
(3) attending the commission.

11.10   If the circumstances justify it, the court will exercise its discretion to order that only a proportion of the costs of the commission are recoverable.[8]

11.11   The party instructing the commission will be responsible for the fee of the commissioner, their clerk and the shorthand writer.[9] It is the party not the agent who is personally liable for these costs.[10] However, the position is different in relation to the costs of citing the haver. The agent for a party, or a party litigant as the case may be, shall be personally liable, in the first instance, for the fees and expenses of a haver cited to appear at a commission for that party.[11]

11.12   Notwithstanding the general rule that the expenses occasioned by commission will usually be awarded in favour of the successful party, there is now the exception to that rule created for personal injury actions where the rules on qualified one-way cost shifting (QOCS) apply. In actions subject to the QOCS rules, the pursuer will not be found liable for the cost of the commission if ultimately unsuccessful with their action unless any of the exceptions to QOCS apply. See Chapter 3.

11.13   A witness attending a commission is entitled to the same payment as they would be entitled to if attending a proof or trial. However, a witness or haver who fails to attend having been properly cited and paid their fee is subject to secondary diligence and may be compelled to attend. The expenses occasioned by that procedure may be decerned for against the witness or haver.

11.14   Optional procedure under RCS rr. 35.3 and 35.3A, OCR rr. 28.3 and 28.3A and SCR rr. 18.2 and 18.2A set out the steps that would normally be taken by a party who has been granted commission and diligence for the recovery of documents prior to execution of a commission for recovery of documents. In essence, service of an optional procedure notice gives the haver the opportunity to produce the document in accordance with the court's interlocutor without the need for a commission hearing. Obviously, optional procedure is significantly less expensive than proceedings with a commission. The costs associated with optional procedure are the costs of serving the

---

8 *Graham v Borthwick* (1875) 2 R 812.
9 RCS r. 35.13(1)(d), OCR r. 28.12(1)(d).
10 RCS r. 35.4(1)(d) and OCR r. 28.4(1)(c).
11 RCS r. 35.4(6) and OCR r. 29.7(5).

optional procedure notice on the haver whereas the costs of proceedings with a commission may run to thousands of pounds when taking into account the fees of agents, counsel, the haver(s), the commissioner and shorthand writer. Unless there are compelling reasons for proceeding immediately to the execution of a commission without first undertaking optional procedure, the cost of the commission would invariably be held by the auditor to be unreasonable and therefore unrecoverable.

FURTHER POINTS RE COMMISSIONS FOR RECOVERY OF DOCUMENTS

11.15 A haver who had to raise an action to recover documents that they had produced in terms of a commission and diligence was awarded expenses against the party who failed to return them.[12]

11.16 A haver is entitled to be represented by a solicitor or person having right of audience before the sheriff at the execution of the commission.

COMMISSIONS TO TAKE EVIDENCE

11.17 It has also been held that the cost of a doctor attending on a witness to confirm their inability to attend a proof due to old age or infirmity is recoverable as part of the commission costs.[13]

11.18 If a witness is examined on commission and then appears and is examined at the proof, the expenses of the commission will not be allowed against the opposite party.[14] However, if a commission is held to take the evidence of a witness to *lie in retentis* (where the evidence is taken to preserve it due to fears that the witness will die prior to the proof) and the witness survives and is able to attend the proof to give evidence, it is suggested that the cost of the commission would be recoverable from the unsuccessful party as it was a necessary step of process. The very fact that the court granted the commission in the first place means it must have been satisfied that there was a real danger that the witness' evidence would be lost prior to proof.

MODE OF ATTENDANCE

11.19 Up until the COVID-19 crisis the norm for any commission, whether for the recovery of documents or to take/preserve evidence of a witness would be for it to be held in person at a mutually acceptable venue. Commissions during the restrictions that applied at the time of the COVID-19 crisis necessitated a different approach and generally all such hearings were held virtually. There were clear benefits in relation to saving on time and expense by conducting commissions over a digital platform. However, going forward, detailed

12 *Muirhead v Alexander Morrison & Co* (1899) 7 SLT 165.
13 *Scot v Craig* (1894) 32 JLR 39.
14 *Napier v Campbell* (1843) 5D 858; *MacLaine v Cooper* (1846) 8D 429; *Parker v North British Railway Company* (1900) 8 SLT 18.

consideration will have to be given to the appropriateness of conducting commission hearings virtually. If the norm of conducting a Proof in person is once again to resume (which, at the time of publication remains uncertain whilst the Scottish Civil Justice Council carry out a re-write of draft court rules to determine the mode of attendance for court hearings in the long term), then any commission to take the evidence of a witness would, as the default position, be justifiably undertaken as an 'in-person hearing' unless there was good reason not to. However, the consultation paper and draft rules in circulation in the latter part of 2021 have, as their starting point, a default position for the vast majority of proofs to be virtual and only those with 'significant issues of credibility' would be held in person. Significant opposition to that proposal is being advanced by both branches of the legal profession. All that can be said at this time is that careful thought will require to be given to the mode of conducting a commission. The party instructing the commission should liaise with the commissioner on whether the commission should be virtual or in person. It is for the commissioner to decide the mode of attendance. It may be prudent for commissioners to express in a preamble to their report the reasons why a commission is held in person to assist the auditor in determining the reasonableness of such a decision, failing which the extra cost associated with an in-person hearing may be subject to abatement. The auditor is entitled to ask the question 'why was a virtual commission not held?' The auditor is unlikely to interfere with the commissioner's decision if there is a clear paper trail to show consideration was given to the pros and cons of holding a commission virtually, but it was considered impractical or unreasonable to do so.

11.20   In relation to commissions for recovery of documents, if there are numerous calls in a specification that are likely to result in a significant volume of documents being produced, it may be unrealistic to expect the commissioner to be able to fulfil their duties and functions unless an in-person hearing is held. On the other hand, if the commission is simply to recover a small bundle of straightforward documents such as wage records, it's difficult to conceive of a situation where an in-person hearing would be required.

11.21   When dealing with commissions to take the evidence of a witness, practical considerations may dictate the mode of attendance. There may be no real alternative to an in-person hearing in the home of the witness if the witness is giving evidence from their death bed. On the other hand, there may be an obvious benefit in holding a commission virtually if the witness is abroad.

Chapter 12

Pursuers' Offers

On 3 April 2017 the Act of Sederunt (Rules of the Court of Session 1994 and Ordinary Cause Rules 1993 Amendment) (Pursuers' Offers) 2017 came into force.[1] This saw the reintroduction of pursuers offers into the rules of the Court of Session and Sheriff Court as a means of allowing a pursuer to make an offer to settle a claim in most types of actions that have a conclusion or crave for money, the exception being conclusions or craves that can only be granted after hearing evidence. **12.01**

Pursuers' offers had been previously introduced back in 1996 but were quickly revoked after the then formulation of the rules was declared *ultra vires* in the case of *Taylor v Marshall's Food Group Ltd (No. 2)*.[2] Notwithstanding the difficulties encountered at that time, the Gill Review in 2009 recommended their reintroduction to provide pursuers with a mechanism of making a settlement offer that has potential financial consequences if not accepted. The aim is to put pursuers on a level playing field with defenders who have the ability to tender. **12.02**

The 2017 Act of Sederunt creates Act of Sederunt (Rules of the Court of Session 1994) 1994 (RCS) r. 34A and Act of Sederunt (Sheriff Court Ordinary Cause Rules) 1993 (OCR) r. 27A to regulate the procedure in the Court of Session and sheriff court respectively. The rules are virtually identical. RCS r. 34A provides: **12.03**

Interpretation of this Chapter
34A.1. In this Chapter—
"appropriate date" means the date by which a pursuer's offer could reasonably have been accepted;
"fees" means fees of solicitors, and includes any additional fee;
"pursuer's offer" means an offer by a pursuer to settle a claim against a defender made in accordance with this Chapter;
"relevant period" means the period from the appropriate date to the date of acceptance of the pursuer's offer or, as the case may be, to the date on which judgment was given, or on which the verdict was applied.

Pursuers' offers
34A.2.—(1) A pursuer's offer may be made in any cause where the summons includes a conclusion for an order for payment of a sum or sums of money, other than an order—

---

1 Act of Sederunt (Rules of the Court of Session 1994 and Ordinary Cause Rules 1993 Amendment) (Pursuers' Offers) 2017 (SSI 2017/52).
2 *Taylor v Marshall's Food Group Ltd (No. 2)* 1998 SC 841.

(a) which the court may not make without evidence; or

(b) the making of which is dependent on the making of another order which the court may not make without evidence.

(2) This Chapter has no effect as regards any other form of offer to settle.

Making of offer

34A.3.—(1) A pursuer's offer is made by lodging in process an offer in the terms specified in rule 34A.4.

(2) A pursuer's offer may be made at any time before—

(a) the court makes avizandum or, if it does not make avizandum, gives judgment; or

(b) in a jury trial, the jury retires to consider the verdict.

(3) A pursuer's offer may be withdrawn at any time before it is accepted by lodging in process a minute of withdrawal.

Form of offer

34A.4. A pursuer's offer must—

(a) state that it is made under this Chapter;

(b) offer to accept—

(i)   a sum or sums of money, inclusive of interest to the date of the offer; and

(ii) the taxed expenses of process; and

(c) specify the conclusion or conclusions of the summons in satisfaction of which the sum or sums and expenses referred to in paragraph (b) would be accepted.

Disclosure of offers

34A.5.—(1) No averment of the fact that a pursuer's offer has been made may be included in any pleadings.

(2) Where a pursuer's offer has not been accepted—

(a) the court must not be informed that an offer has been made until—

(i)   the court has pronounced judgment; or

(ii) in the case of a jury trial, the jury has returned its verdict; and

(b) a jury must not be informed that an offer has been made until it has returned its verdict.

Acceptance of offers

34A.6.—(1) A pursuer's offer may be accepted at any time before—

(a) the offer is withdrawn;

(b) the court makes avizandum or, if it does not make avizandum, gives judgment; or

(c) in the case of a jury trial, the jury retires to consider its verdict.

(2) It is accepted by lodging in process an acceptance of the offer in the form of a minute of acceptance.

(3) A minute of acceptance must be unqualified other than as respects any question of contribution, indemnity or relief.

(4) On acceptance of a pursuer's offer either the pursuer or the defender may apply by motion for decree in terms of the offer and minute of acceptance.

(5) Where a pursuer's offer includes an offer to accept a sum of money in satisfaction of a conclusion for decree jointly and severally against two or more defenders, the offer is accepted only when accepted by all such defenders.

(6) However, the court may, on the motion of the pursuer, and with the consent of any defender who has lodged a minute of acceptance, grant decree in terms of the offer and minute of acceptance.

Late acceptance of offers

34A.7.—(1) This rule applies to the determination of a motion under rule 34A.6(4) where the court is satisfied that a defender lodged a minute of acceptance after the appropriate date.

(2) On the pursuer's motion the court must, except on cause shown—
  (a) allow interest on any sum decerned for from the date on which the pursuer's offer was made; and
  (b) find the defender liable for payment to the pursuer of a sum calculated in accordance with rule 34A.9.

(3) Where the court is satisfied that more than one defender lodged a minute of acceptance after the appropriate date the court may find those defenders liable to contribute to payment of the sum referred to in paragraph (2)(b) in such proportions as the court thinks fit.

(4) Where the court makes a finding under paragraph (2)(b), the pursuer may apply for decerniture for payment of the sum as so calculated no later than 21 days after the later of—
  (a) the date of the Auditor's report of the taxation of the pursuer's account of expenses; and
  (b) the date of the interlocutor disposing of a note of objection.

Non-acceptance of offers
34A.8.—(1) This rule applies where—
  (a) a pursuer's offer has been made, and has not been withdrawn;
  (b) the offer has not been accepted;
  (c) either—
    (i)   the court has pronounced judgment; or
    (ii) in the case of a jury trial, the verdict of the jury has been applied;
  (d) the judgment or verdict, in so far as relating to the conclusions of the summons specified in the pursuer's offer, is at least as favourable in money terms to the pursuer as the terms offered; and
  (e) the court is satisfied that the pursuer's offer was a genuine attempt to settle the proceedings.

(2) For the purpose of determining if the condition specified in paragraph (1)(d) is satisfied, interest awarded in respect of the period after the lodging of the pursuer's offer is to be disregarded.

(3) On the pursuer's motion the court must, except on cause shown, decern against the defender for payment to the pursuer of a sum calculated in accordance with rule 34A.9.

(4) No such motion may be enrolled after the expiry of 21 days after the later of—
  (a) the date of the Auditor's report of the taxation of the pursuer's account of expenses; and
  (b) the date of the interlocutor disposing of a note of objection.

(5) Where more than one defender is found liable to the pursuer in respect of a conclusion specified in the offer, the court may find those defenders liable to contribute to payment of the sum referred to in paragraph (3) in such proportions as it thinks fit.

Extent of defender's liability
34A.9. The sum that may be decerned for under rule 34A.7(2)(b) or rule 34A.8(3) is a sum corresponding to half the fees allowed on taxation of the pursuer's account of expenses, in so far as those fees are attributable to the relevant period, or in so far as they can reasonably be attributed to that period."

A pursuer's offer is made by lodging in Process a written offer that is intimated **12.04** to the opponent. There is no prescribed form. Various styles of minutes of offer and acceptance, depending on whether there are recoupable benefits repayable to the Compensation Recovery Unit, are produced at Appendix 4.

The offer must specify the conclusion or craves of the summons in satisfac- **12.05** tion of which the sums and expenses would be accepted. If there are multiple opponents and the offer is directed only to one or a few, there is no requirement to intimate the offer to those opponents who are not being asked to accept unless the acceptance of the offer will dispose of the whole action.

12.06   A pursuer's offer can be made at any time prior to the court making avizandum or giving a judgment or in the case of a jury trial, prior to the jury retiring to consider its verdict.

12.07   A pursuer's offer must state that it is made under the relevant rule and thereafter offer to accept a sum or sums of money, inclusive of interest, to the date of the offer and must also carry an offer to accept taxed expenses of process.

12.08   In a situation where a pursuer's offer has not been accepted, the court must not be informed of the offer being made until it has pronounced judgement or, in the case of a jury trial, the jury has returned its verdict. Similarly, a jury must not be informed of any such offer being made until it has returned its verdict.

12.09   Any pursuer's offer may be withdrawn at any time before it is accepted by the accepting party and should be withdrawn by the lodging of a minute of withdrawal of the pursuer's offer in process. For a minute of withdrawal style, see Appendix 4.

ACCEPTANCE OF OFFERS

12.10   A pursuer's offer may be accepted at any time prior to the offer being withdrawn or the court makes avizandum or gives judgment in the particular case or, alternatively, in the case of a jury trial, the jury retires to consider its verdict. Acceptance is done by the lodging of a minute of acceptance of the pursuer's offer in process and must be an unqualified acceptance other than in respect of any question of contribution, indemnity or relief. Following upon the offer being accepted, either party can apply to the court by motion for decree in terms of the pursuer's offer and minute of acceptance thereof. Where a pursuer's offer is made in satisfaction of a conclusion or crave for decree jointly and severally against multiple defenders, the offer can only be accepted when so accepted by all defenders except where the pursuer lodges a motion, with the consent of the defender who has accepted an offer in which case the court can grant decree in terms of the offer and acceptance.

LATE OR NON-ACCEPTANCE OF PURSUER'S OFFERS

12.11   Where the court is satisfied that a defender has failed to lodge acceptance of a pursuer's offer within a reasonable period of time or, alternatively, where the court has pronounced judgment or the verdict of the jury has been applied and that judgment or verdict is at least as favourable in monetary terms to the pursuer as the terms offered in the pursuer's offer (disregarding any interest awarded in respect of the period after the lodging of the pursuer's offer), the court must, if satisfied that the offer was a genuine attempt to settle the action, on a motion of the pursuer, find the defender liable for payment to the pursuer of a sum calculated in accordance with RCS r. 34A.9 or OCR r. 27A.9. In terms thereof, a sum corresponding to one-half of the fees allowed upon taxation of the pursuer's account of expenses, insofar as those expenses are attributable to the relevant period post the pursuer's offer or insofar as they can reasonably be attributed to that period, is payable over and above the paying party's liability for taxed expenses. The pursuer may apply for decerniture for payment of this sum within twenty-one days of the auditor's report of the taxation (or within twenty-one days of any interlocutor disposing of a note of objections should that procedure be adopted following upon the taxation of the pursuer's account of expenses). It should be noted that the payment to the pursuer in terms of rr. 34A.9 or 27A.9 is not an expense or part of the judicial account of expenses. It is a payment calculated on recoverable fees as included in the pursuer's judicial account of expenses and, strictly speaking, can only be determined once the pursuer's account of expenses has been agreed or taxed. Any abatements made to the corresponding entries in the pursuer's judicial account of expenses for the period under review are excluded from the 50 per cent 'penalty'. The additional payment is not subject to VAT and is a payment to the pursuer, not the solicitor.

Whether an offer is a genuine attempt to settle may prove contentious. **12.12** Thus far, there is no precedent on the issue. The case of *R (MVN) v London Borough of Greenwich*[3] deals with the similar English provision under their Civil Procedure Rules (CPR r. 36.17(4)). The claimant in that case made an offer to settle for the sum sued for. It was viewed as a tactical ploy with no concession that would have incentivised the defendant to settle. Therefore, notwithstanding the claimant succeeded at trial they failed to obtain the additional amounts that they would have become entitled to had the court viewed their offer as a genuine attempt to settle.

APPEALS

As a pursuer's offer requires to be lodged prior to a sheriff or judge making **12.13** avizandum, or if no avizandum is made, prior to delivering judgment, or prior to a jury retiring to consider its verdict, a pursuer's offer cannot be made in an appeal. This is settled in relation to Court of Session actions per the case of *Anderson v Imrie*[4] although if an interlocutory decision of a Lord Ordinary is reclaimed, the merits of the action not having been disposed of, it appears to still be possible to lodge a pursuer's offer as the merits still have to be decided by the Outer House.[5]

A pursuer's offer lodged timeously in accordance with RCS r. 34A.3(2) and **12.14** the sheriff court equivalent remains valid during an appeal.[6] The relevant period for calculating the uplift due to the pursuer as a result of the opponent failing to accept, or failing to timeously accept, a pursuer's offer runs until the date of the appeal court judgment, not the decision of the court of first instance.[7]

An offer made by a pursuer in respect of a defender's counterclaim is made **12.15** by way of tender, not pursuer's offer.

---

3 *R (MVN) v London Borough of Greenwich* [2015] EWHC 2663 (Admin).
4 *Anderson v Imrie* [2018] CSIH 79.
5 *Anderson v Imrie* per Lord Malcolm, para. 4.
6 *Wright v National Galleries of Scotland* [2020] SAC (Civ) 12.
7 *Wright v National Galleries of Scotland*, para. 13.

Chapter 13

Tenders

13.01   A tender is a judicial offer by a party to pay a part (or in rare cases all) of what their opponent is asking for after a court action is raised.[1] It cannot be made pre-litigation.[2] It differs from extra-judicial, or informal, offers in that a tender carries potential expenses implications if not accepted, or not accepted quickly enough. The use of a tender is designed to put pressure on a pursuer to settle. To be effective in that regard, the tender has to be tempting to a pursuer having regard to the strength of the pursuer's case and a realistic view of its value.

13.02   The tender can be made in the defences where part of the claim is admitted and averments are made tendering the sum admitted to be due. This method is now infrequently used. The much more commonly encountered form of tender is where a defender lodges a minute of tender, without any admission of liability and reserving their whole rights and pleas.

13.03   Various different types of tender are discussed below. Unlike pursuers' offers, tender procedure is not enshrined in rules of court but instead the common law. Tenders usually arise in personal injury or payment actions but can potentially be made in any type of action. A tender does not require to include a monetary offer. A tender has been made in an action of defamation by offering a full retraction of the defamatory remarks but making no offer of damages.[3]

13.04   The courts encourage settlement of actions and have taken the approach of approving innovative or novel wording in tenders.

Lord McCluskey in *Ferguson v MacLennan Salmon Co Ltd*[4] expressed the view '[t]he court will always encourage the settlement of actions rather than their continuation till resolved by the court'. This was the context of:

> 'the creation of minutes ... fashioned on traditional minutes of tender if they are designed to remove from one party the risk of having to pay expenses for a litigation which he can demonstrate would have been unnecessary in whole or in part if the offer contained in the minute had been accepted'.

13.05   There is no prescribed form of tender, although Appendix 4 contains suggested styles. However, there are two basic requirements for a tender to be effective. It must:

(1) be clear and unambiguous – a pursuer must be able to understand exactly what they are being offered. If, for example, benefits are repayable in a

---

1   *Ramsay's Trs v Souter* (1864) 2 M 891 per LJC Inglis at 892.
2   *Stoddart v R J Macleod Ltd* 1963 SLT (Notes) 23.
3   *Davidson v Panti* 1915 1 SLT 273.
4   *Ferguson v MacLennan Salmon Co Ltd* 1990 SLT 428.

personal injuries action the tender must specify whether the offer is gross or net of benefits[5]; and

(2) make an unqualified offer of expenses to the date of tender.[6] In exceptional cases a tender can be made without an offer of expenses, for example, where an action was raised by a pursuer without any pre-litigation notification.[7]

It was stated in *Ferguson*, as above, that: **13.06**

'The principle must be that if one party makes a judicial offer in clear and unambiguous terms which it is open to the other party to accept thereby ending the litigation in whole or in part, and the other party does not accept it, then if after further litigation, the court makes an award which benefits the non-accepting party to no greater extent than he would have benefited by accepting the offer, then, in the absence of other decisive considerations, it is he, not the offeror, who should pay for the unnecessary litigation subsequent to its date.'[8]

DATE OF TENDER

A pursuer is allowed a reasonable period of time to consider a tender. What   **13.07**
constitutes a reasonable period is dependent on the particular circumstances that prevail when the tender is made. A longer period may be allowed at the start of an action where there has been little prior discussion between the parties about valuation of the case compared to the period after a pre-trial meeting. However, tactics of trying to railroad a pursuer into making a quick decision by lodging a tender very late in the case are not viewed favourably by the courts.[9]

The date of the tender is not the date it is intimated or lodged, it is the   **13.08**
date at the end of the reasonable period that is given to the pursuer to make a decision.[10] The date is normally determined by the auditor in the absence of the agreement of the parties,[11] although the court can make the decision if it has all the necessary information to do so.[12] Therefore, reference in an interlocutor to expenses to the date of tender is not the date upon which the tender was lodged or intimated but the date when a pursuer was first in a position to properly consider a tender and decide as to its acceptance or otherwise.

If a pursuer is not in a position to properly consider a tender because it is   **13.09**
insufficiently clear or is ambiguous, the reasonable period allowed to consider the tender does not start running until the lack of clarity or ambiguity is resolved. For example, whilst it is competent to lodge a tender gross of benefits, the reasonable period for consideration would not start to run until a Compensation Recovery Unit certificate is available to tell a pursuer the level

5 *Spence v Wilson (No. 2)* 1998 SLT 959.
6 *Brackencroft v Silvers Marine* 2006 SLT 85.
7 *Lees v Gordon* 1929 SLT 400.
8 *Ferguson v MacLennan Salmon Co Ltd* per Lord McCluskey at pp. 49–51.
9 *Wood v Miller* 1960 SC 86.
10 *Jack v Black* 1911 1 SLT 124.
11 *Smeaton v Dundee Corporation* 1941 SC 600.
12 *Morton v O'Donnell* 1979 SLT (Notes) 26.

of benefits that require to be repaid and, in turn, allow them to calculate what they will receive if the tender is accepted.

13.10   If, upon consideration of a tender, it is determined that further expert evidence is required or some other documentation is needed to enable proper quantification of the claim, intimation should be sent to the defenders that the tender cannot be dealt with until such information is obtained.[13] Clearly, any additional information to enable proper consideration of the tender should be ingathered as promptly as possible.

13.11   Four main scenarios can arise where a basic tender is made:

(1) Acceptance of tender – the pursuer will be awarded the whole expenses of process (excepting any previous awards in favour of the defender) and the action will be disposed of when a motion is lodged to grant decree in terms of the minutes of tender and acceptance.

(2) The pursuer does not accept the tender immediately, carries on with the litigation but then accepts the tender at some point prior to judicial determination. In this scenario the pursuer will be awarded the expenses of process to the date of the tender and the defender will usually be awarded the expenses of process from the date of the tender through to the time the tender is accepted.

(3) Rejection of the tender where the pursuer carries on with the litigation and is ultimately awarded more than had been tendered. In this situation the tender becomes irrelevant and the pursuer will be awarded the expenses of process as if the tender had never been lodged.

(4) Rejection of the tender where the pursuer carries on with the litigation but fails to beat the tender, i.e. they are ultimately awarded a sum equal to or less than the amount that had been tendered. In this situation the pursuer will be awarded the expenses of process up to the date of the tender but the defender will be awarded the expenses of process from the date of the tender through to the conclusion of the case.

13.12   Where a defender wishes to be awarded expenses against a pursuer due to late acceptance of a tender or the pursuer's failure to beat a tender, the defender should lodge a notice of opposition to the pursuer's motion seeking decree for the expenses of the cause. The defender must seek the post-tender expenses no later than the time the court decerns against the defender for the expenses up to the date of the tender. If the contra expenses are not sought by the defender, the court will not grant them.[14]

13.13   Similarly, if the defender has any issue regarding the certification of skilled persons or sanction for counsel, opposition should be made to the pursuer's motion for decree.

13.14   The position in relation to tenders for personal injury actions raised on or after 30 June 2021 and which are subject to the rules on qualified one-way cost shifting, is dealt with in Chapter 3. In such actions, caps apply on the pursuer's liability for any contra award made in favour of the defender where the pursuer fails to beat, or fails to timeously accept, a tender.

---

13 *Smeaton v Dundee Corporation*, as above.
14 *Henderson v Peebleshire CC* 1972 SC 195.

DIFFERENT FORMS OF TENDER

See appendix 4 for Styles

Williamson tenders

In an action involving multiple defenders who are sued jointly and severally, **13.15** one defender can propose to another or others that they admit liability to the pursuer on the basis of contributions between them as specified in the tender relative to any damages and expenses awarded to the pursuer. Such a tender is commonly referred to as a Williamson tender.[15] This is seldom an attractive proposition to the recipient defender unless quantum is also resolved at the same time. Absent any agreement on quantum, they are being asked to accept a specific proportion of a liability for an undetermined amount that the court still requires to rule upon.

Quantification of damages is left open-ended even if the tender is accepted. **13.16** A Williamson tender, even if accepted, has no effect on the liability for expenses associated with the quantification of damages.[16]

If a Williamson tender is accepted to resolve liability and apportionment **13.17** between the defenders, the defenders can then lodge a joint minute of tender and intimate that to the pursuer, which may be accepted by the pursuer, leaving quantification to be determined at proof.[17]

Houston tenders

A defender, who is being sued on a joint and several basis, may lodge a tender **13.18** directed to the other defenders and the pursuer. The purposes are to: (a) propose to the defenders to contribute specific proportions of a sum of damages and taxed expenses; and (b) propose to the pursuer that they settle the action on the basis of the proposal being made between the defenders. Such a tender is known as a Houston tender.[18]

There is no judicial authority on how expenses require to be dealt with if a **13.19** Houston tender is rejected. According to MacPhail:

(1) If a defender fails to accept a Houston tender and they are found liable in a greater proportion than had been proposed in the tender they would be found liable for the tendering defender's expenses after the date of the tender in so far as they relate to the determination and apportionment of liability.[19]

(2) If a pursuer fails to accept a Houston tender and is awarded less than the tender, they may be liable to the defenders from the date of the tender although this is only likely to arise if all defenders had accepted the tender.[20]

---

15 *Williamson v McPherson* 1951 SC 438.
16 *Williamson v McPherson*, as above.
17 *Morton v O'Donnell* 1979 SLT (Notes) 26.
18 *Houston v British Road Services* 1967 SLT 329.
19 MacPhail, *Sheriff Court Practice*, 3rd edn (Edinburgh: W. Green, 2006) para. 14.66.
20 CN McEachran 'The Gentle Art of Tendering' 1969 SLT (News) at p. 56.

TENDERING FOR EXPENSES

13.20   It is not competent to tender for expenses in advance of a taxation[21] if the court has decerned for expenses in favour of the entitled party without any reservation of expenses still to be incurred: *McFarlane v Scottish Borders Council*.[22]

13.21   In *McFarlane*, the defenders had made a proposal to settle the pursuer's judicial account prior to taxation. When the proposal was rejected, the defenders tendered in relation to expenses. The tender was rejected. The purser failed to beat the tender at taxation. The defenders moved the court to grant decree for their costs in having to attend the taxation. The pursuers opposed on the basis that such a motion was incompetent, expenses having been finally disposed of in the interlocutors decerning for expenses in the pursuer's favour.

13.22   The court considered that it would be competent, where the paying party has tendered a sum for expenses, to invite the auditor to disallow any entries in the account that relate to the conduct of the taxation if it is evident that the paying party's offer is higher than the provisional value of the taxed account. If the auditor refused to do so the issue could be canvassed by a note of objections. However, if future expenses are not reserved in the interlocutor dealing with the expenses of the action, that interlocutor is final and future expenses issues cannot be the subject of further awards of expenses.

13.23   Even if there had been no decerniture, Lady Smith stated:

> 'it is plain from a consideration of those interlocutors that they cover not only expense incurred up to that date [the date expenses were decerned for] but also any expenses incurred in remitting the account for taxation and having it taxed'.[23]

13.24   Whilst the foregoing case followed on from decerniture for expenses (in the Court of Session, decerniture arises at the same time as the court makes the award of expenses), decerniture is not the sole factor for rendering a tender for expenses incompetent. The true meaning of the interlocutor granting the entitled party expenses requires to be looked at and if the intention was to dispose of all issues of expenses and achieve finality to the litigation, a tender for expenses would also be incompetent in the sheriff court where expenses are not decerned for until after the diet of taxation. The only potential way round this is for the paying party to seek a reservation of expenses associated with the taxation.

13.25   The position is mitigated now as most court auditors will apportion the fee fund dues/auditor's fee on a pro rata basis having regard to the level of abatements incurred.

INTEREST

13.26   The Interest on Damages (Scotland) Act 1958 s. 1(1B) provides:

> For the avoidance of doubt, it is hereby declared that where, in any action in which it is competent for the court to award interest under this Act, a tender is made in the course of the action, the tender shall, unless otherwise stated therein, be in full

---

21 *Gilmour's Tutor v Renfrew County Council* 1970 SLT 47.
22 *McFarlane v Scottish Borders Council* [2006] CSOH 96.
23 *McFarlane v Scottish Borders Council* para. 18.

satisfaction of any claim to interest thereunder by any person in whose favour the tender is made; and in considering in any such action whether an award is equal to or greater than an amount tendered in the action, the court shall take account of the amount of any interest awarded under this Act, or such part of that interest as the court considers appropriate.

Therefore, a tender in a damages action is inclusive of interest unless it specifically states otherwise. Further, the court will normally add interest to any award it makes following proof but in determining whether a tender has been beaten the court will calculate what the award would be including interest to the date of the tender. In the case of *Manson v Skinner*,[24] a pursuer failed to beat a tender of £3,000 inclusive of interest. They were awarded £2,800 and adding interest to the date of the tender resulted in a value of £2,992. The defender was awarded the expenses from the date of the tender. **13.27**

MULTIPLE PURSUERS

In a case with multiple pursuers who each have separate conclusions or craves, tenders have to be lodged individually.[25] This includes a situation where a pursuer sues in different capacities, such as an individual and executor or guardian.[26] **13.28**

A tender cannot be made for one cumulo sum for all pursuers to decide how to divide between them.[27] Nor can a condition be imposed that requires all pursuers to accept all tenders. It must be open to individual pursuers to accept the tenders directed to them without there being any requirement that all other pursuers follow suit.[28] **13.29**

LAPSE OF TENDER

If there is a material change in circumstances a tender may lapse even though it is not formally withdrawn.[29] This may include the death of the pursuer given that the heads of claim, or at least the value of each head of claim, may radically alter where the pursuer dies, although the point does not appear to have been authoritatively determined. **13.30**

A tender is held to become inoperative after the first instance judgment is issued.[30] A fresh tender would require to be lodged if appropriate after that date, for example, pending the marking of an appeal. **13.31**

Where a defender lodges several tenders over the course of an action, that does not cause the earlier tenders to lapse.[31] **13.32**

---

24 *Manson v Skinner* 2002 SLT 448.
25 *McNeil v National Coal Board* 1966 SC 72.
26 *Wilkinson v Richards* 1967 SLT 270.
27 *Flanagan v Dempster, Moore & Co Ltd* 1928 SC 308.
28 *McNeil v National Coal Board,* as above.
29 *Somerville v National Coal Board* 1963 SC 666.
30 *Bright v Low* 1940 SC 280; *Bond v British Railways Board* 1972 SLT (Notes) 47.
31 *Tait v Campbell* 2004 SLT 187; *Martin v Had-Fab Ltd* 2004 SLT 1192.

WITHDRAWAL OF TENDER

13.33 A minute of tender can be withdrawn at any time until it is accepted. Subject to the position regarding a tender lapsing, a tender can be accepted at any time until final judgment is issued or a jury has returned its verdict.

13.34   The withdrawal of a tender must be done by way of a minute of withdrawal (see style in Appendix 4) and must be lodged with the court and intimated to every other party. *McMillan v Meikleham*[32] is a case where there were failures in following the proper procedure, rendering the withdrawal ineffective.

---

32 *McMillan v Meikleham* 1934 SLT 357.

Chapter 14

Abandonment

Abandonment is the term given to a situation where a party, usually the pursuer, (although it is equally applicable to a defender or other party) gives up on their claim. **14.01**

As counterclaims are treated as separate causes, the abandonment of the pursuer's action has no effect on the counterclaim. Similarly, the pursuer's liability for expenses occasioned by the abandonment does not include the expenses of the counterclaim. **14.02**

Abandonment can arise at common law or under Rules of Court. A minute of abandonment is lodged with the court, accompanied by a motion setting out clearly what the party wishes the court to do. For further consideration of the procedure see MacPhail, *Sheriff Court Practice*.[1] **14.03**

The relevant rules of court provide as below. **14.04**

COURT OF SESSION

CHAPTER 29 ABANDONMENT
Abandonment of actions
29.1.—(1) A pursuer may abandon an action by lodging a minute of abandonment in process and—
    (a) consenting to decree of absolvitor; or
    (b) seeking decree of dismissal.
(2) The court shall not grant decree of dismissal under paragraph (1)(b) unless—
(a) full judicial expenses have been paid to the defender, and to any third party against whom the pursuer has directed any conclusions, within 28 days after the date of intimation of the report of the Auditor on the taxation of the account of expenses of that party; and
    (b) where abandonment is made in a proof or jury trial, the minute of abandonment is lodged before avizandum is made in the proof or the charge to the jury by the presiding judge has begun in the jury trial, as the case may be.
(3) If the pursuer fails to pay the expenses referred to in sub-paragraph (a) of paragraph (2) to the party to whom they are due within the period specified in that sub-paragraph, that party shall be entitled to decree of absolvitor with expenses.

Application of abandonment of actions to counterclaims
29.2 Rule 29.1 shall, with the necessary modifications, apply to the abandonment by a defender of his counterclaim as it applies to the abandonment of an action.

---

1 MacPhail, *Sheriff Court Practice*, 3rd edn (Edinburgh: W. Green, 2006) paras 14.21–14.32.

Abandonment of petitions, minutes and notes

29.3.—(1) A petition, minute or note may be abandoned by the petitioner, minuter or noter, as the case may be—

(a) enrolling a motion for abandonment of the cause; and

(b) intimating the motion to every person who lodged answers.

(2) The court may grant a motion under paragraph (1) subject to such conditions as to expenses or otherwise, if any, as it thinks fit.

SHERIFF COURT ORDINARY ACTIONS

CHAPTER 29 ABANDONMENT

Abandonment of clauses

23.1.—(1) A pursuer may abandon a cause at any time before decree of absolvitor or dismissal by lodging a minute of abandonment and—

(a) consenting to decree of absolvitor; or

(b) seeking decree of dismissal.

(2) The sheriff shall not grant decree of dismissal under paragraph (1)(b) unless full judicial expenses have been paid to the defender, and any third party against whom the pursuer has directed any crave, within 28 days after the date of taxation.

(3) If the pursuer fails to pay the expenses referred to in paragraph (2) to the party to whom they are due within the period specified in that paragraph, that party shall be entitled to decree of absolvitor with expenses.

Application of abandonment to counterclaims

23.2. Rule 23.1 shall, with the necessary modifications, apply to the abandonment by a defender of his counterclaim as it applies to the abandonment of a cause.

COMMENTARY

14.05   The use of the word 'full' judicial expenses in RCS r. 29.1(2) and OCR r. 23.1(2) does not confer any entitlement to a defender or third party beyond normal party/party expenses, unless the court specifically grants a motion to allow expenses on a different scale, e.g. agent/client.[2]

14.06   Abandonment can be made in relation to one opponent but preserving the action against another/others.

14.07   Abandonment should be accompanied by an offer to pay the judicial expenses of the party against whom the action is being abandoned.

14.08   As taxation of the expenses is necessary in accordance with the court rules, the court is not empowered to modify the expenses.

14.09   The party abandoning is only entitled to seek dismissal of their action (as opposed to giving their opponent absolvitor) if they pay the taxed judicial expenses to their opponent(s) within twenty-eight days of the diet of taxation. Dismissal is of course the disposal of choice for a pursuer if they wish to at least preserve the right to re-raise the proceedings.

14.10   Earlier awards of expenses are not recalled or overridden in any way by abandonment.[3]

---

2 *Lord Hamilton v Glasgow Dairy Co* 1933 SLT 7; *P v P* 1940 SC 389.
3 *Hayward v Edinburgh Royal Infirmary* 1955 SLT (Notes) 69.

Abandonment in the context of personal injury actions raised on or after 30 **14.11** June 2021 is subject to the special rules that apply to qualified one-way cost shifting.[4]

Where there are special considerations on expenses that require to be **14.12** reflected in any settlement agreement *vis a vis* the parties it is submitted that the appropriate course to follow is not to abandon but instead to reflect the specific terms of settlement in a joint minute that will dispose of the action, thus allowing the court to pronounce an interlocutor that gives effect to any such agreement.

4 See Chapter 3 on qualified one-way cost shifting.

Chapter 15

Interest on Expenses

15.01 Another significant change brought about by Act of Sederunt (Rules of the Court of Session, Sheriff Appeal Court Rules and Ordinary Cause Rules Amendment) (Taxation of Judicial Expenses) 2019 was the introduction of rules in the Court of Session and Sheriff Court providing for interest on expenses. Until the introduction of these rules, there was no specific provision to enable the courts to award interest on expenses. Although the courts always had a discretion to deal with expenses as they saw fit, it was not the norm for interest to be awarded on judicial expenses.

15.02 The Sheriff Court rule provides:

> **32.5.**—(1) Paragraph (2) applies where the sheriff grants decree for payment of—
> (a) expenses as taxed; and
> (b) interest thereon.
> (2) Without prejudice to the sheriff's other powers in relation to interest, the decree pronounced may require the party decerned against to pay interest on the taxed expenses, or any part thereof, from a date no earlier than 28 days after the date on which the account of expenses was lodged.[1]

15.03 The Court of Session rule provides:

> **42.4A.**—(1) At any time before extract of a decree for payment of expenses as taxed by the Auditor the court may, on the application of the party to whom expenses are payable, grant decree against the party decerned against for payment of interest on the taxed expenses, or any part thereof, from a date no earlier than 28 days after the date on which the account of expenses was lodged.
> (2) Paragraph (1) is without prejudice to the court's other powers in relation to expenses.[2]

15.04 The Sheriff Court rule does not make specific reference to the award of interest following on from an application by the entitled party but it is implicit that is the case. The timing of the award of interest in the sheriff court rule must be at the time the decree for expenses is made by the court. The position in the Court of Session is different as the application for interest can be made by the entitled party at any time prior to the decree for payment of expenses as taxed being extracted.

15.05 The application should be made by motion. There is nothing to stop parties reflecting an agreement to pay interest in a joint minute.

15.06 The interest awarded under OCR r. 32.5 or RCS r. 42.4A runs from a date that can be no earlier than twenty-eight days after the entitled party's account

---

1 Act of Sederunt (Sheriff Court Ordinary Cause Rules) 1993 (OCR) r. 32.5.
2 Act of Sederunt (Rules of the Court of Session 1994) (RCS) r. 42.4A.

is lodged for taxation. This clearly encourages early lodging and intimation of accounts.

Both rules are framed to give the courts discretion as to whether to award **15.07** interest and do not interfere with any other discretionary power that the courts have in making orders relative to expenses. It will be noted that interest is only applicable on taxed expenses. Any extrajudicial agreement regarding an entitled party's account of expenses would require specific provision in that agreement for interest to apply.

Chapter 16

Employment Cases

16.01 The vast majority of employment disputes are dealt with by employment tribunals. The employment tribunal has exclusive jurisdiction over a large number of statutory claims. The types of statutory claims that can be advanced before a tribunal include claims relating to:

- dismissal;
- redundancy rights and business transfers;
- maternity, adoption, paternity and parental leave and flexible working;
- discrimination and equal pay;
- trade unions and union members;
- working time and holiday pay;
- unlawful deduction of wages.

16.02 The general rule applied before the civil courts that an award of expenses follows success in a case does not apply in employment tribunal claims. The Employment Tribunal (Constitution and Rules of Procedure) Regulations 2013[1] at rr. 74–84, provide a statutory framework whereby a party to proceedings can apply for a costs order to recover at least part of their outlay in the event that they are successful in pursuing or defending a claim. The rules are in the following terms:

COSTS ORDERS, PREPARATION TIME ORDERS AND WASTED COSTS ORDERS

Definitions
74.—(1) "Costs" means fees, charges, disbursements or expenses incurred by or on behalf of the receiving party (including expenses that witnesses incur for the purpose of, or in connection with, attendance at a Tribunal hearing). In Scotland all references to costs (except when used in the expression "wasted costs") shall be read as references to expenses.

(2) "Legally represented" means having the assistance of a person (including where that person is the receiving party's employee) who—
  (a) has a right of audience in relation to any class of proceedings in any part of the Senior Courts of England and Wales, or all proceedings in county courts or magistrates' courts;
  (b) is an advocate or solicitor in Scotland; or
  (c) is a member of the Bar of Northern Ireland or a solicitor of the Court of Judicature of Northern Ireland.

---

1 Employment Tribunal (Constitution and Rules of Procedure) Regulations 2013 (SI 2013/1237).

(3) "Represented by a lay representative" means having the assistance of a person who does not satisfy any of the criteria in paragraph (2) and who charges for representation in the proceedings.

Costs orders and preparation time orders

75.—(1) A costs order is an order that a party ("the paying party") make a payment to—

    (a) another party ("the receiving party") in respect of the costs that the receiving party has incurred while legally represented or while represented by a lay representative;

    (b) the receiving party in respect of a Tribunal fee paid by the receiving party; or

    (c) another party or a witness in respect of expenses incurred, or to be incurred, for the purpose of, or in connection with, an individual's attendance as a witness at the Tribunal.

(2) A preparation time order is an order that a party ("the paying party") make a payment to another party ("the receiving party") in respect of the receiving party's preparation time while not legally represented. "Preparation time" means time spent by the receiving party (including by any employees or advisers) in working on the case, except for time spent at any final hearing.

(3) A costs order under paragraph (1)(a) and a preparation time order may not both be made in favour of the same party in the same proceedings. A Tribunal may, if it wishes, decide in the course of the proceedings that a party is entitled to one order or the other but defer until a later stage in the proceedings deciding which kind of order to make.

When a costs order or a preparation time order may or shall be made

76.—(1) A Tribunal may make a costs order or a preparation time order, and shall consider whether to do so, where it considers that—

    (a) a party (or that party's representative) has acted vexatiously, abusively, disruptively or otherwise unreasonably in either the bringing of the proceedings (or part) or the way that the proceedings (or part) have been conducted; or

    (b) any claim or response had no reasonable prospect of success; or

    (c) a hearing has been postponed or adjourned on the application of a party made less than 7 days before the date on which the relevant hearing begins.

(2) A Tribunal may also make such an order where a party has been in breach of any order or practice direction or where a hearing has been postponed or adjourned on the application of a party.

(3) Where in proceedings for unfair dismissal a final hearing is postponed or adjourned, the Tribunal shall order the respondent to pay the costs incurred as a result of the postponement or adjournment if—

    (a) the claimant has expressed a wish to be reinstated or re-engaged which has been communicated to the respondent not less than 7 days before the hearing; and

    (b) the postponement or adjournment of that hearing has been caused by the respondent's failure, without a special reason, to adduce reasonable evidence as to the availability of the job from which the claimant was dismissed or of comparable or suitable employment.

(4) A Tribunal may make a costs order of the kind described in rule 75(1)(b) where a party has paid a Tribunal fee in respect of a claim, employer's contract claim or application and that claim, counterclaim or application is decided in whole, or in part, in favour of that party.

(5) A Tribunal may make a costs order of the kind described in rule 75(1)(c) on the application of a party or the witness in question, or on its own initiative, where a witness has attended or has been ordered to attend to give oral evidence at a hearing.

Procedure
77. A party may apply for a costs order or a preparation time order at any stage up to 28 days after the date on which the judgment finally determining the proceedings in respect of that party was sent to the parties. No such order may be made unless the paying party has had a reasonable opportunity to make representations (in writing or at a hearing, as the Tribunal may order) in response to the application.

The amount of a costs order
78.—(1) A costs order may—
  (a) order the paying party to pay the receiving party a specified amount, not exceeding £20,000, in respect of the costs of the receiving party;
  (b) order the paying party to pay the receiving party the whole or a specified part of the costs of the receiving party, with the amount to be paid being determined, in England and Wales, by way of detailed assessment carried out either by a county court in accordance with the Civil Procedure Rules 1998, or by an Employment Judge applying the same principles; or, in Scotland, by way of taxation carried out either by the auditor of court in accordance with the Act of Sederunt (Fees of Solicitors in the Sheriff Court) (Amendment and Further Provisions) 1993, or by an Employment Judge applying the same principles;
  (c) order the paying party to pay the receiving party a specified amount as reimbursement of all or part of a Tribunal fee paid by the receiving party;
  (d) order the paying party to pay another party or a witness, as appropriate, a specified amount in respect of necessary and reasonably incurred expenses (of the kind described in rule 75(1)(c)); or
  (e) if the paying party and the receiving party agree as to the amount payable, be made in that amount.
(2) Where the costs order includes an amount in respect of fees charged by a lay representative, for the purposes of the calculation of the order, the hourly rate applicable for the fees of the lay representative shall be no higher than the rate under rule 79(2).
(3) For the avoidance of doubt, the amount of a costs order under sub-paragraphs (b) to (e) of paragraph (1) may exceed £20,000.

The amount of a preparation time order
79.—(1) The Tribunal shall decide the number of hours in respect of which a preparation time order should be made, on the basis of—
  (a) information provided by the receiving party on time spent falling within rule 75(2) above; and
  (b) the Tribunal's own assessment of what it considers to be a reasonable and proportionate amount of time to spend on such preparatory work, with reference to such matters as the complexity of the proceedings, the number of witnesses and documentation required.
(2) The hourly rate is £33 and increases on 6 April each year by £1.
(3) The amount of a preparation time order shall be the product of the number of hours assessed under paragraph (1) and the rate under paragraph (2).

When a wasted costs order may be made
80.—(1) A Tribunal may make a wasted costs order against a representative in favour of any party ("the receiving party") where that party has incurred costs—
  (a) as a result of any improper, unreasonable or negligent act or omission on the part of the representative; or
  (b) which, in the light of any such act or omission occurring after they were incurred, the Tribunal considers it unreasonable to expect the receiving party to pay.
Costs so incurred are described as "wasted costs".

(2) "Representative" means a party's legal or other representative or any employee of such representative, but it does not include a representative who is not acting in pursuit of profit with regard to the proceedings. A person acting on a contingency or conditional fee arrangement is considered to be acting in pursuit of profit.

(3) A wasted costs order may be made in favour of a party whether or not that party is legally represented and may also be made in favour of a representative's own client. A wasted costs order may not be made against a representative where that representative is representing a party in his or her capacity as an employee of that party.

Effect of a wasted costs order

81. A wasted costs order may order the representative to pay the whole or part of any wasted costs of the receiving party, or disallow any wasted costs otherwise payable to the representative, including an order that the representative repay to its client any costs which have already been paid. The amount to be paid, disallowed or repaid must in each case be specified in the order.

Procedure

82. A wasted costs order may be made by the Tribunal on its own initiative or on the application of any party. A party may apply for a wasted costs order at any stage up to 28 days after the date on which the judgment finally determining the proceedings as against that party was sent to the parties. No such order shall be made unless the representative has had a reasonable opportunity to make representations (in writing or at a hearing, as the Tribunal may order) in response to the application or proposal. The Tribunal shall inform the representative's client in writing of any proceedings under this rule and of any order made against the representative.

Allowances

83. Where the Tribunal makes a costs, preparation time, or wasted costs order, it may also make an order that the paying party (or, where a wasted costs order is made, the representative) pay to the Secretary of State, in whole or in part, any allowances (other than allowances paid to members of the Tribunal) paid by the Secretary of State under section 5(2) or (3) of the Employment Tribunals Act to any person for the purposes of, or in connection with, that person's attendance at the Tribunal.

Ability to pay

84. In deciding whether to make a costs, preparation time, or wasted costs order, and if so in what amount, the Tribunal may have regard to the paying party's (or, where a wasted costs order is made, the representative's) ability to pay.

Generally, the tribunal is restricted in making a costs order to situations where **16.03** a party has acted vexatiously, abusively, disruptively or otherwise unreasonably in either the bringing of proceedings or the way in which the proceedings have been conducted. Additionally, the tribunal may make a costs order if a claim or a response to that claim had no reasonable prospect of success. The tribunal therefore has a wide discretion as to whether to grant a costs order but it should be noted that costs in the employment tribunal are still the exception rather than the rule.[2]

The employment tribunal has a concurrent jurisdiction with the civil courts **16.04** where a claimant seeks damages in respect of a breach of contract provided the claimant's employment has terminated. The employment tribunal's

---

2 *Yerrakalva v Barnsley Metropolitan Council* [2012] ICR 420.

jurisdiction in this regard only extends to claims where the value of the claim is no greater than £25,000.[3]

16.05   In these circumstances, the prospective litigant needs to weigh up which forum they litigate in. If they lose their employment tribunal claim, then the likelihood is there will be no award of costs against the unsuccessful party. However, if they proceed in the civil courts, expenses will normally follow success.

16.06   Breach of contract actions and interdict actions in an employment setting are commonplace in the civil courts. Interdict actions arise mainly where a restrictive covenant within a contract of employment is allegedly being breached and interdict and interim interdict are sought to prevent the breach. In these types of action, the general rule of costs following success would apply. Interdict proceedings are generally short-lived but they can have additional craves for damages that may prolong the proceedings with resultant costs implications.

---

3 Industrial Tribunals Extension of Jurisdiction (Scotland) Order 1994 (SI 1994/1624).

Chapter 17

Group Proceedings

Historically, it was not possible to raise group proceedings or class actions   **17.01**
in Scotland. The introduction of the Civil Litigation (Expenses and Group
Proceedings) (Scotland) Act 2018 changed the landscape in that regard and
introduced group proceedings to Scottish litigation, at least in the Court of
Session.

Previously, the norm in such cases was for one action, or a select few   **17.02**
actions, to be proceeded with. The remaining actions relating to the group,
whilst still having to be raised if there were time bar considerations, would
be sisted pending the outcome of the lead action(s). Such procedure did
not fit well with the recovery of expenses. Whilst possible to identify which
court procedure related to which particular action, a difficulty arose insofar
as how the work generic to all actions, including those sisted pending the
outcome of the lead action(s), should be dealt with. Generally, an account of
expenses in each of the sisted actions would be prepared on a block fee basis
given the limited court procedure as this would prove more remunerative
insofar as the sisted actions were concerned. Strictly speaking, each sisted
action's share of the generic work undertaken for all actions would be sub-
sumed within the block fees charged in each account of expenses. A difficulty
arose in that the generic work undertaken in relation to all actions within the
group could only be properly quantified by preparation of a detailed account
of expenses, therefore falling foul of the rules of court dictating that a solicitor
cannot charge his account partly on a detailed basis and partly on a block fee
basis.

In one instance, a case proceeded as the lead case with all remaining actions   **17.03**
relating to the same subject matter being sisted pending the outcome of the
lead case. Generic settlement discussions ensued, resulting in settlement of
the lead case and also the various sisted actions. As the settlement discussions took place solely within the lead action, all work, including counsel's
charges were included in the judicial account of expenses for the lead action.
Upon taxation of the account of expenses the auditor of the Court of Session
determined that the generic settlement discussions required to be apportioned
between all cases. To include all work in the account for the lead case would
result in the receiving party recovering expenses relating to one process in
another action, which is not possible.

In another instance, an agreement was reached between parties that the   **17.04**
generic work common to all actions would be included in a separate account
of expenses calculated on a detailed basis and treated as a stand-alone account
of expenses and entirely separate from the accounts of expenses relating to
each individual action.

17.05   The lack of specific court procedure or direction insofar as how expenses in such circumstances should be treated resulted generally in various different approaches to the recovery of expenses on a party/party basis being explored.

17.06   Introduction of Part 4 of the Civil Litigation (Expenses in Group Proceedings) (Scotland) Act 2018 permitted, for the first time, the raising of group proceedings, also referred to as multi-party actions or class actions in the Court of Session. Sections 20–22 of the Act provide:

Group proceedings

20.—(1) There is to be a form of procedure in the Court of Session known as "group procedure", and proceedings subject to that procedure are to be known as "group proceedings".

(2) A person (a "representative party") may bring group proceedings on behalf of two or more persons (a "group") each of whom has a separate claim which may be the subject of civil proceedings.

(3) A person may be a representative party in group proceedings—
    (a) whether or not the person is a member of the group on whose behalf the proceedings are brought,
    (b) only if so authorised by the Court.

(4) There is to be no more than one representative party in group proceedings.

(5) Group proceedings may be brought only with the permission of the Court.

(6) The Court may give permission—
    (a) only if it considers that all of the claims made in the proceedings raise issues (whether of fact or law) which are the same as, or similar or related to, each other,
    (b) only if it is satisfied that the representative party has made all reasonable efforts to identify and notify all potential members of the group about the proceedings, and
    (c) in accordance with provision made in an act of sederunt under section 21(1).

(7) An act of sederunt under section 21(1) may provide for group proceedings to be brought as—
    (a) opt-in proceedings,
    (b) opt-out proceedings, or
    (c) either opt-in proceedings or opt-out proceedings.

(8) In subsection (7)—
    (a) "opt-in proceedings" are group proceedings which are brought with the express consent of each member of the group on whose behalf they are brought,
    (b) "opt-out proceedings" are group proceedings which are brought on behalf of a group, each member of which has a claim which is of a description specified by the Court as being eligible to be brought in the proceedings and—
        (i) is domiciled in Scotland and has not given notice that the member does not consent to the claim being brought in the proceedings, or
        (ii) is not domiciled in Scotland and has given express consent to the claim being brought in the proceedings.

(9) In group proceedings, the representative party may—
    (a) make claims on behalf of the members of the group,
    (b) subject to provision made in an act of sederunt under section 21(1), do anything else in relation to those claims that the members would have been able to do had the members made the claims in other civil proceedings.

(10) Section 11 of the Court of Session Act 1988 (jury actions) does not apply to group proceedings.

Group procedure: rules

21.—(1) The Court of Session may make provision by act of sederunt about group procedure.

(2) Without limiting that generality, the power in subsection (1) includes power to make provision for or about—

(a) persons who may be authorised to be a representative party,

(b) action to be taken by a representative party in connection with group proceedings (whether before or after the proceedings are brought),

(c) the means by which a person may—

(i) give consent for the person's claim to be brought in group proceedings,

(ii) give notice that the person does not consent to the person's claim being brought in group proceedings,

(d) types of claim that may not be made in group proceedings,

(e) circumstances in which permission to bring group proceedings may be refused,

(f) appeals against the granting or refusal of such permission,

(g) the disapplication or modification of section 39 of the Courts Reform (Scotland) Act 2014 (exclusive competence of the sheriff court) in relation to group proceedings,

(h) the making of an additional claim in group proceedings after the proceedings have been brought (including the transfer of a claim made in other civil proceedings),

(i) the exclusion of a claim made in group proceedings from the proceedings (including the transfer of the claim to other civil proceedings),

(j) the replacement of a representative party,

(k) steps that may be taken by a representative party only with the permission of the Court.

(3) Nothing in an act of sederunt under subsection (1) is to derogate from section 20.

(4) An act of sederunt under subsection (1) may make—

(a) incidental, supplementary, consequential, transitional, transitory or saving provision,

(b) provision amending, repealing or revoking any enactment relating to matters with respect to which an act of sederunt under subsection (1) may be made,

(c) different provision for different purposes.

(5) This section is without prejudice to—

(a) any enactment that enables the Court to make rules (by act of sederunt or otherwise) regulating the practice and procedure to be followed in proceedings to which this section applies, or

(b) the inherent powers of the Court.

(6) In subsection (2), "representative party" is to be construed in accordance with section 20(2).

Group proceedings: further provision

22.—(1) The Scottish Ministers may by regulations make further provision in connection with group proceedings.

(2) Regulations under subsection (1) may, in particular, make provision for or about—

(a) circumstances in which a person is domiciled in Scotland for the purposes of section 20(8)(b),

(b) prescriptive or limitation periods in relation to claims brought in group proceedings,

(c) the assessment, apportionment and distribution of damages in connection with such proceedings, including the appointment of persons to give advice about those matters.

(3) Regulations under subsection (1) may modify any enactment.

17.07 The regulations that have been introduced to deal with group proceedings are contained in the Act of Sederunt (Rules of the Court of Session 1994 Amendment) (Group Proceedings) 2020.[1] The regulations are produced in full at Appendix 1. The Scottish statutory instrument creates RCS r. 26A, which sets out the procedure to be followed in relation to group groceedings. Failure to follow the procedure allows the Lord Ordinary to make such order at their own instance:

 (a) to refuse to extend any period of compliance with a provision in these Rules or an order of the court;
 (b) to dismiss the action, as the case may be, in whole or in part;
 (c) to grant decree in respect of all or any of the conclusions of the summons, as the case may be; or
 (d) to make an award of expenses, as the Lord Ordinary thinks fit.[2]

17.08 There is no corresponding provision for Sheriff Court cases. Unfortunately, whilst introducing specific procedure, the status quo remains insofar as expenses are concerned and no direction is provided as to how expenses in such proceedings should be dealt with. The lack of specific rules or direction regarding expenses is by design rather than oversight on the basis that it will be necessary for the rules to be in existence and utilised for some time, which will, in turn, allow the collection of data as to the cost of servicing the new procedure and thereafter allow a policy on the provision of specific fees to be considered. It is the intention that a review will be carried out at a future date to determine what provision for expenses is required. At the time of introduction of the rules, the court retains its discretion to apply the general rule that expenses follow success and, where necessary, determine the liability of each member of the group for any adverse expenses incurred by the group representative (being a person as set out in s. 20(3) and (4) above.

17.09 The rules on qualified one-way cost shifting (see Chapter 3) apply to parties represented in group proceedings if the claims relate to personal injury.

---

1 Act of Sederunt (Rules of the Court of Session 1994 Amendment) (Group Proceedings) 2020 (SSI 2020/208).
2 Act of Sederunt (Rules of the Court of Session 1994) (RCS) r. 26A.29.

Chapter 18

Family Proceedings

Family actions are often marked by high-conflict where legal disputes require **18.01** to be resolved in the context of difficult and stressful emotional issues. In such circumstances, it is inevitable that parties to the litigation sometimes conduct it in an unreasonable manner. It is also perhaps inappropriate to regard one party as 'the winner' in an action concerning relationship breakdown or in respect of children where both parties have sought orders that they consider to be best for their children.

As a result, the usual rule that expenses follow success does not automatically **18.02** apply in family actions and instead judicial discretion is applied flexibly.[1] That said, there have been recent examples of where the court has been persuaded to award expenses where there has been clear success by one party over another.

ACTIONS OF DIVORCE/DISSOLUTION OF CIVIL PARTNERSHIPS

Prior to the Family Law (Scotland) Act 1985, a husband was liable for a wife's **18.03** expenses. The 1985 Act abolished that rule and the starting position is that each party is liable for their own expenses whether pursuing or defending an action.[2]

The most recent leading authority on expenses in divorce actions is *Sweeney* **18.04** *v Sweeney*.[3] In its decision, the Inner House confirmed that in defended actions of divorce the normal rule of expenses following success is not irrelevant but should not be applied to its full vigour. That said, the court may well award expenses where the other party secures an award 'significantly greater' than any outstanding offer (and in this the court will pay close attention to offers from the paying party). The court is also entitled to consider the conduct of the parties, but where there has been full disclosure and agreement as to valuations of matrimonial property the just award may be no expenses due to or by either party. The court also considered whether awards of expenses would disrupt the financial provision being made.

In advising clients, consideration should be given to the following: **18.05**

(1) Whilst *Sweeney* and earlier cases are helpful in establishing general principles, the determination of expenses is a matter for the decision-maker in each case.

---

1 *Little v Little* 1990 SLT 785 per Lord President Hope (pp. 790B–790D).
2 Family Law (Scotland) Act 1985 s. 22.
3 *Sweeney v Sweeney* 2007 SC 396.

(2) No guarantee can therefore be given that an award of expenses will be made. Beating an extrajudicial settlement offer does not itself lead to an award of expenses – much depends on the conduct of the parties during the litigation and the gap between the pre-proof offer and final orders made.

(3) Parties should be advised that so long as the litigation is conducted reasonably they ought to expect to bear their own expenses. Similarly, because many defended actions are resolved shortly before proof, settlement agreements usually provide for each party to bear their own expenses, with an undefended divorce to follow on a 'no expenses due to or by' basis.

(4) The paying party should be advised to consider making a comprehensive offer in settlement prior to proof. It is appreciated that deadlines for acceptance may focus negotiations, but an offer only provides the paying party with protection for so long as it remains on the table.

(5) Whilst decision-makers are reluctant to grant awards of expenses against the receiving party that would disrupt the financial provision being made, it does happen and the client should be advised to conduct the litigation reasonably.[4]

(6) Anecdotal evidence from some family court practitioners is that although decisions tend to be unreported, the direction of travel is for a party to be awarded expenses occasioned by the proof where the paying party's offer was less than the financial orders granted by the judge.

ACTIONS IN RELATION TO CHILDREN

18.06 For actions concerning children, the starting point again is that there should be no expenses due to or by either party. However, the question of expenses is a matter of discretion for the court to be determined after proof.

18.07 The court is more likely to consider making an award of expenses against the unsuccessful party in single-issue actions (such as aliment or responsibility for payment of school fees) and/or winner-take-all outcomes (such as relocation actions, where the specific issue order sought by the party looking to remove the child from the jurisdiction will either be granted or refused). The reasonableness and conduct of the parties to the action remains a factor. Wholly unreasonable conduct may render it more likely that an award of expenses will be made.[5]

OTHER ISSUES

18.08 The issue of expenses in family actions formed part of the Taylor report. Having reviewed the relevant authorities, Sheriff Principal Taylor was persuaded that the approach to expenses in family proceedings worked well:

' ... the Scottish judiciary has been much more willing to exercise its discretion when called upon to make awards of expenses in divorce actions and actions involving

---

4 For example, *Hodge v Hodge* 2008 Fam. L.R. 51.
5 For example, *AB v BB* [2011] CSOH 198.

children. Awards of expenses, particularly in cases in which one party has behaved unreasonably, are becoming more frequent. I consider such a move to be sensible. Although this will result in it being more difficult to predict the expenses of a family action, I consider that this is outweighed by the fact that the power to make such an award may serve to temper the behaviour of the parties and may contribute to a further reduction in the cost of family actions'.[6]

The Civil Litigation (Expenses and Group Proceedings) (Scotland) Act 2018 **18.09** expressly prohibits damages-based agreements from being entered into in family proceedings.[7] It is, however, possible to fund family actions under conditional fee arrangements, i.e. where the success fee is calculated as a percentage of the fee element of the judicial account, though this is not common. Family proceedings are excluded from the provisions that will oblige disclosure of third party funding.[8]

It is possible to seek an award of expenses to be met by the Scottish Legal **18.10** Aid Board against an unsuccessful assisted party who is in receipt of civil legal aid.[9]

6 Taylor, *Review of Expenses and Funding of Civil Litigation in Scotland* (September 2013), para. 93.
7 Civil Litigation (Expenses and Group Proceedings) (Scotland) Act 2018 s. 5; the Civil Litigation (Expenses and Group Proceedings) (Scotland) Act 2018 (Success Fee Agreements) Regulations 2020 (SSI 2020/110).
8 Civil Litigation (Expenses and Group Proceedings) (Scotland) Act 2018 s. 10.
9 Legal Aid (Scotland) Act 1986 s. 19.

Chapter 19

Interim Awards of Expenses

19.01 There seems to be little doubt now that a motion for an interim award of judicial expenses is competent in the Court of Session, which award can be for a specific sum without the need for taxation. The position, however, is less clear for Sheriff Court proceedings due to the different wording of the relevant rules.

19.02 Motions for interim awards of expenses are relatively rare, there being only a handful of reported decisions, all from the Court of Session.

19.03 The rules of the Court of Session provide that where expenses are found due to a party in any cause the court shall:

(a) pronounce an interlocutor finding that party entitled to expenses and subject to there being no modification in legal aid cases, remit the cause to the auditor for taxation; and

(b) unless satisfied there is special cause for not doing so, pronounce an interlocutor decerning against the party found liable in expenses as taxed by the auditor. This is without prejudice to the right to object to the auditor's report.[1]

19.04 Therefore, on the face of it, a taxation is required for any award of expenses, whether interim or final.

19.05 It is commonplace for awards of expenses to be made against a party who, for example, is unsuccessful in moving or opposing a motion, or who loses a procedure roll hearing, or who creates needless procedure during the course of an action. And all practitioners in the Court of Session will be familiar with the standard wording of the interlocutor that follows on from that, 'remits the account to the auditor to tax and report. And decerns'.

19.06 Decerniture simply means a decree or sentence of a court. So, the rule simply confirms that as soon as the account of expenses is taxed, and in the absence of any objections to the auditor's report, a decree for the taxed amount shall automatically follow.

19.07 The position in Sheriff Court ordinary actions is set out in the two versions of the Act of Sederunt (Sheriff Court Ordinary Cause Rules) 1993 (OCR) r. 32.1.

For actions commenced prior to 29 April 2019 the rule states:

> 32.1 Expenses allowed in any cause, whether in absence or *in foro contentioso*, unless modified at a fixed amount, shall be taxed before decree is granted for them.

---

1   Act of Sederunt (Rules of the Court of Session 1994) (RCS) r. 41.1(1)(a) and (b).

For actions commenced on or after 29th April 2019 the rule is in the same terms but subject to OCR 7.4(2) which relates to undefended actions. Where the pursuer elects, in the minute for decree, to claim expenses comprising—

(a) the inclusive charges set out in Part 1 of Table I in schedule 4 of the Act of Sederunt (Taxation of Judicial Expenses Rules) 2019; and
(b) outlays comprising only—
   (i) the court fee for warranting the initial writ;
   (ii) postal charges incurred in effecting, or attempting to effect, service of the initial writ by post; and
   (iii) where applicable, a sheriff officer's fee for service of the initial writ,

the sheriff may grant decree for payment of such expenses without the necessity of taxation

This is where the subtle difference between the Court of Session and Sheriff **19.08** Court rules arises. In the latter there is no interlocutor decerning for the taxed expenses at the time of the remit to the auditor. The matter comes back before the sheriff after the Sheriff Court auditor taxes the account and only then is the Sheriff empowered to pronounce an interlocutor decerning for the taxed expenses.

THE RELEVANT CASE LAW

It will be seen from the following cases that whilst it has always been held to **19.09** be competent to seek interim awards of expenses in the Court of Session, the approach taken in terms of what is required to justify such awards has differed.

Martin & Co (UK) Ltd Petitioners[2]   **19.10**

Lord Drummond Young had granted, at an earlier stage in the proceedings, an unopposed motion for the expenses of process to date on an agent-client, client paying basis. The petitioners followed up with a motion for an interim award of expenses for £50,000 and immediate extract. The diet of taxation had still to be allocated. The respondents argued that the interlocutors relating to expenses did not decern for a particular sum of money, so the petitioner could not obtain inhibition on the dependence to prevent the respondent disposing of certain heritable assets. (There were no conclusions in the summons for payment other than expenses.) Lord Drummond Young stated:

'[5] I am ... satisfied that an order for interim payment of part of the expenses is competent. Such orders are dealt with in MacLaren on Expenses, in two passages. First, at page 43, it is stated: (4) Interim Award. It is within the discretion of the judge to give an interim award of expenses upon a point distinct and separate from the rest of the cause ...

If ... the interim award is unqualified, it is simply regarded as a payment to account Authority for the latter proposition is found in *Cameron and Waterston v Muir & Son*[3]. The second reference to interim expenses in MacLaren is found at pages 302-303, where in relation to consistorial cases it is stated that if a wife had no separate estate she was entitled to an interim award for the purpose of defending an

2   *Martin & Co (UK) Ltd Petitioners* [2013] CSOH 124.
3   *Cameron and Waterston v Muir & Son* 1861 23 D 535.

action of divorce brought against her; the final authority cited for this proposition is
Jaffray v Jaffray[4]. That is obviously based on a state of the law of matrimonial property that has long since gone, but the important point for present purposes is that
the court was in the habit of making interim awards of expenses as a case proceeded.
Thus, the competency of such an award is clear.

[6] I was also referred to the case of *Mars UK Ltd v Teknowledge Ltd*[5], a decision
of Jacob J. in the English High Court. In England the Rules of the Supreme Court
make express provision for payment of costs on account; thus there was no issue
as to the competency of such an order. Jacob J. nevertheless required to consider
whether he should make an order. He stated (at pages 46-47):

"There is no guidance in the Practice Direction. So, I approach the matter as a
question of principle. Where a party has won and has got an order for costs, the
only reason that he does not get the money straightaway is because of the need for
detailed assessment. Nobody knows how much it should be. If a detailed assessment
were carried out instantly he would get the order instantly. So, the successful party
is entitled to the money. In principle he ought to get it as soon as possible. It does
not seem to me to be a good reason for keeping him out of some of his costs that you
need time to work out the total amount. A payment of some lesser amount which he
will almost certainly collect is a closer approximation to justice. So, I hold that where
a party is successful the court should on a rough and ready basis also normally order
an amount to be paid on account, the amount being a lesser sum then the likely full
amount".

What is said there appears to me to be equally applicable in Scotland, except that
here there is no normal practice of making such orders. In general, in Scotland it
will be necessary to show special reasons for making an interim award. Nevertheless,
I am of opinion that such an award is appropriate in the present case in order to
protect the petitioners' right to expenses. There is evidence, narrated above, that the
first respondent is at least reluctant to make payment of expenses, and perhaps lacks
the liquidity to do so. If diligence had been competent on the dependence of the
petition I have no doubt that it would be justified, and the interim award of expenses
is intended to permit the petitioners to do diligence.

[7] As to the amount of the award, I was referred to a letter from the law accountant who is acting in respect of the petitioners' account of expenses. This described
how an award of expenses on an agent and client basis is taxed, and indicated that
the taxation of such an account is usually more straightforward than other cases.
Moreover, such an award (if it is, as here, agent and client, client paying) will
invariably result in total recovery of expenses at taxation. In the present case, the
account was for a sum slightly in excess of £78,000; the law accountant thought that
the Auditor of Court was unlikely to challenge any of the fees or expenses, and he
would not expect the taxed account to be less than £50,000. I accordingly consider
it appropriate to make an interim award of expenses for that amount. Finally, I
should record that the petitioners undertook that, in the event that the Auditor
of Court assessed their account at less than the sum recovered by way of interim
payment, they would repay the excess with interest at the judicial rate from the date
when any payment is received by them. Such an obligation would almost certainly
be implied, or would arise under the law of unjustified enrichment; nevertheless, the
undertaking has been recorded in the minute of proceedings.'

19.11   The court therefore held that such awards were competent, decree could
be pronounced for a specific sum prior to taxation, but special reasons were
required for interim awards.

---

4   *Jaffray v Jaffray* 1909 SC 577.
5   *Mars UK Ltd v Teknowledge Ltd* [1999] 2 Costs LR 44.

Further, an undertaking had been offered by the petitioners that if their **19.12** account was taxed at a sum less than the interim expenses award, they would repay the difference with interest. The court noted that such an obligation would either be implied or would arise under the principles of unjustified enrichment.

It was a pyrrhic victory as the respondent then declared himself bankrupt. **19.13** However, the decision did bring matters to a head a lot quicker than would otherwise have been the case and avoided significant further litigation expense for the petitioner, including the 5 per cent audit fee payable to the auditor if a taxation had been necessary.

Martin & Co (Inner House – unreported on the issue of interim expenses)

The only Inner House case that is known to have dealt with interim awards of **19.14** expenses also stems from the *Martin & Co* case where the Division made an interim award against one of the other respondents. The competency of such procedure was not challenged by their senior counsel. Relying on the outer house *dicta*, it was argued for the petitioner that special reasons continued and were easily demonstrated. The Inner House did not have to consider the matter in detail and simply made the order, which, unfortunately, was not a reported decision on this point. It can be assumed, however, that the court would have, of its own volition, raised any question of competency had it considered it necessary to do so.

Tods Murray WS v Arakin Ltd

Soon after the first instance decision in *Martin*, Lord Woolman, in the case of **19.15** *Tods Murray WS v Arakin Ltd*,[6] followed the reasoning of Lord Drummond Young by making an order for interim payment of expenses, finding that special reasons existed.

The pursuer sought an interim payment of £250,000 toward its expenses. **19.16** Lord Woolman observed that '[a]lthough unusual in Scotland, such an order may be made if special reasons are present', referring to the *Martin* case above.

In considering the level of interim expenses to award, Lord Woolman had **19.17** regard to the fact the pursuer's insurers and the pursuer themselves had paid a total of over £1 million (exclusive of VAT) in respect of fees and outlays, the likely costs in the preparation of an account in this case are likely to be substantial and may take about four months to prepare.

At para. 50 of his opinion, Lord Woolman stated: **19.18**

'I conclude that special reasons do exist in this case. Given the whole history of this litigation and the approach which [the minuter] continues to adopt, in my view it is reasonable to infer that he will resist payment as long as possible. Given the estimated expenses in this case, there is also a question (I put it no higher than that) of whether he has the funds available to satisfy the claim. In those circumstances I shall adopt a conservative approach and order him to make an interim payment of £150,000.'

6   *Tods Murray WS v Arakin Ltd* [2013] CSOH 134.

Higherdelta Ltd v Covea Insurance Plc

19.19　The next time the issue was considered by the Outer House was in 2017 in the case of *Higherdelta Ltd v Covea Insurance Plc*,[7] where a full argument on the matter was held before Lord Bannatyne. Whilst the decision is unreported, there is a useful commentary of the case, and the wider jurisprudence relating to interim damages awards, in a note prepared by the senior acting for Higherdelta, to be found on Compass Chambers website.[8]

In this case, the pursuer sought to challenge the need to show special reasons to justify an award of interim expenses. An 'esto' position was argued that if special reasons had to be established, they existed. It was held by the court that no special reasons were required. Generally speaking, expenses are a matter of judicial discretion. There was no dispute in the case that such an order was competent, it was simply a question of whether an order should be made. The court had to look at the issue of expenses having regard to 'fairness and substantive justice. All of the circumstances should be looked at'.

The arguments of fairness and substantive justice advanced on behalf of the pursuer related to: (a) the fact that the pursuer was obliged to pay his own legal costs of around £140,000 plus VAT; and (b) there would be a delay of around six months before the pursuer could obtain an enforceable decree for expenses following taxation; and (c) the pursuer was obliged to pay interest to his legal advisers under the Late Payments of Commercial Debts (Interest) Act 1998 on his unpaid invoices, yet cannot recover interest on sums due by way of expenses from the opponent until decree for those expenses is pronounced. The court considered that each of these factors alone meant that the interests of justice favoured the pursuer. They justified the making of the order for interim expenses and 'when taken together it is clear that such an order should be made'.

The court further held that even if special reasons were required, they were established by the specific circumstances and factors mentioned above.

19.20　The *Higherdelta* case was therefore a departure from the test laid down in *Martin*. Instead of requiring special reasons, Lord Bannatyne simply required reasons to establish that it was fair and in the interests of justice that an interim award be made.

19.21　An award of £100,000 was therefore made by the court, payable within fourteen days, having regard to a letter produced by the pursuer's law accountant whose view was that that would be a conservative estimate of what would be awarded at taxation.

Kidd v Paul & Williamson LLP and Burness Paul LLP

19.22　There then swiftly followed a further Outer House decision, this time from Lord Tyre in *Kidd v Paul & Williamson LLP and Burness Paul LLP*.[9]

In advance of a proof diet, the court found the defenders liable to the pursuer for the expenses of: (1) an amendment procedure; (2) a discharged

7　*Higherdelta Ltd v Covea Insurance Plc* unreported 30 June 2017.
8　Compass Chambers, *Interim awards of expenses in the Court of Session and the sheriff court: A significant decision that affects all practitioners*, found at https://www.compasschambers.com/perch/resources/paperoninterimawardsofexpenses.pdf (last accessed 11 February 2022)/
9　*Kidd v Paul & Williamson LLP and Burness Paul LLP* [2017] CSOH 124.

diet of proof; and (3) half of the expenses of the action to date except as otherwise dealt with. Each of the awards was on an agent-client, client paying basis. The court had also granted an additional fee on those expenses under various heads of RCS r. 42.14 (3). That interlocutor was pronounced on 25 November 2016. Some ten months later, at the time the motion was argued, no account of expenses had been lodged for taxation. Of course, the requirement to lodge a judicial account for taxation within four months only arises when the final interlocutor making a finding of expenses is made. So, there was no compulsion on the part of the pursuer to lodge an account for interim expense awards prior to seeking a decree for interim expenses.

The pursuer sought an interim award of expenses in the sum of £2,000,000.   **19.23**
No issue was taken by the defenders over the competency of the motion. The pursuer argued that no special reasons were required to justify the award, that it was simply a matter within the discretion of the court. If special reasons were required they existed: (1) because of the conduct of the defenders (and the fact that expenses had been awarded on an agent-client, client paying basis); (2) the size of the sum due by way of expenses; (3) the complexity of the task of making up the pursuer's judicial account coupled with the length of the taxation; and (4) the prejudice to the pursuer in having to fund large sums of legal costs to continue with a litigation, where the court had already found him entitled to the expenses of a significant proportion of the proceedings. The defenders argued that there should only be an interim award if special circumstances existed and none did in this case. Further, if they were success-ful with their defence there would be a substantial contra account to be offset against the pursuer's expenses award and, in any event, the amount sought was excessive.

Lord Tyre opined: **19.24**

'[12] I have already noted that it was not in dispute that it was competent for the court to order an interim payment of part of a party's expenses before an account has been lodged and, if necessary, taxed by the Auditor of Court. There is equally, in my view, no difficulty with regard to the competency of ordering payment of a specified sum by way of interim payment. The cases of *Cameron & Waterston v Muir & Sons* and *Jaffray v Jaffray* provide examples of cases in which the court has, in particular circumstances of no current relevance, made orders for payment of specified sums by way of expenses. I see no reason why the practice should not be regarded as compe-tent more broadly. The question that arises in the present case is whether, and if so in what circumstances, an order for interim payment should be made where expenses have been awarded but where the account has not yet been lodged and taxed.

[13] In *Martin & Co (UK) Ltd*, Lord Drummond Young identified a need to show "special reasons" for making an interim award. I do not, for my part, read this obser-vation as meaning that an order will only be made in exceptional circumstances. It does no more than acknowledge that the rules of court provide a mechanism whereby an award of expenses may be made, quantified by the Auditor of Court in case of dispute, extracted and in due course enforced. This is the "ordinary way" to which reference was made in *Byres' Trs v Gemmell* and *Jaffray v Jaffray*: the proce-dure normally regarded by the rules of court as appropriate for recovery of expenses. But, as with other aspects of expenses, it is in my opinion within the discretion of the court to depart from the "ordinary way", provided the court is satisfied that there is sufficient reason for so doing.

[14] In the present case, four features were relied upon by the pursuer as special reasons for granting the motion for interim payment. The first was the defenders'

conduct which had justified the award of expenses on an agent and client, client paying basis. I reject that contention. The court has already expressed its disapproval of the defenders' conduct by making an award on that basis; there is no good reason to order interim payment as, in effect, a further instalment of punishment. The other three features relied upon were:

1. the size of the sum likely to be found due: the greater the amount of money which the receiving party is kept out of for an extended period, the greater the injustice;

2. the scale, complexity and cost of the process of preparation and taxation of the account: the solicitors' correspondence file ran to 50 volumes, with hundreds of thousands of pages of documents in electronic form. The taxation would be complicated and lengthy; 3. the litigation was ongoing and cost continued to accrue: there was no good reason for the pursuer to have to fund that cost while being kept out of the sum owed to him by the defenders.

[15] In my opinion these three features together afford sufficient reason to grant the pursuer's motion for an interim payment. The present litigation is exceptional in respect of the amount of documents that have been recovered and perused. If taxation of the pursuer's account is required, this is likely to result in a very substantial award and/or a very lengthy process of taxation, depending on the extent to which the account is challenged. Having regard also to the pursuer's need to fund the continuing litigation, it is not in the interests of justice that he should be deprived for an indefinite period of the whole of the expenses to which he has been found entitled. I am not persuaded by the defenders' argument that the possibility of a substantial, and possibly equally large, contra-award were the pursuer's case ultimately to fail, constitutes a good reason for refusing an interim award. The fact that a litigation is continuing does not preclude a party from having an account of expenses taxed in order to enable him to obtain an extract decree and enforce it, even though a future contra-award remains a possibility.'

19.25 Lord Tyre went on to consider the amount of the interim payment:

'[16] The sum sought in the present case by way of an interim payment of expenses (£2,000,000) is very large indeed. Little detail of its composition was provided. In support of it, the pursuer founded upon (i) a letter from the law accountant instructed to prepare the pursuer's account; and (ii) a report by another experienced law accountant not otherwise involved in this litigation. They were both of the opinion (a) that the rates charged by the agents for work in respect of which expenses were awarded to the pursuer were reasonable; (b) that because expenses had been awarded on the agent and client, client paying basis, it was unlikely that there would be any significant taxing off of fees by the Auditor; (c) that an uplift of at least 150% was likely to be allowed in respect of the additional fee; and (d) that it was likely that the outlays, consisting principally of counsel's fees, would be taxed as recoverable in full. The total according to the Pursuer's law accountant's calculation (assuming that the figure of £479,307 at page 2 of her letter represents one half of the total solicitors' fees exclusive of VAT for the period in question) was £1,998,120. The total according to the other law accountant's calculation was said to be £1,909,301 but according to my arithmetic was £1,684,451, although this figure does not appear to include fees charged by the pursuer's previous agents. These totals were regarded by the respective law accountants as underestimates of the sum likely to be awarded.

[17] I accept, on the basis of the views expressed by two experienced law accountants, that fees and outlays are much less likely to be taxed off an account of expenses awarded on an agent and client, client paying basis than on a party and party basis. I also accept that the arithmetic effect of the additional fee uplift will be very significant. The Auditor will nevertheless require to be satisfied both that any expense was reasonably incurred and that the rate charged is reasonable. One may anticipate that an account of this magnitude will be challenged and closely scrutinised. It is appropriate,

especially in the absence of any detailed exposition of the fees and outlays incurred, for the court when exercising its discretion to adopt a conservative approach. In all of the circumstances I shall grant the motion to the extent of ordering the defenders to make an interim payment to the pursuer of the sum of £1,000,000, with interest accruing thereon at the judicial rate after 14 days from the date of my interlocutor.

[18] The pursuer offered a formal undertaking to the court that in the event that the interim award turns out to exceed the taxed award, the excess will be repaid with interest at the judicial rate from the date of the interim payment until the date of repayment of the excess. As Lord Drummond Young observed in *Martin & Co (UK) Ltd* (para 7), such an obligation is almost certainly to be implied, but I shall record the undertaking in the minute of proceedings.'

SHERIFF COURT PROCEEDINGS

As outlined in para. 19.07 above the position in the Sheriff Court is regulated by OCR r. 32 and, for actions raised on or after 29 April 2019, OCR r. 7.4(2).   **19.26**

There are currently no reported cases from the sheriff court on interim awards of expenses. However, a sheriff, like a Court of Session judge, has a wide discretion on how to handle issues of expenses and appeals on expenses are discouraged. In addition, there is nothing in the rationale of any of the Court of Session decisions that would suggest that the issue of competency of interim expenses awards is reserved exclusively to the Court of Session.   **19.27**

Further, it could be argued that there are additional reasons why the sheriff court is likely to consider interim awards of expenses to be competent: **19.28**

(1) OCR r. 32.1 does not require a taxation where expenses are modified for a fixed sum. Any award of interim expenses is likely to be for a fixed sum.
(2) Modification in the context of interim awards does not mean the court is making a final determination of the expenses up to the date of the interim award. As per Maclaren on expenses[10], applied in *Kidd*, the interim award is simply treated as a payment to account in the same way that an interim award of damages is not a final determination of quantum and simply an up-front payment of damages that are likely to ultimately become due.

COMMENTARY

Whilst the Scottish precedent on interim awards of expenses emanates solely from the Court of Session, there is little reason to doubt that such awards are competent in Sheriff Court litigation. The Court of Session precedent gives ample authority for the competency of interim expenses motions. The principles of fairness and the interests of justice extend to all courts and it would be iniquitous if such a remedy was only open to those litigating in the Court of Session.   **19.29**

What is needed to justify an award, and in particular whether special reasons have to be established, is less clear given the conflicting authorities. It is respectfully suggested that the approach adopted by Lord Tyre in *Kidd* is the correct approach. It does not bind or hinder the decision-maker in having to   **19.30**

---

10 Maclaren, *Expenses in the Supreme and Sheriff Court* (Edinburgh, 1912).

find special reasons before making an award. Imposing such a requirement simply fetters the wide discretion of the courts to make such findings of expenses as are just and reasonable. If the *Kidd* approach is correct the party seeking the interim award simply needs to set out sufficient, as opposed to special, reasons for an interim award. The reasons will be case specific.

19.31   There is no need for the preparation of a detailed judicial account in advance of arguing the motion. A letter from a law accountant with an estimated total and their conservative views on what is likely to be allowed by the auditor at taxation is all that is required.

Chapter 20

Additional Fees and Charges

A solicitor may apply to the court for an increase in the charges to be allowed **20.01** at taxation in respect of work carried out by the entitled party's solicitor, i.e. the party in whose favour an award of expenses has been made. The purpose of the application is to reflect the responsibility undertaken by the solicitor in the conduct of the proceedings. The additional fee or charge is only applied to the solicitor's fee element of the judicial account (plus VAT), not to outlays. Therefore, counsel's fees cannot attract an additional fee or charge. If the application is granted it has the effect of increasing the fee element of the judicial account by the percentage determined by the court or auditor.

Such an application is competent whether the account of expenses is pre- **20.02** pared on a detailed itemised basis or on a block fee basis.

For actions commenced prior to 29 April 2019, RCS r. 42.14 governed the **20.03** Court of Session position and para. 5(b) of the general regulations schedule to the Act of Sederunt (Fees of Solicitors in the Sheriff Court) (Amendment and Further Provisions) 1993,[1] as amended, governed the Sheriff Court position.[2] These provisions remain in force for actions raised pre-29 April 2019. The Act of Sederunt (Rules of the Court of Session, Sheriff Appeal Court Rules and Ordinary Cause Rules Amendment) (Taxation of Judicial Expenses) 2019[3] states that all the provisions except those mentioned in r. 2(2) and 2(3) apply from the date the Act of Sederunt comes into force, i.e. 29 April 2019. None of the provisions listed under r. 2(2) or 2(3) affect Part 2 of Ch. 42 (which covers additional fee applications in the Court of Session). Rule 4(14) of the 2019 Act of Sederunt says that Part 2 of Ch. 42 is omitted but as that only applies to actions commenced on or after 29 April 2019, Part 2 of Chapter 42 remains in force for actions commenced prior to that date, notwithstanding it has been deleted from the rules section on the Scottish Courts website. The 2019 Act of Sederunt, in r. 7, specifically saves the provisions in the 1993 Act of Sederunt for sheriff court actions raised prior to 29 April 2019.

---

1 Act of Sederunt (Fees of Solicitors in the Sheriff Court) (Amendment and Further Provisions) 1993 (SI 1993/3080).
2 SI 1193/3080 as amended most recently by Act of Sederunt (Fees of Solicitors in the Court of Session, Sheriff Appeal Court and Sheriff Court) (Amendment) 2018 (SSI 2018/186) (effective 24 September 2018).
3 Act of Sederunt (Rules of the Court of Session, Sheriff Appeal Court Rules and Ordinary Cause Rules Amendment) (Taxation of Judicial Expenses) 2019 (SSI 2019/74).

20.04   For actions raised on or after 29 April 2019 rr. 3.9 and 5.2 of the Act of
Sederunt (Taxation of Judicial Expenses Rules) 2019 (the 2019 Rules) govern
the position in all courts.

20.05   Applications in actions commenced prior to 29 April 2019 are for an additional fee. Applications in actions commenced on or after that date are for an
additional charge.

20.06   As the terms of the 2019 Rules to a large extent mirror the terms of the
earlier rules the focus here will be on the position under the 2019 Rules. These
are as follows.

Additional Charge

3.9. Where, on an application under rule 5.2 (additional charge)—
  (a) the court grants the application and specifies a percentage increase in charges in
       accordance with paragraph (4) of that rule, the charges allowed by the Auditor
       under this Chapter are to be increased by the percentage specified;
  (b) the Court of Session remits to the Auditor to determine if an increase should
       be allowed, or to determine the level of an increase, the charges allowed by the
       Auditor under this Chapter are to be increased by such additional charge, if any,
       as the Auditor may determine.

5.2. (1) An entitled party may apply to the court for an increase in the charges
to be allowed at taxation in respect of work carried out by the entitled party's
solicitor.
  (2) Where the application is made to the Court of Session the court may, instead of
       determining the application, remit the application to the Auditor to determine if
       an increase should be allowed, and the level of any increase.
  (3) The court or, as the case may be, the Auditor must grant the application when
       satisfied that an increase is justified to reflect the responsibility undertaken by
       the solicitor in the conduct of the proceedings.
  (4) On granting an application the court must, subject to paragraph (5), specify a
       percentage increase in the charges to be allowed at taxation.
  (5) The Court of Session may instead remit to the Auditor to determine the level
       of increase.
  (6) In considering whether to grant an application, and the level of any increase, the
       court or, as the case may be, the Auditor is to have regard to—
       (a) the complexity of the proceedings and the number, difficulty or novelty of
            the questions raised;
       (b) the skill, time and labour and specialised knowledge required of the
            solicitor;
       (c) the number and importance of any documents prepared or perused;
       (d) the place and circumstances of the proceedings or in which the work of
            the solicitor in preparation for, and conduct of, the proceedings has been
            carried out;
       (e) the importance of the proceedings or the subject matter of the proceedings
            to the client;
       (f) the amount or value of money or property involved in the proceedings;
       (g) the steps taken with a view to settling the proceedings, limiting the matters
            in dispute or limiting the scope of any hearing.

20.07   Any such uplift or additional charge is to reflect the responsibility undertaken
by the solicitor in the conduct of the proceedings. It is not for the purpose of lessening any differential between agent/client expenses and what is
recoverable on a party/party basis.

COURT OF SESSION

Unlike the Sheriff Court, where an application is made to the Court of Session **20.08** the court may determine the application itself or, alternatively, remit the application to the auditor of court to determine if an increase should be allowed along with the level of any increase.

If the court itself grants the application for an additional charge the court **20.09** must specify a percentage increase in the charges to be allowed at taxation or, alternatively, remit the issue of the percentage increase to the auditor of court to determine the level to be allowed.

SHERIFF COURT

Where the court grants a party's application for an additional charge, it is **20.10** the court's function to specify the percentage increase rather than remitting determination of the level of increase to the auditor of court.

CRITERIA FOR ADDITIONAL CHARGE

The applicability of any criteria is very much dependent on the facts and **20.11** circumstances of the specific case. Generally, the more criteria that apply, the higher the percentage for the additional charge will be. All the criteria have to be looked at in the context of the responsibility of the solicitor in the conduct of the litigation. The question the court or auditor has to answer in determining an application for an additional charge is: 'is the responsibility of the solicitor in the conduct of the litigation evidenced by the additional charge criteria'. If yes, the court or auditor will normally indicate which of the criteria apply. The basic question that the solicitor should address when framing the application is 'what are the specific circumstances of this case which will enable me to satisfy a court that my responsibility in this case, with specific reference to the relevant criteria, justifies an additional charge?'

Motions for additional charges will set out the criteria relied upon, with detailed reasons (if necessary on a paper apart) to justify the motion. If opposed, or if the court, *ex proprio motu*, requires it to call, the solicitor should consider making available to the court any documentation that independently verifies the basis of the argument, such as a draft judicial account to show the level of work undertaken. There is no limit to the percentage that a court or auditor can grant for the additional charge. In the most complex cases, several hundred percent has been allowed as an uplift.

The seven criteria that apply to an additional charge application are set out in paras 20.12–20.18.

Complexity/number, difficulty or novelty of the questions raised

Different weight may be placed on this criterion in the Court of Session **20.12** compared to the Sheriff Court where the complexity and importance of proceedings in the former is frequently greater than in the latter. The fact that senior and/or junior counsel are involved is no bar to the solicitor moving for an additional fee where the solicitor plays a proactive role in complex Court of Session litigation or where the case will set a precedent. One such example is a medical negligence case where there are various allegations of fault on the part of doctors from different medical disciplines, which in turn means the causal effects of each episode of alleged negligence require to be considered and quantified.

Skill, time and labour/specialised knowledge

20.13   To succeed under this criterion, the solicitor will have undertaken work that goes beyond the norm. Exceptional performance is not a pre-requisite but certainly helps the argument. Evidencing high levels of skill in tackling the issues that arise, particularly where that skill has had a bearing on the outcome, may satisfy this criterion as would undertaking significant hours of work and/or working to tight timescales. The fact that the solicitor is an accredited specialist in the area of law that gives rise to the litigation is unlikely to be sufficient. It would generally be necessary to show that specialisation has been applied to the case and played a part in the outcome.

Where a solicitor conducts a litigation in the Sheriff Court personally, i.e. without the involvement of counsel, that may assist in justifying the granting of an additional fee, particularly in a case where counsel's involvement would probably have been sanctioned.

Number and importance of documents prepared/perused

20.14   Again, the forum may influence the success of an application under this criterion. Identify what might be seen as the norm in terms of volume of documentation in the court where the case is being litigated and ask the question 'is the documentation prepared or perused in this case, in terms of volume or importance, evidence of the responsibility which I have borne?' If there was a significant degree of responsibility constituted by having to consider or prepare voluminous and/or important documentation, there would be a basis for including this criterion in the application.

Place and circumstance

20.15   There are two parts to this criterion:

(1) the place and circumstances of the proceedings; or
(2) the place in which the work of the solicitor in preparation for, and conduct of, the proceedings has been carried out.

Out of all the criteria, it may be expected that this one will be the least relied upon to justify an additional charge but practical difficulties in getting instructions from a client such as one who lives abroad or is in hospital or prison, or one who experiences issues with digital exclusion may form a basis for an application, particularly where those difficulties persist over a prolonged period of time. Other examples may involve taking the evidence of a pursuer or a crucial witness on commission to lie *in retentis* from their hospital bed, having to carry out extensive work in some remote accident *locus*, such as photographing the scene of the accident and surrounding area followed by precognition of local police officers, or having to carry out extensive investigations or interviews in a different jurisdiction. With the upsurge in use of virtual platforms such as WebEx, MS Teams and Zoom, some of the previously encountered difficulties are likely to be mitigated.

Importance of the proceedings or subject matter of the proceedings to the client

Arguably every case is important to the client and it is commonplace for Sheriffs to make that point when dealing with arguments that rely on this criterion. There are, however, many situations that can arise that create an added importance for a particular party. For example, fatal claims where liability is disputed, serious allegations of wrongdoing where the party's reputation is on the line, precedent-setting or law-changing cases and cases where the client has taken substantial financial risks to vindicate their rights in a situation where an unsuccessful outcome would have left them in financial difficulties.

20.16

The amount or value of money or property involved in the proceedings

This criterion will clearly only apply where the case has a significant value or involves significant amounts of property. The privative jurisdiction of the sheriff court is £100,000. The criterion applies to Sheriff Court proceedings just as it does to those in the Court of Session. Therefore, it is open to make an application under this criterion in Sheriff Court cases with a value of less than £100,000. In Court of Session cases with values running into the hundreds of thousands or millions of pounds the position will normally be self-evident. There is no hard and fast rule on what value is required. Again, it comes down to how the solicitor's responsibility is affected by the value of the claim. There may be a degree of overlap between this criterion and 'importance to the client'.

20.17

Steps taken with a view to settling the proceedings, limiting the matters in dispute or limiting the scope of any hearing

It is to be expected in any action that parties will engage, to some extent, in trying to see what can be agreed and whether there is the potential for settlement. That is not unusual and does not justify an additional charge. Indeed, it is the whole point of the pre-trial meeting. Making a pursuer's offer is but one tiny cog in the wheel and of itself would not be a basis for seeking an additional charge. What is envisaged here is work that goes above and beyond the norm: steps that proactively try to resolve the case in its entirety or agree evidence and thereby restrict the time needed in court. This can arise through early disclosure of liability and quantum reports, serving detailed Notices to Admit, regular constructive dialogue with the opponent's agent and trying to engage in early settlement discussions where that is appropriate. It may be that a combination of factors, evidenced throughout the litigation, are required to show that this criterion applies.

20.18

GENERAL COMMENTS

20.19   Whilst not strictly necessary, it is good practice for an application for an additional charge to be made at the same time as the question of expenses is dealt with. This can be included in the motion to have a joint minute received to dispose of the action or in the motion to have decree pronounced in terms of a tender and acceptance or pursuer's offer and acceptance. In addition, as a matter of contract, the parties can agree between them a percentage for an additional charge and the auditor will give effect to any such agreement without the agreement being reflected in an interlocutor. Agreement can also be reached in principle on entitlement to an additional charge but the agreement states that it will be left to the auditor to determine the percentage. It is competent for a motion seeking an additional charge to be made at any time until the diet of taxation.[4] It is incompetent, however, to seek any additional charge once the auditor has issued their decision.

20.20   Where earlier awards of expenses have been dealt with between parties either by way of negotiation or taxation and regardless of whether those expenses have been paid, the additional charge granted at the end of the proceedings requires to be calculated on those earlier findings of expenses.[5]

20.21   Where an action involves the work of a foreign solicitor, any additional charge granted does not apply to the foreign agent's account as that work is incorporated within the entitled party's account as an outlay.[6]

20.22   It is also competent for the court to allow an additional charge when expenses have been awarded on an agent and client basis. The same procedure applies and the auditor will assess any additional charge by way of a percentage uplift.

SHERIFF APPEAL COURT

20.23   The Act of Sederunt (Fees of Solicitors in the Sheriff Appeal Court) 2015 makes no provision for an entitled party to make an application for an additional charge and any application in that forum would be incompetent. It is respectfully suggested that this is a lacuna in the rules which will hopefully be addressed by the Scottish Civil Justice Council in the near future.

---

4 *UCB Bank Plc v Dundas & Wilson CS* 1991 SLT 90.
5 *Masterton v Thomas Smith & Sons (Kirkoswald) Ltd* 1998 SLT 699.
6 *Wimpey Construction (UK) Ltd v Martin Black & Co (Wire Ropes) Ltd* 1988 SC 264.

Chapter 21

Taxation of Expenses

AWARD OF EXPENSES

In any litigation between parties, the general rule of thumb, subject to the **21.01** new qualified one-way cost shifting rules,[1] is that expenses follow success. However, an award of expenses lies solely in the discretion of the court and an interlocutor will be issued by the court setting out the paying party's liability for expenses. Unless the interlocutor from the court specifies a specific mode of taxation, then the expenses must be taxed on a party and party basis that is restricted to proper expenses of process and governed by the question of reasonableness.

PARTY/PARTY EXPENSES

Such a finding of expenses is the most common mode of taxation of an account **21.02** between parties, albeit the most restrictive basis of taxation. Regardless of which court the litigation is being conducted in, the governing factor of party/party taxation is the question of reasonableness and it is only those expenses that are deemed reasonable for conducting the cause in a proper manner that shall be allowed. Despite overall success in a litigation or part thereof, the auditor has an overriding discretion to disallow expenses either in whole or in part if they deem the receiving or entitled party to have been unsuccessful in a particular part of the procedure or if the expense has been incurred through the party's own fault or if the auditor determines that such work was unnecessary. However, Lord Bonomy in the case of *Malpas v Fife Council*[2] stated:

'The Rule of Court governing the Auditor's work is 42.10.(1) which provides: "Only such expenses as are reasonable for conducting the cause in a proper manner shall be allowed." It follows that, when the Auditor disallows an item, he does so because it was not reasonable for the party to incur that expense. In his initial submission to me Mr Bowie suggested that it was entirely a matter for the Auditor, in the exercise of his discretion based on his own wide experience of practice and taking into account any material he considered relevant, to decide what charges were reasonable. In my opinion that cannot be the test. If it were, agents would have no basis on which to gauge whether expenses incurred might be recoverable in the event of

1 See Chapter 3 on qualified one-way cost shifting.
2 *Malpas v Fife Council* 1999 SLT 499.

success ... In deciding whether to allow or disallow any particular item, the Auditor is undertaking a task similar to mine and should only disallow an item if it can truly be said that to incur that expense was not reasonable, in the sense that a competent solicitor acting reasonably would not have incurred it.'

This was said in the context of the auditor having disallowed fees of senior counsel in what he had held to be a relatively straightforward case. In upholding the pursuer's note of objections Lord Bonomy went onto state:

I can find no clear indication in the Auditor's Minute that he clearly focused in his own mind the crucial question raised ... in the Note of Objections. That is whether it was reasonable for the pursuer's agents to instruct senior counsel when three days before the proof no offer in settlement had been received, no indication had been given of the level at which an offer might be made, and there was an outstanding minute of amendment before the Court. However, even if he did, I am satisfied he erred in the way I have described in his approach to it.'

21.03　The case of *Marshall v Fife Health Board*[3] followed Lord Bonomy's dicta in *Malpas*. Lord Glennie, holding that the recovery of counsel's fees during the pre-litigation stages was justified, confirmed that the test for recoverability on a party and party basis is not whether a particular item of work is agent/client in nature but whether the work was reasonably undertaken:

'The only relevant test in deciding what expenses should be allowed is that of reasonableness. The Auditor should only disallow an item if it can truly be said that it was unreasonable to incur the expense in the sense that a competent Solicitor acting reasonably would not have incurred it.'

21.04　Therefore any suggestion that the auditor has a discretion to disallow entries in an entitled party's account is subject to that discretion only being exercised if they are satisfied that a competent solicitor acting reasonably would not have incurred the expense.

21.05　In compliance with a finding of expenses on a party/party basis, the receiving or entitled party has the option to prepare an account of expenses on a detailed basis setting out each particular item of work undertaken or, alternatively, on a block or inclusive fee basis whereby a particular fee covers a particular part of process or procedure. However, it is incompetent for a successful party to charge partly on one basis and partly on the other.

21.06　An account prepared on a party/party basis requires to be prepared as if one solicitor were acting. If a local agent instructs an Edinburgh agent, only one account of expenses can be prepared incorporating the work of both firms of solicitors involved. Correspondence between both firms is irrecoverable, as are any discussions and the like. Local agents' attendances at consultations and court hearings where the Edinburgh agent is in attendance are similarly irrecoverable unless there are exceptional circumstances to justify the attendance of both, as is the Edinburgh agent's attendance at meetings with the client at local level. All expenses incurred must fall within the definition of expenses of process. Any related or connected expenses such as attendances at criminal

---

3　*Marshall v Fife Health Board* 2013 CSOH 140.

trials carrying out a watching brief or attending fatal accident inquiries are not recoverable in terms of the expenses of process despite being connected to the subject matter of the litigation.

EXPENSES WITHIN PARTY/PARTY EXPENSES

Despite a successful party having an overall finding of expenses in their favour, **21.07** there are a number of sub-findings that can apply to particular parts of process. It has to be emphasised that a general award of expenses of process in favour of a successful party does not overturn any earlier finding of expenses for particular parts of process.

Expenses in favour of a party

Where an interlocutor awards expenses in favour of a party for a particular **21.08** part of the litigation, the auditor has no discretion over the principle of the work covered by that award of expenses being recovered regardless of success or otherwise. It is for the auditor to give effect to all the procedure that has taken place and only to audit the particular charges subject to the question of reasonableness. The auditor's discretion only extends to the individual charges included within an account of expenses that make up the overall claim for expenses for that particular part of the proceedings.

Expenses in the cause

Where expenses of a particular part of procedure have been found to be in the **21.09** cause, the successful party, as a matter of right, is entitled to recover those expenses for that particular part of the proceedings in terms of their account of expenses relating to the general award of expenses in their favour. Where the court finds expenses of any part of the procedure to be expenses in the cause, the auditor has no discretion insofar as those expenses are concerned even where it can be shown that the party recovering those expenses was truly unsuccessful in that part of the cause. The court when awarding expenses in the cause is, in fact, removing the auditor's discretion.[4]

Reserved expenses

Similar to expenses in the cause, the general rule of thumb is that reserved **21.10** expenses follow success. Proper procedure dictates that when a successful party is enrolling a motion for a final award of expenses, those earlier awards that have been reserved should be revisited at that stage and dealt with in terms of the final interlocutor. This is to ensure that the Auditor is left in no doubt as to which party is entitled to the previously reserved expenses. Where a final interlocutor is silent in relation to any earlier reserved awards of expenses, that work can properly be included within a successful party's account of expenses but is then subject to the discretion of

4 *Turner v Thomson* 1991 GWD19-1159.

the auditor insofar as modification or disallowance of expenses is concerned. Unlike an award in a party's favour or an award of expenses in the cause, the auditor's discretionary power does extend to the principle of the successful party recovering the work covered by the earlier reserved award, subject to the auditor applying the correct test laid down in *Malpas*, See para 21.02.

No expenses due to or by either party

21.11   Such a finding of expenses for a particular part of the proceedings prohibits any party from including any work relating to that particular part of the proceedings in their account of expenses.

Expenses against successful party

21.12   As with an award on a 'no expenses due to or by' basis, the successful party is prohibited from including any work in their account of expenses relating to a part of the litigation where they have been found liable for the expenses. However, the party who has been awarded expenses against the successful party is entitled to recover those expenses in terms of a contra account of expenses. As mentioned previously, an award of expenses in favour of a party upon conclusion of the proceedings does not supersede any previous adverse findings of expenses against that party unless by specific negotiation as part of any settlement agreement, e.g. the waiving of the right to lodge a contra account.

AGENT/CLIENT, CLIENT-PAYING

21.13   A finding of expenses on an 'agent client, client paying' basis is in total contrast to a finding of expenses on a party/party basis and, with the exception of a full indemnity basis, is the most remunerative basis of taxation. A finding against a party on an agent/client, client-paying basis is normally indicative of the court's displeasure at the conduct of a party and is generally seen as being a penalty for unreasonable behaviour. All expenses incurred on behalf of a successful party are recoverable in terms of the account of expenses even where expenses may have been considered to be unreasonable on a party/party basis. By way of example, a client is entitled to hold as many consultations with counsel and with whatever counsel they so desire and whilst that may be considered unreasonable on a party/party view, those costs would be recoverable from the unsuccessful opponent under this mode of taxation. Similarly, a party is entitled to instruct whatever expert they consider to be required regardless of the instruction of other experts in that particular field and expect to recover such expense from the unsuccessful opponent. Generally speaking, where work is undertaken on the direct or even indirect instruction of the client, that work is recoverable on this basis of taxation. Where expenses are awarded on a full agent/client, client-paying indemnity basis, then all discretion or argument is removed and all work is recoverable from the paying party regardless of reasonableness. It would simply have to be a valid charge that the entitled party is liable to pay to their own solicitor.

AGENT/CLIENT BASIS

Where expenses between parties are found to be payable on an agent/client **21.14** basis without further specification, it is to be construed to mean agent/client, client-paying.[5]

AGENT/CLIENT, THIRD PARTY PAYING

Such expenses are deemed to be those that a prudent person of business **21.15** would incur without special instructions from the client in the knowledge that their account would be taxed. Whilst a more generous mode of taxation than party/party, this mode of taxation is not as wide as taxation on an agent/client or agent/client, full indemnity basis. Charging in terms of the letter of engagement entered into with the client is permitted insofar as rates are concerned rather than in terms of the judicial tables of fees in the Acts of Sederunt prescribing solicitors' fees in the Court of Session and sheriff courts. A more generous amount of work is recoverable. For example, if a local agent and Edinburgh agent are involved, then separate accounts for both agents are allowable, including all work between those agents, and therefore the one solicitor acting rule does not apply. However, expenses on this basis are limited to proper expenses of process and therefore the auditor's discretion relating to modification or disallowance of expenses can be exercised where it appears to them that a party, whilst found entitled to expenses, has been unsuccessful in that particular part of process or the work has been recovered through a party's own fault. The auditor may therefore disallow various charges in an account of expenses that would otherwise be recoverable in an account of expenses taxed on a solicitor/client, client-paying basis. The taxation of an account of expenses on an agent/client, third party paying basis will reflect more closely the taxation of an account of expenses on a party/party basis than an account on an agent/client, client-paying basis.

TAXATION OF ENGLISH OR FOREIGN AGENTS' ACCOUNTS OF EXPENSES

In taxation between parties, it is permissible to seek recovery of an English or **21.16** foreign agents' charges in terms of a judicial account of expenses against an unsuccessful opponent. The foreign agents' charges must be included as an outlay in any account of expenses and therefore any award of an additional charge in terms of: (a) r. 5.2 of the Act of Sederunt (Taxation of Judicial Expenses Rules) 2019; or (b) Act of Sederunt (Rules of the Court of Session 1994) 1994 (RCS) r. 42.14 or Act of Sederunt (Fees of Solicitors in the Sheriff Court) (Amendment and Further Provisions) 1993 General Regulation 5 (Sheriff Court) cannot apply to the foreign agents' charges. Vouching in respect of the foreign agents' charges must be in a form that makes it clear what items of work have been undertaken by the foreign agent, thus enabling

5 *Milligan v Tinne's Trustees* 1994 SLT (Notes) 64; *Trunature Ltd v Scotnet (1974) Ltd and Scobie & Junor (Est 1919) Ltd* 2008 SLT 653.

the auditor of court to determine what work is allowable in terms of a party/
party account of expenses. Following upon determination of the admissible
items of work, the auditor then requires to ascertain what charges are appropriate for that work, having regard to the law and practice of the foreign jurisdiction.[6] In determining the appropriate charges for the admissible work, the
auditor can rely on their own experience or, if necessary, may obtain advice
or evidence from any reliable source they consider appropriate, for example,
the Taxing Master or Costs judge in the case of an English agents' account of
expenses. The court determined that this was entirely a matter for the auditor
and that he did not require any order of the court to enable him to seek advice
or evidence from any reliable source.

---

6 *Wimpey Construction (UK) Ltd v Martin Black & Co (Wire Ropes) Ltd* 1988 SLT 637.

Chapter 22

Taxation Procedure

PREPARATION OF JUDICIAL ACCOUNTS OF EXPENSES

It is the responsibility of the entitled party to have an account of expenses **22.01** prepared in accordance with r. 2.1 of the Act of Sederunt (Taxation of Judicial Expenses Rules) 2019 (the 2019 Rules), which states:

> An account of expenses must—
> (a) set out in chronological order all items in respect of which payment is claimed;
> (b) list in separate columns—
>   (i)   the charges claimed for work carried out by the entitled party's solicitor; and
>   (ii) the outlays claimed; and
> (c) include a statement as to whether or not the entitled party will bear the burden of the value added tax referred to in rule 6.1.

Rule 6.1 provides:

> (1) Where work done by a solicitor constitutes a supply of services in respect of which value added tax is chargeable by the solicitor, there may be added to the charges allowed in respect of that work under Chapter 3 an amount equal to the value added tax chargeable on those charges, unless the entitled party will not bear the burden of the value added tax.
> (2) Where an outlay allowed under Chapter 4 is a charge for the supply of goods or services on which the supplier has charged value added tax, the amount of the value added tax charged may only be allowed as an outlay when the entitled party will bear the burden of the value added tax.

The account will therefore normally contain four columns. The left column **22.02** showing the date of the work, the next column containing a concise narrative of the work undertaken, the next column showing outlays incurred and the fourth column showing fees. The columns for outlays and fees are totalled, VAT – if applicable – is added and a total is shown at the end (see 23.16). The auditor will mark any abatements or additions on the left side of the account. However, it is not normal practice for the auditor to append reasons for any abatements.

Any outlays claimed within the account of expenses require to be supported by **22.03** suitable vouching presented in chronological order and numbered appropriately to correspond with the relevant item being claimed in the account of expenses.

LODGING – COURT OF SESSION

The entitled party, in terms of RCS r. 42.1(2), must lodge the account of **22.04** expenses not later than four months after the date of the final interlocutor, failing which it is necessary for the entitled party to obtain an order from the court to allow late lodging of the account of expenses subject to such conditions as the court deems fit to impose:

> **42.1(2).**—Any party found entitled to expenses shall—
> (a) lodge an account of expenses in process not later than four months after the final interlocutor in which a finding in respect of expenses is made; or
> (b) lodge such account at any time with leave of the court but subject to such conditions (if any) as the court thinks fit to impose.

LODGING – SHERIFF COURT

22.05 In the sheriff court, for proceedings where the date of final judgment is on or after 29 April 2019, Act of Sederunt (Sheriff Court Ordinary Cause Rules) 1993 (OCR) r. 32.1A was introduced, thus aligning the Sheriff Court with the Court of Session in relation to timescales for lodging:

> **32.1A**—(1) A party found entitled to expenses shall lodge an account of expenses in process—
> (a) not later than four months after the final judgment; or
> (b) at any time with permission of the sheriff, but subject to such conditions, if any, as the sheriff thinks fit to impose.
> (2) Where an account of expenses is lodged by the Scottish Legal Aid Board in reliance on regulation 39(2)(a) of the Civil Legal Aid (Scotland) Regulations 2002, paragraph (1)(a) applies as if the period specified is eight months.
> (3) In this rule, "final judgment" has the meaning assigned by section 136(1) of the Courts Reform (Scotland) Act 2014.

22.06 Final judgment means a decision that, taken by itself or along with previous decisions, disposes of the subject matter of proceedings, even though judgment may not have been pronounced on every question raised or expenses found due may not have been modified, taxed or decerned for.[1]

MULTI-PARTY ACTIONS

22.07 In an action involving multiple parties, the period for calculating the four month rule is governed by the final interlocutor or judgement disposing of the proceedings against each particular party regardless of whether the action continues against one or other of the parties and the proceedings are disposed of against those remaining parties at a later date.[2] Accordingly, in a situation where a minute of tender is being accepted or a settlement is negotiated on behalf of one, but not all pursuers, it may be prudent for parties to agree that disposal of the court action for that particular pursuer be dealt with at the end of the proceedings by way of an agreement reached with the paying party. Failure to do so renders it necessary to prepare and lodge a judicial account of expenses relating to that particular entitled party within four months of disposal of the proceedings relating to that party. This would then require the apportioning of various charges where they relate to the action as a whole and

---

1 Courts Reform (Scotland) Act 2014 s. 136(1).
2 *Robina King v Global Marine (UK) Ltd and Macgregor Energy Services Ltd* 2003 SC 269.

may make a taxation unnecessarily contentious or complex. The disadvantage, of course, particularly where pursuers are represented by different agents, is that the party settling the action would have to wait to recover their judicial expenses.

PROCEDURE PRIOR TO DIET OF TAXATION

Court of Session

The position in the Court of Session is governed by RCS r. 42.2, which provides: **22.08**

> **42.2.**—(1) Subject to paragraph (2), the Auditor shall fix a diet of taxation on receipt of—
>> (a) the process of the cause;
>> (b) vouchers in respect of all outlays, including counsel's fees; and
>> (c) a letter addressed to the Auditor confirming that the items referred to in subparagraph (b) have been intimated to the party found liable in expenses.
> (2) The Auditor may fix a diet of taxation or within such reasonable period of time thereafter as the Auditor may allow, notwithstanding that paragraphs (1)(b) and (c) have not been complied with.
> (3) The Auditor shall intimate the diet of taxation to—
>> (a) the party found entitled to expenses; and
>> (b) the party found liable in expenses.
> (4) The party found liable in expenses shall, not later than 4.00pm on the fourth business day before the diet of taxation, intimate to the Auditor and to the party found entitled to expenses, particular points of objection, specifying each item objected to and stating concisely the nature and ground of objection.
> (5) Subject to paragraph (6), if the party found liable in expenses fails to intimate points of objection under paragraph (4) within the time limit set out there, the Auditor shall not take account of them at the diet of taxation.
> (6) The Auditor may relieve a party from the consequences of a failure to comply with the requirement contained in paragraph (5) because of mistake, oversight or other excusable cause on such conditions, if any, as the Auditor thinks fit.
> (7) At the diet of taxation, the party found entitled to expenses shall make available to the Auditor all documents, drafts or copies of documents sought by the Auditor and relevant to the taxation.
> (8) In this rule, a "business day" means any other than a Saturday, Sunday, or public holiday as directed by the Lord President of the Court of Session.

Sheriff court: procedure for taxation for accounts lodged on or after 29 April 2019 (largely now mirroring Court of Session procedure)

The old procedure under OCR r. 32.3 related to accounts lodged for taxation prior to 29 April 2019 and now has little relevance. All accounts lodged for taxation in the Sheriff Court on or after 29 April 2019 are dealt with in the new version of OCR r. 32.3: **22.09**

> **32.3.**—(1) Where an account of expenses awarded in a cause is lodged for taxation, the sheriff clerk must transmit the account and the process to the auditor of court.
> (2) Subject to paragraph (3), the auditor of court must fix a diet of taxation on receipt of—

    (a) the account of expenses;

    (b) the process;

    (c) vouchers in respect of all outlays claimed in the account, including counsel's fees; and

    (d) a letter addressed to the auditor of court—

        (i) confirming that the items referred to in sub-paragraph (c) have been intimated to the party found liable in expenses; and

        (ii) providing such information as is required to enable the auditor of court to give intimation to the party found liable in expenses in accordance with paragraph (4)(b).

(3) The auditor of court must fix a diet of taxation where paragraphs (2)(c) and (d) have not been complied with.

(4) The auditor of court shall intimate the diet of taxation to—

    (a) the party found entitled to expenses; and

    (b) the party found liable in expenses.

(5) The party found liable in expenses shall, not later than 4.00 pm on the fourth business day before the diet of taxation, intimate to the auditor of court and to the party found entitled to expenses particular points of objection, specifying each item objected to and stating concisely the nature and ground of objection.

(6) Subject to paragraph (7), if the party found liable in expenses fails to intimate points of objection under paragraph (5) within the time limit set out there, the auditor of court must not take account of them at the diet of taxation.

(7) Where a failure to comply with the requirement contained in paragraph (5) was due to mistake, oversight or other excusable cause, the auditor of court may relieve a party of the consequences of such failure on such conditions, if any, as the auditor thinks fit.

(8) At the diet of taxation, or within such reasonable period of time thereafter as the auditor of court may allow, the party found entitled to expenses shall make available to the auditor of court all documents, drafts or copies of documents sought by the auditor and relevant to the taxation.

(9) In this rule, "business day" means any day other than a Saturday, Sunday or public or court holiday.

22.10 When lodging an account of expenses for taxation, the account of expenses must have appended to it vouching for all outlays claimed in the account, including counsel's fees. The auditor cannot allow an outlay that has not been properly vouched.[3] All vouching should be numbered separately and correspond with the numbered entry in the account of expenses. Following upon lodging of the account of expenses, the sheriff clerk will transmit the account of expenses and the process to the auditor of court. Notwithstanding the requirement to lodge vouching and the letter/information required by OCR r. 32.3(2) (c) and (d), the auditor is obliged, in terms of r. 32.3(3) to fix a diet of taxation if those documents do not accompany the account, although in practice the auditor's clerk will contact the lodging party to request the missing vouching before the diet is fixed. Upon receipt of the account of expenses, process and relevant vouching, the auditor of court will then fix a diet of taxation, the date for which is intimated to both the entitled and the paying party.

22.11 For all Court of Session accounts, and for Sheriff Court accounts lodged on or after 29 April 2019, not later than 16:00 on the fourth business day prior to the diet of taxation, the paying party is required to intimate to the auditor of court and to the entitled party points of objection specifying each

---

3 *Goldie v Mohr* 1993 GWD 1–40.

item objected to and stating concisely the nature and the grounds of objection. If the paying party fails to timeously intimate such points of objection, then the auditor must not take account of them at the diet of taxation. However, where the failure to comply with the requirement to lodge points of objection is due to a mistake, oversight or other excusable cause, the auditor may allow a paying party to lodge points of objection late, thus relieving the paying party of the consequences of failing to lodge objections, subject to such conditions that the auditor may deem appropriate.

DIET OF TAXATION

At the diet of taxation, the auditor hears oral submissions from parties on the points of Objection and will either give their decision thereon as they arise or, alternatively, take matters to avizandum to take time to consider the submissions along with any information presented to them at the diet. There is a duty on parties appearing before the auditor to make full submissions to the auditor to assist them in reaching their decision.[4] **22.12**

In terms of r. 2.2 of the 2019 Rules: **22.13**

2.2.—(1) The Auditor is to allow only such expenses as are reasonable for conducting the proceedings in a proper manner.
(2) The Auditor may in particular refuse to allow—
    (a) expenses that the Auditor considers to have been incurred as a result of fault or error on the part of the entitled party or the entitled party's representative; and
    (b) expenses relating to a part of the proceedings in which the Auditor considers that the entitled party was unsuccessful.

In determining what is reasonable the auditor has to apply the test laid down in *Malpas v Fife Council* and *Marshall v Fife Health Board* (see Chapter 21.02–21.04).

The auditor has a duty not only to tax off items they deem excessive or unreasonable but also to make additions should they be persuaded that such additions are reasonable. **22.14**

The auditor's fee for taxing the account of expenses, referred to as fee fund dues, is calculated as 5 per cent of the total of the account as lodged for taxation, plus any additional fee that is allowed. However, the normal practice is for the auditor to apportion the fee fund dues on a pro rata basis having regard to the level of abatements. For example, if the account is lodged for a total of £20,000 and there is no additional fee, the fee fund dues amount to £1,000. If the auditor abates £5,000, their fee will be apportioned and only £750 of the fee will be added to the account of expenses. The entitled party will therefore have to bear the shortfall of £250 without being able to recover that from the opponent. **22.15**

---

4 *Griffiths v Kerr* 1991 SLT 1024; Practice Note No. 3 of 1993 – Office of the Auditor of the Court of Session.

POST-TAXATION PROCEDURE

22.16 Following upon the auditor's taxation of the account of expenses, a statement of the taxed amount of expenses is prepared by the auditor. The taxed account, statement and process is transmitted by the auditor back to the court and intimation of their so doing is made to each party. Thereafter the entitled party must, within seven days of intimation, remit a copy of the taxed account to the paying party.[5]

NOTES OF OBJECTION TO TAXED ACCOUNT

22.17 Procedure for objecting to the auditor's report differs depending on whether the proceedings were raised in the Court of Session or Sheriff Court.

22.18 In the Court of Session the applicable rule is RCS r. 42.4:

42.4.—(1) Any party to a cause who has appeared or been represented at the diet of taxation may object to the Auditor's statement by lodging in process a note of objection within 14 days after the date of the statement.

(2) A party lodging a note of objection shall—

(a) intimate a copy of the note and a motion under subparagraph (b) to the Auditor and to any party who appeared or was represented at the diet of taxation;

(b) apply by motion for an order allowing the note to be received; and

(c) intimate forthwith to the Auditor a copy of the interlocutor pronounced on a motion under subparagraph (b).

(2A) Within 14 days after the date of receipt of intimation under paragraph (2)(c), the Auditor shall lodge a minute stating the reasons for his or her decision in relation to the items to which objection is taken in the note.

(3) After the minute of the Auditor has been lodged in process, the party who lodged the note of objection shall, in consultation with any other party wishing to be heard, arrange with the Keeper of the Rolls for a diet of hearing before the appropriate court.

(4) At the hearing on the note of objection, the court may–

(a) sustain or repel any objection in the note or remit the account of expenses to the Auditor for further consideration; and

(b) find any party liable in the expenses of the procedure on the note.

22.19 The Sheriff Court has two versions of OCR r. 32.4, one for accounts lodged pre-29 April 2019, which is now redundant, and one for accounts lodged on or after that date. The latter version provides:

32.4.—(1) A party to a cause who has appeared or been represented at a diet of taxation may object to the auditor of court's statement by lodging in process a note of objection within 14 days after the date of the statement.

(2) The party lodging a note of objection is referred to in this rule as "the objecting party".

(3) On lodging the note of objection the objecting party must apply by motion for an order—

(a) allowing the note of objection to be received; and

(b) allowing a hearing on the note of objection.

---

5 RCS r. 42.3 and OCR r. 32.3A (for accounts lodged on or after 29 April 2019).

(4) On the granting of the order mentioned in paragraph (3), the objecting party must intimate to the auditor of court—
  (a) the note of objection; and
  (b) the interlocutor containing the order.

(5) Within 14 days after receipt of intimation of the items mentioned in paragraph (4) the auditor of court must lodge in process a statement of reasons in the form of a minute stating the reasons for the auditor's decision in relation to the items to which objection is taken in the note.

(6) On the lodging of the statement of reasons the sheriff clerk must fix a hearing on the note of objection.

(7) At the hearing, the sheriff may—
  (a) sustain or repel any objection or remit the account of expenses to the auditor of court for further consideration; and
  (b) find any party liable in the expenses of the procedure on the note of objection.

In summary, a party who has appeared or been represented at the diet of taxation may object to the auditor of court's statement by lodging in process a note of objection within fourteen days of the auditor's statement (the previous timescale was seven days in the case of sheriff court accounts lodged prior to 29 April 2019). **22.20**

A note of objection requires to be lodged with the court together with a motion seeking an order allowing the note to be received and a hearing thereon. Upon granting of the order by the court, the objecting party thereafter requires to intimate the note of objection and relevant interlocutor to the auditor of court. Within fourteen days of receipt of intimation of the note of objection, the auditor of court must lodge in process a minute stating the reasons for their decision in relation to the items to which objection is taken. Thereafter, a hearing is fixed on the note of objection, at which time the court may sustain or repel any objection or remit the account back to the auditor of court for further consideration. The court is slow to interfere with the auditor's decisions and will only do so if the auditor has mis-directed themselves by taking irrelevant material into account, or failed to take relevant material into account or has misunderstood or misdirected themselves as to the facts of the case or law. It is not the function of the court to carry out a rehearing of matters debated before the auditor and to substitute its own assessment. For examples of the court sustaining notes of objection see Chapter 21.02–21.04. **22.21**

Chapter 23

Practical Example of Judicial Account

23.01 This chapter provides some practical information on how to deal with a judicial account. It sets out the salient facts of a case, followed by an example of a judicial account and the potential abatements that might arise. The account relates to an action raised post-29 April 2019 and therefore the rates charged are those set out in the Act of Sederunt (Taxation of Judicial Expenses Rules) 2019, which sets out the rates that are based on a particular number of units for each area of work undertaken. A unit currently has a value of £16.40 and is subject to periodic change. For accounts that relate to actions raised pre-29th April 2019 the charges are those set out in the schedules to the Act of Sederunt (Fees of Solicitors in the Sheriff Court) (Amendment and Further Provisions) 1993 as amended.

CASE BACKGROUND

23.02 On 12 September 2018, the pursuer was working in the course of his employment with the defenders and suffered an accident whereby he slipped and fell to the floor, landing on his right hip. The pursuer was subsequently conveyed to the local accident and emergency department where he was examined, X-rayed and treated. The pursuer continued to suffer significant pain in his injured hip and continued to consult his general practitioner (GP) for treatment.

23.03 A claim was intimated by the pursuer's agent upon the defenders in terms of the compulsory pre-accident protocol for personal injury claims and pre-litigation negotiations continued in terms of the protocol.

23.04 During the pre-litigation stages, a report was obtained from the consultant in Accident & Emergency who treated the pursuer upon his attendance at the department. Thereafter, due to the pursuer's ongoing symptoms, medical records were recovered from the GP and hospital with a view to instructing a report from an independent consultant orthopaedic aurgeon. That report opined that the pursuer would continue to suffer from the effects of the injuries sustained for some time and would possibly require to undergo operative procedures at some time in the future.

23.05 During the course of the compulsory pre-action protocol negotiations with the insurers, liability was denied. Precognitions were thereafter obtained from liability witnesses, along with a precognition from the pursuer's spouse in regard to the services provided to the pursuer as a result of the injuries sustained in the accident.

23.06 In light of the denial of liability, agents instructed a report from a further skilled person, namely a consulting engineer, as to the circumstances surrounding the accident.

As pre-litigation negotiations proved unsuccessful in achieving a settlement, **23.07** proceedings were raised against the defenders with counsel being instructed to frame the initial writ. A specification of documents was drafted and subsequently served on the GP and local hospital in order to obtain the pursuer's medical records.

Following upon the lodging of defences, it became clear that the pursuer **23.08** had erroneously designed the defenders and required to lodge a minute of amendment in order to rectify the error.

The defences lodged on behalf of the defender also referred to liability **23.09** documentation and the pursuer lodged a further specification for the recovery thereof.

The proceedings thereafter followed the timetable issued by the court until **23.10** it became necessary for the pursuer to enrol for a variation of the timetable due to the defenders' failure to produce the relevant documentation in terms of the specification of documents. Upon production of the documentation, the record closed with a proof diet being set down for four days.

As a result of the continuing difficulties being experienced by the pursuer **23.11** as a result of the injuries sustained in the accident, it was necessary for the pursuer to undergo operative procedure to improve his condition. Following the further treatment, an additional report was obtained from the independent orthopaedic surgeon to provide an update on these matters, including a revised prognosis.

The pursuer thereafter lodged a minute of amendment to aver the salient **23.12** points of the new medical evidence. The record was amended in terms of the minute of amendment and the defender's answers thereto. The interlocutor giving effect to the amendment was ultimately silent on the question of expenses.

In preparation for the proof diet, the pursuer lodged a list of witnesses that **23.13** included the pursuer's spouse and witnesses A and B, along with the treating consultant in accident and emergency medicine and the two skilled persons who had reported, namely the consultant orthopaedic surgeon and consulting engineer. The defenders likewise lodged a list of witnesses that, amongst others, listed witness C.

During the proof preparation stages, the pursuer's agent lodged a notice **23.14** to admit. Subsequent correspondence and negotiations with the defenders resulted in liability being admitted and medical evidence being agreed, leaving only the issue of quantum at stake.

A pre-trial meeting was arranged and conducted between the agents, at **23.15** which time the pursuer's claim settled in the sum of £15,000. Witnesses under citation were thereafter cancelled and authority interponed to the joint minute with a final interlocutor being granted sanctioning the proceedings as suitable for the employment of counsel and certifying the orthopaedic surgeon and consulting engineer as skilled persons instructed on behalf of the pursuer.

Thereafter, the following account of expenses was prepared and intimated **23.16** to the defenders' agents. The left column of figures relates to outlays incurred and the right column relates to the fees being claimed. A sheet consists of 250 words or part thereof.

SHERIFFDOM OF LOTHIAN AND BORDERS AT EDINBURGH FOR DETERMINATION IN THE ALL
SCOTLAND SHERIFF PERSONAL INJURY COURT AT EDINBURGH

ACCOUNT OF EXPENSES

Incurred PURSUER

to

PRACTICAL EXAMPLE SOLICITORS

In Causa PURSUER A

against DEFENDER B

PAYING PARTY/SOLICITOR REF.: Defender's Agents 123456
ACCOUNT AND VOUCHING PER RULE 42.2C INTIMATED
ON: 18/08/2021 EST. DURATION OF
TAXATION: 30 MIN

2019						
Mar	13	Fee for precognition of pursuer - 5 shs			410	00
May	20	Fee for Report of Treating Consultant in Accident and Emergency medicine - 4 sheets			164	00
		Paid Treating Consultant in Accident and Emergency fee for Report (Voucher 1)	400	00		
Nov	19	Fee for Report of Consultant Orthopaedic Surgeon - 6 shs			246	00
		Paid Consultant Orthopaedic Surgeon fee for Report (Voucher 2)	500	00		
	26	Fee for precognition of pursuer's Spouse - 5 shs			410	00
		Fee for precognition of witness A - 4 shs			328	00
		Fee for precognition of witness B - 3 shs			246	00
		Fee for precognition of witness C - 5 shs			410	00
2020						
Jul	29	Fee for Report of Consulting Engineer - 26 shs			1066	00
		Paid Consulting Engineer fee for Report (Voucher 3)	2500	00		
Aug	04	Fee for supplementary precognition of pursuer - 4 shs			328	00
Oct	20	Fee for all work undertaken in contemplation of Proceedings (£574.00 plus 3.5% of settlement sum of £15,000)			1099	00
		Fee on Instructions			902	00
		Paid Advocate framing Initial Writ (Voucher 4)	500	00		
		VAT	100	00		
		Paid Dues lodging Initial Writ (ledger)	227	00		
		Fee for Pursuers Specification of Documents			82	00
		Optional Procedure adopted on 2 Havers			32	80
Dec	09	Paid Dues fixing Proof Diet (ledger)	62	00		
	11	Fee for pursuer's first Inventory of Productions			82	00
		Carried Forward £	4289	00	5805	80

		Brought Forward £	4289	00	5805	80
2020						
Dec	11	Fee for pursuer's Minute of Amendment - no Answers lodged			164	00
		Paid Dues enrolling Motion (ledger)	57	00		
	18	Fee for pursuer's Specification of Documents			164	00
		Paid Dues enrolling Motion (ledger)	57	00		
		Optional procedure adopted on one haver			16	40
2021						
Jan	05	Instructing Counsel to revise the Pleadings			82	00
	17	Attendance at Consultation on Pleadings - 1 hour			205	00
		Paid Advocate attending Consultation on Pleadings (Voucher 5)	800	00		
		VAT	160	00		
	24	Fee for pursuer's second Inventory of Productions			82	00
Feb	03	Paid Advocate framing Adjustments (Voucher 5)	250	00		
		VAT	50	00		
	12	Fee for pursuer's Statement of Valuation of Claim			246	00
		Paid Advocate framing Statement of Valuation of Claim (Voucher 6)	350	00		
		VAT	70	00		
	16	Fee for pursuer's Motion to vary Court Timetable			82	00
		Paid Dues enrolling Motion (ledger)	57	00		
May	21	Adjustment fee			492	00
		Paid Dues lodging Record (ledger)	113	00		
	23	Perusing and considering documentation recovered from defenders in terms of Specification of Documents - 1 hour			164	00
	27	Fee for pursuer's second Inventory of Productions			82	00
		Carried Forward £	6253	00	7585	20

Prepared by Alex Quinn & Partners - Law Accountants

2021							
		Brought Forward £	6253	00	7585	20
May	27	Fee for pursuer's Motion to allow Proof			82	00
		Paid Dues enrolling Motion (ledger)	57	00		
		Fee for Incidental Procedure with Diet of Proof being fixed to take place on 31 August 2021 and three ensuing days			205	00
		Paid Advocate framing Note on the Line of Evidence (Voucher 7)	750	00		
		VAT	150	00		
Jun	02	Fee for defender's Statement of Valuation of Claim			246	00
		Fee for defender's Inventory of Productions			41	00
	19	Fee for Report of Consultant Orthopaedic Surgeon - 10 shs			410	00
		Paid Orthopaedic Surgeon fee for Report (Voucher 8)	500	00		
Jul	01	Fee for pursuer's Minute of Amendment			164	00
		Paid Dues enrolling Motion (ledger)	57	00		
	08	Fee for defender's Answers			82	00
	30	Hearing Limitation fee - to cover all correspondence with defenders including preparation and lodging Notice to Admit, resulting in liability being admitted and Medical evidence being agreed			287	00
Aug	04	Fee preparing for Proof			512	50
	10	Arranging Pre-Trial Meeting			82	00
	16	Preparing for Pre-Trial Meeting			328	00
		Attendance at Pre-Trial Meeting - 1 hr 10 mins			196	80
		Paid Advocate conducting Pre-Trial Meeting (Voucher9)	1250	00		
		VAT	250	00		
		Fee for Extra-Judicial Settlement - £15,000			307	50
		Fee for Final Procedure			102	50
		Carried Forward £	9267	00	10631	50

		Brought Forward £	9267	00	10631	50
2021						
Aug	16	Paid Consultant Orthopaedic Surgeon Cancellation Fee (Voucher 10)	500	00		
		Fee for pursuer's Motion			82	00
		Paid Dues enrolling Motion (ledger)	57	00		
	18	Fee for Account of Expenses			328	00
		Paid Dues lodging Account of Expenses for Taxation	46	00		
		Preparing for Taxation - 1 hour			164	00
		Attendance at Taxation - 30 mins			82	00
		Paid Audit fee	0	00		
			9870	00	11287	50
		Add VAT @ 20% on 11287.50			2257	50
		Add Outlays			9870	00
		£			23415	00

Prepared by Alex Quinn & Partners - Law Accountants

COMMENTARY ON ACCOUNT OF EXPENSES AND PROPOSED ABATEMENTS

As the action was commenced post-29 April 2019, the fees charged are per **23.17** the Act of Sederunt (Taxation of Judicial Expenses Rules) 2019. Therefore even though some work in the account pre-dates 29 April 2019, the 2019 table covers all entries in the account.

In relation to the pre-litigation fee, as the action was handled under **23.18** the compulsory pre-action protocol for personal injury claims, the entitled party can charge: (a) a fixed fee of £574; plus (b) 3.5 per cent of the value of the settlement. They can also charge up to 50 per cent of the total of (a) and (b) for work carried out prior to the commencement of the proceedings if:

(1) the work was not required for the purpose of complying with the protocol;
(2) involved the sharing of information with the opposing party; and
(3) was not included anywhere else in Part 2A of the table of fees.

Any such additional amount requires to be justified at taxation. In our practical example the pre-litigation fee is confined to the fixed fee and 3.5 per cent of settlement.

REPORT OF TREATING CONSULTANT IN ACCIDENT & EMERGENCY

As will be noted from the general overview of the proceedings, the final inter- **23.19** locutor certified the orthopaedic surgeon and consulting engineer as skilled persons but made no mention of the accident and emergency consultant. However, the charges relating to the accident and emergency report would still form a recoverable charge in the pursuer's account of expenses as the accident and emergency consultant's evidence was of a factual nature, i.e. speaking to his treatment of the pursuer upon his admission to hospital. Factual witnesses do not require to be certified by the court.

PRECOGNITION OF WITNESS C

Witness C was not listed on the pursuer's list of witnesses lodged as part of the **23.20** proof preparation. That would normally invite an objection to the precognition charge being included in the account. However, the precognition charge is rightly included within the account of expenses as the recovery of any precognition is governed by the question of reasonableness. Whether or not the witness is subsequently included on the list of witnesses is immaterial insofar as the recovery of the precognition is concerned. In addition, witness C was included within the defender's list of witnesses, thus entitling the pursuer's agent to precognosce the witness.

PURSUER'S SPECIFICATION OF DOCUMENTS

23.21   As part of the pre-litigation work undertaken, medical records were recovered from the GP and hospital attended to enable the instruction of skilled person evidence. At the time of raising the proceedings, the pursuer's agent sought recovery of the up-to-date records by way of specification of documents. The case of *Zdrzalka v Sabre Insurance*[1] dealt with *inter alia* recovery of medical records by way of specification when there had been a previous recovery during the pre-litigation stages. The costs of a specification in that case were not recoverable from the opponent as the specification simply recovered the same records as had been previously obtained.

23.22   This can be contrasted with the case study above. The pursuer had ongoing issues, had consulted his GP and continued to attend upon the treating consultant. Therefore, in this instance, it would be considered reasonable to recover the updated records by way of specification. If the pursuer had no ongoing symptoms, then a valid objection could be made at taxation to the expenses associated with the specification of documents and optional procedure. The objection would most likely be upheld by the auditor.

PURSUER'S MINUTE OF AMENDMENT

23.23   The purpose of the minute of amendment was to rectify an error made by the pursuer's agents in the designation of the defender. Accordingly, unless the court has otherwise directed, the expense of that minute of amendment procedure should not be laid at the door of the paying party as it is an expense caused through the actings and the fault of the pursuer's agents.

It should be borne in mind that the rules of the Court of Session and the Sheriff Court rules both provide that the court:

> 'shall find the party making an amendment liable in the expenses occasioned by the amendment unless it is shown that it is just and equitable that the expenses occasioned by the amendment should be otherwise dealt with, and may attach such other conditions as it thinks fit'.[2]

Therefore, in situations where an amending party considers that they should not be found liable for the expenses of the amendment, the justification for departing from the default position must be clearly set out in the motion accompanying the minute of amendment.

PURSUER'S FURTHER SPECIFICATION OF DOCUMENTS

23.24   Consideration should be given to the documentation called for in the further specification of documents. If the documentation sought could have been included within the earlier specification of documents then the commission and diligence procedure and all work thereanent could rightly be objected to and abated. If, however, the documentation was outwith the scope of

---

1 *Mariola Zdrzalka v Sabre Insurance* (2018) SC Edin 57, 2018 WLUK 362.
2 RCS r. 24.4 and OCR r. 18.6.

the specification lodged with the initial writ, then the further specification procedure would be rightly chargeable. In our practical example, the documentation relating to liability only came to light following upon the lodging of defences and therefore the further specification procedure would be considered a reasonable step of process and chargeable within the entitled party's account of expenses.

PURSUER'S MOTION TO VARY COURT TIMETABLE

Consideration would have to be given to the reasons why such a motion was **23.25** necessary. In this instance, the necessity to vary arose due to the defender's failure to produce documentation timeously and therefore such a motion to vary the court timetable would be considered reasonable and rightly chargeable.

PURSUER'S FURTHER MINUTE OF AMENDMENT

Following upon the pursuer undergoing operative procedures to rectify the **23.26** injuries sustained, an updated expert report from the consultant orthopaedic surgeon was obtained. It was thereafter necessary to amend the pleadings to introduce that new information into the pleadings. Accordingly, on the basis that the court has not otherwise directed, the pursuer's agents would be acting reasonably in seeking the expense of the amendment procedure. The purpose of the amendment was to introduce new evidence that was not available at the time of the closing of the record. The pursuer has to give fair notice to his opponent about the points in issue. His medical condition was developing and the prognosis was altering, all of which is relevant to quantum. As quantum was the only live issue for proof it was reasonable, indeed necessary, for the pursuer to amend and, as such, the costs of doing so would be recoverable from the opponent. Note, however, para, 23.23 above regarding the need to specifically move the court to find the expenses occasioned by the amendment to be expenses in the cause, failing which the party amending should automatically be found liable for the expenses.

HEARING LIMITATION FEE

The hearing limitation fee is designed to cover work not covered elsewhere in **23.27** the table of fees, undertaken with a view to limiting the scope of any hearing and includes the exchange of documents, precognitions and expert reports, agreeing any fact, statement or document not in dispute, preparing and intimating any notice to admit or notice of non-admission (and consideration thereof) and preparing and lodging any joint minute.

As the litigation progressed significant areas of agreement were reached, **23.28** thus restricting the scope of the proof diet. In particular, liability was conceded and medical evidence was agreed, meaning the only issue left for proof was quantum. A notice to admit had been served that led to the concession on liability. There is therefore a basis to argue for a full hearing limitation fee.

Where less effort is made to limit the areas of disagreement there is scope for a defender to argue that the hearing limitation fee should be wholly or partially abated.

CONSULTANT ORTHOPAEDIC'S CANCELLATION FEE

23.29   Once liability is conceded and medical evidence is agreed, all witnesses cited to deal with liability and the medical evidence should have their citations for the proof diet promptly cancelled unless for some reason there is a specific need to call a witness to assist with determination of quantum. Failure to do so may incur avoidable cancellation charges that would be abated at taxation.

In our example, due to an oversight by the pursuer's agents, the orthopaedic consultant's citation was not cancelled until final settlement terms were agreed, despite the medical evidence being agreed. Accordingly, the cancellation fee could be rightly objected to and removed from the account given the fee only became payable due to delay in countermanding the citation.

UNINCURRED ITEMS

23.30   It is a standard objection to an account that does not proceed to taxation for unincurred items, such as preparation for and conduct of the taxation, and, if appropriate, the account lodging fee, to be abated. This is invariably agreed during the pre-taxation negotiations.

Auditor's fee

23.31   On lodging an account for taxation a fee (currently £46) for lodging dues is payable. The fee fund dues for taxing accounts are payable on issue of the auditor's report and are currently 5 per cent of the total of the account as lodged rounded up to the nearest £100. For accounts that total less than £400 a fixed sum of £21 is payable. Lodging dues and fee fund dues must be paid to the auditor's office. The auditor's office will issue an invoice for the collection of lodging dues and this requires to be paid prior to a diet of taxation being fixed. An invoice for the fee fund dues is issued on completion of the taxation and must be paid within fourteen days.

CANCELLATION FEES

23.32   Where the diet of taxation has been cancelled less than three working days prior to the date the diet is fixed to take place, the auditor is entitled to charge a cancellation fee, as follows:

- Three days prior to the diet = 2.5 per cent.
- Two days prior to the diet = 2.5 per cent.
- The day before or the day of the diet = 3.75 per cent.

The cutoff point to avoid a cancellation fee is 16:00 on the fourth working day prior to the diet, i.e. if the taxation is fixed to take place on a Thursday the cutoff point is 16:00 on the preceding Friday. It is important to note that cancellation of the diet of taxation must be made by the receiving party in writing by 16:00 as stipulated above.

Chapter 24

Vexatious Litigant Orders

24.01 In terms of s. 101(1) of the Courts Reform (Scotland) Act 2014,[1] the Inner House of the Court of Session may make a vexatious litigant order if satisfied that a person has habitually and persistently, without any reasonable ground for doing so: (a) instituted vexatious civil proceedings; or (b) made vexatious applications to the court in the course of civil proceedings (whether or not instituted by the person).

24.02 There clearly has to be a pattern of conduct in raising or conducting litigation in a vexatious manner.

24.03 The critical question is whether the conduct in question can be classified as 'vexatious'. Delivering the opinion of the court in the petition by the Lord Advocate for a vexatious litigant order against Aslam the Lord Justice Clerk stated:

> ' … it is not enough for an individual to be classed as a vexatious litigant that actions which he has instituted, or applications made, have not succeeded or been abandoned: it is not persistent failure which is the key, rather that the failure in question has been based on there being no merit even to commence the litigation or make the application. The critical finding will be that repeated litigations and applications have failed for reasons of competence, irrelevance and the like. It is the fact that repeated actions were commenced with there being no reasonable grounds for doing so which can render them vexatious'.[2]

24.04 The court adopts a two stage test in determining whether to grant such an order. First, it requires to be satisfied that the s. 101(1) test has been met. Secondly, it requires to be satisfied that it is in the interests of justice to grant the order.[3]

24.05 Such an order interferes with the rights of a citizen to access the courts. However, the interference is limited and designed to prevent abuses of court processes. The order does not prevent a person from raising court actions, simply that they have to satisfy an Outer House judge that there is a reasonable basis for raising the proceedings.

24.06 The court will balance the *prima facie* right of citizens to invoke the jurisdiction of the civil courts, the availability of other powers to deal with abuses of process, the overall conduct of the person accused of acting in a vexatious manner, the need to obtain permission from a Lord Ordinary to raise future

---

1 Reproduced in Appendix 1.
2 *Petition by Lord Advocate for an Order in terms of Section 100 of the Courts Reform (Scotland) Act 2014 against Mohammed Aslam* [2019] CSIH 17 per Lady Dorrian at para. 10.
3 Petition by Lord Advocate for order against *Politakis* [2021] CSIH 34 per Lord Woolman paras 22–24.

proceedings, the need to protect the person whom they might sue and the finite resources of the court itself.

There are therefore several different interests, namely those of the 'vexatious' person, those aggrieved by the vexatious conduct and the court. Does the vexatious litigant order procedure adequately protect those who are the victims of repeated abuses of process? Such victims have no right to raise the petition under the Courts Reform (Scotland) Act 2014. That has to be instigated by the Lord Advocate who will be advised by the legal department of the Scottish Government. Unless the court makes the Government aware of concerns that it has about vexatious conduct, the procedure is dependent on an aggrieved party being aware of the Lord Advocate's ability to seek a vexatious litigant order and to contact the relevant government department to consider the merits of such an application. As at the date of publication, only around twelve such orders have been granted by the court under the 2014 Act.   **24.07**

Further, other remedies for abuse of process are sparingly exercised. They afford little protection in the short-term against the likes of appeals being made against summary dismissal of an unmeritorious claim containing scandalous allegations or appeals following on from a decree by default due to a failure to comply with an order for caution for expenses.   **24.08**

The order will only be sought where there has been habitual and persistent conduct. Multiple actions over a number of years through the courts at first instance and various appeal stages may have to be endured by one or more defenders before the test under s. 101 is met. The expenses awards made at various stages are generally never met by the vexatious person. Costs of taxation require to be borne by the aggrieved party with little prospect of any recovery.   **24.09**

Permission is required from a Court of Session judge to proceed with an appeal from the Sheriff Appeal Court. A simple solution would be to create rules of court that would remove an automatic right of appeal against final decisions where the judge or sheriff has made a finding that the litigation is devoid of any merit, incompetent or wholly irrelevant. Where such a finding is made it should place the onus onto the unsuccessful party to show sufficient cause before being permitted to appeal. Any appeal should be subject to a sift to determine whether it has any reasonable prospect of success and if the sift appeal judge refuses permission to appeal that would be the end of the matter. This largely mirrors the requirements for a party who is subject to a vexatious litigation order in seeking permission to raise fresh proceedings but would remove protracted abuses of process at a much earlier stage.   **24.10**

Chapter 25

Simple Procedure

25.01 Simple procedure was introduced by the Courts Reform (Scotland) Act 2014 to replace the procedure for small claims as well as some summary cause actions raised on or after 28 November 2016.[1] The Simple Procedure Rules (SPR) are set out in Sch. 1 to the Act of Sederunt (Simple Procedure) 2016.[2] The various forms to be used in simple procedure are set out in Sch. 2. It should be noted that the small claims rules still apply to actions raised before 28 November 2016.

25.02 The underlying principles of simple procedure are set out in SPR r. 1.2:

> **1.2**—(1) Cases are to be resolved as quickly as possible, at the least expense to parties and the courts.
> (2) The approach of the court to a case is to be as informal as is appropriate, taking into account the nature and complexity of the dispute.
> (3) Parties are to be treated even-handedly by the court.
> (4) Parties are to be encouraged to settle their disputes by negotiation or alternative dispute resolution, and should be able to do so throughout the progress of a case.
> (5) Parties should only have to come to court when it is necessary to do so to progress or resolve their dispute.

25.03 Simple procedure must now be used for any new case raised if it is a type of case listed in s. 72(3) of the Courts Reform (Scotland) Act 2014 as a relevant claim namely:

- (a) proceedings for payment of a sum of money not exceeding £5,000,
- (b) actions of multiplepoinding where the value of the fund or property that is the subject of the action does not exceed £5,000,
- (c) actions of furthcoming where the value of the arrested fund or subject does not exceed £5,000,
- (d) actions ad factum praestandum, other than actions in which there is claimed, in addition or as an alternative to a decree ad factum praestandum, a decree for payment of a sum of money exceeding £5,000,
- (e) proceedings for the recovery of possession of heritable property or moveable property, other than proceedings in which there is claimed, in addition or as an alternative to a decree for such recovery, a decree for payment of a sum of money exceeding £5,000.

25.04 No types of proceedings other than those listed under s. 72(3) may be raised as a simple procedure case. A relevant claim essentially has the same definition as a small claim, which specifically excludes personal injury claims and therefore that prevents personal injury actions being dealt with under simple procedure.

---

1 Courts Reform (Scotland) Act 2014 ss. 72–83.
2 Act of Sederunt (Simple Procedure) 2016 (SSI 2016/200).

Also currently excluded from simple procedure are actions for eviction and actions for aliment (unless the aliment claim falls within the scope of s. 74 of the Courts Reform (Scotland) Act 2014, i.e. where the aliment sought is £100 per week or less for a child aged under 18 or £200 per week or less in any other case. However, the Simple Procedure Special Claims Rules are pending with an anticipated introduction date of mid-2022. If, and when, they are introduced, they will extend the categories of cases that can be dealt with under simple procedure to include personal injury.

The detailed terms of SPR are beyond the scope of this book. The focus **25.05** here will be on the issues that pertain to expenses. However, it should be borne in mind that the Civil Online portal must be used for registering simple procedure claim forms until at least 31 March 2022. That mandatory requirement may well continue on a permanent basis.[3] The electronic submission is done either through the portal on the Scottish Courts and Tribunal Service (SCTS) website or the SCTS internet interface to its case management system.[4] If neither of those options are possible, the claim will only be registered if: (1) a paper version of the claim form is sent to the court with a note explaining why it could not be sent electronically in one of the two ways mentioned; and 2) the Sheriff considers, from the explanation in the note, that the claimant could not have sent it using either the portal or the interface.[5]

The position in relation to expenses in simple procedure actions is set out in **25.06** SPR r. 14, which is in the following terms:

14.1 What is this Part about?
(1) This Part is about the expenses of a claim which the sheriff can order a party to pay for.
14.2 What orders about expenses can the sheriff make?
(1) Once a claim has been resolved, the sheriff must make an order about expenses, such as:
  (a) that no payments are to be made in respect of the expenses of any party,
  (b) that a payment is to be made to a party or to a party's solicitor.
(2) Expenses incurred by a party to do with a courtroom supporter may not be part of an order about expenses
14.3 When will the sheriff make an order about expenses?
(1) In a case where the expenses of a claim are capped, the sheriff must make an order about expenses when deciding the claim.
(2) In any other case, the sheriff must, if able to, make an order about expenses when deciding the claim.
(3) If not able to make an order about expenses when deciding the claim, the sheriff may make an order about expenses after deciding the claim.
14.4 What if the sheriff does not make an order about expenses when deciding the claim?
(1) If the sheriff makes an order about expenses after deciding the claim, then the sheriff must not set out the final decision in a case in a Decision Form until the order about expenses is made.

3 Act of Sederunt (Simple Procedure Amendment) (Civil Online) 2020 (SSI 2020/293) as amended by Act of Sederunt (Simple Procedure Amendment) (Civil Online) 2021 (SSI 2021/295).
4 SPR r. 3.7(1).
5 SPR r. 3.7(1A).

(2) If the sheriff does not make an order about expenses when deciding the claim, the sheriff must give the parties written orders.

(3) Those orders must arrange an expenses hearing.

(4) Those orders may require a party to send an account of expenses to the court and to each other before the expenses hearing.

(5) Those orders may then require the sheriff clerk to assess the level of expenses (if any) that should be awarded to a party and to send notice of that assessment to the parties before the expenses hearing.

14.5 What is an expenses hearing?

(1) The purpose of an expenses hearing is to assess the level of expenses (if any) that should be awarded to a party.

(2) At the expenses hearing, the sheriff must make an order about expenses, such as:

    (a) that no payments are to be made in respect of the expenses of any party,

    (b) that a payment is to be made to a party or to a party's solicitor.

25.07 The onus is therefore on the sheriff to make an expenses order as soon as the case is decided. This is mandatory if the case is one where the expenses are to be capped (see Para 25.09). If the expenses are not to be capped the Sheriff should make the expenses order, if possible, when deciding the case but can make the order later, if necessary, in which case an expenses hearing must be fixed. The Sheriff can, but is not obliged to, order that a party sends an account of expenses to the court and intimates it to the other opponents in advance of the expenses hearing. The Sheriff will then decide at the expenses hearing whether: (1) any expenses should be payable; and if so (2) whether they are payable by one party to another or the other's solicitor and whether they are payable for a fixed sum or on the simple procedure scale. The Sheriff must make an order about expenses at the expenses hearing.

SECTION 81 OF THE COURTS REFORM (SCOTLAND) ACT 2014

25.08 Section 81 permits Scottish Ministers to introduce regulations to set out how expenses are to be dealt with in certain categories of cases. It also states that the normal rules in relation to caps on expenses do not apply in certain situations, which include situations where the defender has not stated a defence, or having stated a defence has not proceeded with it, or having stated and proceeded with a defence has not acted in good faith in relation to the merits of the defence. The caps are also disapplied in appeals to the Sheriff Appeal Court from any decision in a simple procedure case or if the Sheriff grants an application made by any party that the caps should not apply. Section 81 is in the following terms:

Expenses in simple procedure cases

81.—(1) The Scottish Ministers may by order provide that—

    (a) in such category of simple procedure cases as may be prescribed in the order, no award of expenses may be made,

    (b) in such other category of simple procedure cases as may be so prescribed, any expenses awarded may not exceed such sum as may be so prescribed.

(2) The categories of simple procedure cases mentioned in subsection (1) may be prescribed by reference to—

    (a) the value of the claim in the cases,

    (b) the subject matter of the claim in the cases.

(3) Categories may be prescribed subject to specified exceptions.

(4) An order under subsection (1) does not apply—
    (a) to simple procedure cases such as those mentioned in subsection (5),
    (b) in relation to an appeal to the Sheriff Appeal Court from any decision in a simple procedure case, or
    (c) to a simple procedure case in respect of which a direction under subsection (7) is made.
(5) The simple procedure cases referred to in subsection (4)(a) are those in which—
    (a) the defender—
        (i) has not stated a defence,
        (ii) having stated a defence, has not proceeded with it, or
        (iii) having stated and proceeded with a defence, has not acted in good faith as to its merits, or
    (b) a party to the case has behaved in a manner which is manifestly unreasonable in relation to the case.
(6) Subsection (7) applies where the sheriff in a simple procedure case is of the opinion that a difficult question of law, or a question of fact of exceptional complexity, is involved.
(7) The sheriff may, at any stage, on the application of any party to the case, direct that an order under subsection (1) is not to apply in relation to the case.

THE SHERIFF COURT SIMPLE PROCEDURE (LIMITS ON AWARD OF EXPENSES) ORDER 2016[6] AS AMENDED BY THE SHERIFF COURT SIMPLE PROCEDURE (LIMITS ON AWARD OF EXPENSES) AMENDMENT ORDER 2019[7]

The 2016 and 2019 Orders give effect to s. 81 and set out the specific rules as to when no awards, or capped awards, of expenses may be made in simple procedure cases. The 2019 Order simply increases figures in the 2016 order from £200 to £300. The salient provisions are:

25.09

Category of simple procedure cases in which no award of expenses may be made
2. No award of expenses may be made in a simple procedure case in which the value of the claim is less than or equal to £300. (£200 for actions commenced prior to 1st April 2019).

Categories of simple procedure cases in which expenses awarded may not exceed prescribed sum
3. In any simple procedure case in which the value of the claim is:
    (a) greater than £300 (£200 for actions commenced prior to 1st April 2019)[8] but less than or equal to £1,500, the expenses awarded by the sheriff may not exceed £150;
    (b) greater than £1,500 but less than or equal to £3,000, the expenses awarded by the sheriff may not exceed 10% of the value of the claim.

Exceptions
4. This Order does not apply to the following types of simple procedure case— (a) actions in respect of aliment and interim aliment;

---

6 Sheriff Court Simple Procedure (Limits on Award of Expenses) Order 2016 (SSI 2016/388).
7 Sheriff Court Simple Procedure (Limits on Award of Expenses) Amendment Order 2019 (SSI 2019/79).
8 Sheriff Court Simple Procedure (Limits on Award of Expenses) Amendment Order 2019 art. 3.

(b) actions of defamation; or

(c) actions for personal injury to which section 17 or 18 of the Prescription and
     Limitation (Scotland) Act 1973 apply.[9]

OUTLAYS

25.10   The question arises whether the capped expenses include VAT and outlays.
Unfortunately, there are conflicting authorities on the point and there is no
appellate authority to resolve the issue.

In the case of *Gowans v Miller*,[10] decided in 2017, the Sheriff held that the
cap did include VAT and outlays. However, in the case of *Martin v Southern
Rock Insurance Company Ltd*[11] the court held that the court dues for registering
the case and VAT are payable in addition to the capped expenses, effectively
treating the capped expenses as the fee element of the account. Whilst there
is an element of judicial discretion in expenses matters, and it is within the
general power of a Sheriff to order that no expenses are payable in a simple
procedure case,[12] this is an issue of legal interpretation and it would be beneficial for parties and agents if a consistent approach is taken to provide certainty.
The matter will hopefully be clarified once the Scottish Civil Justice Council
have completed a review, currently ongoing, of simple procedure.

EXCEPTIONS TO THE CAP

Failing to proceed with a defence

25.11   This is perhaps the most common exception that will be encountered and
can be said to effectively be a re-enactment of s. 36B(3) of the Sheriff Courts
(Scotland) Act 1971, which governed expenses in summary cause/small claims
procedures. The Courts Reform (Scotland) Act 2014 provides an exception to
the expenses cap in cases where the respondent, 'having stated a defence, has
not proceeded with it'.[13]

25.12   The question therefore arises, as it did with summary cause/small claims
procedure, 'when can it reasonably be said that a defence has not proceeded?'
The question often arises when a claim is settled or when a tender is accepted.

25.13   In summary cause/small claims procedure, the cases of *Gilmour v Paterson*;
Glover v Deighan; *Fenton v Uniroyal Englebert Tyres Ltd*; *Tallo v Clark*; *Hamilton
v Sullivan*; *and Semple v Black* provide decisions in relation to whether settlement of a claim, prior to the evidential hearing, justifies removal of the cap on
expenses. With some exceptions, the trend was to hold that this constitutes
not proceeding with a defence and therefore the cap should not apply.[14]

---

9 Sheriff Court Simple Procedure (Limits on Award of Expenses) Order 2016 arts 2–4.
10 *Gowans v Miller* 2018 SLT (Sh Ct) 11.
11 *Martin v Southern Rock Insurance Company Ltd* [2018] SC EDIN 10.
12 SPR r. 14.2(1)(a).
13 Courts Reform (Scotland) Act 2014 s. 81(5)(a)(ii).
14 *Gilmour v Paterson* 1992 SLT 10, *Glover v Deighan* 1992 SLT 88, *Fenton v Uniroyal Englebert
    Tyres Ltd* 1995 SLT 21, *Tallo v Clark* 2015 S.L.T 181 but see also *Hamilton v Sullivan* 1993
    SCLR 969 and *Semple v Black* 2000 SCLR 1098.

There have been three simple procedure cases at the time of writing that **25.14**
have considered this issue. In all three cases quantum was at issue and settlement was achieved before any hearing on evidence took place.

In the case of *Graham v Farrell*,[15] a tender was accepted in the sum of **25.15**
£3,000. It was argued by the respondent that the cap should apply and
that the acceptance of a tender was not necessarily a failure to proceed with
the defence. The Sheriff in Edinburgh preferred the reasoning outlined in
the case of *Tallo v Clark*, a decision of the Sheriff Principal for Lothian and
Borders, which had been determined in a small claims action. He followed
Tallo when stating '[i]n my opinion, the meaning of ["has not proceeded with
a defence"] was definitively determined in Tallo to mean " ... not proceeding
with the hearing on evidence and obtaining a decision or judgement of the
court".'

However, in the case of *Davis v Skyfire Insurance*[16] the Summary Sheriff in **25.16**
Edinburgh held: (1) that while *Tallo* and *Graham* were not strictly binding
(presumably because they were decisions in small claim cases) *Semple v Black*
and *Glover v Deighan*, together with *Tallo*, were all Sheriff Principal appeal
cases with so small a difference in procedure that they had to be highly per-
suasive; (2) that there was no difference in statutory interpretation whether
the defence was to liability or quantum or both: the respondent had therefore
stated a defence and not proceeded with it, and the cap on expenses in s. 81 of
the Courts Reform (Scotland) Act 2014 did not apply but it could not make
sense, applying the principles of simple procedure, to punish a party who
avoided a hearing and ultimately was at least partially, if not wholly, successful
in a defence and who negotiated a settlement without taking up court and parties' time and resources with a hearing; the difference in the award of expenses
between the cap, namely £170, and the likely assessed expenses, perhaps in
advance of £2,000, meant that punishment, if the claimant was right in this
argument, was excessive and did nothing to encourage negotiation throughout
the progress of the case; (3) that while the Summary Sheriff was bound by the
strict interpretation of s. 81(5)(a)(ii) in terms of the case law and statutory
interpretation, and in a position that Chapter V had to be applied, there was a
discretion in terms of arts 3A and 5 of the Act of Sederunt (Fees of Solicitors
in the Sheriff Court) (Amendment and Further Provisions) 1993[17] and the
award of expenses was also an equitable matter. It was noted that the sum
sued for was in excess of £3,000. By the eve of the hearing the respondents
had successfully persuaded the claimant that the sum sued for was excessive
and the eventual settlement was lower than any counter offer made thereby,
there could be little difference between the costs incurred by the parties in
preparing their cases, and applying the principles of simple procedure to the
question of discretion in respect of expenses, the award of assessed expenses
would be contrary to the Sheriff's duties set out in SPR r. 1.4. Expenses were
therefore awarded to the claimant in the sum of £170, as if it had been a
capped expenses case.

---

15 *Graham v Farrell* 2018 Rep. L.R. 36.
16 *Davis v Skyfire Insurance* 2019 SLT (Sh Ct) 272.
17 Act of Sederunt (Fees of Solicitors in the Sheriff Court) (Amendment and Further Provisions)
    1993 (SI 1993/3080).

25.17   The third case is *McKinlay v Aviva Insurance Ltd*[18] a decision of the Sheriff in Falkirk, where the court held:

(1) that the claimant having settled the case for a sum well below that originally claimed (settlement of £1,200 compared to a sum claimed of almost £3,700), was clearly indicative of the fact that the respondent had proceeded with his defence, and the cap on expenses should not be removed; and

(2) that even if this view was wrong, the court had a discretion in relation to the question of expenses, which followed from the principles of simple procedure actions that were to encourage parties to settle their disputes by negotiation. An interpretation of the rules that led to the result that a negotiated settlement by a respondent would always result in an award of uncapped expenses would be completely counter to that principle. An award of capped expenses would therefore also have been made by applying that discretion. Capped expenses of £284 were awarded to the claimant.

It was observed by the Sheriff that if liability is disputed, i.e. the line being taken by the defender is 'I'm not paying anything' in the lead up to any settlement, or if the agreed settlement is very close to the sum sued for, the position may well be different and the court may take the view the caps should not apply.

Exceptions due to complexity

25.18 If a difficult question of law or a question of fact of exceptional complexity is involved a party may apply to the court for an order that the normal rules for no awards of expenses or capped expenses do not apply to the case.[19] This will be determined having regard to the specific circumstances of the case.

SCALES OF FEES WHERE NO CAPS APPLY

Cases commenced pre-29 April 2019

25.19 Claims raised prior to 29 April 2019 are regulated by Chapter V of the Act of Sederunt (Fees of Solicitors in the Sheriff Court) (Amendment and Further Provisions) 1993 (as amended). Chapter V is split into two parts. Part one deals with admitted claims and part two deals with disputed claims. In admitted claims, an inclusive fee for all work is prescribed. A further small fee can be claimed if reservice of the claim form is required. A table of fees sets out what can be charged in a disputed claim and, if necessary, will be assessed by the auditor of court at a diet of assessment.

25.20   Unless the Sheriff orders otherwise[20]:

---

18 *McKinlay v Aviva Insurance Ltd* 2021 Rep. L.R. 95.
19 Courts Reform (Scotland) Act 2014 s. 81(6) and (7).
20 Act of Sederunt (Fees of Solicitors in the Sheriff Court) (Amendment and Further Provisions) 1993 Sch. 1 para. 3A.

(1) there will be no award if the value of the claim is less than or equal to £300 (£200 if the case was raised prior to 1 April 2019)[21];

(2) where the total value of the claim is £1,000 or less, those expenses must be reduced by 50 per cent; and

(3) where the total value of the claim is more than £1,000 and not more than £2,500, those expenses must be reduced by 25 per cent.

Cases commenced on or after 29 April 2019

Cases commenced after 29 April 2019 are subject to the fees prescribed by Sch. 5 of the Act of Sederunt (Taxation of Judicial Expenses Rules) 2019.[22] This provides fees for both admitted and disputed claims and the charges are based on multiples of the unit (currently valued at £16.40 as at November 2021) for each work item listed. **25.21**

Rule 3.7 of the 2019 Rules provides:

3.7.—(1) This rule applies where an account of expenses falls to be taxed by reference to a table of charges in schedule 5.

(2) All charges allowed by the Auditor are to be reduced by 10%.

(3) Unless the court otherwise directs, where the total value of the claim is £2500 or less, all charges allowed by the Auditor, as reduced in accordance with paragraph (2), are to be further reduced—

    (a) where the total value of the claim is less than £1000, by 50%;

    (b) otherwise by 25%.

In summary: **25.22**

(1) Precedent exists from cases decided by Sheriffs Principal, in small claim cases, to the effect that settlement of an action prior to an evidential hearing will lead to the court holding that a defence has not been proceeded with and therefore lead to a disapplication of the caps.

(2) The precedent in small claims cases has been followed in one simple procedure case but distinguished in two others. The latest decisions suggest that the courts will look at the specific circumstances of the case in reaching a decision as to whether to apply the caps or not. A discretion exists that permits the court to apply the caps in cases that do not proceed to an evidential hearing. Factors such as whether the only issue in dispute was quantum and the value of any settlement relative to the sum sued for have been held to be relevant considerations in determining whether the discretion should be exercised in applying the caps.

(3) Other exceptions relating to a party's conduct apply that would result in the caps being disapplied namely where no defence is stated at all or where any party has behaved unreasonably in relation to the case. The court in the former scenario will require to assess the nature of the defence being advanced to determine whether it could be construed as constituting a partial or complete defence or no defence at all and in the latter scenario whether the conduct is such as to justify a finding that the caps should be disapplied.

---

21 The Sheriff Court Simple Procedure (Limits on Award of Expenses) Order 2016 art. 2 as amended by art. 2 of the Sheriff Court Simple Procedure (Limits on Award of Expenses) Amendment Order 2019.

22 Act of Sederunt (Taxation of Judicial Expenses Rules) 2019 r. 3.3(4).

(4) There are no caps in a case where the value of the claim exceeds £3,000. The value is based on what is agreed by way of settlement or the sum that the court finds the claimant entitled to, not the sum sued for.

(5) A distinction should be noted between art. 3 of the Sheriff Court Simple Procedure (Limits on Award of Expenses) Order 2016 order where expenses are capped at 10 per cent of the value of the claim and r. 3.7 of the Act of Sederunt (Taxation of Judicial Expenses Rules) 2019 that applies where expenses have not been capped but instead have been assessed by the auditor of court.

Chapter 26

Miscellaneous Expenses Issues

CURATOR AD LITEM'S CHARGES

Where a *curator ad litem* is appointed on behalf of a pursuer, the remuneration **26.01** of the *curator ad litem* can be properly included in the judicial account of expenses as an expense of process.[1] The *curator ad litem* is entitled to receive professional remuneration for examining and superintending the proceedings.

A *curator ad litem* cannot be made personally liable to any opponent for **26.02** expenses and is invariably entitled to an award of expenses even though he is unsuccessful. The recovery of the curator's charges will be made on a complete indemnity basis from any source available.[2]

A curator's appointment commences following a motion being granted by **26.03** the court to appoint the curator and the administration of the oath *de fideli administratione officii.*

RESTORATION OF COMPANY TO THE REGISTER

It is often necessary for the pursuer's agent, in an action for damages, to restore **26.04** a defender company to the Companies Register. It should be noted that the cost of the restoration proceedings is not a proper expense within the damages action. It is necessary for a separate judicial account of expenses to be prepared in respect of the recovery process and for that account to be incorporated within the pursuer's claim as a separate head of claim. It follows that the author of the account in the restoration process would then be a witness on behalf of the pursuer at proof should it not be possible to agree the restoration costs.

EXPENSES AWARDS AND ROAD TRAFFIC ACT INSURERS:

Lisa Clarke v Robert Keenan,[3] involves a decision of Sheriff Braid in the All- **26.05** Scotland Personal Injury Court (ASPIC). This is an unusual case where the defender had not entered the process but his insurers, Sky Fire Insurance

---

1 *Campbell v Alexander & Sons Ltd* 1934 SLT 52.
2 Hastings, *Expenses in the Supreme and Sheriff Courts of Scotland* (Edinburgh: W. Green, 1989) p. 125, para. 12; *Dunlop v Brown* (1903) 11 SLT 522.
3 *Lisa Clarke v Robert Keenan* [2019] SC EDIN 74.

Company, had entered the process as party minuters. They had refused to indemnify the defender. However, they had the writ intimated to them under s. 151 of the Road Traffic Act 1988, which they believed would require them to satisfy any judgment against the defender.

26.06 The pursuer had moved the court to grant decree in absence against the defender for a sum just over £5,000 together with expenses as taxed, including certification of a skilled person and dismissal in favour of the party minuters with no expenses due to or by them. However, there was no crave against the party minuters and therefore the action could not be dismissed against them.

26.07 It was recognised that it was commonplace for insurers in these circumstances to become party minuters to an action and for them to effectively take over the negotiations and resolution of the claim. It was acknowledged that all the party minuters were seeking to achieve was the right to go against the defender to recover whatever they had to pay to the pursuer.

26.08 There seemed to be no doubt that the intervention of the party minuters was beneficial to the swift resolution of the action and had the effect of reducing the amount that had to be paid to the pursuer.

26.09 Sheriff Braid's concerns were whether it was competent for a Scottish court to make an award of the whole expenses of process against a party, in this case the defender, who had not entered the process and who had in no way contributed to the expenses incurred apart from the expenses of an undefended action.

26.10 The principle is that an unsuccessful party is liable in expenses only for the expenditure that they have caused to the successful party. In the case in question, that extended only to the raising of the action and the taking of the decree in absence. He therefore held that it was not competent for him to make the expenses award that was sought.

PROTECTIVE EXPENSES ORDERS IN ENVIRONMENTAL APPEALS AND JUDICIAL REVIEWS

26.11 Special rules exist in the Court of Session that can afford a level of protection against adverse costs in environmental appeals and judicial reviews if certain conditions are met. The position is regulated by the Act of Sederunt (Rules of the Court of Session 1994) 1994 (RCS) r. 58A, which provides:

CHAPTER 58A PROTECTIVE EXPENSES ORDERS IN ENVIRONMENTAL APPEALS AND JUDICIAL REVIEWS
Application and interpretation of this Chapter
58A.1—(1) This Chapter applies to applications for protective expenses orders in:
   (a) an appeal under section 56 of the Freedom of Information (Scotland) Act 2002 as modified by regulation 17 of the Environmental Information (Scotland) Regulations 2004;
   (b) relevant proceedings which include a challenge to a decision, act or omission which is subject to, or said to be subject to, the provisions of Article 6 of the Aarhus Convention;
   (c) relevant proceedings which include a challenge to an act or omission on the grounds that it contravenes the law relating to the environment.
(2) In this Chapter:
"the Aarhus Convention" means the United Nations Economic Commission for Europe Convention on Access to Information, Public Participation in

Decision-Making and Access to Justice in Environmental Matters done at Aarhus, Denmark on 25th June 1998;

"protective expenses order" means an order which regulates the liability for expenses in the proceedings, including as to the future, of all or any of the parties to them;

"the public" and "the public concerned" have the meanings given by Article 2 of the Aarhus Convention;

"relevant proceedings" means— (a) applications to the supervisory jurisdiction of the court, including applications under section 45(b) (specific performance of a statutory duty) of the Act of 1988; (b) appeals under statute.

(3) Proceedings are to be considered prohibitively expensive for the purpose of this Chapter if the costs and expenses likely to be incurred by the applicant for a protective expenses order:
   (a) exceed the financial means of the applicant; or
   (b) are objectively unreasonable having regard to:
       (i)   the situation of the parties;
       (ii) whether the applicant has reasonable prospects of success;
       (iii) the importance of what is at stake for the applicant;
       (iv) the importance of what is at stake for the environment;
       (v)   the complexity of the relevant law and procedure; and
       (vi) whether the case is frivolous.

(4) The costs and expenses mentioned in paragraph (3) are:
   (a) the costs incurred by the applicant in conducting the proceedings; and
   (b) the expenses for which the applicant would be liable if the applicant was found liable for the taxed expenses of process, without modification.

Appeals relating to requests for environmental information
58A.2—(1) This rule applies to an application for a protective expenses order in proceedings mentioned in rule 58A.1(1)(a).
(2) Where the person who requested the environmental information is a party to the appeal, that person may apply for a protective expenses order.
(3) The application must be made, except on cause shown:
   (a) where the applicant is the appellant, no later than is reasonably practicable after the applicant becomes aware that the appeal is defended;
   (b) where the applicant is the respondent, no later than the expiry of the period allowed for the lodging of answers.
(4) Where the court is satisfied that the proceedings are prohibitively expensive, it must make a protective expenses order.

Public participation in decisions on specific environmental activities
58A.3—(1) This rule applies to an application for a protective expenses order in proceedings mentioned in rule 58A.1(1)(b).
(2) An application for a protective expenses order may be made by the petitioner or the appellant.
(3) The application must be made, except on cause shown, no later than is reasonably practicable after the applicant becomes aware that the petition or appeal is defended.
(4) The court must make a protective expenses order where it is satisfied that:
   (a) the applicant is a member of the public concerned;
   (b) the applicant has a sufficient interest in the subject matter of the proceedings; and
   (c) the proceedings are prohibitively expensive.

Contravention of the law relating to the environment
58A.4—(1) This rule applies to an application for a protective expenses order in proceedings mentioned in rule 58A.1(1)(c).

(2) An application for a protective expenses order may be made by the petitioner or the appellant.

(3) The application must be made, except on cause shown, no later than is reasonably practicable after the applicant becomes aware that the petition or appeal is defended.

(4) The court must make a protective expenses order where it is satisfied that:
   (a) the applicant is a member of the public; and
   (b) the proceedings are prohibitively expensive.

Applications for protective expenses orders

58A.5—(1) A protective expenses order is applied for by motion.

(2) Intimation of the motion and of the documents mentioned in paragraph (3) must be given to every other party not less than 14 days before the date of enrolment.

(3) The applicant must lodge with the motion:
   (a) a statement setting out:
       (i)   the grounds for seeking the order;
       (ii) the terms on which the applicant is represented;
       (iii) an estimate of the expenses that the applicant will incur in relation to the proceedings;
       (iv) an estimate of the expenses of each other party for which the applicant may be liable in relation to the proceedings; and
       (v)   in the case of an application for liability in expenses to be limited to an amount lower or, as the case may be, higher than a sum mentioned in rule 58A.7(1), the grounds on which the lower or higher amount is applied for; and
   (b) any documents or other materials on which the applicant seeks to rely.

(4) A party opposing an application for a protective expenses order must lodge with the notice of opposition:
   (a) a statement setting out the grounds for opposing the application; and
   (b) any documents or other materials on which the party seeks to rely.

Determination of applications

58A.6—(1) Unless the Lord Ordinary or, as the case may be, the procedural judge otherwise directs:
   (a) an application for a protective expenses order is to be determined in chambers without appearance;
   (b) the motion is not to be starred; and
   (c) rule 23.4(6) (opposition to motions) is disapplied.

(2) Unless granting an unopposed application, the Lord Ordinary or, as the case may be, the procedural judge must give brief reasons in writing.

Terms of protective expenses orders

58A.7—(1) A protective expenses order must:
   (a) limit the applicant's liability in expenses to the respondent to the sum of £5,000, or such other sum as may be justified on cause shown; and
   (b) limit the respondent's liability in expenses to the applicant to the sum of £30,000, or such other sum as may be justified on cause shown.

(2) Where the applicant is the respondent in proceedings mentioned in rule 58A.1(1)(a):
   (a) paragraph (1)(a) applies as if the reference to the applicant's liability in expenses to the respondent was a reference to the applicant's liability in expenses to the appellant; and
   (b) paragraph (1)(b) applies as if the reference to the respondent's liability in expenses to the applicant was a reference to the appellant's liability in expenses to the applicant.

(3) In paragraph (1), "the respondent" means—
    (a) all parties that lodge answers in an application to the supervisory jurisdiction of the court; and
    (b) all respondents in an appeal under statute.

Expenses protection in reclaiming motions

58A.8—(1) Paragraph (2) applies where:
    (a) the court has made a protective expenses order in relation to proceedings in the Outer House; and
    (b) a decision of the Lord Ordinary is reclaimed at the instance of a party whose liability in expenses is limited in accordance with rule 58A.7(1)(b).
(2) Subject to any review of the protective expenses order by the Inner House, the limits on the parties' liability in expenses set by the order include liability for expenses occasioned by the reclaiming motion.
(3) Paragraphs (4) and (5) apply for the purposes of any other reclaiming motion from a decision of the Lord Ordinary in proceedings mentioned in rule 58A.1(1)(b) or (c).
(4) A party who would have been entitled to apply for a protective expenses order in the Outer House proceedings (whether or not the party did so apply) may apply for a protective expenses order in relation to the reclaiming motion in which event rule 58A.3(4) or, as the case may be, rule 58A.4(4) applies to the application.
(5) The application must be made, except on cause shown, no later than is reasonably practicable after the reclaiming motion has been marked.

Expenses of application

58A.9—(1) Paragraph (2) applies where, in proceedings in which an application for a protective expenses order has been refused:
    (a) the applicant is found liable for payment of expenses; and
    (b) the expenses for which the applicant has been found liable comprise or include the expenses occasioned by the application.
(2) On the motion of the applicant the court must, other than on exceptional cause shown, limit the applicant's total liability in expenses, in so far as occasioned by the application, to the sum of £500.

26.12 The requirement to be directly and individually concerned, which was a requirement of the Aarhus Convention, was removed on 28 October 2021 as a result of EU Regulation 2021/1767 coming into force.

CASE LAW

26.13 The following are two cases where issues relevant to the granting of protective expenses orders have been considered:

R. (on the application of Edwards) v Environment Agency[4]

26.14 The court held:

(1) that the assessment of whether the costs of judicial proceedings were 'prohibitively expensive' within the meaning of art. 10a of Council Directive 85/337/EEC and art. 15a of Council Directive 96/61/EC was not a matter

4 Decision of European Court of Justice Fourth Chamber C-260/11.

for national law alone; that account should be taken of the objective of European Union law to preserve, protect and improve the quality of the environment and to ensure that, to that end, the public played an active role and had wide access to justice; that members of the public covered by the requirement that judicial proceedings should not be prohibitively expensive should not be prevented from seeking, or pursuing a claim for, a review by the courts of an environmental decision by reason of the financial burden that might arise as a result; that where a national court was called upon to make a costs order against a member of the public who was an unsuccessful claimant in an environmental dispute or, more generally, where it was required to state its views, at an earlier stage of proceedings, on the possible capping of the costs for which the unsuccessful party might be liable, it had to satisfy itself that that requirement had been complied with, taking into account both the interest of the person wishing to defend their rights and the public interest in the protection of the environment.

(2) That, where the national court was required to determine whether judicial proceedings in environmental matters were prohibitively expensive for a claimant within the meaning of art. 10a of Council Directive 85/337/EEC and art. 15a of Council Directive 96/61/EC, it could not act solely on the basis of that claimant's financial situation but had also to carry out an objective analysis of the amount of costs, particularly since members of the public and associations were required to play an active role in protecting the environment; that, therefore, the costs of proceedings had neither to exceed the financial resources of the claimant nor to appear to be objectively unreasonable; that the court could also take into account the situation of the parties concerned, whether the claimant had a reasonable prospect of success, the importance of what was at stake for the claimant and for the protection of the environment, the complexity of the relevant law and procedure, the potentially frivolous nature of the claim at its various stages, and the existence of a national legal aid scheme or a costs protection regime; that, moreover, the fact that the claimant had not been deterred, in practice, from asserting their claim was not in itself sufficient to establish that the proceedings were not prohibitively expensive for them; and that the assessment could not be conducted according to different criteria depending on whether it was carried out at the conclusion of first instance proceedings, an appeal or a second appeal.

Carroll v Scottish Borders Council[5]

26.15 A homeowner appealed against a decision of the local planning authority granting planning permission to the owners of a nearby site, as an interested party, for the erection of two wind turbines. The appellant also enrolled a motion for a protective expenses order in terms of RCS r. 58A, which failing at common law, to limit her potential liability in expenses to the respondent and the interested party to a cumulative total of £5,000 and to limit the respondent and the interested party's liability in expenses to the appellant to £30,000. The latter two parts of the motion were not opposed and the motion for a protective expenses order was determined.

5 *Carroll v Scottish Borders Council* 2014 SLT 659.

'Held, (1) that for the purposes of the order, the respondent and the interested party had to be taken together so that the appellant's liability was limited to a cumulative total of £5,000 to both, correspondingly, the limit of £30,000 on the liability incurred to the appellant should relate to both the respondent and the interested party; (2) that the application for a protective expenses order should be treated as a separate hearing for the purposes of expenses accordingly, the respondent and the interested party were liable to the appellant in the expenses of the hearing, which would not form part of the £30,000 limit placed on their liability to her, as that sum was clearly designed to relate to the expenses of the substantive challenge to the planning decision; (3) that a protective expenses order under r.58A was justified: the appellant clearly had an interest in the subject matter of the proceedings and it could not be said that the proceedings had no real prospect of success, and the court had been provided with adequate financial information about the appellant's resources and an apparently realistic estimate of the expenses of the litigation, from which it could be concluded that without the order the proceedings would be prohibitively expensive for the appellant; The protective expenses order was pronounced.

The court observed: 26.16

(1) that the words in parentheses in the text of the opening part of RCS r. 58A.5(1), namely 'subject to rule 58A.3(1)', did not appear to make sense and had to be a drafting error, and the words 'rule 58A.4' should be substituted as that was clearly what had been intended;

(2) that it was clear that RCS r. 58A had to be interpreted according to its own terms, in light of Directive 2011/92 and European Court of Justice cases dealing with the requirements of the directive, and it also had to be given an interpretation that was both purposive and contextual;

(3) that four particular features were of importance in determining whether an order under RCS r. 58A should be made:
  (i) the person seeking the order had to establish that the intended proceedings fell within the scope of the rule and the proceedings had to be subject to the public participation provisions of the relevant Directive;
  (ii) the applicant had to demonstrate that they had a sufficient interest in the proposed proceedings;
  (iii) an order could not be made if the court considered that the proposed proceedings had no real prospect of success; and
  (iv) the court had to consider the likely expenses of the proposed proceedings and the applicant's financial resources, with a wholly objective approach to be adopted in respect of the former, and a partly subjective and partly objective approach in relation to the latter;

(4) that where there might be a number of persons wishing to challenge a proposed development, the normal approach would be to treat each of them as a separate applicant for the purposes of the liability limit in RCS r. 58A.4(1);

(5) the test of a 'real prospect of success' was a low hurdle, consequently, if one or more of the standard grounds of judicial review appeared *prima facie* to be stateable, that should suffice.

The court offered the following opinion: 26.17

(1) that the financial limits specified in RCS r. 58A could be varied, however, the figures selected appeared to have been chosen to represent a realistic amount in a 'standard environmental' case;

(2) that RCS r. 58A.3(4) gave a general indication of the documents required in an application for a general expenses order, and those lodged by the appellant were sufficient to determine the application, and it was to be envisaged that similar documents would be lodged in any future application.

COURT OF SESSION AND SHERIFF COURT FEES ORDERS

26.18   Unless exempt from paying lodging dues, a fee is payable to Scottish Courts and Tribunal Service (SCTS) for most forms of interaction with the courts such as lodging writs and motions, citing a jury, etc. A party is exempt from paying the court dues if they are in receipt of certain types of benefits, in receipt of civil legal aid or the work is covered under legal aid special urgency provisions or where a principal remedy is a specified form of interdict or an exclusion order. An exemption form can be downloaded from the SCTS website.

26.19   A fee exemption cannot be applied for if the party is:

- making an application in relation to commissary proceedings (dealing with a deceased person's estate) unless the estate of the deceased person is exempt from inheritance tax by virtue of s. 153A (death of emergency service personnel, etc.), s. 154 (death in active service, etc.) or s. 155A (death of constables and service personnel targeted because of their status) of the Inheritance Tax Act 1984 in which case there will be no fee in respect of the inventory of that estate; and
- lodging a petition for removal of disqualification from driving under the Road Traffic Offenders Act 1988.

26.20   Fees orders for the Court of Session, Sheriff Appeal Court and Sheriff Court, including the ASPIC can be found on the SCTS website.

26.21   Solicitors will normally have a fee charging account with SCTS and will be billed in arrears on a monthly basis. Party litigants can pay by debit card, cheque, postal order or cash. The clerks of court will refuse to accept the document being lodged if the fee is not paid or an exemption form is not lodged.

26.22   The fees paid to the court are treated as outlays and are recoverable from an opponent in a judicial account unless the fees have been paid in error, e.g. for a legally aided party. In that situation, SCTS will reimburse the court dues on production of an exemption form.

Appendices

Appendix 1

Legislation and Protocols

COURTS REFORM (SCOTLAND) ACT 2014

(ASP 18)

Simple procedure

72.—(1) For the purposes of the procedure and practice in civil proceedings in the sheriff court, there is to be a form of procedure to be known as "simple procedure".

(2) Subject to the provisions of this Part, further provision about simple procedure is to be made by act of sederunt under section 104(1).

(3) The following types of proceedings may only be brought subject to simple procedure (and no other types of proceedings may be so brought:

(a) proceedings for payment of a sum of money not exceeding £5,000,

(b) actions of multiplepoinding where the value of the fund or property that is the subject of the action does not exceed £5,000,

(c) actions of furthcoming where the value of the arrested fund or subject does not exceed £5,000,

(d) actions ad factum praestandum, other than actions in which there is claimed, in addition or as an alternative to a decree ad factum praestandum, a decree for payment of a sum of money exceeding £5,000,

(e) proceedings for the recovery of possession of heritable property or moveable property, other than proceedings in which there is claimed, in addition or as an alternative to a decree for such recovery, a decree for payment of a sum of money exceeding £5,000.

(4) Subsection (3) is subject to sections 78 (transfer of cases to simple procedure), 80 (transfer of cases from simple procedure) and 83 (transitional provision: summary cause).

(5) Subsection (3)(a) is subject to sections 73 and 74.

(6) The calculation of a sum for the time being mentioned in subsection (3) is to be determined in accordance with provision made by the Court of Session by act of sederunt.

(7) An act of sederunt under subsection (6) may make different provision for different purposes.

(8) An act of sederunt under section 104(1) may make provision for the purposes of this Act for determining whether proceedings are of a type mentioned in subsection (3).

(9) Proceedings that:

(a) are subject to simple procedure under subsection (3) or by virtue of any other enactment,

(b) are brought subject to simple procedure under section 74, or

(c) are continued subject to simple procedure by virtue of section 78 or 79, are referred to in this Part as a "simple procedure case".

(10) Subsection (9) is subject to section 80.

(11) References in subsection (3) to a sum of money is to that amount exclusive of interest and expenses.

(12) The Scottish Ministers may by order substitute for any sum for the time being specified in this section a different sum.

Proceedings in an all-Scotland sheriff court

73.—(1) Section 72(3), so far as requiring any relevant proceedings to be brought subject to simple procedure, does not apply to any such proceedings in an all-Scotland sheriff court, and no such proceedings may be brought or continued in such a court subject to simple procedure.

(2) Subsection (1) does not affect the application of section 72(3) in relation to any relevant proceedings brought in any other sheriff court.

(3) In this section, "relevant proceedings" means proceedings of a type mentioned in section 72(3)(a) so far as they are also of a type specified in an order under section 41(1).

Proceedings for aliment of small amounts under simple procedure

74.—(1) Subsection (2) applies to a claim for aliment only (whether or not expenses are also sought) under section 2 of the Family Law (Scotland) Act 1985 (actions for aliment).

(2) The claim may be brought subject to simple procedure if the aliment claimed does not exceed:

(a) in respect of a child under the age of 18 years, the sum of £100 per week, and

(b) in any other case, the sum of £200 per week.

(3) A provision such as is mentioned in subsection (4) does not apply in relation to a claim brought subject to simple procedure under subsection (2).

(4) The provision referred to in subsection (3) is provision in any enactment:

(a) limiting the jurisdiction of a sheriff in a simple procedure case by reference to any amount, or

(b) limiting the period for which a decree granted by a sheriff is to have effect. (5) The Scottish Ministers may by order substitute for any sum for the time being mentioned in subsection (2) a different sum.

1. Section 74 not yet in force.

Rule-making: matters to be taken into consideration

75. The power to make provision relating to simple procedure by act of sederunt under section 104(1) is to be exercised so far as possible with a view to ensuring that the sheriff before whom a simple procedure case is conducted

(a) is able to identify the issues in dispute,

(b) may facilitate negotiation between or among the parties with a view to securing a settlement,

(c) may otherwise assist the parties in reaching a settlement,

(d) can adopt a procedure that is appropriate to and takes account of the particular circumstances of the case.

Service of documents

76.—(1) An act of sederunt under section 104(1) may permit a party to a simple procedure case, in such circumstances as may be specified in the act, to require the sheriff clerk to effect service of any document relating to the case on behalf of the party.

(2) In subsection (1):

(a) the reference to a party to a simple procedure case includes a reference to a description of such a party as may be specified in an act of sederunt mentioned in that subsection, (b) the reference to any document relating to the case includes a reference to a description of any such document as may be so specified.

[1]Evidence in simple procedure cases

Partially In Force Version as of 28 November 2016

77.—(1) Any enactment or rule of law that prevents evidence being led on grounds of admissibility before a court of law does not apply in simple procedure cases.

(2) The evidence, if any, given in simple procedure cases is not to be recorded.

1. Section 77 partially in force as at 28 November 2016.

Transfer of cases to simple procedure

78.—(1) This section applies to any civil proceedings in the sheriff court that are being conducted otherwise than as a simple procedure case.

(2) The parties to the proceedings may, at any stage, make a joint application for the proceedings to continue subject to simple procedure if the proceedings are of a type that, if brought at the time when the application is made

(a) would or could be brought subject to simple procedure by virtue of any enactment, or

(b) would or could be so brought but for the fact that a financial limit specified in section 72(3) or 74(2) is exceeded.

(3) Where such a joint application is made, the sheriff must direct that the proceedings are to continue subject to simple procedure for all purposes (including appeal).

Proceedings in an all-Scotland sheriff court: transfer to simple procedure

79.—(1) This section applies to any relevant proceedings in an all-Scotland sheriff court.

(2) A party to the proceedings may, at any stage, make an application for the proceedings to continue subject to simple procedure in another sheriff court.

(3) Where such an application is made, the sheriff may, on special cause shown

(a) direct that the proceedings are to continue subject to simple procedure for all purposes (including appeal), and

(b) make an order transferring the proceedings to another sheriff court having jurisdiction in relation to the proceedings.

(4) Where a sheriff makes a direction under section 78(3) in relation to proceedings to which this section applies, the sheriff must make an order

transferring the proceedings to another sheriff court having jurisdiction in relation to the proceedings.

(5) In this section, "relevant proceedings" has the same meaning as in section 73.

¹Transfer of cases from simple procedure

80.—(1) A party to a simple procedure case may, at any stage, make an application for the case not to proceed subject to simple procedure.

(2) Where such an application is made, the sheriff may direct that the proceedings are no longer subject to simple procedure.

(3) Where a direction is made under subsection (2), the proceedings are to continue for all purposes (including appeal) subject to such procedure as would have been applicable to them had they not been subject to simple procedure.

1. Section 80 partially in force as at 28 November 2016.

¹Expenses in simple procedure cases

81.—(1) The Scottish Ministers may by order provide that
  (a) in such category of simple procedure cases as may be prescribed in the order, no award of expenses may be made,
  (b) in such other category of simple procedure cases as may be so prescribed, any expenses awarded may not exceed such sum as may be so prescribed.

(2) The categories of simple procedure cases mentioned in subsection (1) may be prescribed by reference to
  (a) the value of the claim in the cases,
  (b) the subject matter of the claim in the cases.

(3) Categories may be prescribed subject to specified exceptions.

(4) An order under subsection (1) does not apply
  (a) to simple procedure cases such as those mentioned in subsection (5), (b) in relation to an appeal to the Sheriff Appeal Court from any decision in a simple procedure case, or
  (c) to a simple procedure case in respect of which a direction under subsection (7) is made.

(5) The simple procedure cases referred to in subsection (4)(a) are those in which
  (a) the defender—
    (i) has not stated a defence,
    (ii) having stated a defence, has not proceeded with it, or
    (iii) having stated and proceeded with a defence, has not acted in good faith as to its merits, or
  (b) a party to the case has behaved in a manner which is manifestly unreasonable in relation to the case.

(6) Subsection (7) applies where the sheriff in a simple procedure case is of the opinion that a difficult question of law, or a question of fact of exceptional complexity, is involved.

(7) The sheriff may, at any stage, on the application of any party to the case, direct that an order under subsection (1) is not to apply in relation to the case.

1. Section 81 partially in force as at 30 June 2021.

¹Appeals from simple procedure cases

82.—(1) An appeal may be taken to the Sheriff Appeal Court under section 110 on a point of law only against a decision of the sheriff constituting final judgment in a simple procedure case.

(2) Any other decision of the sheriff in such a case is not subject to review.

Section 83 Transitional provision: summary causes Not Yet In Force - Date to be appointed

(a) Any reference, however expressed, in a pre-commencement enactment to proceedings being subject to summary cause procedure is, on and after the coming into force of this section, to be construed as a reference to proceedings being subject to simple procedure.

(b) Accordingly, any reference to proceedings being taken by way of summary cause is to be construed as a reference to proceedings being subject to simple procedure.

(c) In subsection (1), "pre-commencement enactment" means any enactment passed or made before this section comes into force.

1. Section 83 partially in force as at 28 November 2016.

[...]

Key defined terms

95.—(1) This section applies for the purposes of the interpretation of this Chapter.

(2) "Non-natural person" means

(a) a company (whether incorporated in the United Kingdom or elsewhere),

(b) a limited liability partnership,

(c) any other partnership,

(d) an unincorporated association of persons.

(3) "Lay representative" means an individual who is not a legal representative.

(4) "Legal representative" means:

(a) a solicitor,

(b) an advocate, or

(c) a person having a right to conduct litigation, or a right of audience, by virtue of section 27 of the Law Reform (Miscellaneous Provisions) (Scotland) Act 1990.

(5) An individual holds a relevant position with a non-natural person if the individual

(a) in the case of a company, is a director or secretary of the company,

(b) in the case of a limited liability partnership, is a member of the partnership,

(c) in the case of any other partnership, is a partner in the partnership,

(d) in the case of an unincorporated association, is a member or office holder of the association.

(6) For the purposes of section 96, an individual also holds a relevant position with a nonnatural person if the individual is an employee of the non-natural person.

(7) References to conducting proceedings are references to exercising, in relation to the proceedings, a function or right (including a right of audience) that a legal representative could exercise in the proceedings.

Lay representation in simple procedure cases

96.—(1) This section applies in any simple procedure case to which a non-natural person is a party.

(2) A lay representative may conduct proceedings in the case on behalf of the non-natural person if

(a) the lay representative holds a relevant position with the non-natural person,

(b) the responsibilities of the lay representative in that position do not consist wholly or mainly of conducting legal proceedings on behalf of the non-natural person or another person,

(c) the lay representative is authorised by the non-natural person to conduct the proceedings,

(d) the lay representative does not have a personal interest in the subject matter of the proceedings, and

(e) the lay representative is not the subject of an order such as is mentioned in section 98(2)(f).

(3) In subsection (2)(d), "personal interest" means an interest other than one that anyone holding the position that the lay representative holds with the non-natural person would have.

(4) Subsection (2) is subject to provision made by an act of sederunt under section 98.

1. Section 96 partially in force as at 28 November 2016.

¹Lay representation in other proceedings

97.—(1) This section applies in civil proceedings (other than a simple procedure case) to which a non-natural person is a party.

(2) A lay representative may, if the court grants permission, conduct the proceedings on behalf of the non-natural person.

(3) The court may grant permission if satisfied that

(a) the non-natural person is unable to pay for the services of a legal representative to conduct the proceedings,

(b) the lay representative is a suitable person to conduct the proceedings, and

(c) it is in the interests of justice to grant permission.

(4) For the purposes of subsection (3)(b), a lay representative is a suitable person to conduct the proceedings if

(a) the lay representative holds a relevant position with the non-natural person,

(b) the responsibilities of the lay representative in that position do not consist wholly or mainly of conducting legal proceedings on behalf of the non-natural person or another person,

(c) the lay representative is authorised by the non-natural person to conduct the proceedings,

(d) the lay representative does not have a personal interest in the subject matter of the proceedings,

(e) the lay representative is not the subject of an order such as is mentioned in section 98(2)(f).

(5) In subsection (4)(d), "personal interest" means an interest other than one that anyone holding the position that the lay representative holds with the non-natural person would have.

(6) For the purposes of subsection (3)(c), in deciding whether it is in the interests of justice to grant permission, the court must have regard, in particular, to
  (a) the non-natural person's prospects of success in the proceedings, and
  (b) the likely complexity of the proceedings.
(7) Subsection (2) is subject to provision made by an act of sederunt under section 98.
(8) In this section— "civil proceedings" means civil proceedings in
  (a) the Court of Session,
  (b) the Sheriff Appeal Court, or
  (c) the sheriff court, "the court", in the case of proceedings in the sheriff court, means the sheriff.
1. Section 97 partially in force as at 28 November 2016.

Lay representation: supplementary provision
98.—(1) The Court of Session may, by act of sederunt, make further provision about
  (a) the granting of permission under section 97, and
  (b) the conduct of proceedings by lay representatives by virtue of this Chapter.
(2) Provision under subsection (1) may include, in particular, provision
  (a) about the procedure to be followed in considering applications for permission under section 97 (including provision for applications to be considered in chambers and without hearing the parties),
  (b) regulating the conduct of lay representatives in exercising a function or right by virtue of this Chapter,
  (c) about the authorisation of lay representatives for the purposes of this Chapter,
  (d) imposing conditions on the exercise by lay representatives of a function or right by virtue of this Chapter or enabling the court to impose such conditions in particular cases,
  (e) enabling the court, in particular cases, to withdraw a lay representative's right to exercise a function or right by virtue of this Chapter if the representative contravenes provision made by virtue of the act of sederunt,
  (f) enabling the court to make an order preventing a lay representative from conducting any proceedings before any court on behalf of non-natural persons,
  (g) enabling the court, in awarding expenses against a non-natural person in any case, to find a lay representative jointly and severally liable for the expenses.
(3) An act of sederunt under subsection (1) may make different provision for different purposes.
(4) In this section, "the court", in the case of proceedings in the sheriff court, means the sheriff.
  [...]

Vexatious litigation orders
100.—(1) The Inner House may, on the application of the Lord Advocate, make a vexatious litigation order in relation to a person (a "vexatious litigant").

(2) A vexatious litigation order is an order which has either or both of the following effects

    (a) the vexatious litigant may institute civil proceedings only with the permission of a judge of the Outer House,

    (b) the vexatious litigant may take a specified step in specified ongoing civil proceedings only with such permission.

(3) In subsection (2)(b)

    (a) "specified ongoing civil proceedings" means civil proceedings which

        (i) were instituted by the vexatious litigant before the order was made, and

        (ii) are specified in the order,

    (b) "specified step" means a step specified in the order.

(4) A vexatious litigation order has effect

    (a) during such period as is specified in the order, or

    (b) if no period is so specified, indefinitely.

(5) In this section and section 101

    (a) "the Inner House" means the Inner House of the Court of Session,

    (b) "the Outer House" means the Outer House of the Court of Session,

    (c) "vexatious litigant" means, in relation to a vexatious litigation order, the person to whom the order relates,

    (d) "vexatious litigation order" means an order made under subsection (1).

Vexatious litigation orders: further provision Law In Force 28 November 2016

101.—(1) The Inner House may make a vexatious litigation order in relation to a person only if satisfied that the person has habitually and persistently, without any reasonable ground for doing so

    (a) instituted vexatious civil proceedings, or

    (b) made vexatious applications to the court in the course of civil proceedings (whether or not instituted by the person).

(2) For the purpose of subsection (1), it does not matter whether the proceedings

    (a) were instituted in Scotland or elsewhere,

    (b) involved the same parties or different parties.

(3) A copy of a vexatious litigation order must be published in the Edinburgh Gazette.

(4) A judge of the Outer House may grant permission to a vexatious litigant to institute civil proceedings or, as the case may be, to take a step in such proceedings only if satisfied that there is a reasonable ground for the proceedings or the taking of the step.

(5) The decision of the judge to refuse to grant permission under subsection (4) is final.

(6) Subsection (7) applies in relation to civil proceedings instituted in any court by a vexatious litigant before the Inner House makes a vexatious litigation order in relation to the vexatious litigant.

(7) The court may make such order as it sees fit in consequence of the vexatious litigation order.

(8) In subsection (7), "the court" means
  (a) the court which is dealing with the proceedings,
  (b) in the case of proceedings in the sheriff court, the sheriff.

Vexatious litigation orders: further provision

102.—(1) The Scottish Ministers may by regulations confer on the Court of Session, a sheriff or the Sheriff Appeal Court the power to make an order of a kind mentioned in subsection (2) in relation to a person who has behaved in a vexatious manner in civil proceedings before the Court of Session, sheriff or, as the case may be, Sheriff Appeal Court.

(2) The order referred to in subsection (1) is an order that the person may do any of the following only with the permission of a court or a judge of any court
  (a) take such a step in those proceedings as is specified in the order,
  (b) take such a step as is so specified in such other civil proceedings (whether or not those proceedings are before the Court of Session, sheriff or, as the case may be, Sheriff Appeal Court) as are so specified,
  (c) institute civil proceedings in such a court as is so specified.

(3) For the purpose of subsection (1), a person behaves in a vexatious manner in civil proceedings if the person
  (a) institutes the proceedings and they are vexatious, or
  (b) makes a vexatious application in the course of the proceedings (whether or not they were instituted by the person).

(4) Regulations under subsection (1) may include provision for
  (a) an order to be made on the application of a party to the proceedings or on the Court's or, as the case may be, sheriff's own initiative,
  (b) circumstances in which the Court or sheriff may make an order, and the requirements as to permission which may be imposed in an order in those circumstances,
  (c) the factors which the Court or sheriff may take into account in deciding whether to make an order (including the person's behaviour in other civil proceedings, whether in Scotland or elsewhere),
  (d) the courts in relation to which an order may have effect,
  (e) the maximum period for which an order may have effect,
  (f) the effect of an order in any other respects.

(5) The Scottish Ministers must consult the Lord President of the Court of Session before making regulations under subsection (1).

(6) Regulations under subsection (1)
  (a) are subject to the negative procedure,
  (b) may make different provision for different purposes,
  (c) may make incidental, supplemental, consequential, transitional, transitory or saving provision.

  [...]

Power to regulate fees in the Court of Session

105.—(1) The Court of Session may, in relation to any proceedings in the Court (including any execution or diligence following such proceedings), by act of sederunt make provision for or about the fees of
  (a) solicitors,
  (b) messengers-at-arms,

    (c)   persons acting under the Execution of Diligence (Scotland) Act 1926,

    (d)   witnesses,

    (e)   shorthand writers,

    (f)   such other persons, or persons of such descriptions, as the Scottish Ministers may by order specify.

(2) An act of sederunt under subsection (1) may not make any provision for or about the fees that the Scottish Ministers may regulate under or by virtue of section 33 of the Legal Aid (Scotland) Act 1986 (fees and outlays of solicitors and counsel).

(3) An act of sederunt under subsection (1) and an order under subsection (1)(f) may make

    (a)   incidental, supplemental, consequential, transitional, transitory or saving provision,

    (b)   different provision for different purposes.

Power to regulate fees in the sheriff court and the Sheriff Appeal Court

106.—(1) The Court of Session may, in relation to civil proceedings in the sheriff court or the Sheriff Appeal Court (including any execution or diligence following such proceedings), by act of sederunt make provision for or about the fees of

    (a)   solicitors,

    (b)   sheriff officers,

    (c)   persons acting under the Execution of Diligence (Scotland) Act 1926,

    (d)   witnesses,

    (e)   shorthand writers,

    (f)   such other persons, or persons of such descriptions, as the Scottish Ministers may by order specify.

(2) An act of sederunt under subsection (1) may not make any provision for or about the fees that the Scottish Ministers may regulate under or by virtue of section 33 of the Legal Aid (Scotland) Act 1986 (fees and outlays of solicitors and counsel).

(3) An act of sederunt under subsection (1) may make

    (a)   incidental, supplemental, consequential, transitional, transitory or saving provision,

    (b)   different provision for different purposes.

(4) Before making an order under subsection (1)(f), the Scottish Ministers must consult the Lord President of the Court of Session.

(5) An act of sederunt under subsection (1) is subject to the negative procedure.

[...]

Sanction for counsel in the sheriff court and Sheriff Appeal Court

108.—(1) This section applies in civil proceedings in the sheriff court or the Sheriff Appeal Court where the court is deciding, for the purposes of any relevant expenses rule, whether to sanction the employment of counsel by a party for the purposes of the proceedings.

(2) The court must sanction the employment of counsel if the court considers, in all the circumstances of the case, that it is reasonable to do so.

(3) In considering that matter, the court must have regard to

(a) whether the proceedings are such as to merit the employment of counsel, having particular regard to
  (i) the difficulty or complexity, or likely difficulty or complexity, of the proceedings,
  (ii) the importance or value of any claim in the proceedings, and
(b) the desirability of ensuring that no party gains an unfair advantage by virtue of the employment of counsel.

(4) The court may have regard to such other matters as it considers appropriate.

(5) References in this section to proceedings include references to any part or aspect of the proceedings.

(6) In this section

"counsel" means

(a) an advocate,
(b) a solicitor having a right of audience in the Court of Session under section 25A of the Solicitors (Scotland) Act 1980,

"court", in relation to proceedings in the sheriff court, means the sheriff,

"relevant expenses rule" means, in relation to any proceedings mentioned in subsection (1), any provision of an act of sederunt requiring, or having the effect of requiring, that the employment of counsel by a party for the purposes of the proceedings be sanctioned by the court before the fees of counsel are allowable as expenses that may be awarded to the party.

(7) This section is subject to an act of sederunt under section 104(1) or 106(1).

SCOTTISH STATUTORY INSTRUMENTS

2016 No. 215

SHERIFF COURT

Act of Sederunt (Sheriff Court Rules Amendment) (Personal Injury Pre-Action Protocol) 2016

Made - - - -	*20th July 2016*
Laid before the Scottish Parliament	*22nd July 2016*
Coming into force - -	*28th November 2016*

In accordance with section 4 of the Scottish Civil Justice Council and Criminal Legal Assistance Act 2013(**a**), the Court of Session has approved draft rules submitted to it by the Scottish Civil Justice Council with such modifications as it thinks appropriate.

The Court of Session therefore makes this Act of Sederunt under the powers conferred by section 104(1) of the Courts Reform (Scotland) Act 2014(**b**) and all other powers enabling it to do so.

Citation and commencement, etc.

1.—(1) This Act of Sederunt may be cited as the Act of Sederunt (Sheriff Court Rules Amendment) (Personal Injury Pre-Action Protocol) 2016.

(2) It comes into force on 28th November 2016.

(3) A certified copy is to be inserted in the Books of Sederunt.

Amendment of the Ordinary Cause Rules 1993

2.—(1) The Ordinary Cause Rules 1993(**c**) are amended in accordance with this paragraph.

(2) After Chapter 3 (commencement of causes) insert—

(**a**)   2013 asp 3. Section 4 was amended by the Courts Reform (Scotland) Act 2014 (asp 18), schedule 5, paragraph 31(3) and the Inquiries into Fatal Accidents and Sudden Deaths etc. (Scotland) Act 2016, schedule 1, paragraph 1(4).
(**b**)   2014 asp 18.
(**c**)   The Ordinary Cause Rules 1993 are in schedule 1 of the Sheriff Courts (Scotland) Act 1907 (c.51). Schedule 1 was substituted by S.I. 1993/1956 and last amended by S.S.I. 2016/194.

"CHAPTER 3A

PERSONAL INJURY PRE-ACTION PROTOCOL

Application and interpretation

3A.1.—(1) This Chapter applies to an action of damages for, or arising from, personal injuries.

(2) In this Chapter "the Protocol" means the Personal Injury Pre-Action Protocol set out in Appendix 4, and references to the "aims of the Protocol", "requirements of the Protocol" and "stages of the Protocol" are to be construed accordingly.

Requirement to comply with the Protocol

3A.2. In any case where the Protocol applies, the court will normally expect parties to have complied with the requirements of the Protocol before proceedings are commenced.

Consequences of failing to comply with the Protocol

3A.3.—(1) This rule applies where the sheriff considers that a party ("party A")—

   (a) failed, without just cause, to comply with the requirements of the Protocol; or

   (b) unreasonably failed to accept an offer in settlement which was—

      (i) made in accordance with the Protocol; and

      (ii) lodged as a tender during the period beginning with the commencement of proceedings and ending with the lodging of defences.

(2) The sheriff may, on the sheriff's own motion, or on the motion of any party, take any steps the sheriff considers necessary to do justice between the parties, and may in particular—

   (a) sist the action to allow any party to comply with the requirements of the Protocol;

   (b) make an award of expenses against party A;

   (c) modify an award of expenses; or

   (d) make an award regarding the interest payable on any award of damages.

(3) A motion made by a party under paragraph (2) must include a summary of—

   (a) the steps taken by parties under the Protocol with a view to settling the action; and

   (b) that party's assessment of the extent to which parties have complied with the requirements of the Protocol.

(4) In considering what steps (if any) to take under paragraph (2), the sheriff must take into account—

   (a) the nature of any breach of the requirements of the Protocol; and

   (b) the conduct of the parties during the stages of the Protocol.

(5) In assessing the conduct of the parties, the sheriff must have regard to the extent to which that conduct is consistent with the aims of the Protocol.

(6) This rule does not affect any other enactment or rule of law allowing the sheriff to make or modify awards regarding expenses and interest.".

(3) After Appendix 3 (schedule of timetable under personal injuries procedure) insert Appendix 4 as set out in schedule 1 of this Act of Sederunt.

2

Amendment of the Summary Cause Rules 2002

3.—(1) The Summary Cause Rules 2002(a) are amended in accordance with this paragraph.

(2) After Chapter 4 (commencement of action), insert—

"CHAPTER 4A

PERSONAL INJURY PRE-ACTION PROTOCOL

Application and interpretation

4A.1.—(1) This Chapter applies to an action of damages for, or arising from, personal injuries.

(2) In this Chapter "the Protocol" means the Personal Injury Pre-Action Protocol set out in Appendix 3, and references to the "aims of the Protocol", "requirements of the Protocol" and "stages of the Protocol" are to be construed accordingly.

Requirement to comply with the Protocol

4A.2. In any case where the Protocol applies, the court will normally expect parties to have complied with the requirements of the Protocol before proceedings are commenced.

Consequences of failing to comply with the Protocol

4A.3.—(1) This rule applies where the sheriff considers that a party ("party A")—

    (a) failed, without just cause, to comply with the requirements of the Protocol; or

    (b) unreasonably failed to accept an offer in settlement which was—

        (i) made in accordance with the Protocol; and

        (ii) lodged as a tender during the period beginning with the commencement of proceedings and ending with the lodging of defences.

(2) The sheriff may, on the sheriff's own motion, or on the motion of any party, take any steps the sheriff considers necessary to do justice between the parties, and may in particular—

    (a) sist the action to allow any party to comply with the requirements of the Protocol;

    (b) make an award of expenses against party A;

    (c) modify an award of expenses; or

    (d) make an award regarding the interest payable on any award of damages.

(3) A motion made by a party under paragraph (2) must include a summary of—

    (a) the steps taken by parties under the Protocol with a view to settling the action; and

    (b) that party's assessment of the extent to which parties have complied with the requirements of the Protocol.

(4) In considering what steps (if any) to take under paragraph (2), the sheriff must take into account—

    (a) the nature of any breach of the requirements of the Protocol; and

    (b) the conduct of the parties during the stages of the Protocol.

(5) In assessing the conduct of the parties, the sheriff must have regard to the extent to which that conduct is consistent with the aims of the Protocol.

(a) The Summary Cause Rules 2002 are in schedule 1 of the Act of Sederunt (Summary Cause Rules) 2002 (SSI 2002/132), last amended by S.S.I. 2015/419.

(6) This rule does not affect any other enactment or rule of law allowing the sheriff to make or modify awards regarding expenses and interest."

(3) After Appendix 1 (forms) insert Appendix 1A as set out in schedule 2 of this Act of Sederunt.

Saving

4. Paragraphs 2 and 3 do not apply to an action where the accident or other circumstance giving rise to the liability to which the action relates occurred before 28th November 2016.

CJM SUTHERLAND
Lord President
I.P.D.

Edinburgh
20th July 2016

SCHEDULE 1   Paragraph 2(3)

APPENDIX 4

THE PERSONAL INJURY PRE-ACTION PROTOCOL

Application of the Protocol

1.   This Protocol applies to claims for damages for, or arising from personal injuries, unless:

   (a)   the claimant reasonably estimates that the total liability value of the claim, exclusive of interest and expenses, exceeds £25,000;

   (b)   the accident or other circumstance giving rise to the liability occurred before 28th November 2016;

   (c)   the claimant is not represented by a solicitor during the stages of the Protocol; or

   (d)   the injuries for which damages are claimed—

      (i)   arise from alleged clinical negligence;

      (ii)   arise from alleged professional negligence; or

      (iii)   take the form of a disease.

In this paragraph—

"clinical negligence" has the same meaning as in rule 36.C1 of the Ordinary Cause Rules 1993; and

"disease" includes—

   (a)   any illness, physical or psychological; and

   (b)   any disorder, ailment, affliction, complaint, malady or derangement, other than a physical or psychological injury solely caused by an accident or other similar single event.

Definitions

2.   In this Protocol:

"claimant" means the person who is seeking damages from the defender;

"defender" means the person against whom a claim is made.

"next-day postal service which records delivery" means a postal service which—

   (a)   seeks to deliver documents or other things by post no later than the next working day in all or the majority of cases; and

   (b)   provides for the delivery of documents or other things by post to be recorded.

Aims of the Protocol

3.   The aims of the Protocol are to assist parties to avoid the need for, or mitigate the length and complexity of, civil proceedings by encouraging:

- the fair, just and timely settlement of disputes prior to the commencement of proceedings; and

- good practice, as regards:

  – early and full disclosure of information about the dispute;

  – investigation of the circumstances surrounding the dispute; and

  – the narrowing of issues to be determined through litigation in cases which do not reach settlement under the Protocol.

Protocol rules

4.   Where, in the course of completing the stages of the Protocol, the claimant reasonably estimates that the total value of the claim, exclusive of interest and expenses, has increased beyond £25,000, the claimant must advise the defender that the Protocol threshold has been exceeded. Parties may agree to continue following the stages of the Protocol on a voluntary basis with a view to facilitating settlement before commencing proceedings.

5.   Anything done or required to be done by a party under this Protocol may be done by a solicitor, insurer or other representative dealing with the claim for, or on behalf of, that party.

6.   Where a party is required under this Protocol to intimate or send a document to another party, the document may be intimated or sent to the solicitor, insurer or other representative dealing with the claim for, or on behalf of, that party.

7.   Documents that require to be intimated or sent under the Protocol, should, where possible, be intimated or sent by email using an email address supplied by the claimant or defender. Alternatively, such documents are to be sent or intimated using a next-day postal service which records delivery.

8.   Where there is a number of days within which or a date by which something has to be done (including being sent or intimated), it must be done or sent so that it will be received before the end of that period or that day.

9.   The claimant is expected to refrain from commencing proceedings unless:

- all stages of the Protocol have been completed without reaching settlement;

- the defender fails to complete a stage of the Protocol within the specified period;

- the defender refuses to admit liability, or liability is admitted on the basis that the defender does not intend to be bound by the admission in any subsequent proceedings;

- the defender admits liability but alleges contributory negligence and the fact or level of contributory negligence is disputed by the claimant (see paragraph 18).

- settlement is reached but the defender fails to pay damages and agreed expenses/outlays within 5 weeks of settlement (see paragraph 35 below); or

- it is necessary to do so for time-bar reasons (in which case, proceedings should be commenced and a sist applied for to allow the stages of the Protocol to be followed).

10.   Parties are expected to co-operate generally with each other with a view to fulfilling the aims of the Protocol.

The stages of the Protocol

Stage 1 – issuing of Claim Form

11.   The claimant must send a Claim Form to the defender as soon as sufficient information is available to substantiate a claim. The Claim Form should contain a clear summary of the facts on which the claim is based, including allegations of negligence, breaches of common law or statutory duty and an indication of injuries suffered and financial loss incurred. A suggested template for the Claim Form can be found in **Annex A** at the end of this Appendix.

Stage 2 – the defender's acknowledgement of Claim Form

12.   The defender must acknowledge the Claim Form within 21 days of receipt.

Stage 3 – the defender's investigation of the claim and issuing of Response

13.   The defender has a maximum of three months from receipt of the Claim Form to investigate the merits of the claim. The defender must send a reply during that period, stating whether liability is admitted or denied, giving reasons for any denial of liability, including any alternative version of events relied upon. The defender must confirm whether any admission made is intended to be a binding admission. Paragraph 9 above confirms that the claimant may raise proceedings if a non-binding admission is made.

14.   If the defender denies liability, in whole or in part, they must disclose any documents which are relevant and proportionate to the issues in question at the same time as giving their decision on liability.

15.   Paragraph 14 does not apply to documents that would never be recoverable in the course of proceedings, or that the defender would not be at liberty to disclose in the absence of an order from the court.

16.   A suggested list of documents which are likely to be material in different types of claim is included in **Annex B** at the end of this Appendix.

17.   If an admission of liability is made under this Protocol, parties will be expected to continue to follow the stages of the Protocol, where:

- the admission is made on the basis that the defender is to be bound by it (subject to the claim subsequently being proved to be fraudulent); and

- the admission is accepted by the claimant.

Stage 4 – disclosure of documents and reports following admission of liability

18.   Where the defender admits liability to make reparation under the Protocol but alleges contributory negligence, the defender must give reasons supporting the allegations and disclose the documents which are relevant and proportionate to the issue of contributory negligence. The claimant must respond to the allegation of contributory negligence before proceedings are raised.

19. Medical reports are to be instructed by the claimant at the earliest opportunity but no later than 5 weeks from the date the defender admits, in whole or part, liability (unless there is a valid reason for not obtaining a report at this stage).

20. Any medical report on which the claimant intends to rely must be disclosed to the other party within 5 weeks from the date of its receipt. Similarly, any medical report on which the defender intends to rely must be disclosed to the claimant within 5 weeks of receipt.

21. Parties may agree an extension to the issuing of medical reports if necessary.

Stage 5 – issuing of Statement of Valuation of Claim

22. The claimant must send a Statement of Valuation of Claim to the defender (in the same form as Form P16 in Appendix 1 of the Ordinary Cause Rules), together with supporting documents. The Statement of Valuation of Claim should be sent as soon as possible following receipt of all the other relevant information, including medical reports, wage slips, etc.

23. If the defender considers that additional information is required in order to consider whether to make an offer in settlement, the defender may request additional information from the claimant. Any such request is to be made promptly following receipt of the Statement of Valuation of Claim and supporting documents. The claimant must provide the information requested within 14 days of receipt of the request.

Stage 6 – offer of settlement

24. Any offer in settlement to be made by the defender may be made within 5 weeks from the date of receipt of the Statement of Valuation of Claim, medical reports and supporting evidence (including any additional information requested under paragraph 23).

25. Where the claimant's injuries are minor and no formal medical treatment is sought, a settlement offer may be made in the absence of medical evidence; otherwise, settlement offers may only be made following the submission of satisfactory medical evidence of injury.

26. An offer in settlement is only valid for the purposes of this Protocol if it includes an offer to pay expenses in accordance with the expenses provisions (at paragraphs 30-33) in the event of acceptance.

Stage 7 – claimant's response to offer of settlement

27. If a settlement offer is made, the claimant must either accept the offer or issue a reasoned response within 14 days of receipt of the offer. Alternatively, if the claimant considers that additional information is required to allow full and proper consideration of the settlement offer, the claimant may make a request for additional information from the defender within 14 days of the receipt of the offer.

28. Where additional information or documentation is requested to allow the claimant to give full and proper consideration to the settlement offer, the claimant must accept the offer or issue a reasoned response within 21 days of receipt of the additional information or documentation.

29. In any reasoned response issued, the claimant must:

- reject the offer outright, giving reasons for the rejection; or

- reject the offer and make a counter-offer, giving reasons.

30.   The expenses to be paid to the claimant in the event of settlement comprise—

  (a)   a payment in respect of the claimant's liability for solicitors' fees calculated in
          accordance with paragraph 31, and

  (b)   reimbursement of all other reasonably incurred outlays.

31.   The payment in respect of liability for solicitors' fees is the sum of—

  (a)   £546;

  (b)   3.5% of the total amount of agreed damages up to £25,000;

  (c)   25% of that part of the agreed damages up to £3,000;

  (d)   15% of the excess of the agreed damages over £3,000 up to £6,000;

  (e)   7.5% of the excess of the agreed damages over £6,000 up to £12,000;

  (f)   5% of the excess of the agreed damages over £12,000 up to £18,000;

  (g)   2.5% of the excess of the agreed damages over £18,000; and

  (h)   a figure corresponding to the VAT payable on the sum of the foregoing.

32.   Where an expert report has been instructed, any associate agency fee is not a reasonably
        incurred outlay for the purpose of paragraph 30(b).

33.   Any deduction from damages in accordance with section 7 of the Social Security
        (Recovery of Benefits) Act 1997 is to be disregarded for the purpose of paragraph 31.

Stage 8 – stocktaking period

34.   The claimant must not raise proceedings until at least 14 days after the defender receives
        the claimant's reasoned response (even in cases where the settlement offer is rejected
        outright). This period allows parties to take stock of their respective positions and to
        pursue further settlement negotiations if desired.

Stage 9 – payment

35.   Damages and Protocol expenses must be paid within 5 weeks of settlement (with interest
        payable thereafter at the judicial rate).

Annex A

1. This form is to be used where the details of the defender's insurers are known:

Pre-Action Protocol Claim Form
TO: (*name of insurance company*)
FROM: (*name of solicitor and firm representing claimant*)
DATE: (*date of issue of Claim Form*)
This is a claim which we consider to be subject to the terms of the Personal Injury Pre-Action Protocol as set out in the Act of Sederunt (Sheriff Court Rules Amendment) (Personal Injury Pre-Action Protocol) 2016. **Please acknowledge receipt of this claim within 21 days of the date of this Form.**
CONTACT: (*postal and email address of solicitor representing claimant*)

Claimant's details	
Claimant's Full Name	
Claimant's Full Address	
Claimant's Date of Birth	
Claimant's Payroll or Reference Number	
Claimant's Employer (name and address)	
Claimant's National Insurance Number	

Details of Claim

We are instructed by the above named to claim damages in connection with: [*state nature of accident* an accident at work/road traffic accident/tripping accident] on [Xth] day of [year] at [*state place of accident* – which must be sufficiently detailed to establish location].

The circumstances of the accident are:-

[*provide brief outline and simple explanation* e.g. defective machine, vicarious liability].

Your insured failed to:- [*provide brief details of the common law and/or statutory breaches*].

Our client's injuries are as follows:- [*provide brief outline*].

i.   Our client received treatment for the injuries at [*give name and address of GP/treating hospital*].

[In cases of road accidents…]

ii.   Our client's motor insurers are:-

Our client is still suffering from the effects of his/her injury. We invite you to participate with us in addressing his/her immediate needs by use of rehabilitation.

He/she is employed as [*insert occupation*] and has had the following time off work [*provide dates of absence*]. His/her approximate weekly income is [*insert if known*].

Reports

We are obtaining a police report and will let you have a copy of same upon your undertaking to meet half the fee.

At this stage of our enquiries we would expect the undernoted documents to be relevant to this claim.

(…)

2.   This form is to be used where the details of the defender's insurers are not known:

<table>
<tr><td colspan="2" align="center">**Pre –Action Protocol Claim Form**</td></tr>
<tr><td colspan="2">**TO:** (*name of defender*)</td></tr>
<tr><td colspan="2">**FROM:** (*name of solicitor and firm representing claimant*)</td></tr>
<tr><td colspan="2">**DATE:** (*date of issue of Claim Form*)</td></tr>
<tr><td colspan="2">This is a claim which we consider to be subject to the terms of the Personal Injury Pre-Action Protocol as set out in the Act of Sederunt (Sheriff Court Rules Amendment) (Personal Injury Pre-Action Protocol) 2016.

You should acknowledge receipt of this claim and forward it to your Insurers as soon as possible, asking them to contact us within 21 days of the date of this Form.</td></tr>
<tr><td colspan="2">**CONTACT:** (*postal and email address of solicitor representing claimant*)</td></tr>
<tr><td colspan="2" align="center">**Claimant's details**</td></tr>
<tr><td>**Claimant's Full Name**</td><td></td></tr>
<tr><td>**Claimant's Full Address**</td><td></td></tr>
<tr><td>**Claimant's Payroll or Reference Number**</td><td></td></tr>
<tr><td>**Claimant's Employer (name and address)**</td><td></td></tr>
<tr><td colspan="2">We are instructed by the above named to claim damages in connection with: [*state nature of accident* an accident at work/road traffic accident/tripping accident] on [Xth] day of [year] at [*state place of accident* – which must be sufficiently detailed to establish location].

The circumstances of the accident are:-

[*provide brief outline and simple explanation* e.g. defective machine, vicarious liability].

You failed to:- [*provide brief details of the common law and/or statutory breaches*].

Our client's injuries are as follows:- [*provide brief outline*].

i.   Our client received treatment for the injuries at [*give name and address of GP/treating hospital*].

[In cases of road accidents…]

ii.   Our client's motor insurers are:-

Our client is still suffering from the effects of his/her injury. We invite you to participate with us in addressing his/her immediate needs by use of rehabilitation.

He/she is employed as [*insert occupation*] and has had the following time off work [*provide dates of absence*]. His/her approximate weekly income is [*insert if known*].</td></tr>
</table>

Reports
We are obtaining a police report and will let you have a copy of same upon your undertaking to meet half the fee.
At this stage of our enquiries we would expect the undernoted documents to be relevant to this claim. (…)

Annex B – Standard Disclosure

1.   Road Traffic Cases

Section A – cases where liability is at issue

(i)   Documents identifying nature, extent and location of damage to defender's vehicle where there is any dispute about point of impact.

(ii)   MOT certificate where relevant.

(iii)   Maintenance records where vehicle defect is alleged or it is alleged by defender that there was an unforeseen defect which caused or contributed to the accident.

Section B - accidents involving a potential defender's commercial vehicle

(i)   Tachograph charts or entry from individual control book, where relevant.

(ii)   Maintenance and repair records required for operators' licence where vehicle defect is alleged or it is alleged by defender that there was an unforeseen defect which caused or contributed to the accident.

Section C - cases against local authorities where a highway design defect is alleged

(i)   Documents produced to comply with section 39 of the Road Traffic Act 1988 in respect of the duty designed to promote road safety to include studies into road accidents in the relevant area and documents relating to measures recommended to prevent accidents in the relevant area.

2.   Road/footway tripping claims

Documents from the Highway Authority or local authority for a period of 12 months prior to the accident–

(i)   Records of inspection for the relevant stretch of road/footway.

(ii)   Maintenance records including records of independent contractors working in relevant area.

(iii)   Statement of the Roads Authority's policy under the Code of Practice for Highway Maintenance Management (2005) or alternatively records of the Minutes of Highway Authority or Local Authority meetings where maintenance or repair policy has been discussed or decided.

(iv)   Records of complaints about the state of roads/footway at the accident locus for a 12 month period prior to the accident.

(v)   Records of other accidents which have occurred on the relevant stretch of road/footway within 12 months of the accident.

3.   Workplace claims – general

(i)   Accident book entry.

(ii)   First aider report.

(iii)   Surgery record.

(iv)   Foreman/supervisor accident report.

(v)   Safety representatives' accident report.

(vi)   RIDDOR (Reporting of Injuries, Disease and Dangerous Occurrences Regulations 2013) report to the Health and Safety Executive (HSE).

(vii)   Other communications between defenders and HSE.

(viii)   Minutes of Health and Safety Committee meeting(s) where accident/matter considered.

(ix)   Report to the Department for Work and Pensions.

(x)   Documents listed above relative to any previous accident/matter identified by the claimant and relied upon as proof of negligence.

(xi)   Earnings information where defender is employer.

4.   Workplace claims -

Documents produced to comply with requirements of the Management of Health and Safety at Work Regulations 1991/3242

(i)   Pre-accident Risk Assessment required by Regulation 3.

(ii)   Post-accident Re-Assessment required by Regulation 3.

(iii)   Accident Investigation Report prepared in implementing the requirements of Regulation 5.

(iv)   Health Surveillance Records in appropriate cases required by Regulation 6.

(v)   Information provided to employees under Regulation 10.

(vi)   Documents relating to the employee's health and safety training required by Regulation 13.

5.   Workplace claims – Disclosure where specific regulations apply

Section A – Manual Handling Operations Regulations 1992/2793

(i)   Manual Handling Risk Assessment carried out to comply with the requirements of Regulation 4(1)(b)(i).

(ii)   Re-assessment carried out post-accident to comply with requirements of Regulation 4(1)(b)(i).

(iii)   Documents showing the information provided to the employee to give general indications related to the load and precise indications on the weight of the load and the heaviest side of the load if the centre of gravity was not positioned centrally to comply with Regulation 4(1)(b)(iii).

(iv)   Documents relating to training in respect of manual handling operations and training records.

(v)   All documents showing or tending to show the weight of the load at the material time.

Section B – Personal Protective Equipment at Work Regulations 1992/2966

(i)   Documents relating to the assessment of Personal Protective Equipment to comply with Regulation 6.

(ii)   Documents relating to the maintenance and replacement of Personal Protective Equipment to comply with Regulation 7.

(iii)   Record of maintenance procedures for Personal Protective Equipment to comply with Regulation 7.

(iv)   Records of tests and examinations of Personal Protective Equipment to comply with Regulation 7.

(v)   Documents providing information, instruction and training in relation to the Personal Protective Equipment to comply with Regulation 9.

(vi)   Instructions for use of Personal Protective Equipment to include the manufacturers' instructions to comply with Regulation 10.

Section C – Workplace (Health Safety and Welfare) Regulations 1992/3004

(i)   Repair and maintenance records required by Regulation 5.

(ii)   Housekeeping records to comply with the requirements of Regulation 9.

(iii)   Hazard warning signs or notices to comply with Regulation 17.

Section D – Provision and Use of Work Equipment Regulations 1998/2306

(i)   Manufacturers' specifications and instructions in respect of relevant work equipment establishing its suitability to comply with Regulation 4.

(ii)   Maintenance log/maintenance records required to comply with Regulation 5.

(iii)   Documents providing information and instructions to employees to comply with Regulation 8.

(iv)   Documents provided to the employee in respect of training for use to comply with Regulation 9.

(v)   Any notice, sign or document relied upon as a defence to alleged breaches of Regulations 14 to 18 dealing with controls and control systems.

(vi)   Instruction/training documents issued to comply with the requirements of Regulation 22 insofar as it deals with maintenance operations where the machinery is not shut down.

(vii)   Copies of markings required to comply with Regulation 23.

(viii) Copies of warnings required to comply with Regulation 24.

Section E – Lifting Operations and Lifting Equipment Regulations 1998/2307

(i)   All documents showing the weight of any load to establish lifting equipment of adequate strength and stability to comply with Regulation 4.

(ii)   All notices and markings showing the safe working load of machinery and accessories to comply with Regulation 7.

(iii)   All documents showing lifting operations have been planned by a competent person, appropriately supervised and carried out in a safe manner to comply with Regulation 8.

(iv)   All defect reports to comply with Regulation 10.

Section F – Pressure Systems Safety Regulations 2000/128

(i)   Information and specimen markings provided to comply with the requirements of Regulation 5.

(ii)   Written statements specifying the safe operating limits of a system to comply with the requirements of Regulation 7.

(iii)   Copy of the written scheme of examination required to comply with the requirements of Regulation 8.

(iv)   Examination records required to comply with the requirements of Regulation 9.

(v)   Instructions provided for the use of operator to comply with Regulation 11.

(vi)   Records kept to comply with the requirements of Regulation 14.

Section G – Control of Substances Hazardous to Health Regulations 2002/2677

(i)   Risk assessment carried out to comply with the requirements of Regulation 6.

(ii)   Reviewed risk assessment carried out to comply with the requirements of Regulation 6.

(iii)   Copy labels from containers used for storage handling and disposal of carcinogenics to comply with the requirements of Regulation 7.

(iv)   Warning signs identifying designation of areas and installations which may be contaminated by carcinogenics to comply with the requirements of Regulation 7.

(v)   Documents relating to the assessment of the Personal Protective Equipment to comply with Regulation 7.

(vi)   Documents relating to the maintenance and replacement of Personal Protective Equipment to comply with Regulation 7.

(vii)   Record of maintenance procedures for Personal Protective Equipment to comply with Regulation 7.

(viii)   Records of tests and examinations of Personal Protective Equipment to comply with Regulation 7.

(ix)   Documents providing information, instruction and training in relation to the Personal Protective Equipment to comply with Regulation 7.

(x)   Instructions for use of Personal Protective Equipment to include the manufacturers' instructions to comply with Regulation 7.

(xi)   Air monitoring records for substances assigned a maximum exposure limit or occupational exposure standard to comply with the requirements of Regulation 7.

(xii)   Maintenance examination and test of control measures records to comply with Regulation 9.

(xiii)   Monitoring records to comply with the requirements of Regulation 10.

(xiv)   Health surveillance records to comply with the requirements of Regulation 11.

(xv)   Documents detailing information, instruction and training including training records for employees to comply with the requirements of Regulation 12.

(xvi)   Labels and Health and Safety data sheets supplied to the employers to comply with the CLP (Classification, Labelling and Packaging) Regulations.

Section H – Control of Noise at Work Regulations 2005/1643

(i)   Any risk assessment records required to comply with the requirements of Regulation 5.

(ii)   Manufacturers' literature in respect of all ear protection made available to claimant to comply with the requirements of Regulation 7.

(iii)   Health surveillance records relating to the claimant to comply with the requirements of Regulation 9.

(iv)   All documents provided to the employee for the provision of information to comply with Regulation 10.

Section I – Construction (Design and Management) Regulations 2015/51

(i)   All documents showing the identity of the principal contractor, or a person who controls the way in which construction work is carried out by a person at work, to comply with the terms of Regulation 5.

(ii)   Notification of a project form (HSE F10) to comply with the requirements of Regulation 6.

(iii)   Construction Phase Plan to comply with requirements of Regulation 12.

(iv)   Health and Safety file to comply with the requirements of Regulations 4 and 12.

(v)   Information and training records provided to comply with the requirements of Regulations 4, 14 and 15.

(vi)   Records of consultation and engagement of persons at work to comply with the requirements of Regulation 14.

(vii)   All documents and inspection reports to comply with the terms of Regulations 22, 23 and 24.

SCHEDULE 2   Paragraph 3(3)

APPENDIX 1A

THE PERSONAL INJURY PRE-ACTION PROTOCOL

Application of the Protocol

1.   This Protocol applies to claims for damages for, or arising from personal injuries, unless:

      (a)   the claimant reasonably estimates that the total liability value of the claim, exclusive of interest and expenses, exceeds £25,000;

      (b)   the accident or other circumstance giving rise to the liability occurred before 28th November 2016;

      (c)   the claimant is not represented by a solicitor during the stages of the Protocol; or

      (d)   the injuries for which damages are claimed—

            (i)   arise from alleged clinical negligence;

            (ii)   arise from alleged professional negligence; or

            (iii)   take the form of a disease.

In this paragraph—

"clinical negligence" has the same meaning as in rule 36.C1 of the Ordinary Cause Rules 1993; and

"disease" includes—

      (a)   any illness, physical or psychological; and

      (b)   any disorder, ailment, affliction, complaint, malady or derangement, other than a physical or psychological injury solely caused by an accident or other similar single event.

Definitions

2.   In this Protocol:

"claimant" means the person who is seeking damages from the defender;

"defender" means the person against whom a claim is made.

"next-day postal service which records delivery" means a postal service which—

      (a)   seeks to deliver documents or other things by post no later than the next working day in all or the majority of cases; and

      (b)   provides for the delivery of documents or other things by post to be recorded.

Aims of the Protocol

3.   The aims of the Protocol are to assist parties to avoid the need for, or mitigate the length and complexity of, civil proceedings by encouraging:

- the fair, just and timely settlement of disputes prior to the commencement of proceedings; and

- good practice, as regards:

  – early and full disclosure of information about the dispute;

  – investigation of the circumstances surrounding the dispute; and

  – the narrowing of issues to be determined through litigation in cases which do not reach settlement under the Protocol.

Protocol rules

4.   Where, in the course of completing the stages of the Protocol, the claimant reasonably estimates that the total value of the claim, exclusive of interest and expenses, has increased beyond £25,000, the claimant must advise the defender that the Protocol threshold has been exceeded. Parties may agree to continue following the stages of the Protocol on a voluntary basis with a view to facilitating settlement before commencing proceedings.

5.   Anything done or required to be done by a party under this Protocol may be done by a solicitor, insurer or other representative dealing with the claim for, or on behalf of, that party.

6.   Where a party is required under this Protocol to intimate or send a document to another party, the document may be intimated or sent to the solicitor, insurer or other representative dealing with the claim for, or on behalf of, that party.

7.   Documents that require to be intimated or sent under the Protocol, should, where possible, be intimated or sent by email using an email address supplied by the claimant or defender. Alternatively, such documents are to be sent or intimated using a next-day postal service which records delivery.

8.   Where there is a number of days within which or a date by which something has to be done (including being sent or intimated), it must be done or sent so that it will be received before the end of that period or that day.

9.   The claimant is expected to refrain from commencing proceedings unless:

- all stages of the Protocol have been completed without reaching settlement;

- the defender fails to complete a stage of the Protocol within the specified period;

- the defender refuses to admit liability, or liability is admitted on the basis that the defender does not intend to be bound by the admission in any subsequent proceedings;

- the defender admits liability but alleges contributory negligence and the fact or level of contributory negligence is disputed by the claimant (see paragraph 18).

- settlement is reached but the defender fails to pay damages and agreed expenses/outlays within 5 weeks of settlement (see paragraph 35 below); or

- it is necessary to do so for time-bar reasons (in which case, proceedings should be commenced and a sist applied for to allow the stages of the Protocol to be followed).

10.   Parties are expected to co-operate generally with each other with a view to fulfilling the aims of the Protocol.

The stages of the Protocol

Stage 1 – issuing of Claim Form

11.   The claimant must send a Claim Form to the defender as soon as sufficient information is available to substantiate a claim. The Claim Form should contain a clear summary of the facts on which the claim is based, including allegations of negligence, breaches of common law or statutory duty and an indication of injuries suffered and financial loss incurred. A suggested template for the Claim Form can be found in **Annex A** at the end of this Appendix.

Stage 2 – the defender's acknowledgement of Claim Form

12.   The defender must acknowledge the Claim Form within 21 days of receipt.

Stage 3 – the defender's investigation of the claim and issuing of Response

13.   The defender has a maximum of three months from receipt of the Claim Form to investigate the merits of the claim. The defender must send a reply during that period, stating whether liability is admitted or denied, giving reasons for any denial of liability, including any alternative version of events relied upon. The defender must confirm whether any admission made is intended to be a binding admission. Paragraph 9 above confirms that the claimant may raise proceedings if a non-binding admission is made.

14.   If the defender denies liability, in whole or in part, they must disclose any documents which are relevant and proportionate to the issues in question at the same time as giving their decision on liability.

15.   Paragraph 14 does not apply to documents that would never be recoverable in the course of proceedings, or that the defender would not be at liberty to disclose in the absence of an order from the court.

16.   A suggested list of documents which are likely to be material in different types of claim is included in **Annex B** at the end of this Appendix.

17.   If an admission of liability is made under this Protocol, parties will be expected to continue to follow the stages of the Protocol, where:

- the admission is made on the basis that the defender is to be bound by it (subject to the claim subsequently being proved to be fraudulent); and

- the admission is accepted by the claimant.

Stage 4 – disclosure of documents and reports following admission of liability

18.   Where the defender admits liability to make reparation under the Protocol but alleges contributory negligence, the defender must give reasons supporting the allegations and disclose the documents which are relevant and proportionate to the issue of contributory negligence. The claimant must respond to the allegation of contributory negligence before proceedings are raised.

19.   Medical reports are to be instructed by the claimant at the earliest opportunity but no later than 5 weeks from the date the defender admits, in whole or part, liability (unless there is a valid reason for not obtaining a report at this stage).

20.   Any medical report on which the claimant intends to rely must be disclosed to the other party within 5 weeks from the date of its receipt. Similarly, any medical report on which the defender intends to rely must be disclosed to the claimant within 5 weeks of receipt.

21.   Parties may agree an extension to the issuing of medical reports if necessary.

Stage 5 – issuing of Statement of Valuation of Claim

22.   The claimant must send a Statement of Valuation of Claim to the defender (in the same form as Form P16 in Appendix 1 of the Ordinary Cause Rules), together with supporting documents. The Statement of Valuation of Claim should be sent as soon as possible following receipt of all the other relevant information, including medical reports, wage slips, etc.

23.   If the defender considers that additional information is required in order to consider whether to make an offer in settlement, the defender may request additional information from the claimant. Any such request is to be made promptly following receipt of the Statement of Valuation of Claim and supporting documents. The claimant must provide the information requested within 14 days of receipt of the request.

Stage 6 – offer of settlement

24.   Any offer in settlement to be made by the defender may be made within 5 weeks from the date of receipt of the Statement of Valuation of Claim, medical reports and supporting evidence (including any additional information requested under paragraph 23).

25.   Where the claimant's injuries are minor and no formal medical treatment is sought, a settlement offer may be made in the absence of medical evidence; otherwise, settlement offers may only be made following the submission of satisfactory medical evidence of injury.

26.   An offer in settlement is only valid for the purposes of this Protocol if it includes an offer to pay expenses in accordance with the expenses provisions (at paragraphs 30-33) in the event of acceptance.

Stage 7 – claimant's response to offer of settlement

27.   If a settlement offer is made, the claimant must either accept the offer or issue a reasoned response within 14 days of receipt of the offer. Alternatively, if the claimant considers that additional information is required to allow full and proper consideration of the settlement offer, the claimant may make a request for additional information from the defender within 14 days of the receipt of the offer.

28.   Where additional information or documentation is requested to allow the claimant to give full and proper consideration to the settlement offer, the claimant must accept the offer or issue a reasoned response within 21 days of receipt of the additional information or documentation.

29.   In any reasoned response issued, the claimant must:

   •   reject the offer outright, giving reasons for the rejection; or

   •   reject the offer and make a counter-offer, giving reasons.

30.   The expenses to be paid to the claimant in the event of settlement comprise—

    (a)   a payment in respect of the claimant's liability for solicitors' fees calculated in accordance with paragraph 31, and

    (b)   reimbursement of all other reasonably incurred outlays.

31.   The payment in respect of liability for solicitors' fees is the sum of—

    (a)   £546;

    (b)   3.5% of the total amount of agreed damages up to £25,000;

    (c)   25% of that part of the agreed damages up to £3,000;

    (d)   15% of the excess of the agreed damages over £3,000 up to £6,000;

    (e)   7.5% of the excess of the agreed damages over £6,000 up to £12,000;

    (f)   5% of the excess of the agreed damages over £12,000 up to £18,000;

    (g)   2.5% of the excess of the agreed damages over £18,000; and

    (h)   a figure corresponding to the VAT payable on the sum of the foregoing.

32.   Where an expert report has been instructed, any associate agency fee is not a reasonably incurred outlay for the purpose of paragraph 30(b).

33.   Any deduction from damages in accordance with section 7 of the Social Security (Recovery of Benefits) Act 1997 is to be disregarded for the purpose of paragraph 31.

Stage 8 – stocktaking period

34.   The claimant must not raise proceedings until at least 14 days after the defender receives the claimant's reasoned response (even in cases where the settlement offer is rejected outright). This period allows parties to take stock of their respective positions and to pursue further settlement negotiations if desired.

Stage 9 – payment

35.   Damages and Protocol expenses must be paid within 5 weeks of settlement (with interest payable thereafter at the judicial rate).

Annex A

1.   This form is to be used where the details of the defender's insurers are known:

Pre-Action Protocol Claim Form
TO: (*name of insurance company*)
FROM: (*name of solicitor and firm representing claimant*)
DATE: (*date of issue of Claim Form*)
This is a claim which we consider to be subject to the terms of the Personal Injury Pre-Action Protocol as set out in the Act of Sederunt (Sheriff Court Rules Amendment) (Personal Injury Pre-Action Protocol) 2016. **Please acknowledge receipt of this claim within 21 days of the date of this Form.**
CONTACT: (*postal and email address of solicitor representing claimant*)

Claimant's details	
Claimant's Full Name	
Claimant's Full Address	
Claimant's Date of Birth	
Claimant's Payroll or Reference Number	
Claimant's Employer (name and address)	
Claimant's National Insurance Number	

Details of Claim

We are instructed by the above named to claim damages in connection with: [*state nature of accident* an accident at work/road traffic accident/tripping accident] on [Xth] day of [year] at [*state place of accident* – which must be sufficiently detailed to establish location].

The circumstances of the accident are:-

[*provide brief outline and simple explanation* e.g. defective machine, vicarious liability].

Your insured failed to:- [*provide brief details of the common law and/or statutory breaches*].

Our client's injuries are as follows:- [*provide brief outline*].

i.   Our client received treatment for the injuries at [*give name and address of GP/treating hospital*].

[In cases of road accidents…]

ii.   Our client's motor insurers are:-

Our client is still suffering from the effects of his/her injury. We invite you to participate with us in addressing his/her immediate needs by use of rehabilitation.

He/she is employed as [*insert occupation*] and has had the following time off work [*provide dates of absence*]. His/her approximate weekly income is [*insert if known*].

Reports

We are obtaining a police report and will let you have a copy of same upon your undertaking to meet half the fee.

At this stage of our enquiries we would expect the undernoted documents to be relevant to this claim.

(…)

2. This form is to be used where the details of the defender's insurers are not known:

Pre –Action Protocol Claim Form
TO: (*name of defender*)
FROM: (*name of solicitor and firm representing claimant*)
DATE: (*date of issue of Claim Form*)
This is a claim which we consider to be subject to the terms of the Personal Injury Pre-Action Protocol as set out in the Act of Sederunt (Sheriff Court Rules Amendment) (Personal Injury Pre-Action Protocol) 2016. **You should acknowledge receipt of this claim and forward it to your Insurers as soon as possible, asking them to contact us within 21 days of the date of this Form.**
CONTACT: (*postal and email address of solicitor representing claimant*)
Claimant's details

Claimant's Full Name	
Claimant's Full Address	
Claimant's Payroll or Reference Number	
Claimant's Employer (name and address)	

We are instructed by the above named to claim damages in connection with: [*state nature of accident* an accident at work/road traffic accident/tripping accident] on [Xth] day of [year] at [*state place of accident* – which must be sufficiently detailed to establish location].

The circumstances of the accident are:-

[*provide brief outline and simple explanation* e.g. defective machine, vicarious liability].

You failed to:- [*provide brief details of the common law and/or statutory breaches*].

Our client's injuries are as follows:- [*provide brief outline*].

i. Our client received treatment for the injuries at [*give name and address of GP/treating hospital*].

[In cases of road accidents…]

ii. Our client's motor insurers are:-

Our client is still suffering from the effects of his/her injury. We invite you to participate with us in addressing his/her immediate needs by use of rehabilitation.

He/she is employed as [*insert occupation*] and has had the following time off work [*provide dates of absence*]. His/her approximate weekly income is [*insert if known*].

Reports
We are obtaining a police report and will let you have a copy of same upon your undertaking to meet half the fee.
At this stage of our enquiries we would expect the undernoted documents to be relevant to this claim. (...)

Annex B – Standard Disclosure

1.   **Road Traffic Cases**

Section A – cases where liability is at issue

(i)   Documents identifying nature, extent and location of damage to defender's vehicle where there is any dispute about point of impact.

(ii)   MOT certificate where relevant.

(iii)   Maintenance records where vehicle defect is alleged or it is alleged by defender that there was an unforeseen defect which caused or contributed to the accident.

Section B - accidents involving a potential defender's commercial vehicle

(i)   Tachograph charts or entry from individual control book, where relevant.

(ii)   Maintenance and repair records required for operators' licence where vehicle defect is alleged or it is alleged by defender that there was an unforeseen defect which caused or contributed to the accident.

Section C - cases against local authorities where a highway design defect is alleged

(i)   Documents produced to comply with section 39 of the Road Traffic Act 1988 in respect of the duty designed to promote road safety to include studies into road accidents in the relevant area and documents relating to measures recommended to prevent accidents in the relevant area.

2.   **Road/footway tripping claims**

Documents from the Highway Authority or local authority for a period of 12 months prior to the accident–

(i)   Records of inspection for the relevant stretch of road/footway.

(ii)   Maintenance records including records of independent contractors working in relevant area.

(iii)   Statement of the Roads Authority's policy under the Code of Practice for Highway Maintenance Management (2005) or alternatively records of the Minutes of Highway Authority or Local Authority meetings where maintenance or repair policy has been discussed or decided.

(iv)   Records of complaints about the state of roads/footway at the accident locus for a 12 month period prior to the accident.

(v)   Records of other accidents which have occurred on the relevant stretch of road/footway within 12 months of the accident.

3.   **Workplace claims – general**

(i)   Accident book entry.

(ii)   First aider report.

(iii)   Surgery record.

(iv)   Foreman/supervisor accident report.

(v)   Safety representatives' accident report.

(vi)   RIDDOR (Reporting of Injuries, Disease and Dangerous Occurrences Regulations 2013) report to the Health and Safety Executive (HSE).

(vii)   Other communications between defenders and HSE.

(viii)   Minutes of Health and Safety Committee meeting(s) where accident/matter considered.

(ix)   Report to the Department for Work and Pensions.

(x)   Documents listed above relative to any previous accident/matter identified by the claimant and relied upon as proof of negligence.

(xi)   Earnings information where defender is employer.

4.   Workplace claims -

Documents produced to comply with requirements of the Management of Health and Safety at Work Regulations 1991/3242

(i)   Pre-accident Risk Assessment required by Regulation 3.

(ii)   Post-accident Re-Assessment required by Regulation 3.

(iii)   Accident Investigation Report prepared in implementing the requirements of Regulation 5.

(iv)   Health Surveillance Records in appropriate cases required by Regulation 6.

(v)   Information provided to employees under Regulation 10.

(vi)   Documents relating to the employee's health and safety training required by Regulation 13.

5.   Workplace claims – Disclosure where specific regulations apply

Section A – Manual Handling Operations Regulations 1992/2793

(i)   Manual Handling Risk Assessment carried out to comply with the requirements of Regulation 4(1)(b)(i).

(ii)   Re-assessment carried out post-accident to comply with requirements of Regulation 4(1)(b)(i).

(iii)   Documents showing the information provided to the employee to give general indications related to the load and precise indications on the weight of the load and the heaviest side of the load if the centre of gravity was not positioned centrally to comply with Regulation 4(1)(b)(iii).

(iv)   Documents relating to training in respect of manual handling operations and training records.

(v)   All documents showing or tending to show the weight of the load at the material time.

Section B – Personal Protective Equipment at Work Regulations 1992/2966

(i)   Documents relating to the assessment of Personal Protective Equipment to comply with Regulation 6.

(ii)   Documents relating to the maintenance and replacement of Personal Protective Equipment to comply with Regulation 7.

(iii)   Record of maintenance procedures for Personal Protective Equipment to comply with Regulation 7.

(iv)   Records of tests and examinations of Personal Protective Equipment to comply with Regulation 7.

(v)   Documents providing information, instruction and training in relation to the Personal Protective Equipment to comply with Regulation 9.

(vi)   Instructions for use of Personal Protective Equipment to include the manufacturers' instructions to comply with Regulation 10.

Section C – Workplace (Health Safety and Welfare) Regulations 1992/3004

(i)   Repair and maintenance records required by Regulation 5.

(ii)   Housekeeping records to comply with the requirements of Regulation 9.

(iii)   Hazard warning signs or notices to comply with Regulation 17.

Section D – Provision and Use of Work Equipment Regulations 1998/2306

(i)   Manufacturers' specifications and instructions in respect of relevant work equipment establishing its suitability to comply with Regulation 4.

(ii)   Maintenance log/maintenance records required to comply with Regulation 5.

(iii)   Documents providing information and instructions to employees to comply with Regulation 8.

(iv)   Documents provided to the employee in respect of training for use to comply with Regulation 9.

(v)   Any notice, sign or document relied upon as a defence to alleged breaches of Regulations 14 to 18 dealing with controls and control systems.

(vi)   Instruction/training documents issued to comply with the requirements of Regulation 22 insofar as it deals with maintenance operations where the machinery is not shut down.

(vii)   Copies of markings required to comply with Regulation 23.

(viii) Copies of warnings required to comply with Regulation 24.

Section E – Lifting Operations and Lifting Equipment Regulations 1998/2307

(i)   All documents showing the weight of any load to establish lifting equipment of adequate strength and stability to comply with Regulation 4.

(ii)   All notices and markings showing the safe working load of machinery and accessories to comply with Regulation 7.

(iii)   All documents showing lifting operations have been planned by a competent person, appropriately supervised and carried out in a safe manner to comply with Regulation 8.

(iv)   All defect reports to comply with Regulation 10.

Section F – Pressure Systems Safety Regulations 2000/128

(i)   Information and specimen markings provided to comply with the requirements of Regulation 5.

(ii)   Written statements specifying the safe operating limits of a system to comply with the requirements of Regulation 7.

(iii)   Copy of the written scheme of examination required to comply with the requirements of Regulation 8.

(iv)   Examination records required to comply with the requirements of Regulation 9.

(v)   Instructions provided for the use of operator to comply with Regulation 11.

(vi)   Records kept to comply with the requirements of Regulation 14.

Section G – Control of Substances Hazardous to Health Regulations 2002/2677

(i)   Risk assessment carried out to comply with the requirements of Regulation 6.

(ii)   Reviewed risk assessment carried out to comply with the requirements of Regulation 6.

(iii)   Copy labels from containers used for storage handling and disposal of carcinogenics to comply with the requirements of Regulation 7.

(iv)   Warning signs identifying designation of areas and installations which may be contaminated by carcinogenics to comply with the requirements of Regulation 7.

(v)   Documents relating to the assessment of the Personal Protective Equipment to comply with Regulation 7.

(vi)   Documents relating to the maintenance and replacement of Personal Protective Equipment to comply with Regulation 7.

(vii)   Record of maintenance procedures for Personal Protective Equipment to comply with Regulation 7.

(viii)   Records of tests and examinations of Personal Protective Equipment to comply with Regulation 7.

(ix)   Documents providing information, instruction and training in relation to the Personal Protective Equipment to comply with Regulation 7.

(x)   Instructions for use of Personal Protective Equipment to include the manufacturers' instructions to comply with Regulation 7.

(xi)   Air monitoring records for substances assigned a maximum exposure limit or occupational exposure standard to comply with the requirements of Regulation 7.

(xii)   Maintenance examination and test of control measures records to comply with Regulation 9.

(xiii)   Monitoring records to comply with the requirements of Regulation 10.

(xiv)   Health surveillance records to comply with the requirements of Regulation 11.

(xv)   Documents detailing information, instruction and training including training records for employees to comply with the requirements of Regulation 12.

(xvi)   Labels and Health and Safety data sheets supplied to the employers to comply with the CLP (Classification, Labelling and Packaging) Regulations.

Section H – Control of Noise at Work Regulations 2005/1643

(i)   Any risk assessment records required to comply with the requirements of Regulation 5.

(ii)   Manufacturers' literature in respect of all ear protection made available to claimant to comply with the requirements of Regulation 7.

(iii)   Health surveillance records relating to the claimant to comply with the requirements of Regulation 9.

(iv)   All documents provided to the employee for the provision of information to comply with Regulation 10.

Section I – Construction (Design and Management) Regulations 2015/51

(i)   All documents showing the identity of the principal contractor, or a person who controls the way in which construction work is carried out by a person at work, to comply with the terms of Regulation 5.

(ii)   Notification of a project form (HSE F10) to comply with the requirements of Regulation 6.

(iii)   Construction Phase Plan to comply with requirements of Regulation 12.

(iv)   Health and Safety file to comply with the requirements of Regulations 4 and 12.

(v)   Information and training records provided to comply with the requirements of Regulations 4, 14 and 15.

(vi)   Records of consultation and engagement of persons at work to comply with the requirements of Regulation 14.

(vii)   All documents and inspection reports to comply with the terms of Regulations 22, 23 and 24.

EXPLANATORY NOTE

(This note is not part of the Act of Sederunt)

This Act of Sederunt amends the Ordinary Cause Rules and Summary Cause Rules in respect of personal injury actions. It introduces a requirement on parties to certain actions of damages for personal injury to follow a Personal Injury Pre-Action Protocol ("the Protocol") with a view to settling the action before proceedings are raised.

Paragraph 2 inserts a new Chapter 3A into the Ordinary Cause Rules which introduces the new Protocol (the Protocol itself is set out in schedule 1 of this instrument and is inserted as Appendix 4 of the Ordinary Cause Rules). Chapter 3A provides that where the Protocol applies, the court will normally expect parties to have complied with the Protocol requirements before commencing proceedings. The Protocol will not apply where the total liability value of the claim is reasonably estimated to be more than £25,000, the claimant is not represented by a solicitor, or the injuries for which damages are claimed arise from clinical negligence, professional negligence or take the form of a disease (paragraph 1 of the Protocol).

Where proceedings are commenced and the sheriff considers that a party has failed to comply with the Protocol, or has unreasonably failed to accept a settlement offer made under the Protocol and subsequently lodged as a tender following the commencement of proceedings, the sheriff can take steps to do justice between the parties (rule 3A.3 as inserted by paragraph 2 of this instrument). In doing so, the sheriff must take into account the conduct of the parties during the stages of the Protocol and the nature of any breach of Protocol requirements.

Paragraph 3 inserts a new Chapter 4A into the Summary Cause Rules which applies the new Protocol to relevant Summary Cause cases (the Protocol itself is set out in schedule 2 of this instrument and is inserted as Appendix 3 of the Summary Cause Rules). The provision made in the new Chapter 4A and Appendix 3 of the Summary Cause Rules is in identical terms to that made in the Ordinary Cause Rules.

Saving provision is included in paragraph 4 to preserve the existing law as regards actions where the accident or circumstance giving rise to the claim for damages occurred before 28th November 2016; there will accordingly be no requirement to follow the Protocol prior to commencing proceedings in such cases.

VOLUNTARY PRE-ACTION PROTOCOL IN SCOTLAND FOR PERSONAL INJURY CLAIMS

The full terms of the Protocol as agreed between the Law Society of Scotland and the Forum of Scottish Claims Managers

1. PURPOSE OF VOLUNTARY PROTOCOL

The Voluntary Protocol has been kept deliberately simple to promote ease of use and general acceptability.   **1.1**

The aims of the Voluntary Protocol are: **1.2**

- To put parties in a position where they may be able to settle cases fairly and early without litigation;
- To ensure the early provision of reliable information reasonably required to enter into meaningful discussions re liability and quantum;
- To enable appropriate offers to be made either before or after litigation commences.

It also sets out good practice making it easier for the parties to obtain and rely upon information required.   **1.3**

The Voluntary Protocol encourages the joint exploration of rehabilitation at an early stage, in appropriate cases, without prejudice to liability.   **1.4**

The standards within the Voluntary Protocol are to be regarded as the normal, reasonable approach to pre-action conduct in relation to Voluntary Protocol cases.   **1.5**

2. INTRODUCTION

A Voluntary Pre-Action Protocol in Scotland

Unlike England, there is no statutory basis for a pre-action protocol. The   **2.1**
Protocol will therefore require to be entered into voluntarily on an individual case by case basis by mutual agreement. It will be for the pursuer's agent to intimate the claim in the general format of specimen letter A1 or A2 which will invite the defender or insurer to agree on a case by case basis that conduct of the pre-action negotiations is to be undertaken in terms of the Voluntary Protocol. When a defender or Insurer accepts, a letter in the general format of specimen letter B will be sent within 21 days of receipt of the letter of

claim. Thereafter the claim will proceed in terms of the Voluntary Protocol in respect of the negotiations, disclosure, repudiation of liability, settlement and calculation of fees.

2.2   The agent may wish to notify the insurer as soon as they know a claim is likely to be made but before they are able to send a detailed letter of claim, particularly for instance, when the insurer has no or limited knowledge of the incident giving rise to the claim or where the claimant is incurring significant expenditure as a result of the accident which he/she hopes the insurer might pay for, in whole or in part. If the pursuer's agent chooses to do this, it will not start the timetable for responding.

2.3   The Voluntary Protocol if entered into will apply in all cases which include a claim for personal injury (excepting clinical negligence and disease and illness cases) and will apply not merely to the personal injury element of a claim but also to other heads of loss and damage. It is primarily designed for road traffic, tripping and slipping and accident at work cases where the value of the claim is up to £10,000. The Protocol is voluntary and there is nothing to prevent parties by mutual agreement dealing with any claim of a higher value under the Protocol.

2.4   Where proceedings are raised in a Voluntary Protocol case, whether for the payment of damages or for the recovery of evidence and other orders under the Administration of Justice (Scotland) Act 1972, without prejudice to any existing rule of law, it shall be open to any party to lodge Voluntary Protocol communications for the sole purpose of assisting the court in any determination of expenses.

3. LETTER OF CLAIM

3.1   The agent shall send to the proposed defender (or to his insurer if known) a letter of claim as soon as sufficient information is available to substantiate a claim and before issues of quantum are addressed in detail. The letter should ask for details of the insurer if not known and the letter should request that a copy should be sent by the proposed defender to the insurer where appropriate. If the insurer is known, a copy shall be sent directly to the insurer.

3.2   The letter shall contain a clear summary of the facts on which the claim is based, including allegations of negligence, breaches of common law or statutory duty, together with an indication of the nature of any injuries suffered and of any financial loss incurred, so far as known. In all cases the letter should provide the name and address of the hospital where treatment has been obtained and where appropriate, the name and address of the claimant's own motor insurer.

3.3   Agents are recommended to use a standard format for such a letter, specimen letter A1 or A2: this can be amended to suit the particular case.

3.4   Sufficient information should be given in order to enable the insurer to commence investigations and at least put a broad valuation on the "risk".

3.5   The insurer should acknowledge the letter of claim within 21 days of the date of receipt of the letter. The insurer should advise in a letter in the terms of specimen B whether it is agreed that the case is suitable for the Voluntary Protocol. If there has been no reply by the defender or insurer within 21 days, the claimant will be entitled to issue proceedings.

Where liability is admitted, the insurer will be bound by this admission **3.6** for all Protocol claims with a personal injury value, as laid down in 2.3, of less than £10,000. The exception to this will be when, subsequently, there is evidence that the claim is fraudulent.

The insurer will have a maximum of three months from the date of specimen **3.7** letter B to investigate the merits of the claim. Not later than the end of that period, the insurer shall reply, stating whether liability is admitted or denied and giving reasons for their denial of liability, including any alternative version of events relied upon and all available documents supporting their position.

Documents

The aim of early disclosure of documents by the insurer is to promote an early **3.8** exchange of relevant information to help in clarifying or resolving the issues in dispute. If the insurer denies liability, in whole or in part, they will at the same time as giving their decision on liability, disclose any documents which are relevant and proportionate to the issues in question, with reference to those identified in the letter of claim.

Attached at Appendix A are specimen, but not exhaustive, lists of docu- **3.9** ments likely to be material in different types of claim. Where the pursuer's agent's investigation of the case is well advanced, the letter of claim should indicate which classes of documents are considered relevant for early disclo- sure. Where this is not practical, these should be identified as soon as practical but disclosure will not affect the timetable.

Where the insurer admits primary liability but alleges contributory negli- **3.10** gence by the pursuer, the insurer should give reasons supporting these allega- tions and disclose those documents from Appendix A which are relevant and proportionate to the issues in dispute. The pursuer's agent should respond to the allegation of contributory negligence before proceedings are issued.

Medical reports

A medical report will be instructed at the earliest opportunity but no later **3.11** than five weeks from the date the insurer admits, in whole or part, liability unless there is a valid reason for not obtaining a report at this stage. In those circumstances, the pursuer's agent will advise accordingly and agree an amended timetable with the insurers or withdraw the case from the Protocol. Any medical report obtained and on which the pursuer intends to rely will be disclosed to the other party within five weeks from the date of its receipt. By mutual consent, the insurers may ask the examiner, via the pursuer's agent, supplementary questions.

The pursuer's agent will normally instruct a medical report, will organise **3.12** access to all relevant medical records, and will send a letter of instruction to a medical expert in general terms of specimen letter C. Where it has been agreed that the insurer will obtain the medical report, the pursuer's agent will agree to disclosure of all medical records relevant to the accident. Pre-accident medical records will be disclosed only with the specific agreement of the pursuer's agent and if relevant to the claim. Any medical report on which the insurer intends to rely will be disclosed to the pursuer's agent within five weeks of receipt.

Damages

3.13   The pursuer's agents will send to the insurer a Statement of Valuation of Claim ("the Statement of Valuation") with supporting documents, where the insurer has admitted liability. The pursuer's agents are recommended to use a standard format for the Statement of Valuation. An example is at specimen D. This can be amended to suit the particular case.

4. SETTLEMENT

4.1   Where the insurer admits liability, in whole or in part, before proceedings are issued, any medical reports, supporting documentary evidence and Statement of Valuation obtained under this Voluntary Protocol on which a party relies, should be disclosed to the other party. The pursuer's agent should delay issuing proceedings for five weeks from the date the insurer receives the statement of valuation to enable the parties to consider whether the claim is capable of settlement.

4.2   Where a Statement of Valuation with supporting documents has been disclosed under 3.12, the insurer shall offer to settle the claim based on their reasonable valuation of it within five weeks of receipt of such disclosure, serving a counter-schedule of valuation if they dispute the pursuer's agent's valuation.

4.3   The pursuer's agent will advise insurers whether or not their offer is to be accepted or rejected, prior to the raising of proceedings and in any event within five weeks of receipt.

4.4   Where a Voluntary Protocol case settles, cheques for both damages and agreed expenses must be paid within five weeks of receipt of the settlement. The date of settlement will be the date when the insurer receives notification of settlement. Thereafter, interest will be payable on both damages and expenses due and payable in accordance with the agreed settlement terms at the prevailing judicial rate from the date of settlement until payment is made in full.

APPENDIX A
STANDARD DISCLOSURE LISTS

RTA cases

SECTION A

In all cases where liability is at issue –
(i)   Documents identifying nature, extent and location of damage to defender's vehicle where there is any dispute about point of impact
(ii)   MOT certificate where relevant
(iii) Maintenance records where vehicle defect is alleged or it is alleged by defender that there was an unforeseen defect which caused or contributed to the accident

SECTION B

Accident involving commercial vehicle as potential defender –
(i)   Tachograph charts or entry from individual control book, where relevant
(ii) Maintenance and repair records required for operators' licence where vehicle defect is alleged or it is alleged by defendants that there was an unforeseen defect which caused or contributed to the accident

SECTION C

Cases against local authorities where highway design defect is alleged –
(i)   Documents produced to comply with section 39 of the Road Traffic Act 1988 in respect of the duty designed to promote road safety, to include studies into road accidents in the relevant area and documents relating to measures recommended to prevent accidents in the relevant area

Road/footway tripping claims

Documents from the highway authority or local authority for a period of 12 months prior to the accident –
(i)   Records of inspection for the relevant stretch of road/footway
(ii) Maintenance records including records of independent contractors working in relevant area
(iii) Statement of the roads authority's policy under the Code of Practice for Delivering Best Value in Highway Maintenance 2001 or alternatively records of the minutes of Highway Authority or Local Authority meetings where maintenance or repair policy has been discussed or decided
(iv) Records of complaints about the state of roads/footway at the accident locus for a 12 month period prior to the accident
(v)   Records of other accidents which have occurred on the relevant stretch of road/footway within 12 months of the accident

Workplace claims

(i)   Accident book entry
(ii)   First aider report
(iii) Surgery record
(iv)   Foreman/supervisor accident report
(v)   Safety representatives accident report
(vi)   RIDDOR report to HSE
(vii) Other communications between defenders and HSE
(viii) Minutes of Health and Safety Committee meeting(s) where accident/matter considered
(ix)   Report to DSS
(x)   Documents listed above relative to any previous accident/matter identified by the claimant and relied upon as proof of negligence
(xi)   Earnings information where defender is employer

Documents produced to comply with requirements of the Management of Health and Safety at Work Regulations 1999 –

(i)   Pre-accident risk assessment required by regulation 3
(ii) Post-accident re-assessment required by regulation 3

(iii) Accident investigation report prepared in implementing the requirements of regulation 5
(iv) Health surveillance records in appropriate cases required by regulation 6
(v) Information provided to employees under regulation 10
(vi) Documents relating to the employee's health and safety training required by regulation 13

Workplace claims – disclosure where specific regulations apply

SECTION A

WORKPLACE (HEALTH SAFETY AND WELFARE) REGULATIONS 1992

(i) Repair and maintenance records required by regulation 5
(ii) Housekeeping records to comply with the requirements of regulation 9
(iii) Hazard warning signs or notices to comply with regulation 17 (traffic routes)

SECTION B

PROVISION AND USE OF WORK EQUIPMENT REGULATIONS 1998

(i) Manufacturers' specifications and instructions in respect of relevant work equipment establishing its suitability to comply with regulation 4
(ii) Maintenance log/maintenance records required to comply with regulation 5
(iii) Documents providing information and instructions to employees to comply with regulation 8
(iv) Documents provided to the employee in respect of training for use to comply with regulation 9
(v) Any notice, sign or document relied upon as a defence to alleged breaches of regulations 14 to 18 dealing with controls and control systems
(vi) Instruction/training documents issued to comply with the requirements of regulation 22 insofar as it deals with maintenance operations where the machinery is not shut down.
(vii) Copies of markings required to comply with regulation 23
(viii) Copies of warnings required to comply with regulation 24

SECTION C

PERSONAL PROTECTIVE EQUIPMENT AT WORK REGULATIONS 1992

(i) Documents relating to the assessment of the personal protective equipment to comply with regulation 6
(ii) Documents relating to the maintenance and replacement of personal protective equipment to comply with regulation 7
(iii) Record of maintenance procedures for personal protective equipment to comply with regulation 7
(iv) Records of tests and examinations of personal protective equipment to comply with regulation 7

(v) Documents providing information, instruction and training in relation to the personal protective equipment to comply with regulation 9

(vi) Instructions for use of personal protective equipment to include the manufacturers' instructions to comply with regulation 10

SECTION D

MANUAL HANDLING OPERATIONS REGULATIONS 1992

(i)   Manual handling risk assessment carried out to comply with the requirements of regulation 4(1)(b)(i)

(ii) Re-assessment carried out post-accident to comply with requirements of regulation 4(1)(b)(i)

(iii) Documents showing the information provided to the employee to give general indications related to the load and precise indications on the weight of the load and the heaviest side of the load if the centre of gravity was not positioned centrally to comply with regulation 4(1)(b)(iii)

(iv) Documents relating to training in respect of manual handling operations and training records

(v)   All documents showing or tending to show the weight of the load at the material time

SECTION E

HEALTH AND SAFETY (DISPLAY SCREEN EQUIPMENT) REGULATIONS 1992

(i)   Analysis of work stations to assess and reduce risks carried out to comply with the requirements of regulation 2

(ii) Re-assessment of analysis of work stations to assess and reduce risks following development of symptoms by the claimant

(iii) Documents detailing the provision of training including training records to comply with the requirements of regulation 6

(iv) Documents providing information to employees to comply with the requirements of regulation 7

SECTION F

CONTROL OF SUBSTANCES HAZARDOUS TO HEALTH REGULATIONS 2002

(i)   Risk assessment carried out to comply with the requirements of regulation 6

(ii) Reviewed risk assessment carried out to comply with the requirements of regulation 6

(iii) Copy labels from containers used for storage handling and disposal of carcinogenics to comply with the requirements of regulation 7(2A)(h)

(iv) Warning signs identifying designation of areas and installations which may be contaminated by carcinogenics to comply with the requirements of regulation 7

(v)   Documents relating to the assessment of the personal protective equipment to comply with regulation 7

(vi)   Documents relating to the maintenance and replacement of personal protective equipment to comply with regulation 7

(vii)   Record of maintenance procedures for personal protective equipment to comply with regulation 7

(viii) Records of tests and examinations of personal protective equipment to comply with regulation 7

(ix)   Documents providing information, instruction and training in relation to the personal protective equipment to comply with regulation 7

(x)   Instructions for use of personal protective equipment to include the manufacturers' instructions to comply with regulation 7

(xi)   Air monitoring records for substances assigned a maximum exposure limit or occupational exposure standard to comply with the requirements of regulation 7

(xii)   Maintenance examination and test of control measures records to comply with regulation 9

(xiii) Monitoring records to comply with the requirements of regulation 10

(xiv) Health surveillance records to comply with the requirements of regulation 11

(xv)   Documents detailing information, instruction and training including training records for employees to comply with the requirements of regulation 12

(xvi) Labels and health and safety data sheets supplied to the employers to comply with the CHIP Regulations.

SECTION G

CONSTRUCTION (DESIGN AND MANAGEMENT) (AMENDMENT) (REGULATIONS 2000

(i)   Notification of a project form (HSE Fl 0) to comply with the requirements of regulation 7

(ii)   Health and safety plan to comply with requirements of regulation 15

(iii) Health and safety file to comply with the requirements of regulations 12 and 14

(iv)   Information and training records provided to comply with the requirements of regulation 17

(v)   Records of advice from and views of persons at work to comply with the requirements of regulation 18

SECTION H

PRESSURE SYSTEMS AND TRANSPORTABLE GAS CONTAINERS REGULATIONS 1989

(i) Information and specimen markings provided to comply with the requirements of regulation 5

(ii) Written statements specifying the safe operating limits of a system to comply with the requirements of regulation 7

(iii) Copy of the written scheme of examination required to comply with the requirements of regulation 8

(iv) Examination records required to comply with the requirements of regulation 9

(v) Instructions provided for the use of operator to comply with regulation 11
(vi) Records kept to comply with the requirements of regulation 13
(vii) Records kept to comply with the requirements of regulation 22

SECTION I

LIFTING OPERATIONS AND LIFTING EQUIPMENT REGULATIONS 1998

(i) All documents showing the weight of any load to establish lifting equipment of adequate strength and stability to comply with regulation 4
(ii) All notices and markings showing the safe working load of machinery and accessories to comply with regulation 7
(iii) All documents showing lifting operations have been planned by a competent person, appropriately supervised and carried out in a safe manner to comply with regulation 8
(iv) All defect reports to comply with regulation 10

SECTION K

CONSTRUCTION (HEAD PROTECTION) REGULATIONS 1989

(i) Pre-accident assessment of head protection required to comply with regulation 3(4)
(ii) Post-accident re-assessment required to comply with regulation 3(5)

SECTION L

GAS CONTAINERS REGULATIONS 1989

(i) Information and specimen markings provided to comply with the requirements of regulation 5
(ii) Written statements specifying the safe operating limits of a system to comply with the requirements of regulation 7
(iii) Copy of the written scheme of examination required to comply with the requirements of regulation 8
(iv) Examination records required to comply with the requirements of regulation 9
(v) Instructions provided for the use of operator to comply with regulation 11
(vi) Records kept to comply with the requirements of regulation 13
(vii) Records kept to comply with the requirements of regulation 22

SECTION M

CONSTRUCTION (HEALTH, SAFETY AND WELFARE) REGULATIONS 1996

(i) All documents showing the identity of the principal contractor, or a person who controls the way in which construction work is carried out by a person at work, to comply with the terms of regulation 4
(ii) All documents and inspection reports to comply with the terms of sections 29 and 30

APPENDIX B
PERSONAL INJURY CASES – PROTOCOL FEES FROM
1 JANUARY 2006

The fees for claims intimated after 1 January 2006 and dealt with entirely under the Protocol comprise the following elements:

1. **INVESTIGATION FEE**
   On settlements up to and including £1,500 £ 300
   On settlements over £1,500 £ 660
2. **NEGOTIATION AND COMPLETION FEE**
   On settlements up to £2,500 25 %
   On the excess over £2,500 up to £5,000 15 %
   On the excess over £5,000 up to £10,000 7.5 %
   On the excess over £10,000 up to £20,000 5 %
   On the excess over £20,000 2.5%

NOTES
(1) In addition, VAT (on all elements) and outlays will be payable.
(2) In cases including payment to CRU the Protocol fee will be calculated in accordance with the following examples:
   (i) Solatium £5,000
      Wage loss £5,000
      CRU repayment £2,000
      Sum paid to pursuer £8,000
      In these circumstances the Protocol fee will be based on £10,000 being the total value of the pursuer's claim.
   (ii) Settlement as above but repayment to the CRU is £6,000 and only £5,000 can be offset. Payment to the pursuer is £5,000 and £6,000 to the CRU. The protocol fee will be on £10,000 being the value of the pursuer's claim, as opposed to the total sum paid by the insurer – £11,000.
(3) In cases involving refundable sick pay the Protocol fee will be calculated by including any refundable element.

APPENDIX C
MEMBERSHIP OF THE FSCM

The following insurers are currently members of the FSCM:

- NFU
- E-sure
- Halifax
- Sainsbury's Bank
- First Alternative
- Zurich Municipal
- Zurich Commercial
- Eagle Star Direct
- Zurich London
- Zurich Personal Lines Insurance

- Norwich Union
- Norwich Union Direct
- Ford Insure
- AIG Europe (UK) Ltd on behalf of New Hampshire Insurance Co
- Landmark Insurance Co
- Allianz Cornhill
- RSA
- More Than
- Direct Line
- Churchill
- Prudential
- Tesco
- Privilege
- Devitt
- UKI Insurance – (Peugeot, Citroen, Barclay, Nat-West, BMW Fleet, Vauxhall, eg and Renault)
- Pearl
- NIG
- Nationwide
- Lloyds TSB
- AXA
- QBE
- CIS General Insurance Society Ltd
- Marsh (on behalf of self insured clients)
- AON (on behalf of self insured clients)

SCOTTISH STATUTORY INSTRUMENTS

2017 No. 52

COURT OF SESSION
SHERIFF COURT

Act of Sederunt (Rules of the Court of Session 1994 and Ordinary Cause Rules 1993 Amendment) (Pursuers' Offers) 2017

Made - - - -	*28th February 2017*
Laid before the Scottish	
Parliament - - - -	*2nd March 2017*
Coming into force - -	*3rd April 2017*

In accordance with section 4 of the Scottish Civil Justice Council and Criminal Legal Assistance Act 2013(1), the Court of Session has approved draft rules submitted to it by the Scottish Civil Justice Council with such modification as it thinks appropriate.

The Court of Session therefore makes this Act of Sederunt under the powers conferred by section 103(1) and 104(1) of the Courts Reform (Scotland) Act 2014(2), and all other powers enabling it to do so.

Citation and commencement, etc.

1.—(1) This Act of Sederunt may be cited as the Act of Sederunt (Rules of the Court of Session 1994 and Ordinary Cause Rules 1993 Amendment) (Pursuers' Offers) 2017.

(2) It comes into force on 3rd April 2017.

(3) A certified copy is to be inserted in the Books of Sederunt.

Amendment of the Rules of the Court of Session 1994

2.—(1) The Rules of the Court of Session 1994(3) are amended in accordance with this paragraph.

(2) After Chapter 34 (reports to Inner House), insert—

---

(1) 2013 asp 3. Section 4 was amended by the Courts Reform (Scotland) Act 2014 (asp 18), schedule 5, paragraph 31(3) and by the Inquiries into Fatal Accidents and Sudden Deaths etc. (Scotland) Act 2016 (asp 2), schedule 1, paragraph 1(4).
(2) 2014 asp 18.
(3) The Rules of the Court of Session 1994 are in schedule 2 of the Act of Sederunt (Rules of the Court of Session 1994) 1994 (S.I. 1994/1443), last amended by S.S.I. 2017/26.

Document Generated: 2017-08-05

"CHAPTER 34A(4)

PURSUERS' OFFERS

Interpretation of this Chapter

34A.1. In this Chapter—

"appropriate date" means the date by which a pursuer's offer could reasonably have been accepted;

"fees" means fees of solicitors, and includes any additional fee;

"pursuer's offer" means an offer by a pursuer to settle a claim against a defender made in accordance with this Chapter;

"relevant period" means the period from the appropriate date to the date of acceptance of the pursuer's offer or, as the case may be, to the date on which judgment was given, or on which the verdict was applied.

Pursuers' offers

34A.2.—(1) A pursuer's offer may be made in any cause where the summons includes a conclusion for an order for payment of a sum or sums of money, other than an order—

(a) which the court may not make without evidence; or

(b) the making of which is dependent on the making of another order which the court may not make without evidence.

(2) This Chapter has no effect as regards any other form of offer to settle.

Making of offer

34A.3.—(1) A pursuer's offer is made by lodging in process an offer in the terms specified in rule 34A.4.

(2) A pursuer's offer may be made at any time before—

(a) the court makes avizandum or, if it does not make avizandum, gives judgment; or

(b) in a jury trial, the jury retires to consider the verdict.

(3) A pursuer's offer may be withdrawn at any time before it is accepted by lodging in process a minute of withdrawal.

Form of offer

34A.4. A pursuer's offer must—

(a) state that it is made under this Chapter;

(b) offer to accept—

(i) a sum or sums of money, inclusive of interest to the date of the offer; and

(ii) the taxed expenses of process; and

(c) specify the conclusion or conclusions of the summons in satisfaction of which the sum or sums and expenses referred to in paragraph (b) would be accepted.

---

(4) The rules previously comprising Chapter 34A were revoked by S.I. 1996/2769.

2

Document Generated: 2017-08-05

Status: *This is the original version (as it was originally made). This item of legislation is currently only available in its original format.*

Disclosure of offers

34A.5.—(1) No averment of the fact that a pursuer's offer has been made may be included in any pleadings.

(2) Where a pursuer's offer has not been accepted—

  (a) the court must not be informed that an offer has been made until—

    (i) the court has pronounced judgment; or

    (ii) in the case of a jury trial, the jury has returned its verdict; and

  (b) a jury must not be informed that an offer has been made until it has returned its verdict.

Acceptance of offers

34A.6.—(1) A pursuer's offer may be accepted any time before—

  (a) the offer is withdrawn;

  (b) the court makes avizandum or, if it does not make avizandum, gives judgment; or

  (c) in the case of a jury trial, the jury retires to consider its verdict.

(2) It is accepted by lodging in process an acceptance of the offer in the form of a minute of acceptance.

(3) A minute of acceptance must be unqualified other than as respects any question of contribution, indemnity or relief.

(4) On acceptance of a pursuer's offer either the pursuer or the defender may apply by motion for decree in terms of the offer and minute of acceptance.

(5) Where a pursuer's offer includes an offer to accept a sum of money in satisfaction of a conclusion for decree jointly and severally against two or more defenders, the offer is accepted only when accepted by all such defenders.

(6) However, the court may, on the motion of the pursuer, and with the consent of any defender who has lodged a minute of acceptance, grant decree in terms of the offer and minute of acceptance.

Late acceptance of offers

34A.7.—(1) This rule applies to the determination of a motion under rule 34A.6(4) where the court is satisfied that a defender lodged a minute of acceptance after the appropriate date.

(2) On the pursuer's motion the court must, except on cause shown—

  (a) allow interest on any sum decerned for from the date on which the pursuer's offer was made; and

  (b) find the defender liable for payment to the pursuer of a sum calculated in accordance with rule 34A.9.

(3) Where the court is satisfied that more than one defender lodged a minute of acceptance after the appropriate date the court may find those defenders liable to contribute to payment of the sum referred to in paragraph (2)(b) in such proportions as the court thinks fit.

(4) Where the court makes a finding under paragraph (2)(b), the pursuer may apply for decerniture for payment of the sum as so calculated no later than 21 days after the later of—

  (a) the date of the Auditor's report of the taxation of the pursuer's account of expenses; and

  (b) the date of the interlocutor disposing of a note of objection.

Document Generated: 2017-08-05

Non-acceptance of offers

34A.8.—(1) This rule applies where—

(a) a pursuer's offer has been made, and has not been withdrawn;

(b) the offer has not been accepted;

(c) either—

(i) the court has pronounced judgment; or

(ii) in the case of a jury trial, the verdict of the jury has been applied;

(d) the judgment or verdict, in so far as relating to the conclusions of the summons specified in the pursuer's offer, is at least as favourable in money terms to the pursuer as the terms offered; and

(e) the court is satisfied that the pursuer's offer was a genuine attempt to settle the proceedings.

(2) For the purpose of determining if the condition specified in paragraph (1)(d) is satisfied, interest awarded in respect of the period after the lodging of the pursuer's offer is to be disregarded.

(3) On the pursuer's motion the court must, except on cause shown, decern against the defender for payment to the pursuer of a sum calculated in accordance with rule 34A.9.

(4) No such motion may be enrolled after the expiry of 21 days after the later of—

(a) the date of the Auditor's report of the taxation of the pursuer's account of expenses; and

(b) the date of the interlocutor disposing of a note of objection.

(5) Where more than one defender is found liable to the pursuer in respect of a conclusion specified in the offer, the court may find those defenders liable to contribute to payment of the sum referred to in paragraph (3) in such proportions as it thinks fit.

Extent of defender's liability

34A.9. The sum that may be decerned for under rule 34A.7(2)(b) or rule 34A.8(3) is a sum corresponding to half the fees allowed on taxation of the pursuer's account of expenses, in so far as those fees are attributable to the relevant period, or in so far as they can reasonably be attributed to that period.".

Amendment of the Ordinary Cause Rules 1993

3.—(1) The Ordinary Cause Rules 1993(5) are amended in accordance with this paragraph.

(2) After Chapter 27 (caution and security), insert—

"CHAPTER 27A

PURSUERS' OFFERS

Interpretation of this Chapter

27A.1. In this Chapter—

---

(5) The Ordinary Cause Rules 1993 are in schedule 1 of the Sheriff Courts (Scotland) Act 1907 (c.51). Schedule 1 was substituted by S.I. 1993/1956 and last amended by S.S.I. 2016/415.

Document Generated: 2017-08-05

"appropriate date" means the date by which a pursuer's offer could reasonably have been accepted;

"fees" means fees of solicitors, and includes any additional fee;

"pursuer's offer" means an offer by a pursuer to settle a claim against a defender made in accordance with this Chapter;

"relevant period" means the period from the appropriate date to the date of acceptance of the pursuer's offer or, as the case may be, to the date on which judgment was given, or on which the verdict was applied.

Pursuers' offers

27A.2.—(1) A pursuer's offer may be made in any cause where the initial writ includes a crave for an order for payment of a sum or sums of money, other than an order—

(a) which the sheriff may not make without evidence; or

(b) the making of which is dependent on the making of another order which the sheriff may not make without evidence.

(2) This Chapter has no effect as regards any other form of offer to settle.

Making of offer

27A.3.—(1) A pursuer's offer is made by lodging in process an offer in the terms specified in rule 27A.4.

(2) A pursuer's offer may be made at any time before—

(a) the sheriff makes avizandum or, if the sheriff does not make avizandum, gives judgment; or

(b) in a jury trial, the jury retires to consider the verdict.

(3) A pursuer's offer may be withdrawn at any time before it is accepted by lodging in process a minute of withdrawal.

Form of offer

27A.4. A pursuer's offer must—

(a) state that it is made under this Chapter;

(b) offer to accept—

(i) a sum or sums of money, inclusive of interest to the date of the offer; and

(ii) the taxed expenses of process; and

(c) specify the crave or craves of the initial writ in satisfaction of which the sum or sums and expenses referred to in paragraph (b) would be accepted.

Disclosure of offers

27A.5.—(1) No averment of the fact that a pursuer's offer has been made may be included in any pleadings.

(2) Where a pursuer's offer has not been accepted—

(a) the sheriff must not be informed that an offer has been made until—

(i) the sheriff has pronounced judgment; or

(ii) in the case of a jury trial, the jury has returned its verdict; and

Document Generated: 2017-08-05

(b) a jury must not be informed that an offer has been made until it has returned its verdict.

Acceptance of offers

27A.6.—(1) A pursuer's offer may be accepted any time before—

(a) the offer is withdrawn;

(b) the sheriff makes avizandum or, if the sheriff does not make avizandum, gives judgment; or

(c) in the case of a jury trial, the jury retires to consider its verdict.

(2) A pursuer's offer is accepted by lodging in process an acceptance of the offer in the form of a minute of acceptance.

(3) A minute of acceptance must be unqualified other than as respects any question of contribution, indemnity or relief.

(4) On acceptance of a pursuer's offer either the pursuer or the defender may apply by motion for decree in terms of the offer and minute of acceptance.

(5) Where a pursuer's offer includes an offer to accept a sum of money in satisfaction of a crave for decree jointly and severally against two or more defenders, the offer is accepted only when accepted by all such defenders.

(6) However, the sheriff may, on the motion of the pursuer, and with the consent of any defender who has lodged a minute of acceptance, grant decree in terms of the offer and minute of acceptance.

Late acceptance of offers

27A.7.—(1) This rule applies to the determination of a motion under rule 27A.6(4) where the sheriff is satisfied that a defender lodged a minute of acceptance after the appropriate date.

(2) On the pursuer's motion the sheriff must, except on cause shown—

(a) allow interest on any sum decerned for from the date on which the pursuer's offer was made; and

(b) find the defender liable for payment to the pursuer of a sum calculated in accordance with rule 27A.9.

(3) Where the sheriff is satisfied that more than one defender lodged a minute of acceptance after the appropriate date the sheriff may find those defenders liable to contribute to payment of the sum referred to in paragraph (2)(b) in such proportions as the sheriff thinks fit.

(4) Where the sheriff makes a finding under paragraph (2)(b), the pursuer may apply for decerniture for payment of the sum as so calculated no later than the granting of decree for expenses as taxed.

Non-acceptance of offers

27A.8.—(1) This rule applies where—

(a) a pursuer's offer has been made, and has not been withdrawn;

(b) the offer has not been accepted;

(c) either—

(i) the sheriff has pronounced judgment; or

(ii) in the case of a jury trial, the verdict of the jury has been applied;

(d) the judgment or verdict, in so far as relating to the craves specified in the pursuer's offer, is at least as favourable in money terms to the pursuer as the terms offered; and

(e) the sheriff is satisfied that the pursuer's offer was a genuine attempt to settle the proceedings.

(2) For the purpose of determining if the condition specified in paragraph (1)(d) is satisfied, interest awarded in respect of the period after the lodging of the pursuer's offer is to be disregarded.

(3) On the pursuer's motion the sheriff must, except on cause shown, decern against the defender for payment to the pursuer of a sum calculated in accordance with rule 27A.9.

(4) Such a motion must be lodged no later than the granting of decree for expenses as taxed.

(5) Where more than one defender is found liable to the pursuer in respect of a crave specified in the offer, the sheriff may find those defenders liable to contribute to payment of the sum referred to in paragraph (3) in such proportions as the sheriff thinks fit.

Extent of defender's liability

27A.9. The sum that may be decerned for under rule 27A.7(2)(b) or rule 27A.8(3) is a sum corresponding to half the fees allowed on taxation of the pursuer's account of expenses, in so far as those fees are attributable to the relevant period, or in so far they can reasonably be attributed to that period.".

CJM SUTHERLAND
Lord President
Edinburgh
28th February 2017   I.P.D.

Document Generated: 2017-08-05

EXPLANATORY NOTE

(This note is not part of the Act of Sederunt)

This Act of Sederunt amends the Rules of the Court of Session 1994 and the Ordinary Cause Rules 1993 by inserting rules that provide for a formal system of pursuers' offers.

A pursuer's offer can be made in any case in which the summons or initial writ includes a pecuniary conclusion or crave, other than a conclusion or crave that cannot be granted without evidence. The offer, which is lodged in process, must offer to accept a sum or sums of money, inclusive of interest to the date of the offer, along with the taxed expenses of process. It must also specify the conclusions or craves in satisfaction of which the sum or sums would be accepted.

A pursuer's offer is accepted by lodging a minute of acceptance in process. The acceptance must be unqualified other than as regards any question of contribution, indemnity or relief. On the acceptance of an offer, either party may apply by motion for decree in terms of the offer and acceptance. Where the offer relates to a conclusion or crave for decree against more than one defender, it is only accepted when accepted by all such defenders, but the pursuer may nevertheless seek decree against an accepting defender, with the consent of that defender, although the offer has not been accepted by all defenders.

Where an offer is accepted, and the court is satisfied that it was accepted later than it could reasonably have been accepted, the rules provide for the defender to be found liable for interest on the principal sum from the date of the offer, and for payment of an additional sum to the pursuer.

The rules also provide for the defender to be found liable for payment of an additional sum to the pursuer where an offer is not accepted, where the judgement or verdict is at least as favourable to the pursuer as the terms offered, and where the court is satisfied that the offer was a genuine attempt to settle.

The additional sum for which the defender is found liable in these circumstances is calculated by reference to the pursuer's taxed expenses, being a sum corresponding to half the fees allowed on taxation that are attributable to the period following the making of the offer.

Civil Litigation (Expenses and Group Proceedings) (Scotland) Act 2018

2018 asp 10

The Bill for this Act of the Scottish Parliament was passed by the Parliament on 1st May 2018 and received Royal Assent on 5th June 2018

An Act of the Scottish Parliament to make provision about success fee agreements; to make provision about expenses in civil litigation; to make provision about the offices of the Auditor of the Court of Session, the auditor of the Sheriff Appeal Court and the auditor of the sheriff court; and to make provision about the bringing of civil proceedings on behalf of a group of persons.

PART 1

SUCCESS FEE AGREEMENTS

1   Success fee agreements

(1) In this Part, a "success fee agreement" is an agreement between a person providing relevant services (the "provider") and the recipient of those services (the "recipient") under which the recipient—

    (a)   is to make a payment (the "success fee") to the provider in respect of the services if the recipient obtains a financial benefit in connection with a matter in relation to which the services are provided, but

    (b)   is not to make any payment, or is to make a payment of a lower amount than the success fee, in respect of the services if no such benefit is obtained.

(2) In this section—

    "claims management services" means services consisting of the provision of advice or services, other than legal services, in connection with the making of a claim for damages or other financial benefit, including—

        (a)   advice or services in relation to—

            (i)   legal representation,

            (ii)   the payment or funding of costs associated with making the claim,

        (b)   referring or introducing one person to another,

Legislation and Protocols   239

2   *Civil Litigation (Expenses and Group Proceedings) (Scotland) Act 2018 asp 10*
                                                        PART 1 – SUCCESS FEE AGREEMENTS
                                                           Document Generated: 2021-04-01

(c) making inquiries,

"legal services" means services consisting of the provision of legal advice, assistance or representation,

"payment" includes a transfer of assets and any other transfer of money's worth,

"relevant services" means legal services or claims management services provided in connection with a matter—

> (a) which is the subject of civil proceedings to which the recipient is a party before a Scottish court or tribunal, or
>
> (b) in relation to which such proceedings are in contemplation,

"Scottish court or tribunal" means a court or tribunal established under the law of Scotland.

(3) In this Part, the following terms, in relation to a success fee agreement, are to be construed in accordance with this section—

> "payment",
>
> "provider",
>
> "recipient",
>
> "relevant services",
>
> "success fee".

2   Enforceability

(1) A success fee agreement is not unenforceable by reason only that it is a pactum de quota litis (that is, an agreement for a share of the litigation).

(2) Subsection (1) does not affect any other ground on which a success fee agreement may be unenforceable.

3   Expenses in the event of success

(1) This section applies where the recipient of relevant services under a success fee agreement—

> (a) is awarded expenses in civil proceedings concerned with a matter to which the agreement relates, or
>
> (b) agrees with another person that the recipient is entitled to recover expenses from that person in relation to such a matter.

(2) Unless the success fee agreement provides otherwise—

> (a) the provider is entitled to recover and retain the expenses so far as those expenses relate to the relevant services provided by the provider in relation to the matter, and
>
> (b) the amount of the success fee to be paid under the agreement is not affected by the amount of expenses recovered and retained by the provider.

(3) Subsection (2) is subject to section 17(2A) of the Legal Aid (Scotland) Act 1986 (which makes provision for circumstances in which expenses recovered are to be paid to the Scottish Legal Aid Board).

Civil Litigation (Expenses and Group Proceedings) (Scotland) Act 2018 asp 10
PART 1 – SUCCESS FEE AGREEMENTS
Document Generated: 2021-04-01   3

Status: *This is the original version (as it was originally enacted).*

4   Power to cap success fees

(1) The Scottish Ministers may by regulations make provision for or about the maximum amounts of success fees that may be provided for under success fee agreements.

(2) Regulations under subsection (1) may specify maximum amounts or provide for them to be determined in accordance with the regulations.

(3) Subsection (4) applies where the maximum amount of the success fee that may be provided for under a success fee agreement is restricted—

    (a)   by provision made in regulations under subsection (1), and

    (b)   by, or in accordance with, another enactment.

(4) The maximum amount of the success fee that may be paid under the agreement is the lower of the amounts allowed for by, or in accordance with, the enactments mentioned in subsection (3)(a) and (b).

(5) A success fee agreement is unenforceable to the extent that it provides for a success fee of an amount that is higher than the maximum amount allowed for by virtue of this section.

5   Exclusion for certain matters

(1) A success fee agreement must not be entered into in connection with a matter which may be the subject of civil proceedings of a description specified by the Scottish Ministers in regulations.

(2) Regulations under subsection (1) may relate to all success fee agreements or to success fee agreements of a description specified by the Scottish Ministers in the regulations.

6   Personal injury claims

(1) This section applies to a success fee agreement entered into in connection with a claim for damages for—

    (a)   personal injuries, or

    (b)   the death of a person from personal injuries.

(2) The agreement must provide that the recipient of the relevant services is not liable to make any payment (including outlays incurred in providing the services) to the provider in respect of the services, apart from the success fee, regardless of whether any damages are obtained.

(3) In subsection (2), "outlays" do not include any sums paid in respect of insurance premiums in connection with the claim to which the agreement relates.

(4) The agreement—

    (a)   may provide that any damages for future loss obtained in connection with the claim (the "future element") will be included in the amount of damages by reference to which the success fee is to, or may, be calculated (the "relevant amount of damages") if the future element is within subsection (5), but

    (b)   otherwise, must provide that any future element will not be included in the relevant amount of damages.

(5) The future element is within this subsection if it is to be paid in a lump sum and—

    (a)   does not exceed £1,000,000, or

Legislation and Protocols

241

4

Civil Litigation (Expenses and Group Proceedings) (Scotland) Act 2018 asp 10
PART 1 – SUCCESS FEE AGREEMENTS
Document Generated: 2021-04-01

Status: This is the original version (as it was originally enacted).

    (b)   exceeds £1,000,000 and—

        (i) the provider had not advised the recipient to accept that the future element be paid in periodical instalments, and

        (ii) the condition in subsection (6) is met.

(6) The condition is—

    (a)   in the case where the damages are awarded by a court or tribunal, that the court or tribunal in awarding the future element has stated that it is satisfied that it is in the recipient's best interests that the future element be paid as a lump sum rather than in periodical instalments,

    (b)   in the case where the damages are obtained by agreement, that an independent actuary has, after having consulted the recipient personally in the absence of the provider, certified that in the actuary's view it is in the recipient's best interests that the future element be paid as a lump sum rather than in periodical instalments.

(7) The agreement is unenforceable to the extent that it makes provision contrary to subsection (2) or (4).

(8) The Scottish Ministers may by regulations substitute another sum for the sum for the time being specified in subsection (5)(a) and (b).

(9) In subsection (1), "personal injuries" include any disease and any impairment of a person's physical or mental condition.

(10) In subsection (6)(b), "actuary" means an Associate or Fellow of the Institute and Faculty of Actuaries.

7   Form, content etc.

(1) A success fee agreement must be in writing.

(2) A success fee agreement must specify the basis on which the amount of the success fee is to be determined.

(3) The Scottish Ministers may by regulations make further provision about success fee agreements including in particular provision about—

    (a)   their form and content (including their terms),

    (b)   the manner in which they may be entered into,

    (c)   their modification and termination,

    (d)   the resolution of disputes in relation to such agreements,

    (e)   the consequences of failure to comply with the requirements of subsection (1) or (2) or the regulations,

    (f)   the application of this Part, or any provision made under it, where a recipient receives relevant services from more than one provider in connection with the same matter.

(4) Regulations under subsection (3) may modify this section so as to—

    (a)   add text to it,

    (b)   modify any text added under paragraph (a).

Civil Litigation (Expenses and Group Proceedings) (Scotland) Act 2018 asp 10   5
PART 2 – EXPENSES IN CIVIL LITIGATION
Document Generated: 2021-04-01
Status: This is the original version (as it was originally enacted).

PART 2

EXPENSES IN CIVIL LITIGATION

8   Restriction on pursuer's liability for expenses in personal injury claims

(1) This section applies in civil proceedings where—

    (a)   the person bringing the proceedings makes a claim for damages for—

        (i) personal injuries, or

        (ii) the death of a person from personal injuries, and

    (b)   the person conducts the proceedings in an appropriate manner.

(2) The court must not make an award of expenses against the person in respect of any expenses which relate to—

    (a)   the claim, or

    (b)   any appeal in respect of the claim.

(3) Subsection (2) does not prevent the court from making an award in respect of expenses which relate to any other type of claim in the proceedings.

(4) For the purposes of subsection (1)(b), a person conducts civil proceedings in an appropriate manner unless the person or the person's legal representative—

    (a)   makes a fraudulent representation or otherwise acts fraudulently in connection with the claim or proceedings,

    (b)   behaves in a manner which is manifestly unreasonable in connection with the claim or proceedings, or

    (c)   otherwise, conducts the proceedings in a manner that the court considers amounts to an abuse of process.

(5) For the purpose of subsection (4)(a), the standard of proof is the balance of probabilities.

(6) Subsection (2) is subject to any exceptions that may be specified in an act of sederunt under section 103(1) or 104(1) of the Courts Reform (Scotland) Act 2014.

(7) In subsection (1)(a), "personal injuries" include any disease and any impairment of a person's physical or mental condition.

9   Representation free of charge

(1) This section applies in civil proceedings where—

    (a)   a party to the proceedings is represented by a legal representative, and

    (b)   some (or all) of that representation is provided free of charge.

(2) The party must disclose to the court the fact that some (or all) of the representation is provided free of charge.

(3) The court may order a person to make a payment to the charity designated under subsection (5) in respect of the representation which was provided free of charge.

(4) In considering whether to make an order under subsection (3) and the terms of such an order, the court must have regard to—

Legislation and Protocols   243

6   *Civil Litigation (Expenses and Group Proceedings) (Scotland) Act 2018 asp 10*
                                                                PART 2 – EXPENSES IN CIVIL LITIGATION
                                                                      Document Generated: 2021-04-01
                          Status: This is the original version (as it was originally enacted).

    (a)   whether, had the representation not been provided free of charge, the court would have awarded expenses in respect of the representation, and

    (b)   if so, what the terms of the award would have been.

(5) For the purposes of subsection (3), the Lord President of the Court of Session must designate a charity which—

    (a)   is registered in the Scottish Charity Register, and

    (b)   has a charitable purpose (however described) of improving access to justice in respect of civil proceedings in Scotland.

(6) Subsection (3) does not apply in relation to representation provided under section 28 of the Equality Act 2006 (legal assistance).

(7) In this section, "free of charge" means otherwise than for or in expectation of a fee, gain or reward.

10   Third party funding of civil litigation

(1) This section applies where a party to civil proceedings receives financial assistance in respect of the proceedings from another person (whether directly or through an intermediary) who is not a party to the proceedings ("the funder").

(2) The party receiving financial assistance must disclose to the court—

    (a)   if known to the party, the identity of the funder and any intermediary, and

    (b)   the nature of the assistance being provided.

(3) If the funder has a financial interest in respect of the outcome of the proceedings—

    (a)   the party receiving the assistance must disclose that interest to the court once the substantive issues in dispute in the proceedings have been decided or otherwise resolved, and

    (b)   the court may make an award of expenses against the funder and any intermediary.

(4) Subsection (3) does not apply where the assistance is provided—

    (a)   under a success fee agreement (within the meaning of section 1),

    (b)   by a trade union or similar body which represents the interests of workers.

(5) This section does not apply where the assistance is provided in respect of family proceedings by—

    (a)   the spouse or civil partner of the party receiving the assistance,

    (b)   a person living with the party as if they were married to each other,

    (c)   a parent of the party,

    (d)   a child of the party,

    (e)   a sibling of the party (whether of the full-blood or of the half-blood).

(6) For the purposes of this section—

"family proceedings" has the same meaning as in section 135 of the Courts Reform (Scotland) Act 2014,

"financial assistance" does not include a payment from the Scottish Legal Aid Fund.

(7) This section is subject to an act of sederunt under section 103(1) or 104(1) of the Courts Reform (Scotland) Act 2014.

11   Awards of expenses against legal representatives

(1) This section applies in civil proceedings where the court considers that a legal representative of a party to the proceedings has committed a serious breach of that representative's duties to the court.

(2) The court may make an award of expenses against the legal representative.

(3) This section is subject to any limitations that may be specified in an act of sederunt under section 103(1) or 104(1) of the Courts Reform (Scotland) Act 2014.

12   Minor and consequential modifications of the Courts Reform (Scotland) Act 2014

(1) The Courts Reform (Scotland) Act 2014 is amended as follows.

(2) In section 81(5)(b) (expenses in simple procedure cases), for "unreasonably" substitute "in a manner which is manifestly unreasonable".

(3) In section 103(2) (examples of how the power to regulate procedure and practice in the Court of Session may be exercised)—

    (a)   in paragraph (j), for "to parties to" substitute "in",

    (b)   in paragraph (k), after "parties" insert "or persons representing such parties".

(4) In section 104(2) (examples of how the power to regulate procedure and practice in the sheriff court and Sheriff Appeal Court may be exercised)—

    (a)   in paragraph (j), for "to parties to" substitute "in",

    (b)   in paragraph (k), after "parties" insert "or persons representing such parties".

13   Meaning of "legal representative"

In this Part, "legal representative" means—

    (a)   a solicitor enrolled in the roll of solicitors kept under section 7 of the Solicitors (Scotland) Act 1980,

    (b)   a member of the Faculty of Advocates,

    (c)   any other person who may exercise a right of audience or conduct litigation in civil proceedings on behalf of a party to the proceedings.

PART 3

AUDITORS OF COURT

14   Auditors of court

(1) There is to continue to be—

    (a)   an office of the Court of Session called the Auditor of the Court of Session,

    (b)   an office of the Sheriff Appeal Court called the auditor of the Sheriff Appeal Court,

    (c)   an office called the auditor of the sheriff court.

(2) In this Part, the holders of those offices are referred to as the "auditors of court".

(3) The Scottish Courts and Tribunals Service ("the SCTS") has the function of appointing individuals to hold those offices.

(4) A person's appointment as an auditor of court—

    (a)   lasts for such period, and

    (b)   is on such other terms and conditions,

as the SCTS may determine.

(5) The auditors of court are also members of the staff of the SCTS and, accordingly, a reference in any enactment to the staff of the SCTS includes, except where the context requires otherwise, a reference to the auditors of court.

(6) The Auditor of the Court of Session is to continue to be a member of the College of Justice.

(7) The schedule modifies enactments in relation to the auditors of court.

15   Temporary Auditor of the Court of Session

(1) Subsection (2) applies during any period when—

    (a)   the office of the Auditor of the Court of Session is vacant, or

    (b)   the holder of that office is for any reason unable to carry out the functions of the office.

(2) The Lord President of the Court of Session may appoint a person to act as the Auditor of the Court of Session during that period.

(3) A person appointed under subsection (2)—

    (a)   is to be appointed on such terms and conditions as the Lord President determines,

    (b)   while acting as the Auditor of the Court of Session, is to be treated for all purposes, other than those of sections 14(4), (5) and (6) and 18(1) and (6), as the Auditor of the Court of Session.

16   Auditors' functions

(1) An auditor of court—

    (a)   is to tax such accounts of expenses as are remitted to the auditor for taxation by a court or tribunal,

    (b)   has such other functions as are conferred on that office by an enactment (including this Act).

(2) An auditor of court may tax such accounts as are submitted to the auditor for taxation otherwise than on remission from a court or tribunal or where required by an enactment.

(3) An auditor of the sheriff court may—

    (a)   tax an account of expenses remitted to any auditor of the sheriff court by a court or tribunal,

    (b)   exercise the functions of that office in any sheriffdom.

17   Auditors unable to tax account

(1) Where an account of expenses remitted by a court or tribunal for taxation cannot be taxed by an auditor of court—

    (a)   the account must be returned to the court or tribunal, and

    (b)   the court or tribunal must remit the account to a person who is not an auditor of court for taxation.

(2) Where an account is remitted to a person under subsection (1)(b)—

    (a)   the person is to be treated in relation to the taxation of the account as if the person were an auditor of court (but is not to be treated as an auditor for the purposes of section 14),

    (b)   the person is entitled to payment of such sums as the Scottish Courts and Tribunals Service may determine by way of—

        (i)   remuneration in respect of the taxation,

        (ii)   reimbursement of expenses reasonably incurred by the person in connection with the taxation.

18   Guidance

(1) The Auditor of the Court of Session must issue guidance to the auditors of court about the exercise of their functions.

(2) The guidance may, in particular, include guidance relating to the types and levels of expenses that may be allowed in an account of expenses.

(3) When preparing the guidance, the Auditor of the Court of Session must have regard to the desirability of auditors of court exercising their functions in a manner which is consistent and transparent.

(4) An auditor of court (including the Auditor of the Court of Session) must have regard to the guidance when exercising the auditor's functions.

(5) The guidance must—

    (a)   be in writing, and

    (b)   be published (as soon as reasonably practicable after it is issued) in such manner as the Auditor of the Court of Session considers appropriate.

(6) The Auditor of the Court of Session may, from time to time, issue revised guidance (and the references to guidance in subsections (2) to (5) include references to any revised guidance).

19   Reports

(1) The Scottish Courts and Tribunals Service ("the SCTS") must publish, for each financial year, a report setting out the information mentioned in subsection (2) in relation to—

    (a)   the Auditor of the Court of Session,

    (b)   the auditor of the Sheriff Appeal Court,

    (c)   the auditors of the sheriff court,

    (d)   any person to whom an account is remitted under section 17(1)(b), but only where the information relates to such an account.

(2) That information is—

    (a) the number of judicial taxations carried out during the year, and the amount of fees charged in respect of those taxations,

    (b) the number of other taxations carried out during the year, and the amount of fees charged in respect of those taxations,

    (c) the amount of fees charged in respect of any other work carried out during the year.

(3) A report must be published—

    (a) as soon as practicable after the end of the financial year to which it relates,

    (b) in such manner as the SCTS considers appropriate.

(4) For the purposes of subsection (2), a judicial taxation is the taxation of an account of expenses remitted for taxation to an auditor of court by a court or tribunal.

PART 4

GROUP PROCEEDINGS

20 Group proceedings

(1) There is to be a form of procedure in the Court of Session known as "group procedure", and proceedings subject to that procedure are to be known as "group proceedings".

(2) A person (a "representative party") may bring group proceedings on behalf of two or more persons (a "group") each of whom has a separate claim which may be the subject of civil proceedings.

(3) A person may be a representative party in group proceedings—

    (a) whether or not the person is a member of the group on whose behalf the proceedings are brought,

    (b) only if so authorised by the Court.

(4) There is to be no more than one representative party in group proceedings.

(5) Group proceedings may be brought only with the permission of the Court.

(6) The Court may give permission—

    (a) only if it considers that all of the claims made in the proceedings raise issues (whether of fact or law) which are the same as, or similar or related to, each other,

    (b) only if it is satisfied that the representative party has made all reasonable efforts to identify and notify all potential members of the group about the proceedings, and

    (c) in accordance with provision made in an act of sederunt under section 21(1).

(7) An act of sederunt under section 21(1) may provide for group proceedings to be brought as—

    (a) opt-in proceedings,

    (b) opt-out proceedings, or

    (c) either opt-in proceedings or opt-out proceedings.

Civil Litigation (Expenses and Group Proceedings) (Scotland) Act 2018 asp 10   11
PART 4 – GROUP PROCEEDINGS
Document Generated: 2021-04-01
Status: *This is the original version (as it was originally enacted).*

(8) In subsection (7)—

    (a)   "opt-in proceedings" are group proceedings which are brought with the express consent of each member of the group on whose behalf they are brought,

    (b)   "opt-out proceedings" are group proceedings which are brought on behalf of a group, each member of which has a claim which is of a description specified by the Court as being eligible to be brought in the proceedings and—

         (i)   is domiciled in Scotland and has not given notice that the member does not consent to the claim being brought in the proceedings, or

         (ii)   is not domiciled in Scotland and has given express consent to the claim being brought in the proceedings.

(9) In group proceedings, the representative party may—

    (a)   make claims on behalf of the members of the group,

    (b)   subject to provision made in an act of sederunt under section 21(1), do anything else in relation to those claims that the members would have been able to do had the members made the claims in other civil proceedings.

(10) Section 11 of the Court of Session Act 1988 (jury actions) does not apply to group proceedings.

21   Group procedure: rules

(1) The Court of Session may make provision by act of sederunt about group procedure.

(2) Without limiting that generality, the power in subsection (1) includes power to make provision for or about—

    (a)   persons who may be authorised to be a representative party,

    (b)   action to be taken by a representative party in connection with group proceedings (whether before or after the proceedings are brought),

    (c)   the means by which a person may—

         (i)   give consent for the person's claim to be brought in group proceedings,

         (ii)   give notice that the person does not consent to the person's claim being brought in group proceedings,

    (d)   types of claim that may not be made in group proceedings,

    (e)   circumstances in which permission to bring group proceedings may be refused,

    (f)   appeals against the granting or refusal of such permission,

    (g)   the disapplication or modification of section 39 of the Courts Reform (Scotland) Act 2014 (exclusive competence of the sheriff court) in relation to group proceedings,

    (h)   the making of an additional claim in group proceedings after the proceedings have been brought (including the transfer of a claim made in other civil proceedings),

    (i)   the exclusion of a claim made in group proceedings from the proceedings (including the transfer of the claim to other civil proceedings),

    (j)   the replacement of a representative party,

    (k)   steps that may be taken by a representative party only with the permission of the Court.

(3) Nothing in an act of sederunt under subsection (1) is to derogate from section 20.

(4) An act of sederunt under subsection (1) may make—

    (a) incidental, supplementary, consequential, transitional, transitory or saving provision,

    (b) provision amending, repealing or revoking any enactment relating to matters with respect to which an act of sederunt under subsection (1) may be made,

    (c) different provision for different purposes.

(5) This section is without prejudice to—

    (a) any enactment that enables the Court to make rules (by act of sederunt or otherwise) regulating the practice and procedure to be followed in proceedings to which this section applies, or

    (b) the inherent powers of the Court.

(6) In subsection (2), "representative party" is to be construed in accordance with section 20(2).

22 Group proceedings: further provision

(1) The Scottish Ministers may by regulations make further provision in connection with group proceedings.

(2) Regulations under subsection (1) may, in particular, make provision for or about—

    (a) circumstances in which a person is domiciled in Scotland for the purposes of section 20(8)(b),

    (b) prescriptive or limitation periods in relation to claims brought in group proceedings,

    (c) the assessment, apportionment and distribution of damages in connection with such proceedings, including the appointment of persons to give advice about those matters.

(3) Regulations under subsection (1) may modify any enactment.

PART 5

REVIEW OF OPERATION OF ACT

23 Review of operation of Act

(1) The Scottish Ministers must, as soon as practicable after the end of the 5 year period, review the operation of—

    (a) Parts 1 to 3,

    (b) Part 4,

and lay before the Scottish Parliament a report on that review.

(2) The report on the review of Parts 1 to 3 must, in particular, contain information about the effect of the operation of section 8 on access to justice and the administration of Scottish courts.

Civil Litigation (Expenses and Group Proceedings) (Scotland) Act 2018 asp 10   13
PART 6 – GENERAL PROVISION
Document Generated: 2021-04-01
_____
                    Status: *This is the original version (as it was originally enacted).*

(3) The report on the review of Part 4 must, in particular, contain information about the effect of the operation of section 20 on access to justice and the administration of Scottish courts.

(4) Each report must include a statement by the Scottish Ministers setting out—

    (a)   whether they intend to bring forward proposals to modify any provision of this Act, and

    (b)   where no such proposals are to be brought forward, their reasons for not doing so.

(5) The Scottish Ministers must, as soon as practicable after a report has been laid before the Parliament, publish the report in such a manner as they consider appropriate.

(6) In this section, "the 5 year period" means the period of 5 years beginning with—

    (a)   in the case of the review of Parts 1 to 3, the day of Royal Assent,

    (b)   in the case of the review of Part 4, the day on which the first act of sederunt under section 21(1) comes into force.

PART 6

GENERAL PROVISION

24   Regulations

(1) Any power of the Scottish Ministers to make regulations under this Act includes power to make—

    (a)   incidental, supplementary, consequential, transitional, transitory or saving provision,

    (b)   different provision for different purposes.

(2) Regulations under section 4(1), 5(1), 6(8), 7(3) or 22(1) are subject to the affirmative procedure.

(3) Regulations under section 25(1)—

    (a)   which add to, replace or omit any part of the text of an Act are subject to the affirmative procedure,

    (b)   otherwise, are subject to the negative procedure.

(4) This section does not apply to regulations under section 27(3).

25   Ancillary provision

(1) The Scottish Ministers may by regulations make any incidental, supplementary, consequential, transitional, transitory or saving provision they consider appropriate for the purposes of, in connection with or for giving full effect to this Act or any provision made under it.

(2) Regulations under this section may modify any enactment (including this Act).

26   Meaning of "court"

In this Act, in relation to civil proceedings in the sheriff court, a reference to the court includes a reference to the sheriff conducting the proceedings.

27   Commencement

(1) This Part comes into force on the day after Royal Assent.

(2) Part 5 comes into force at the end of the period of 2 months beginning with the day of Royal Assent.

(3) The other provisions of this Act come into force on such day as the Scottish Ministers may by regulations appoint.

(4) Regulations under subsection (3) may—

    (a)   include transitional, transitory or saving provision,

    (b)   make different provision for different purposes.

28   Short title

The short title of this Act is the Civil Litigation (Expenses and Group Proceedings) (Scotland) Act 2018.

Civil Litigation (Expenses and Group Proceedings) (Scotland) Act 2018 asp 10
SCHEDULE – AUDITORS OF COURT: MODIFICATION OF ENACTMENTS
Document Generated: 2021-04-01   15

Status: *This is the original version (as it was originally enacted).*

SCHEDULE

(introduced by section 14)

AUDITORS OF COURT: MODIFICATION OF ENACTMENTS

Court of Session Act 1821

1   The Court of Session Act 1821 is repealed.

Courts of Law Fees (Scotland) Act 1895

2   (1) The Courts of Law Fees (Scotland) Act 1895 is amended in accordance with this
         paragraph.

         (2) In section 3 (taxation of accounts in High Court of Justiciary)—
              (a)   the existing text becomes subsection (1),
              (b)   in that subsection—
                    (i) for "High Court of Justiciary", in both places where it occurs,
                    substitute "relevant court",
                    (ii) for "said High Court" substitute "relevant court",
                    (iii) for "auditor of the Court of Session" substitute "relevant auditor of
                    court",
                    (iv) for "regulations" substitute "rules of court",
                    (v) for "actions in the Court of Session" substitute "relevant civil
                    proceedings",
              (c)   after that subsection insert—

                    "(2) In subsection (1)—
                             "relevant court" means—
                                  (a) the High Court of Justiciary, or
                                  (b) the Sheriff Appeal Court, when exercising its
                                  jurisdiction in criminal proceedings,
                             "relevant auditor of court" means—
                                  (a) where the relevant court is the High Court of
                                  Justiciary, the Auditor of the Court of Session,
                                  (b) where the relevant court is the Sheriff Appeal Court,
                                  the auditor of the Sheriff Appeal Court,
                             "relevant civil proceedings" means—
                                  (a) where the relevant court is the High Court of
                                  Justiciary, proceedings in the Court of Session,
                                  (b) where the relevant court is the Sheriff Appeal Court,
                                  civil proceedings in that Court.".

         (3) The title of section 3 becomes "**Taxation of accounts in criminal proceedings**"

Administration of Justice (Scotland) Act 1933

3   The following provisions of the Administration of Justice (Scotland) Act 1933 are
         repealed—
              (a)   section 25(2),
              (b)   section 26,

Status: This is the original version (as it was originally enacted).

    (c)   section 27(1),

    (d)   section 28.

Solicitors (Scotland) Act 1980

4   In the Solicitors (Scotland) Act 1980, in section 51(3) (complaints to the Scottish Solicitors' Discipline Tribunal), after paragraph (c) insert—

        "(ca)   the auditor of the Sheriff Appeal Court,".

Law Reform (Miscellaneous Provisions) (Scotland) Act 1990

5   In the Law Reform (Miscellaneous Provisions) (Scotland) Act 1990, section 36(4) is repealed.

Legal Profession and Legal Aid (Scotland) Act 2007

6   In the Legal Profession and Legal Aid (Scotland) Act 2007, in section 2(2)(b) (receipt of complaints by Scottish Legal Complaints Commission: preliminary steps), after sub-paragraph (v) insert—

        "(va)   the auditor of the Sheriff Appeal Court,".

Status: This is the original version (as it was originally made). This item of legislation is currently only available in its original format.

SCOTTISH STATUTORY INSTRUMENTS

2019 No. 74

COURT OF SESSION
SHERIFF APPEAL COURT
SHERIFF COURT

Act of Sederunt (Rules of the Court of Session, Sheriff Appeal Court Rules and Ordinary Cause Rules Amendment) (Taxation of Judicial Expenses) 2019

Made - - - -	*27th February 2019*
Laid before the Scottish Parliament - - - -	*1st March 2019*
Coming into force - -	*29th April 2019*

In accordance with section 4 of the Scottish Civil Justice Council and Criminal Legal Assistance Act 2013(**1**), the Court of Session has approved draft rules submitted to it by the Scottish Civil Justice Council.

The Court of Session therefore makes this Act of Sederunt under the powers conferred by section 1(2) of the Litigants in Person (Costs and Expenses) Act 1975(**2**), sections 103(1), 104(1), 105(1) and 106(1) of the Courts Reform (Scotland) Act 2014(**3**) and all other powers enabling it to do so.

Citation and commencement, etc.

1.—(1) This Act of Sederunt may be cited as the Act of Sederunt (Rules of the Court of Session, Sheriff Appeal Court Rules and Ordinary Cause Rules Amendment) (Taxation of Judicial Expenses) 2019.

(2) It comes into force on 29th April 2019.

(3) A certified copy is to be inserted in the Books of Sederunt.

(**1**) 2013 asp 3. Section 4 was amended by the Courts Reform (Scotland) Act 2014 (asp 18), schedule 5, paragraph 31(3), and by the Inquiries into Fatal Accidents and Sudden Deaths etc. (Scotland) Act 2016 (asp 2), schedule 1, paragraph 1(4).

(**2**) 1975 c.47. Section 1(2) was last amended by the Tribunals, Courts and Enforcement Act 2007 (c.15), schedule 8, paragraph 6(2).

(**3**) 2014 asp 18. Sections 105 and 106 were modified by S.S.I. 2018/158.

Document Generated: 2019-04-30

Status: *This is the original version (as it was originally made). This item of legislation is currently only available in its original format.*

Application

2.—(1) Subject to sub-paragraphs (2) and (3), the amendments effected by this Act of Sederunt apply in respect of proceedings commenced on or after the coming into force of this Act of Sederunt.

(2) The amendments effected by paragraphs 3(6) and 5(3) apply in respect of proceedings where the date of the final judgment (as defined in those provisions) is on or after the coming into force of this Act of Sederunt.

(3) The amendments effected by paragraphs 3(7), 4(6), 4(7), 4(8), 4(9), 4(10), 4(11), 4(13) and 5(4) apply in respect of accounts lodged for taxation on or after the coming into force of this Act of Sederunt.

(4) For the purpose of sub-paragraph (1)—

(a) proceedings in the Sheriff Appeal Court; and

(b) proceedings in the Inner House of the Court of Session under Chapters 38, 39 or 40 of the Rules of the Court of Session 1994, other than on a remit from the Sheriff Appeal Court,

are distinct proceedings.

Amendment of the Ordinary Cause Rules 1993

3.—(1) The Ordinary Cause Rules 1993(4) are amended in accordance with this paragraph.

(2) In rule 7.4 (decree for expenses)—

(a) the existing rule becomes paragraph (1);

(b) after paragraph (1), insert—

"(2) Where the pursuer elects, in the minute for decree, to claim expenses comprising —

(a) the inclusive charges set out in Part 1 of Table 1 in schedule 4 of the Act of Sederunt (Taxation of Judicial Expenses Rules) 2019; and

(b) outlays comprising only—

(i) the court fee for warranting the initial writ;

(ii) postal charges incurred in effecting, or attempting to effect, service of the initial writ by post; and

(iii) where applicable, a sheriff officer's fee for service of the initial writ,

the sheriff may grant decree for payment of such expenses without the necessity of taxation.".

(3) In rule 27A.1 (pursuers' offers – interpretation)(5), for the definition of "fees" substitute—

""charges" means charges for work carried out by the pursuer's solicitor, and includes any additional charge;".

(4) In rule 27A.9 (extent of defender's liability), for "fees" in both places where it appears substitute "charges".

(5) In rule 32.1 (taxation before decree for expenses)—

(a) the existing rule becomes paragraph (1);

(b) after paragraph (1) insert—

"(2) Paragraph (1) applies subject to rule 7.4(2).".

---

(4) The Ordinary Cause Rules 1993 are in schedule 1 of the Sheriff Courts (Scotland) Act 1907 (c. 51). Schedule 1 was substituted by S.I. 1993/1956 and last amended by S.S.I. 2017/186.

(5) Rule 27A was inserted by S.S.I. 2017/52.

Document Generated: 2019-04-30

(6) For rule 32.1A (order to lodge account of expenses)(**6**), substitute—

"Time for lodging account of expenses

32.1A.—(1) A party found entitled to expenses must lodge an account of expenses in process—

(a) not later than four months after the final judgment; or

(b) at any time with permission of the sheriff, but subject to such conditions, if any, as the sheriff thinks fit to impose.

(2) Where an account of expenses is lodged by the Scottish Legal Aid Board in reliance on regulation 39(2)(a) of the Civil Legal Aid (Scotland) Regulations 2002(**7**), paragraph (1)(a) applies as if the period specified there is 8 months.

(3) In this rule, "final judgment" has the meaning assigned by section 136(1) of the Courts Reform (Scotland) Act 2014(**8**).".

(7) For rule 32.3 (procedure for taxation) and rule 32.4 (objections to auditor's report), substitute—

"Diet of taxation

32.3.—(1) Where an account of expenses awarded in a cause is lodged for taxation, the sheriff clerk must transmit the account and the process to the auditor of court.

(2) Subject to paragraph (3), the auditor of court must fix a diet of taxation on receipt of—

(a) the account of expenses;

(b) the process;

(c) vouchers in respect of all outlays claimed in the account, including counsel's fees; and

(d) a letter addressed to the auditor of court—

(i) confirming that the items referred to in sub-paragraph (c) have been intimated to the party found liable in expenses; and

(ii) providing such information as is required to enable the auditor of court to give intimation to the party found liable in expenses in accordance with paragraph (4)(b).

(3) The auditor of court must fix a diet of taxation where paragraph (2)(c) or (d), or both, have not been complied with.

(4) The auditor of court shall intimate the diet of taxation to—

(a) the party found entitled to expenses; and

(b) the party found liable in expenses.

(5) The party found liable in expenses may, not later than 4.00 pm on the fourth business day before the diet of taxation, intimate to the auditor of court and to the party found entitled to expenses particular points of objection, specifying each item objected to and stating concisely the nature and ground of objection.

(6) Subject to paragraph (7), if the party found liable in expenses fails to intimate points of objection under paragraph (5) within the time limit set out there, the auditor of court must not take account of them at the diet of taxation.

(**6**)   Rule 32.1A was inserted by S.S.I. 2004/197.

(**7**)   S.S.I. 2002/494.

(**8**)   2014 asp 18.

Document Generated: 2019-04-30

Status: *This is the original version (as it was originally made). This item of legislation is currently only available in its original format.*

(7) Where a failure to comply with the requirement contained in paragraph (5) was due to mistake, oversight or other excusable cause, the auditor of court may relieve a party of the consequences of such failure on such conditions, if any, as the auditor thinks fit.

(8) At the diet of taxation, or within such reasonable period of time thereafter as the auditor of court may allow, the party found entitled to expenses must make available to the auditor of court all documents, drafts or copies of documents sought by the auditor and relevant to the taxation.

(9) In this rule, "business day" means any day other than a Saturday, Sunday or public or court holiday.

Auditor's statement

32.3A.—(1) The auditor of court must—

(a) prepare a statement of the amount of expenses as taxed;

(b) transmit the process, the taxed account and the statement to the sheriff clerk; and

(c) on the day on which the documents referred to in sub-paragraph (b) are transmitted, intimate that fact and the date of the statement to each party to whom the auditor intimated the diet of taxation.

(2) The party found entitled to expenses must, within 7 days after the date of receipt of intimation under paragraph (1)(c), send a copy of the taxed account to the party found liable in expenses.

(3) Where no objections are lodged under rule 32.4 (objections to taxed account), the sheriff may grant decree for the expenses as taxed.

Objections to taxed account

32.4.—(1) A party to a cause who has appeared or been represented at a diet of taxation may object to the auditor of court's statement by lodging in process a note of objection within 14 days after the date of the statement.

(2) The party lodging a note of objection is referred to in this rule as "the objecting party".

(3) On lodging the note of objection the objecting party must apply by motion for an order—

(a) allowing the note of objection to be received; and

(b) allowing a hearing on the note of objection.

(4) On the granting of the order mentioned in paragraph (3), the objecting party must intimate to the auditor of court—

(a) the note of objection; and

(b) the interlocutor containing the order.

(5) Within 14 days after receipt of intimation of the items mentioned in paragraph (4) the auditor of court must lodge in process a statement of reasons in the form of a minute stating the reasons for the auditor's decision in relation to the items to which objection is taken in the note.

(6) On the lodging of the statement of reasons the sheriff clerk must fix a hearing on the note of objection.

(7) At the hearing, the sheriff may—

(a) sustain or repel any objection or remit the account of expenses to the auditor of court for further consideration; and

(b) find any party liable in the expenses of the procedure on the note of objection.

Document Generated: 2019-04-30

Status: *This is the original version (as it was originally made). This
item of legislation is currently only available in its original format.*

Interest on expenses

32.5.—(1) Paragraph (2) applies where the sheriff grants decree for payment of—

(a) expenses as taxed; and

(b) interest thereon.

(2) Without prejudice to the sheriff's other powers in relation to interest, the decree pronounced may require the party decerned against to pay interest on the taxed expenses, or any part thereof, from a date no earlier than 28 days after the date on which the account of expenses was lodged.".

Amendment of the Rules of the Court of Session 1994

4.—(1) The Rules of the Court of Session 1994(**9**) are amended in accordance with this paragraph.

(2) In rule 19.1 (decrees in absence)—

(a) in paragraph (3)(b)(ii), for "under Part I of Chapter III of the Table of Fees in rule 42.16" substitute "in accordance with paragraph (3A)";

(b) after paragraph (3), insert—

"(3A) Where the pursuer elects to claim expenses comprising—

(a) the inclusive charge set out in Part 1 of Table 1 in schedule 2 of the Act of Sederunt (Taxation of Judicial Expenses Rules) 2019; and

(b) outlays not exceeding £471.50 (excluding value added tax),

the court may grant decree for payment of such expenses without the necessity of taxation.".

(3) In rule 34A.1 (pursuers' offers – interpretation)(**10**), for the definition of "fees" substitute—

""charges" means charges for work carried out by the pursuer's solicitor, and includes any additional charge;".

(4) In rule 34A.9 (extent of defender's liability)(**11**), for "fees", in both places where it appears substitute "charges".

(5) The heading of Chapter 42 (taxation of accounts and fees of solicitors) becomes "TAXATION OF ACCOUNTS, ETC.".

(6) In rule 42.1(2) (remit to the Auditor)(**12**)—

(a) at the end of sub paragraph (a) add "or";

(b) in sub-paragraph (b)—

(i) omit "if he has failed to comply with sub paragraph (a),"; and

(ii) for "impose; and", substitute "impose."; and

(c) omit sub-paragraph(c).

(7) After rule 42.1(2) insert—

"(2A) On lodging an account under paragraph (2)(a) or (b), any party found entitled to expenses must intimate a copy of it forthwith to the party found liable to pay those expenses.".

---

(9) The Rules of the Court of Session 1994 are in schedule 2 of the Act of Sederunt (Rules of the Court of Session 1994) 1994 (S.I. 1994/1443), last amended by S.S.I. 2018/348.

(10) Rule 34A.1 was inserted by S.S.I. 2017/52.

(11) Rule 34A.9 was inserted by S.S.I. 2017/52.

(12) Rule 42.1(2) was substituted by S.S.I. 2008/123.

Document Generated: 2019-04-30

(8) In rule 42.2 (diet of taxation)(**13**), in paragraph (7) after "diet of taxation", insert "or within such reasonable period of time thereafter as the Auditor may allow,".

(9) In rule 42.3 (report of taxation)(**14**), for paragraph (1) substitute—

"(1) The Auditor must—

(a) prepare a statement of the amount of expenses as taxed;

(b) transmit the process of the cause, the taxed account and the statement to the appropriate Department of the Office of Court; and

(c) on the day on which the documents mentioned in sub-paragraph (b) are transmitted, intimate that fact and the date of the statement to each party to whom the Auditor intimated the diet of taxation.".

(10) In rule 42.4 (objections to report of the auditor)(**15**), in paragraph (1)—

(a) for "report of the Auditor" substitute "Auditor's statement";

(b) for "date of the report" substitute "date of the statement".

(11) After rule 42.4, insert—

"Interest on expenses

42.4A.—(1) At any time before extract of a decree for payment of expenses as taxed by the Auditor the court may, on the application of the party to whom expenses are payable, grant decree against the party decerned against for payment of interest on the taxed expenses, or any part thereof, from a date no earlier than 28 days after the date on which the account of expenses was lodged.

(2) Paragraph (1) is without prejudice to the court's other powers in relation to expenses."

(12) In rule 42.5 (modification or disallowance of expenses), omit paragraph (2).

(13) In rule 42.7 (taxation of solicitors' own accounts)(**16**)—

(a) for paragraph (7), substitute—

"(7) The Auditor must—

(a) prepare a statement of the fees and outlays as taxed;

(b) transmit the statement and the taxed account to the appropriate Department of the Office of Court; and

(c) send a copy of the statement to the solicitor and the client.";

(b) in paragraph (7A), for "report" substitute "statement"; and

(c) in paragraph (8), for "report of the Auditor" substitute "Auditor's statement".

(14) Omit Part II of Chapter 42 (fees of solicitors).

(15) After Part III of Chapter 42 (fees in speculative causes), insert—

(**13**) Rule 42.2 was substituted by S.S.I 2011/402.

(**14**) Rule 42.3 was amended by S.S.I. 2011/402.

(**15**) Rule 42.4 was amended by S.S.I. 2011/402.

(**16**) Rule 42.7 was amended by S.S.I. 2011/402.

Document Generated: 2019-04-30

Status: *This is the original version (as it was originally made). This item of legislation is currently only available in its original format.*

"PART IV

REMUNERATION OF REPORTERS

Remuneration of reporters

42.18.—(1) This rule applies where any matter in a cause is remitted by the court, at its own instance or on the motion of a party, to a reporter or other person to report to the court.

(2) The party liable to the reporter or other person for payment of that person's fee, and reimbursement of that person's outlays, is—

(a) where the court makes the remit at its own instance, the party so ordained by the court;

(b) where the court makes the remit on the motion of a party, that party.

(3) The solicitor for the liable party is personally liable in the first instance for payment of such fee and outlays.

(4) This rule applies subject to—

(a) any other provision in these Rules;

(b) any order of the court; or

(c) any agreement between a party and that party's solicitor.".

Amendment of the Sheriff Appeal Court Rules

5.—(1) The Act of Sederunt (Sheriff Appeal Court Rules) 2015(**17**) is amended in accordance with this paragraph.

(2) Omit rule 19.2 (additional fee) and rule 19.2A (sanction for the employment of counsel)(**18**).

(3) For rule 19.3 (order to lodge account of expenses), substitute—

"Time for lodging account of expenses

19.3.—(1) A party found entitled to expenses must lodge an account of expenses in process —

(a) not later than 4 months after the final judgment; or

(b) at any time with permission of the court, but subject to such conditions, if any, as the court thinks fit to impose.

(2) Where an account of expenses is lodged by the Scottish Legal Aid Board in reliance on regulation 39(2)(a) of the Civil Legal Aid (Scotland) Regulations 2002(**19**), paragraph (1)(a) applies as if the period specified there is 8 months.

(3) In this rule, "final judgment" has the meaning assigned by section 136(1) of the Courts Reform (Scotland) Act 2014(**20**).".

(4) For rule 19.4 (procedure for taxation of expenses) and rule 19.5 (objections to taxed account), substitute—

(**17**) S.S.I. 2015/356, last amended by S.S.I. 2017/186.
(**18**) Rule 19.2A was inserted by S.S.I. 2015/419.
(**19**) S.S.I. 2002/494.
(**20**) 2014 asp 18.

Document Generated: 2019-04-30

Status: *This is the original version (as it was originally made). This item of legislation is currently only available in its original format.*

"Diet of taxation

19.4.—(1) Where an account of expenses is lodged for taxation, the clerk must transmit the account and the process to the auditor of court.

(2) Subject to paragraph (3), the auditor of court must fix a diet of taxation on receipt of—

(a) the account of expenses;

(b) the process;

(c) vouchers in respect of all outlays claimed in the account, including counsel's fees; and

(d) a letter addressed to the auditor of court—

(i) confirming that the items referred to in sub-paragraph (c) have been intimated to the party found liable in expenses; and

(ii) providing such information as is required to enable the auditor of court to give intimation to the party found liable in expenses in accordance with paragraph (4)(b).

(3) The auditor of court may fix a diet of taxation where paragraph (2)(c) or (d), or both, have not been complied with.

(4) The auditor of court must intimate the diet of taxation to—

(a) the party found entitled to expenses; and

(b) the party found liable in expenses.

(5) The party found liable in expenses must, not later than 4.00 pm on the fourth business day before the diet of taxation, intimate to the auditor of court and to the party found entitled to expenses particular points of objection, specifying each item objected to and stating concisely the nature and ground of objection.

(6) Subject to paragraph (7), if the party found liable in expenses fails to intimate points of objection under paragraph (5) within the time limit set out there, the auditor of court must not take account of them at the diet of taxation.

(7) Where a failure to comply with the requirement contained in paragraph (5) was due to mistake, oversight or other excusable cause, the auditor of court may relieve a party of the consequences of such failure on such conditions, if any, as the auditor thinks fit.

(8) At the diet of taxation, or within such reasonable period of time thereafter as the auditor of court may allow, the party found entitled to expenses must make available to the auditor of court all documents, drafts or copies of documents sought by the auditor and relevant to the taxation.

(9) In this rule, a "business day" means any day other than a Saturday, Sunday or public or court holiday.

Auditor's statement

19.4A.—(1) The auditor of court must—

(a) prepare a statement of the amount of expenses as taxed;

(b) transmit the process, the taxed account and the statement to the clerk; and

(c) on the day on which the documents referred to in sub-paragraph (b) are transmitted, intimate that fact and the date of the report to each party to whom the auditor intimated the diet of taxation.

Document Generated: 2019-04-30

---

(2) The party found entitled to expenses must, within 7 days after the date of receipt of intimation under paragraph (1)(c), send a copy of the taxed account to the party found liable in expenses.

(3) Where no objections are lodged under rule 19.5 (objections to taxed account), the court may grant decree for the expenses as taxed.

Objections to taxed account

19.5.—(1) A party to an appeal who has appeared or been represented at a diet of taxation may object to the auditor of court's statement by lodging in process a note of objection within 14 days after the date of the statement.

(2) The party lodging a note of objection is referred to in this rule as "the objecting party".

(3) On lodging the note of objection the objecting party must apply by motion for an order—

(a) allowing the note to be received; and

(b) allowing a hearing on the note of objection.

(4) On the granting of the order mentioned in paragraph (3), the objecting party must intimate to the auditor of court—

(a) the note of objection; and

(b) the interlocutor containing the order.

(5) Within 14 days after receipt of intimation of the items mentioned in paragraph (4) the auditor of court must lodge in process a statement of reasons in the form of a minute stating the reasons for the auditor's decision in relation to the items to which objection is taken in the note.

(6) On the lodging of the statement of reasons the clerk must fix a hearing on the note of objection.

(7) At the hearing, the court may—

(a) sustain or repel any objection in the note of objection or remit the account of expenses to the auditor of court for further consideration; and

(b) find any party liable in the expenses of the procedure on the note of objection.".

Revocation

6. The following Acts of Sederunt are revoked—

(a) Act of Sederunt (Expenses of Party Litigants) 1976(**21**);

(b) Act of Sederunt (Fees of Witnesses and Shorthand Writers in the Sheriff Court) 1992(**22**);

(c) Act of Sederunt (Fees of Solicitors in the Sheriff Court) (Amendment and Further Provisions) 1993(**23**);

(d) Act of Sederunt (Fees of Members of the Association of Commercial Attorneys in the Sheriff Court) 2009(**24**);

(e) Act of Sederunt (Sanction for the Employment of Counsel in the Sheriff Court) 2011(**25**);

(f) Act of Sederunt (Fees of Solicitors in the Sheriff Appeal Court) 2015(**26**).

(**21**) S.I. 1976/1606, last amended by S.S.I. 2015/419.
(**22**) S.I. 1992/1878, last amended by S.S.I. 2018/126.
(**23**) S.I. 1993/3080, last amended by S.S.I. 2018/186.
(**24**) S.S.I. 2009/162.
(**25**) S.S.I. 2011/404.
(**26**) S.S.I. 2015/387, last amended by S.S.I. 2018/186.

Document Generated: 2019-04-30
Status: *This is the original version (as it was originally made). This item of legislation is currently only available in its original format.*

Saving

7.—(1) The Acts of Sederunt revoked by paragraph 6 are saved in so far as they apply to—

(a) any proceedings commenced before the coming into force of this Act of Sederunt; and

(b) summary cause proceedings in the sheriff court commenced on or after the coming into force of this Act of Sederunt.

(2) For the purpose of sub-paragraph (1)—

(a) proceedings in the Sheriff Appeal Court; and

(b) proceedings in the Inner House of the Court of Session under Chapters 38, 39 or 40 of the Rules of the Court of Session 1994, other than on a remit from the Sheriff Appeal Court,

are distinct proceedings.

(3) In sub-paragraph (1)(b) the reference to summary cause proceedings is to proceedings subject to the procedure introduced by section 35 of the Sheriff Courts (Scotland) Act 1971(**27**).

Edinburgh
27th February 2019

CJM SUTHERLAND
Lord President
I.P.D.

(**27**) 1971 c.58. Section 35 is repealed by the Courts Reform (Scotland) Act 2014 (asp 18), schedule 5, paragraph 6(2) which was brought into force in part by S.S.I. 2016/291.

EXPLANATORY NOTE

(This note is not part of the Act of Sederunt)

This Act of Sederunt makes provision for—

revocations of, and amendments to, rules consequential on the coming into force of the Act of Sederunt (Taxation of Judicial Expenses Rules) 2019; and

amendments to the rules of procedure governing the taxation of accounts of expenses in civil proceedings in the Court of Session, Sheriff Appeal Court and sheriff court.

In this note—

"the Ordinary Cause Rules" means the Ordinary Cause Rules 1993 in schedule 1 of the Sheriff Courts (Scotland) Act 1907;

"the Rules of the Court of Session" means the Rules of the Court of Session 1994 in schedule 2 of Act of Sederunt (Rules of the Court of Session 1994) 1994;

"the Sheriff Appeal Court Rules" means Act of Sederunt (Sheriff Appeal Court Rules) 2015; and

"the Taxation of Judicial Expenses Rules" means Act of Sederunt (Taxation of Judicial Expenses Rules) 2019.

Amendments and revocations consequential on the Taxation of Judicial Expenses Rules

Paragraph 3(2) amends rule 7.4 of the Ordinary Cause Rules to allow the requirement for taxation to be dispensed with when decree has been granted in absence, and where the expenses claimed comprise only the inclusive charge provided for the purpose in the Taxation of Judicial Expenses Rules, a court fee, postal charges, and, where applicable, a sheriff officer's fee for service.

Paragraph 4(2) amends rule 19.1 of the Rules of the Court of Session to allow the requirement for taxation to be dispensed with when decree has been granted in absence, and when the expenses claimed comprise only the inclusive charge provided for the purpose in the Taxation of Judicial Expenses Rules and outlays not exceeding £471.50.

Paragraphs 3(3) and (4), and 4(3) and (4) replace various references to fees with references to charges, consistent with the Taxation of Judicial Expenses Rules.

Paragraphs 4(5), 4(12) and 4(14), 5(2) and 6 provide for the omission of rules and tables, and for the revocation of Acts of Sederunt that are superseded by the Taxation of Judicial Expenses Rules.

Paragraph 4(15) amends the Rules of the Court of Session by inserting rule 42.18 in substitution for the provisions previously set out in rule 42.15. The rule makes provision regarding the remuneration of reporters appointed at the instance of the court.

In terms of paragraph 2(1), the foregoing amendments have effect only in respect of proceedings commenced on or after the coming into force of this Act of Sederunt. In terms of paragraph 7, the Acts of Sederunt revoked by paragraph 6 are saved for the purposes of proceedings commenced before the coming into force of this Act of Sederunt, and for the purposes of summary causes commenced subsequently.

Modification of taxation procedure

Paragraphs 3(6) and 5(3) amend the Ordinary Cause Rules and the Sheriff Appeal Court Rules by inserting rules that require a party found entitled to expenses to lodge an account of expenses

Document Generated: 2019-04-30
Status: *This is the original version (as it was originally made). This
item of legislation is currently only available in its original format.*

for taxation not later than four months after the date of the final judgment, unless the court orders otherwise. The time limit is extended to eight months where the account is lodged by the Scottish Legal Aid Board in reliance on regulation 39(2)(a) of the Civil Legal Aid (Scotland) Regulations 2002.

The rules inserted replace rule 32.1A of the Ordinary Cause Rules and rule 19.3 of the Sheriff Appeal Court Rules. In terms of paragraph 2(2), the rules inserted have effect when the date of the final judgment is on or after the coming into force of this Act of Sederunt.

The amendments set out in paragraphs 3(7) and 5(4) provide for the modification of taxation procedure in sheriff court ordinary causes and in the Sheriff Appeal Court. Paragraph 3(7) omits existing rules 32.3 and 32.4 of the Ordinary Cause Rules and substitutes new rules 32.3, 32.3A, 32.4 and 32.5. Paragraph 5(4) omits existing rules 19.4 and 19.5 of the Sheriff Appeal Court Rules and substitutes new rules 19.4, 19.4A and 19.5.

New rules 32.3 and 19.4 make provision regarding the fixing and intimation of diets of taxation, the provision of vouching and information, and the intimation of points of objection. On receipt of an account of expenses remitted from the court the Auditor is not obliged to fix a diet of taxation until the party lodging the account has also provided vouchers in respect of all outlays claimed, and a letter that both confirms that the vouchers have been intimated to the paying party, and provides the Auditor with such information as is required to enable the Auditor to intimate the diet of taxation on the paying party.

Under the new rules it is for the Auditor to intimate the diet of taxation on both the party lodging the account and the paying party. The paying party must intimate particular points of objection to the account by 4.00 pm on the fourth business day before the diet of taxation. Where a failure to do so was due to mistake or oversight the Auditor may relieve the paying party of the consequences of the failure. Otherwise, the Auditor must not take account of a point of objection that has not been intimated in advance.

In place of the requirement to prepare a report, new rules 32.3A and 19.4A require the Auditor to prepare a statement of the amount of expenses as taxed.

New rules 32.4 and 19.5 introduce more detailed provision regarding the procedure to be followed where a party challenges decisions taken by the Auditor at taxation by way of note of objection. A note of objection must be lodged within fourteen days of the date of the Auditor's statement. The party lodging the note must apply for an order allowing the note to be received, and allowing a hearing on the note. It is for the objecting party to intimate the note and the interlocutor allowing a hearing to the Auditor.

Within fourteen days of intimation the Auditor must lodge a statement of reasons. The sheriff clerk or clerk to the Sheriff Appeal Court then fixes a hearing on the note of objections.

New rule 32.5 of the Ordinary Cause Rules makes provision concerning the payment of interest on expenses by allowing the court to award interest from a date before the date of the Auditor's statement. The earliest date from which interest may be awarded is 28 days after the date on which the account of expenses was lodged.

Paragraphs 4(6), 4(7), 4(8), 4(9), 4(10) and 4(11) provide for amendments to the Rules of the Court of Session relating to taxation procedure. Paragraphs 4(6) and 4(7) amend rule 42.1(2) to allow a party to apply to the court for an extension of the period allowed for the lodging of an account of expenses before that period has expired. Paragraph 4(8) amends rule 42.2(7) to make it possible for the Auditor to allow a party a reasonable period following the diet of taxation to produce documents or information sought in the course of the diet.

Paragraphs 4(9), 4(10) and 4(13) provide for references to the Auditor's report to be replaced with references to a statement of the amount of expenses as taxed. Paragraph 4(11) inserts rule 42.4A which makes provision for awards of interest on expenses to be backdated to a date no earlier than 28 days after the lodging of the account.

Document Generated: 2019-04-30
Status: *This is the original version (as it was originally made). This item of legislation is currently only available in its original format.*

In terms of paragraph 2(3), the foregoing amendments have effect in relation to proceedings where the account of expenses is lodged for taxation on or after the coming into force of this Act of Sederunt.

SCOTTISH STATUTORY INSTRUMENTS

2019 No. 75

COURT OF SESSION
SHERIFF APPEAL COURT
SHERIFF COURT

Act of Sederunt (Taxation of Judicial Expenses Rules) 2019

Made - - - -	*27th February 2019*
Laid before the Scottish	
Parliament - - - -	*1st March 2019*
Coming into force - -	*29th April 2019*

In accordance with section 4 of the Scottish Civil Justice Council and Criminal Legal Assistance Act 2013(**1**), the Court of Session has approved draft rules submitted to it by the Scottish Civil Justice Council.

The Court of Session therefore makes this Act of Sederunt under the powers conferred by section 1(2) of the Litigants in Person (Costs and Expenses) Act 1975(**2**), sections 103(1), 104(1), 105(1) and 106(1) of the Courts Reform (Scotland) Act 2014(**3**) and all other powers enabling it to do so.

CHAPTER 1

CITATION, APPLICATION AND INTERPRETATION ETC.

Citation and commencement, etc.

1.1.—(1) This Act of Sederunt may be cited as the Act of Sederunt (Taxation of Judicial Expenses Rules) 2019.

(2) It comes into force on 29th April 2019.

(3) A certified copy is to be inserted in the Books of Sederunt.

(**1**)   2013 asp 3. Section 4 was amended by the Courts Reform (Scotland) Act 2014 (asp 18), schedule 5, paragraph 31(3), and by the Inquiries into Fatal Accidents and Sudden Deaths etc. (Scotland) Act 2016 (asp 2), schedule 1, paragraph 1(4).
(**2**)   1975 c.47. Section 1(2) was last amended by the Tribunals, Courts and Enforcement Act 2007 (c.15), schedule 8, paragraph 6(2).
(**3**)   2014 asp 18. Sections 105 and 106 were modified by S.S.I. 2018/158.

Document Generated: 2019-04-29

Application

1.2.—(1) Subject to paragraphs (3) and (4), these Rules apply to the taxation of accounts of expenses, and for related purposes, where—

- (a) the expenses were incurred in—

    (i) proceedings in the Court of Session;

    (ii) proceedings in the Sheriff Appeal Court; or

    (iii) proceedings, other than a summary cause, in the sheriff court;

- (b) the proceedings were commenced on or after the coming into force of these Rules; and

- (c) the taxation is pursuant to a finding that a party ("the paying party") is liable in expenses to another party ("the entitled party").

(2) For the purposes of paragraph (1)(b)—

- (a) proceedings in the Sheriff Appeal Court; and

- (b) proceedings in the Inner House of the Court of Session under Chapters 38, 39 or 40 of the Rules of the Court of Session 1994(**4**), other than on remit from the Sheriff Appeal Court,

are distinct proceedings.

(3) Chapter 7 (payments to witnesses and fees of shorthand writers) and schedules 6 and 7 apply in relation to proceedings referred to in paragraphs (1)(a) and (b).

(4) Chapter 8 (diligence) applies where the chargeable work was carried out on or after the coming into force of these Rules.

Interpretation

1.3.—(1) In these Rules—

"counsel" means an advocate or solicitor advocate;

"the court" in relation to proceedings in the sheriff court means the sheriff;

"member of the Association of Commercial Attorneys" means a person who has rights to conduct litigation or rights of audience by virtue of the scheme to which effect was given by Act of Sederunt (Sections 25 to 29 of the Law Reform (Miscellaneous Provisions) (Scotland) Act 1990) (Association of Commercial Attorneys) 2009(**5**);

"paying party" and "entitled party" have the meaning given in rule 1.2(1)(c);

"solicitor advocate" means a solicitor having a right of audience in the Court of Session under section 25A of the Solicitors (Scotland) Act 1980(**6**);

"summary cause" means proceedings, subject to the procedure introduced by section 35 of the Sheriff Courts (Scotland) Act 1971(**7**).

(2) In relation to simple procedure cases—

- (a) references to the taxation of an account of expenses include the assessment of an account of expenses, and

- (b) references to the Auditor include the sheriff clerk.

(**4**) The Rules of the Court of Session 1994 are in schedule 2 of the Act of Sederunt (Rules of the Court of Session 1994) 1994 (S.I. 1994/1443), last amended by S.S.I. 2018/348.

(**5**) S.S.I. 2009/163.

(**6**) 1980 c.46. Section 25A was inserted by the Law Reform (Miscellaneous Provisions) (Scotland) Act 1990 (c.24), section 24, and was last amended by the Enterprise and Regulatory Reform Act 2013 (c.24), schedule 6(1), paragraph 10.

(**7**) 1971 c.58. Section 35 is repealed by the Courts Reform (Scotland) Act 2014 (asp 18), schedule 5, paragraph 6(2) which was brought into force in part by S.S.I. 2016/291.

(3) A charge or a fee relating to a document or communication that is prescribed by reference to a number of words is chargeable in respect of each multiple of that number of words or part thereof.

CHAPTER 2

GENERAL PRINCIPLES

Form of account

2.1. An account of expenses must—

(a) set out in chronological order all items in respect of which payment is claimed;

(b) list in separate columns—

(i) the charges claimed for work carried out by the entitled party's solicitor; and

(ii) the outlays claimed; and

(c) include a statement as to whether or not the entitled party will bear the burden of the value added tax referred to in rule 6.1.

General principles

2.2.—(1) The Auditor is to allow only such expenses as are reasonable for conducting the proceedings in a proper manner.

(2) The Auditor may in particular refuse to allow—

(a) expenses that the Auditor considers to have been incurred as a result of fault or error on the part of the entitled party or the entitled party's representative; and

(b) expenses relating to a part of the proceedings in which the Auditor considers that the entitled party was unsuccessful.

CHAPTER 3

CHARGES FOR WORK CARRIED OUT BY SOLICITORS

Application

3.1.—(1) Subject to rule 3.10 (party litigants), this Chapter, and the tables of charges set out in schedules 1 to 5, apply for the purpose of determining the charges to be allowed on taxation in respect of work carried out by the entitled party's solicitor.

(2) Where the entitled party was represented by a member of the Association of Commercial Attorneys this Chapter, rule 5.2 (additional charge), and the tables of charges in schedules 1, 3, 4 and 5 apply as if the work charged for was carried out by a solicitor.

The unit

3.2. In this Chapter, in Chapter 8, and in schedules 1 to 5, references to a "unit" are to a measure of monetary charge with a value of £16.40.

Document Generated: 2019-04-29

Status: *This is the original version (as it was originally made). This item of legislation is currently only available in its original format.*

Table of charges

3.3.—(1) Paragraph (2) applies to proceedings in respect of which there is a table of inclusive charges applicable to the proceedings in schedule 2, 3 or 4.

(2) The charges to be allowed are those specified in—

    (a) the table of detailed charges in schedule 1; or

    (b) the applicable table of inclusive charges in—

        (i) for proceedings in the Court of Session, schedule 2;

        (ii) for proceedings in the Sheriff Appeal Court, schedule 3; or

        (iii) for ordinary actions in the sheriff court, schedule 4,

as the entitled party may elect, but the entitled party may not elect to have an account taxed partly on one basis and partly on another.

(3) Subject to paragraph (4), the charges to be allowed where there is no table of inclusive charges applicable to the proceedings are those specified in the table of detailed charges in schedule 1.

(4) Subject to rule 3.7 (simple procedure), the charges to be allowed in respect of a simple procedure case in the sheriff court(8) are those specified in the applicable table of inclusive charges in schedule 5.

(5) This rule applies unless the court otherwise directs.

Copying and scanning

3.4.—(1) This rule applies to the copying or scanning of documents carried out by, or at the instance of, the entitled party's solicitor, other than on payment of a charge to a third party (in which event Chapter 4 applies).

(2) Where the Auditor is satisfied that the number of pages reasonably copied or scanned was in excess of 2000, the Auditor may allow the charge mentioned in paragraph (3), but only in respect of those pages which exceed 2000.

(3) The charge is 1 unit per 100 pages copied or scanned, or part thereof.

Travel time

3.5. The Auditor may, on cause shown, and at the Auditor's discretion, allow a charge of 0.9 units per 6 minutes in respect of time engaged in travelling by the entitled party's solicitor.

Modification of inclusive charges

3.6. In appropriate circumstances the Auditor may, in respect of a charge specified in a table of inclusive charges—

    (a) increase or reduce a charge; or

    (b) apportion a charge between parties represented by different solicitors.

Simple procedure

3.7.—(1) This rule applies where an account of expenses falls to be taxed by reference to a table of charges in schedule 5.

(2) All charges allowed by the Auditor are to be reduced by 10%.

---

(8)   Simple procedure was introduced by the Courts Reform (Scotland) Act 2014 (asp 18), section 72.

(3) Unless the court otherwise directs, where the total value of the claim is £2500 or less, all charges allowed by the Auditor, as reduced in accordance with paragraph (2), are to be further reduced—

(a) where the total value of the claim is less than £1000, by 50%;

(b) otherwise by 25%.

Instructing and attending with counsel

3.8.—(1) Subject to paragraph (2), where fees of counsel are allowed as an outlay in the sheriff court or Sheriff Appeal Court, the Auditor is also to allow the applicable charge for instructing counsel.

(2) Where the fees allowed are those of a solicitor advocate, paragraph (1) does not apply unless the solicitor advocate is acting on the instructions of another solicitor.

(3) Paragraph (4) applies where—

(a) a solicitor advocate exercises a right of audience in the Court of Session; or

(b) fees of a solicitor advocate are allowed as an outlay in the sheriff court or Sheriff Appeal Court in accordance with rule 4.3 (fees of counsel in the sheriff court or Sheriff Appeal Court).

(4) Where the solicitor advocate is assisted by another solicitor or a clerk the Auditor may allow the applicable attendance charge.

Additional charge

3.9. Where, on an application under rule 5.2 (additional charge)—

(a) the court grants the application and specifies a percentage increase in charges in accordance with paragraph (4) of that rule, the charges allowed by the Auditor under this Chapter are to be increased by the percentage specified;

(b) the Court of Session remits to the Auditor to determine if an increase should be allowed, or to determine the level of an increase, the charges allowed by the Auditor under this Chapter are to be increased by such additional charge, if any, as the Auditor may determine.

Party litigants

3.10.—(1) Where the entitled party was not represented by a solicitor the Auditor may, subject to paragraph (3), allow a reasonable sum in respect of work done by the entitled party which was reasonably required in connection with the proceedings.

(2) In determining what would be a reasonable sum the Auditor is to have regard to all the circumstances, including—

(a) the nature of the work;

(b) the time required to do the work;

(c) the amount of any earnings lost during that time;

(d) the importance of the proceedings to the entitled party; and

(e) the complexity of the issues involved in the proceedings.

(3) Any sum allowed under this rule must not exceed two thirds of the charges that would be allowed under this Chapter if the same work had been done by a solicitor.

Document Generated: 2019-04-29

CHAPTER 4

OUTLAYS

Application

4.1. This Chapter applies for the purpose of determining the outlays incurred by, or on behalf of, the entitled party that are to be allowed at taxation.

Allowance of outlays

4.2. Subject to rules 4.3 to 4.5, outlays reasonably incurred in order to conduct the proceedings in a proper manner are to be allowed.

Fees of counsel in the sheriff court or Sheriff Appeal Court

4.3.—(1) This rule applies to the taxation of accounts of expenses relating to proceedings in the sheriff court or Sheriff Appeal Court.

(2) No fees are to be allowed for the work of counsel unless the proceedings, or particular work involved in the conduct of the proceedings, have been sanctioned as suitable for the employment of counsel in accordance with rule 5.4 (sanction for the employment of counsel in the sheriff court and Sheriff Appeal Court).

(3) Where particular work has been sanctioned as suitable for the employment of counsel the Auditor is to allow the reasonable fees of counsel for—

    (a) doing that work, and

    (b) subject to paragraph (6), consultations reasonably required in relation to that work.

(4) Where the proceedings have been sanctioned as suitable for the employment of counsel—

    (a) it is for the Auditor to determine the work in relation to which it was reasonable for counsel to be instructed;

    (b) subject to sub-paragraph (c), the Auditor is to allow the reasonable fees of counsel for carrying out that work;

    (c) subject to paragraph (3), no fees are to be allowed for work carried out before the date on which sanction was granted unless the proceedings are—

        (i) proceedings subject to Chapter 36 of the Ordinary Cause Rules 1993(9);

        (ii) a simple procedure case; or

        (iii) proceedings in the Sheriff Appeal Court.

(5) In the determination of reasonable fees for the purposes of paragraphs (3) and (4), the Auditor must disregard the fact that counsel who carried out the work was senior counsel unless the proceedings, or the particular work, have been sanctioned as suitable for the employment of senior counsel.

(6) Except on cause shown, the Auditor is to allow fees for only two consultations in the course of proceedings.

(7) In this rule, references to fees of counsel for carrying out work include, where appropriate in the case of proofs, trials or other hearings that do not proceed, fees reflecting counsel's inability to accept alternative commitments.

---

(9)   The Ordinary Cause Rules 1993 are in schedule 1 of the Sheriff Courts (Scotland) Act 1907 (c.51). Schedule 1 was substituted by S.I. 1993/1956 and last amended by S.S.I. 2017/186.

Document Generated: 2019-04-29

Fees of solicitor advocates in the Court of Session

4.4. Where a solicitor advocate exercises a right of audience in the Court of Session, the Auditor is to allow such fee for each item of work done by the solicitor advocate in the exercise of the right of audience as the Auditor would allow to an advocate for an equivalent item of work.

Skilled persons

4.5.—(1) No charge incurred to a person who has been engaged for the purposes of the application of that person's skill is to be allowed as an outlay unless—

(a) the person has been certified as a skilled person in accordance with rule 5.3 (certification of skilled persons); and

(b) except where paragraph (4) applies, the charge relates to work done, or expenses incurred, after the date of certification.

(2) Where a person has been so certified, the Auditor is to allow charges for work done or expenses reasonably incurred by that person which were reasonably required for a purpose in connection with the proceedings, or in contemplation of the proceedings.

(3) The charges to be allowed under paragraph (2) are such charges as the Auditor determines to be fair and reasonable.

(4) This paragraph applies where—

(a) the account relates to—

(i) proceedings subject to Chapter 43 of the Rules of the Court of Session 1994;

(ii) proceedings subject to Chapter 36 of the Ordinary Cause Rules 1993; or

(iii) a simple procedure case; or

(b) the sheriff has determined in accordance with rule 5.3(5) that the certification has effect for the purposes of work done, or expenses incurred, before the date of certification.

Witnesses

4.6.—(1) Payments relating to the attendance of a witness at a proof or trial, when the witness is not called to give evidence, are to be allowed as an outlay only where the court has granted a motion certifying the witness as being in attendance.

(2) Payments to witnesses are to be aggregated in the account as a single outlay, and the details of the payments are to be entered in a separate schedule appended to the account.

(3) Receipts and vouchers for all payments claimed are to be produced to the paying party prior to the taxation, and to the Auditor if the Auditor so requires.

CHAPTER 5

APPLICATIONS FOR ALLOWANCE OF AN ADDITIONAL FEE, FOR SANCTION FOR THE EMPLOYMENT OF COUNSEL, AND FOR CERTIFICATION OF SKILLED WITNESSES

Application

5.1.—(1) This Chapter applies for the purpose of applications to the court for—

(a) the allowance of an additional charge;

(b) the certification of skilled witnesses; and

Document Generated: 2019-04-29
Status: *This is the original version (as it was originally made). This
item of legislation is currently only available in its original format.*

(c) sanction for the employment of counsel in the sheriff court and Sheriff Appeal Court.

(2) Applications to which this Chapter applies are to be made—

(a) in a simple procedure case by incidental orders application;

(b) otherwise by motion.

Additional charge

5.2.—(1) An entitled party may apply to the court for an increase in the charges to be allowed at taxation in respect of work carried out by the entitled party's solicitor.

(2) Where the application is made to the Court of Session the court may, instead of determining the application, remit the application to the Auditor to determine if an increase should be allowed, and the level of any increase.

(3) The court or, as the case may be, the Auditor must grant the application when satisfied that an increase is justified to reflect the responsibility undertaken by the solicitor in the conduct of the proceedings.

(4) On granting an application the court must, subject to paragraph (5), specify a percentage increase in the charges to be allowed at taxation.

(5) The Court of Session may instead remit to the Auditor to determine the level of increase.

(6) In considering whether to grant an application, and the level of any increase, the court or, as the case may be, the Auditor is to have regard to—

(a) the complexity of the proceedings and the number, difficulty or novelty of the questions raised;

(b) the skill, time and labour and specialised knowledge required of the solicitor;

(c) the number and importance of any documents prepared or perused;

(d) the place and circumstances of the proceedings or in which the work of the solicitor in preparation for, and conduct of, the proceedings has been carried out;

(e) the importance of the proceedings or the subject matter of the proceedings to the client;

(f) the amount or value of money or property involved in the proceedings;

(g) the steps taken with a view to settling the proceedings, limiting the matters in dispute or limiting the scope of any hearing.

Certification of skilled persons

5.3.—(1) On the application of a party the court may certify a person as a skilled person for the purpose of rule 4.5 (skilled persons).

(2) The court may only grant such an application if satisfied that—

(a) the person is a skilled person; and

(b) it is, or was, reasonable and proportionate that the person should be employed.

(3) The refusal of an application under this rule does not preclude the making of a further application on a change of circumstances.

(4) Where the application is made in proceedings other than—

(a) proceedings subject to Chapter 43 of the Rules of the Court of Session 1994;

(b) proceedings subject to Chapter 36 of the Ordinary Cause Rules 1993; or

(c) a simple procedure case,

paragraph (5) applies.

Document Generated: 2019-04-29

*Status: This is the original version (as it was originally made). This
item of legislation is currently only available in its original format.*

(5) Where this paragraph applies, the court may only determine that the certification has effect for the purposes of work already done by the person where the court is satisfied that the party applying has shown cause for not having applied for certification before the work was done.

Sanction for the employment of counsel in the sheriff court and Sheriff Appeal Court

5.4.—(1) This rule applies to proceedings in the sheriff court and Sheriff Appeal Court.

(2) On the application of a party the court may, subject to paragraphs (4) to (6), sanction—

(a) the proceedings;

(b) any part of the proceedings;

(c) particular work involved in the conduct of the proceedings; or

(d) any combination of (a), (b) and (c),

as suitable for the employment of counsel by that party.

(3) Where proceedings or work are sanctioned as suitable for the employment of senior counsel, or as suitable for the employment of more than one counsel, the interlocutor must record that.

(4) Paragraphs (5) and (6) apply where the application is made in proceedings other than—

(a) proceedings subject to Chapter 36 of the Ordinary Cause Rules 1993;

(b) a simple procedure case; or

(c) proceedings in the Sheriff Appeal Court.

(5) An interlocutor sanctioning proceedings, or a part of proceedings, as suitable for the employment of counsel has no effect as regards work carried out by counsel before the date of the interlocutor.

(6) The court may only sanction particular work already carried out as suitable for the employment of counsel when satisfied that the party applying has shown cause for not having applied for sanction before the work was carried out.

(7) The refusal of an application under this rule does not preclude the making of a further application on a change of circumstances.

CHAPTER 6

VALUE ADDED TAX

Value added tax

6.1.—(1) Where work done by a solicitor constitutes a supply of services in respect of which value added tax is chargeable by the solicitor, there may be added to the charges allowed in respect of that work under Chapter 3 an amount equal to the value added tax chargeable on those charges, unless the entitled party will not bear the burden of the value added tax.

(2) Where an outlay allowed under Chapter 4 is a charge for the supply of goods or services on which the supplier has charged value added tax, the amount of the value added tax charged may only be allowed as an outlay when the entitled party will bear the burden of the value added tax.

Document Generated: 2019-04-29

CHAPTER 7

PAYMENTS TO WITNESSES AND FEES OF SHORTHAND WRITERS

Reimbursement of witnesses

7.1. Schedule 6 has effect for the purpose of regulating the liability of a party at whose instance a person was cited or requested to appear as a witness in civil proceedings, to reimburse losses and expenses incurred by that person.

Fees of shorthand writers and transcribers

7.2.—(1) The table in Part 1 of schedule 7 has effect for the purpose of regulating the fees charged by shorthand writers and persons preparing transcripts of evidence.

(2) The table in Part 2 of schedule 7 has effect for the purpose of regulating the expenses that may be charged by a shorthand writer instructed to attend a proof, jury trial or commission, in so far as reasonably incurred.

(3) Value added tax may be added to the fees and expenses chargeable where the shorthand writer or transcriber is required to charge value added tax.

CHAPTER 8

DILIGENCE

Instructing steps in diligence

8.1. Where, in the execution of diligence, the expenses chargeable against a debtor include the expenses incurred by a solicitor in instructing a messenger-at-arms or sheriff officer to take any step, the sum chargeable for each such instruction is 1.25 units.

Edinburgh
27th February 2019

CJM SUTHERLAND
Lord President
I.P.D.

Document Generated: 2019-04-29

Status: *This is the original version (as it was originally made). This item of legislation is currently only available in its original format.*

SCHEDULE 1   Rule 3.3(2)(a)

TABLE OF DETAILED CHARGES

		Units
Time charges		

1.	Time engaged by solicitor, except as otherwise specifically provided, in
	
	    preparing for or conducting any hearing;
	    attendance at any hearing (including waiting time), consultation with counsel, or meeting; or
	    perusing documents,
	
	per 6 minutes (or such other sum as in the opinion of the Auditor is justified)
		1

2.	Time engaged by clerk, one-half of above	
Documents		
3.	Drafting—	
	(a) affidavits and (where ordered by the court) witness summaries and witness statements, per 250 words	2.5
	(b) formal documents	0.75
	(c) other documents, per 250 words	1.25
4.	Perusal of a precognition or report prepared by a skilled person, per 250 words	0.75
5.	Reviewing documents prepared by counsel where counsel's fee for preparing same is allowed as an outlay, per 1250 words	0.75
6.	Certifying or signing a document	0.75
Communications		
7.	Formal written communications	0.5
8.	Other written communications, per 125 words	1.25
9.	Lengthy telephone calls, to be charged at attendance rate	
10.	Other telephone calls	0.75
The process		
11.	Making up and lodging process	1.25
12.	Each necessary lodging in process, uplifting and borrowing from process and return of borrowed item	1.25
Citation and service		
13.	Each citation of party, witness or haver, to include completion of all associated forms and certificate of citation	1.25

Document Generated: 2019-04-29
Status: *This is the original version (as it was originally made). This item of legislation is currently only available in its original format.*

| 14. | Instructing officers to serve, execute or intimate any document, including examining execution and settling fee | 1.25 |
| 15. | Accepting service | 1.25 |

SCHEDULE 2   Rule 3.3(2)(b)(i)

TABLES OF INCLUSIVE CHARGES FOR WORK UNDERTAKEN BY SOLICITORS IN PROCEEDINGS IN THE COURT OF SESSION

TABLE 1

UNDEFENDED ACTIONS

PART 1

UNDEFENDED ACTIONS IN WHICH DECREE IN ABSENCE WAS GRANTED IN ACCORDANCE WITH RULE 19.1 OF THE RULES OF THE COURT OF SESSION 1994

	Units
All work up to and including obtaining extract decree	22.5

PART 2

UNDEFENDED ACTIONS OF DIVORCE OR DISSOLUTION OF CIVIL PARTNERSHIP, OR OF SEPARATION, IN WHICH THE FACTS SET OUT IN SECTION 1(2)(a) OR (b) OF THE DIVORCE (SCOTLAND) ACT 1976 OR IN SECTION 117(3)(a) OF THE CIVIL PARTNERSHIP ACT 2004 WERE RELIED ON AND IN WHICH EVIDENCE WAS GIVEN BY AFFIDAVIT ALONE

	Units
All work up to and including obtaining extract decree	95
Further charge where decree granted in respect of a conclusion relating to an ancillary matter	25
Further charge where the pursuer was represented by a solicitor in Edinburgh and a solicitor outside Edinburgh, and the Auditor is satisfied that it was appropriate for the pursuer to be so represented	22.5

PART 3

UNDEFENDED ACTIONS OF DIVORCE OR DISSOLUTION OF CIVIL PARTNERSHIP, OR OF SEPARATION, IN WHICH THE FACTS SET OUT IN SECTION 1(1)(b), (2)(d) or (2)(e) OF THE DIVORCE (SCOTLAND) ACT 1976 OR IN SECTION 117(2)(b), (3)(c) or (3)(d) OF THE CIVIL PARTNERSHIP ACT 2004 WERE RELIED ON AND IN WHICH EVIDENCE WAS GIVEN BY AFFIDAVIT ALONE

	Units
All work up to and including obtaining extract decree	70
Further charge where decree granted in respect of a conclusion relating to an ancillary matter	25

Document Generated: 2019-04-29

Status: *This is the original version (as it was originally made). This item of legislation is currently only available in its original format.*

Further charge where the pursuer was represented by a solicitor in Edinburgh and a solicitor outside Edinburgh, and the Auditor is satisfied that it was appropriate for the pursuer to be so represented	22.5

PART 4

UNDEFENDED ACTIONS SUBJECT TO SECTION 8(1) OF
THE CIVIL EVIDENCE (SCOTLAND) ACT 1988 IN WHICH
DECREE WAS GRANTED FOLLOWING A PAROLE PROOF

	Units
1. Instruction	
All work (apart from precognitions) up to and including the calling of the summons	30
2. Amendment	
(a) Where summons amended, re-service is not ordered and motion is not starred	5
(b) Where summons amended, re-service is not ordered and motion is starred	6.25
(c) Where summons amended and re-service is ordered	7.5
3. Incidental procedure	
Fixing diet, enrolling action, preparing for proof, citing witnesses etc.	17.5
4. Commission to take evidence on interrogatories	
(a) All work (except as otherwise provided for) up to and including lodging of completed interrogatories	7.5
(b) Attendance at execution of commission (if required), per 6 minutes	1
(c) Charge for completed interrogatories, per 250 words	1.25
5. Commission to take evidence on open commission	
(a) All work up to and including lodging of report of commission, other than attendance at execution of commission	7.5
(b) Attendance at execution of commission, per 6 minutes	1
6. Other matters	
Where applicable, charges under paragraphs 1, 12, 14, 17 and 22 of Table 2 of this schedule	
7. Proof and completion	
All work (except as otherwise provided for) up to and including obtaining extract decree	22.5
8. Accounts	
Framing and lodging account and attending taxation	7.5

TABLE 2

DEFENDED ACTIONS (OTHER THAN THOSE TO WHICH TABLE 3 APPLIES)

	Units

Document Generated: 2019-04-29
Status: This is the original version (as it was originally made). This item of legislation is currently only available in its original format.

1. Precognitions, affidavits and (where ordered by the court) witness summaries and witness statements	
(a) Taking and drawing precognitions, per 250 words	5
(b) Where a skilled person prepares his or her own precognition or report, charge for perusing it (whether or not in the course of doing so the solicitor revises or adjusts it), per 250 words	2.5
(c) Preparation and lodging of affidavits and (where ordered by the court) witness summaries and witness statements, per 250 words	5
(d) Perusing opponent's witness summaries, witness statements and affidavits, per 250 words	2.5
2. Work before commencement of proceedings	
All work (except as otherwise provided for) which the Auditor is satisfied has reasonably been undertaken in contemplation of, or preparatory to, the commencement of proceedings	45
3. Instruction	
(a) All work (apart from precognitions) from commencement until lodgement of open record	45
(b) Instructing re-service where necessary	5
(c) If counterclaim lodged, further charge to each party	10
4. Record	
(a) All work in connection with adjustment and closing of record (including subsequent work in connection with By Order (Adjustment) Roll, except in actions proceeding under Chapter 42A)—	
(i) where cause settled or disposed of before record closed	30
(ii) otherwise	50
(b) If consultation held before record closed, further charges may be allowed as follows—	
(i) arranging consultation	5
(ii) attendance at consultation, per 6 minutes	1
(c) Further charge to each existing party for each pursuer, defender or third party brought in before the record is closed (to include necessary amendments)	15
(d) Further charge to each existing party if an additional pursuer, defender or third party is brought in after the record is closed	22.5
(e) Charge to a new pursuer who requires to be brought in as a result of the death of an existing pursuer	15
5. By Order (Adjustment) Roll in actions proceeding under Chapter 42A	
(a) Preparing for hearing, including instruction of counsel, and attendance not exceeding half an hour	7.5
(b) Thereafter attendance, per 6 minutes	1

Document Generated: 2019-04-29

Status: *This is the original version (as it was originally made). This item of legislation is currently only available in its original format.*

6. Notes of Argument, Statements of Facts or Issues and Notes of Proposals for Further Procedure	
(a) Instructing, perusing and lodging first Note of Arguments (either party)	10
(b) Perusing opponent's Note of Arguments	5
(c) Instructing, perusing and lodging any further Note of Arguments (either party)	5
(d) Instructing, perusing and lodging (each) Statement of Facts or Issues	7.5
(e) Perusing opponent's Statement of Facts or Issues (each)	5
(f) Instructing, revising and lodging (each) Note of Proposals for Further Procedure	7.5
(g) Perusing opponent's Note of Proposals for Further Procedure (each)	5
7. Procedure Roll, preliminary, procedural or other hearing	
(a) Preparing for hearing including all work, incidental work and instruction of counsel	10
(b) Attendance, per 6 minutes	1
(c) Advising and work incidental to it	7.5
8. Adjustment of issues and counter issues	
(a) All work in connection with, and incidental to, the lodging, adjustment and approval of an issue	10
(b) Further charge to pursuer for considering—	
(i) first counter-issue	2.5
(ii) each additional counter-issue	1.25
(c) Charge to defender or third party for—	
(i) all work in connection with and incidental to the lodging, adjustment and approval of a counter-issue	10
(ii) considering issue where no counter-issue lodged	2.5
(iii) considering each additional counter-issue	1.25
9. Incidental Procedure (not chargeable prior to the approval of issue of allowance of proof)	
Fixing diet, obtaining note on the line of evidence etc., borrowing and returning process and all other work prior to the consultation on the sufficiency of evidence	22.5
10. Amendment of record	
(a) Amendment of conclusions only, charge to proposer	7.5
(b) Amendment of conclusions only, charge to opponent	2.5
(c) Amendment of pleadings after record closed, where no answers to the amendment are lodged, charge to proposer	10
(d) In same circumstances as set out in sub-paragraph (c), charge to opponent	5
(e) Amendment of pleadings after record closed, where answers are lodged, charge to proposer and each party lodging answers	25

Document Generated: 2019-04-29
*Status: This is the original version (as it was originally made). This
item of legislation is currently only available in its original format.*

(f) Further charge for adjustment of minute and answers, where applicable, to be allowed to each party	15
11. Lodging productions	
(a) Lodging productions, each inventory	5
(b) Considering opponent's productions, each inventory	2.5
12. Miscellaneous motions and minutes where not otherwise covered by this table	
(a) Where attendance of counsel and/or solicitor not required	2.5
(b) Where attendance of counsel and/or solicitor required, inclusive of instruction of counsel, not exceeding half an hour	7.5
(c) Thereafter attendance, per additional 6 minutes	1
(d) Instructing counsel for a minute (other than a minute ordered by the court), revising and lodging as a separate step in process including any necessary action	7.5
(e) Perusing a minute of admission or abandonment	2.5
13. Valuation of claim in actions proceeding under Chapter 42A	
(a) Valuation of claim	30
(b) Considering opponent's valuation of claim	15
14. Specification of documents or property	
(a) Instructing counsel, revising and lodging and all incidental procedure to obtain a diligence up to and including obtaining interlocutor	10
(b) Charge to opponent	5
(c) Arranging commission, citing havers, instructing commissioner and shorthand writer and preparation for commission	10
(d) Charge to opponent	5
(e) Attendance at execution of commission, per 6 minutes	1
(f) If alternative procedure adopted, charge per person on whom order served	3.75
(g) Perusal of documents or inspection of property recovered under a specification (or by informal means) where not otherwise provided for in this Table, per 6 minutes	1
15. Commission to take evidence on interrogatories	
(a) Applying for commission to cover all work up to and including lodging report of commission with completed interrogatories and cross-interrogatories	20
(b) Charge to opponent—	
(i) if cross-interrogatories lodged	15
(ii) if no cross-interrogatories lodged	6.25
(c) In addition to above, charge to each party for completed interrogatories or cross-interrogatories, per 250 words	1.25
16. Commission to take evidence on open commissions	

Legislation and Protocols 283

Document Generated: 2019-04-29

Status: *This is the original version (as it was originally made). This item of legislation is currently only available in its original format.*

(a) Applying for commission up to and including lodging report of commission	22.5
(b) Charge to opponent	10
(c) Further charge for attendance at execution of commission, per 6 minutes	1
17. Reports obtained under order of court excluding Auditor's report	
(a) All work incidental to the report	10
(b) Further charge for perusal of report, per 6 minutes	1
18. Preparation for proof or jury trial	
To include fixing consultation on the sufficiency of evidence, citing witnesses, all work checking and writing up process and preparing for proof or jury trial—	
(a) if action settled before proof or jury trial, or lasts only one day, to include, where applicable, instruction of counsel	65
(b) for each day or part of day after the first, including instruction of counsel	6.25
(c) preparing for adjourned diets and all work incidental to it as in sub-paragraph (a), if adjourned for more than five days	15
(d) if consultation held before proof or jury trial, attendance, per 6 minutes	1
(e) all work in connection with making up and pagination of joint bundle of medical records in actions proceeding under Chapter 42A	10
19. Pre-trial meeting	
(a) Arranging pre-trial meeting (each occasion)	5
(b) Preparing for pre-trial meeting	27.5
(c) Preparing for continued pre-trial meeting (each occasion)	10
(d) Attending pre-trial meeting, per 6 minutes	1
(e) Joint Minute of pre-trial meeting	2.5
20. Settlement	
(a) Judicial tender or pursuer's offer—	
(i) lodging or considering first tender or pursuer's offer	15
(ii) lodging each further tender or pursuer's offer, subject to the Auditor being satisfied that the tender or offer was a genuine attempt to settle the proceedings	10
(iii) considering each further tender or pursuer's offer	10
(iv) if tender accepted, further charge to each accepting party	10
(v) if pursuer's offer accepted, further charge to offering party	10
(b) Extra-judicial settlement – advising on, negotiating and agreeing extra-judicial settlement (not based on judicial tender or pursuer's offer) to include preparation and lodging of joint minute	25
(c) The Auditor may allow a charge in respect of work undertaken with a view to settlement (whether or not settlement is in fact agreed), including offering settlement	40

Document Generated: 2019-04-29
*Status: This is the original version (as it was originally made). This
item of legislation is currently only available in its original format.*

(d) If consultation held to consider tender, pursuer's offer, extra-judicial settlement or with a view to settlement (whether or not settlement is in fact agreed), attendance, per 6 minutes	1
21. Hearing limitation fee	
To include all work undertaken with a view to limiting the matters in dispute or limiting the scope of any hearing, and including exchanging documents, precognitions and expert reports, agreeing any fact, statement or document, and preparing and lodging any joint minute	50
22. Proof or jury trial	
Attendance, per 6 minutes	1
23. Accounts	
(a) Preparation and lodging of judicial account, to include production of vouchers and adjustment of expenses	20
(b) Preparing for taxation, per 6 minutes	1
(c) Attendance at taxation, per 6 minutes	1
24. Ordering and obtaining extract	**3.75**
25. Final procedure	
All work to close of cause so far as not otherwise provided for—	
(a) if case goes to proof or jury trial, or is settled within 14 days before the diet of proof or jury trial	20
(b) in any other case	6.25

TABLE 3

DEFENDED PERSONAL INJURIES ACTIONS

	Units
1. Precognitions/Expert Reports	
(a) Taking and drawing precognitions, per 250 words	5
(b) Where a skilled person prepares his or her own precognition or report, charge for perusing it (whether or not in the course of doing so the solicitor revises or adjusts it), per 250 words	2.5
2. Work before commencement of proceedings	
All work (except as otherwise provided for in this Table) which the Auditor is satisfied has reasonably been undertaken in contemplation of, or preparatory to, the commencement of proceedings particularly to include communications between parties in relation to areas of medical/quantum/discussion regarding settlement	45
3. Instruction	
(a) All work (except as otherwise specifically provided for in this Table) from commencement to lodging of defences	45
(b) Further charge in the event of the summons being drafted without the assistance of counsel	15

Document Generated: 2019-04-29

Status: *This is the original version (as it was originally made). This item of legislation is currently only available in its original format.*

(c) Specification of documents per Form 43.2-B	7.5
(d) Charge to opponent for considering specification of documents	5
(e) Instructing re-service where necessary	5
(f) If counterclaim lodged, further charge to each party to include Answers	15
(g) Arranging commission to recover documents, citing havers, instructing commissioner and shorthand writer and preparation for commission	10
(h) Charge to opponent where commission arranged	5
(i) Attendance at execution of commission, per 6 minutes	1
(j) If alternative procedure adopted, charge per person on whom order served	3.75
(k) Perusal of documents recovered under a specification of documents (or by informal means) where not otherwise provided for in this Table, per 6 minutes	1
4. Record	
(a) All work in connection with adjustment and closing of record—	
(i) where cause settled or disposed of before record closed	30
(ii) otherwise	50
(b) If consultation held before record closed, further charges may be allowed as follows—	
(i) arranging consultation	5
(ii) attendance at consultation, per 6 minutes	1
(c) Further charge to each existing party for each pursuer, defender or third party brought in before the record is closed (to include necessary amendments)	15
(d) Further charge to each existing party if an additional pursuer, defender or third party is brought in after the record is closed	22.5
(e) Charge to a new pursuer who requires to be brought in as a result of the death of an existing pursuer	15
5. Notes of arguments	
(a) Instructing, perusing and lodging first Note of Arguments, where ordained by the Court (either party)	10
(b) Perusing opponent's Note of Arguments	5
(c) Instructing, perusing and lodging any further Note of Arguments, where ordained by the Court (either party)	5
6. Adjustment of issues and counter-issues	
(a) All work in connection with, and incidental to, the lodging, adjustment and approval of an issue	10
(b) Further charge to pursuer for considering—	
(i) first counter-issue	2.5
(ii) each additional counter-issue	1.25

Document Generated: 2019-04-29
Status: This is the original version (as it was originally made). This item of legislation is currently only available in its original format.

(c) Charge to defender or third party for—	
(i) all work in connection with and incidental to the lodging, adjustment and approval of a counter-issue	10
(ii) considering issue where no counter-issue lodged	2.5
(iii) considering each additional counter-issue	1.25
7. Incidental procedure (not chargeable prior to the approval of issue of allowance of proof)	
Fixing diet, obtaining note on the line of evidence etc., borrowing and returning process and all other work prior to the consultation on the sufficiency of evidence	22.5
8. Amendment of record	
(a) Amendment of conclusions only, charge to proposer	7.5
(b) Amendment of conclusions only, charge to opponent	2.5
(c) Amendment of pleadings after record closed, where no answers to the amendment are lodged, charge to proposer	10
(d) In same circumstances as set out in sub-paragraph (c), charge to opponent	5
(e) Amendment of pleadings after record closed, where answers are lodged, charge to proposer and each party lodging answers	25
(f) Further charge for adjustment of minute and answers, where applicable, to be allowed to each party	15
9. Lodging productions	
(a) Lodging productions, each inventory	5
(b) Considering opponent's productions, each inventory	2.5
10. By Order Roll/variation of timetable order/adjustment on final decree/ interim payment of damages	
(a) Preparing for hearing, including instruction of counsel, and attendance not exceeding half an hour	7.5
(b) Thereafter attendance, per 6 minutes	1
(c) In the event of a separate Advising/Opinion, all work incidental thereto	7.5
11. Miscellaneous motions and minutes where not otherwise covered by this Table	
(a) Where attendance of counsel and/or solicitor not required	2.5
(b) Where attendance of counsel and/or solicitor required, inclusive of instruction of counsel, not exceeding half an hour	7.5
(c) Thereafter attendance, per 6 minutes	1
(d) Instructing counsel for a minute/note on further procedure (if applicable), revising and lodging as a separate step in process including any necessary action	7.5
(e) Perusing a minute of admission or abandonment, a note ordered by the court, or a notice of grounds	2.5
12. Valuation of claim	

Document Generated: 2019-04-29

Status: This is the original version (as it was originally made). This item of legislation is currently only available in its original format.

(a) Statement of valuation of claim	30
(b) Considering opponent's statement of valuation of claim	15
13. Specification of documents or property (if further specification considered necessary)	
(a) Instructing counsel, revising and lodging and all incidental procedure to obtain a diligence up to and including obtaining interlocutor	10
(b) Charge to opponent	5
(c) Arranging commission, citing havers, instructing commissioner and shorthand writer and preparation for commission	10
(d) Charge to opponent	5
(e) Attendance at execution of commission, per 6 minutes	1
(f) If alternative procedure adopted, charge per person on whom order served	3.75
(g) Perusal of documents or inspection of property recovered under a specification (or by informal means) where not otherwise provided for in this Table, per 6 minutes	1
14. Commission to take evidence on interrogatories	
(a) Applying for commission to cover all work up to and including lodging report of commission with completed interrogatories and cross-interrogatories	20
(b) Charge to opponent—	
(i) if cross-interrogatories lodged	15
(ii) if no cross-interrogatories lodged	6.25
(c) In addition to above, charge to each party for completed interrogatories or cross-interrogatories, per 250 words	1.25
15. Commission to take evidence on open commission	
(a) Applying for commission up to and including lodging report of commission	22.5
(b) Charge to opponent	10
(c) Further charge for attendance at execution of commission, per 6 minutes	1
16. Reports obtained under order of court excluding Auditor's report	
(a) All work incidental to the report	10
(b) Further charge for perusal of report, per 6 minutes	1
17. Preparation for proof or jury trial	
To include fixing consultation on the sufficiency of evidence, citing witnesses, all work checking and writing up process and preparing for proof or jury trial—	
(a) if action settled before proof or jury trial, or lasts only one day, to include, where applicable, instruction of counsel	65
(b) for each day or part of day after the first, including instruction of counsel	6.25
(c) preparing for adjourned diets and all work incidental to it as in sub-paragraph (a), if adjourned for more than five days	15

Document Generated: 2019-04-29

Status: This is the original version (as it was originally made). This item of legislation is currently only available in its original format.

(d) if consultation held before proof or jury trial, attendance, per 6 minutes	1
18. Pre-trial meeting	
(a) Arranging pre-trial meeting (each occasion)	5
(b) Preparing for pre-trial meeting	27.5
(c) Preparing for continued pre-trial meeting (each occasion)	10
(d) Attending pre-trial meeting, per 6 minutes	1
(e) Joint Minute of pre-trial meeting	2.5
19. Settlement	
(a) Judicial tender or pursuer's offer—	
(i) lodging or considering first tender or pursuer's offer	15
(ii) lodging each further tender or pursuer's offer, subject to the Auditor being satisfied that the tender or offer was a genuine attempt to settle the proceedings	10
(iii) considering each further tender or pursuer's offer	10
(iv) if tender accepted, further charge to each accepting party	10
(v) if pursuer's offer accepted, further charge to offering party	10
(b) Extra-judicial settlement – advising on, negotiating and agreeing extra-judicial settlement (not based on judicial tender or pursuer's offer) to include preparation and lodging of joint minute	25
(c) The Auditor may allow a charge in respect of work undertaken with a view to settlement (whether or not settlement is in fact agreed), including offering settlement	40
(d) If consultation held to consider tender, pursuer's offer, extra-judicial settlement or with a view to settlement (whether or not settlement is in fact agreed), attendance, per 6 minutes	1
20. Hearing limitation fee	
For any work undertaken to limit matters in dispute not otherwise provided for – subject to details being provided	20
21. Proof or jury trial	
Attendance, per 6 minutes	1
22. Accounts	
(a) Preparation and lodging of judicial account, to include production of vouchers and adjustment of expenses	20
(b) Preparing for taxation, per 6 minutes	1
(c) Attendance at taxation, per 6 minutes	1
23. Ordering and obtaining extract	**3.75**
24. Final procedure	
All work to close of cause so far as not otherwise provided for—	

Document Generated: 2019-04-29

Status: *This is the original version (as it was originally made). This item of legislation is currently only available in its original format.*

(a) if case goes to proof or jury trial, or is settled within 14 days before the diet of proof or jury trial	20
(b) in any other case	6.25

TABLE 4

OUTER HOUSE PETITIONS

	Units
1. Unopposed petition	
(a) All work, including precognitions, up to and obtaining extract decree	45
(b) Where the party has been represented by an Edinburgh solicitor and a solicitor outside Edinburgh, the Auditor may, if satisfied that it was appropriate for the party to be so represented, allow a charge of	60
2. Opposed petition	
(a) All work (other than precognitions) up to and including lodging petition, obtaining and executing warrant for service	35
(b) Where applicable, charges under paragraphs 1, 2, 4, 6(a) – (e), 7, 9, 10, 11, 12 and 14 – 25 of Table 2 of this schedule	
3. Reports in opposed petitions	
(a) Each report by the Accountant of Court	5
(b) Any other report, as under paragraph 17 of Table 2 of this schedule	
4. Obtaining a bond of caution	5

TABLE 5

INNER HOUSE BUSINESS

	Units
1. Reclaiming motions	
(a) Charge to reclaimer for all work (except as otherwise provided for in this Table) up to interlocutor sending cause to Summar Roll	15
(b) Charge to respondent	7.5
(c) Further charge to each party for preparing or reviewing every 50 pages of Appendix	6.25
2. Appeals from inferior courts	
(a) Charge to appellant	17.5
(b) Charge to respondent	8.75
(c) Further charge to each party for preparing or reviewing every 50 pages of Appendix	6.25
3. Special cases, Inner House petitions and appeals other than under paragraph 2 of this Table	
According to circumstances of the case.	

Document Generated: 2019-04-29
Status: *This is the original version (as it was originally made). This item of legislation is currently only available in its original format.*

4. Note of objection	
(a) Instructing, perusing and lodging note of objection	10
(b) Perusing opponent's note of objection	5
(c) Where attendance of counsel inclusive of instruction of counsel, not exceeding half an hour	7.5
(d) Thereafter attendance, per 6 minutes	1
5. Grounds of appeal or cross appeal	
(a) Instructing, perusing and lodging grounds of appeal or cross appeal	10
(b) Perusing opponent's note of appeal or cross appeal	5
6. Incidental procedure	
All work in connection with noting remittance of cause to Summar Roll and fixing of Summar Roll hearing	10
7. Summar Roll	
(a) Preparing for hearing and instructing counsel including instructing and lodging lists of authorities and notes of arguments	15
(b) Attendance, per 6 minutes	1
8. Obtaining a bond of caution	**6.25**
9. Other matters	
Where applicable, charges under Table 2 of this schedule	

SCHEDULE 3   Rule 3.3(2)(b)(ii)

TABLES OF INCLUSIVE CHARGES FOR WORK UNDERTAKEN BY
SOLICITORS IN PROCEEDINGS IN THE SHERIFF APPEAL COURT
UNDER THE ACT OF SEDERUNT (SHERIFF APPEAL COURT RULES) 2015

TABLE 1

APPEALS UNDER THE STANDARD APPEAL PROCEDURE
OR THE ACCELERATED APPEAL PROCEDURE

	Units
Initiation of appeal	
1. All work (except appearances) up to appointment of appeal to standard appeal procedure or accelerated appeal procedure—	
(a) charge for appellant	25
(b) charge for respondent	12.5
Cross appeals	
2. Preparing and lodging—	

Legislation and Protocols

291

Document Generated: 2019-04-29

Status: *This is the original version (as it was originally made). This item of legislation is currently only available in its original format.*

(a) grounds of appeal	10
(b) answers to grounds of appeal	10
3. Considering opponent's grounds of appeal or answers to grounds of appeal	5
Referral of questions about competency of appeal	
4. Preparing and lodging reference	10
5. Considering opponent's reference	5
6. Preparing and lodging note of argument	10
Lodging documents prior to procedural hearing	
7. Lodging all necessary documents (except appendix) as required by the timetable	10
8. Preparing or revising appendix, per 50 pages	6.25
Conduct of and attendance at hearings	
9. Conducting or attending any hearing, per 6 minutes	1
Note: Paragraph 9 does not apply where any other paragraphs in this Part specifies that it includes initial attendance at court, unless that hearing is continued.	
Preparation for appeal hearing	
10. Preparing for appeal hearing where counsel not instructed to conduct the hearing	20
Motions and minutes	
11. Preparing and lodging any written motion or minute, including initial attendance at court to conduct hearing—	
(a) where opposed	12.5
(b) where unopposed	5
12. Considering opponent's written motion or minute, including initial attendance at court to conduct hearing—	
(a) where opposed	12.5
(b) where unopposed	5
Amendment of pleadings	
13. Preparing and lodging motion to amend	10
14. Considering opponent's motion to amend	7.5
15. Preparing and lodging opposition to motion	5
16. Considering opponent's opposition to motion	5
Withdrawal of solicitors	
17. All work preparing for a peremptory hearing fixed under rule 17.3(1), including initial attendance at court to conduct peremptory hearing	10
Expenses	
18. Preparing and lodging account of expenses	15

Document Generated: 2019-04-29
Status: *This is the original version (as it was originally made). This
item of legislation is currently only available in its original format.*

19. Attendance at taxation, per 6 minutes	1
Instruction of counsel	
20. Instructing counsel to attend court to conduct a hearing (to include solicitor's preparation for the hearing)	12.5
21. Arranging and attending consultation with counsel—	
(a) where total time engaged does not exceed one hour	12.5
(b) for each additional 6 minutes	1

TABLE 2

APPLICATIONS FOR NEW TRIAL OR TO ENTER JURY VERDICT

	Units
Initiation of application	
1. All work (except appearances) up to issue of timetable—	
(a) charge for applicant	25
(b) charge for respondent	12.5
Referral of questions about competency of application	
2. Preparing and lodging reference	10
3. Considering opponent's reference	5
4. Preparing and lodging note of argument	10
Lodging documents prior to procedural hearing	
5. Lodging all necessary documents (except appendix) as required by the timetable	10
6. Preparing or revising appendix, per 50 pages	6.25
Conduct of and attendance at hearings	
7. Conducting or attending any hearing, per 6 minutes	1
Note: Paragraph 7 does not apply where any other paragraph in this Part specifies that it includes initial attendance at court, unless that hearing is continued.	
Preparation for hearing required to dispose of application	
8. Preparing for hearing required to dispose of application where counsel not instructed to conduct the hearing	20
Motions and minutes	
9. Preparing and lodging any written motion or minute, including initial attendance at court to conduct hearing—	
(a) where opposed	12.5
(b) where unopposed	5
10. Considering opponent's written motion or minute, including initial attendance at court to conduct hearing—	

(a) where opposed	12.5
(b) where unopposed	5
Amendment of pleadings	
11. Preparing and lodging motion to amend	10
12. Considering opponent's motion to amend	7.5
13. Preparing and lodging opposition to motion	5
14. Considering opponent's opposition to motion	5
Withdrawal of solicitors	
15. All work preparing for a peremptory hearing fixed under rule 17.3(1), including initial attendance at court to conduct peremptory hearing	10
Expenses	
16. Preparing and lodging account of expenses	15
17. Attendance at taxation, per 6 minutes	1
Instruction of counsel	
18. Instructing counsel to attend court to conduct a hearing (to include solicitor's preparation for the hearing)	12.5
19. Arranging and attending consultation with counsel	
(a) where total time engaged does not exceed one hour	12.5
(b) for each additional 6 minutes	1

TABLE 3

APPEALS FROM SIMPLE PROCEDURE CASES

	Units
Preparation for hearing required to dispose of appeal	
1. Preparing for hearing under rule 29.4 of the Sheriff Appeal Court Rules (or rule 16.4 of the Simple Procedure Rules) where counsel not instructed to conduct the hearing	20
Conduct of and attendance at hearings	
2. Conducting or attending any hearing, per 6 minutes	1
Note: Paragraph 2 does not apply where any other paragraph in this Part specifies that it includes initial attendance at court, unless that hearing is continued.	
Motions and minutes	
3. Preparing and lodging any written motion or minute, including initial attendance at court to conduct hearing—	
(a) where opposed	12.5
(b) where unopposed	5

Document Generated: 2019-04-29
*Status: This is the original version (as it was originally made). This
item of legislation is currently only available in its original format.*

4. Considering opponent's written motion or minute, including initial attendance at court to conduct hearing—	
(a) where opposed	12.5
(b) where unopposed	5
Withdrawal of solicitors	
5. All work preparing for a peremptory hearing fixed under rule 17.3(1), including initial attendance at court to conduct peremptory hearing	10
Expenses	
6. Preparing and lodging account of expenses	15
7. Attendance at taxation, per 6 minutes	1
Instruction of counsel	
8. Instructing counsel to attend court to conduct a hearing (to include solicitor's preparation for the hearing)	12.5
9. Arranging and attending consultation with advocate or solicitor advocate	
(a) where total time engaged does not exceed one hour	12.5
(b) for each additional 6 minutes	1

SCHEDULE 4   Rule 3.3(2)(b)(iii)

TABLES OF INCLUSIVE CHARGES FOR WORK UNDERTAKEN
BY SOLICITORS IN ORDINARY CAUSES IN THE SHERIFF COURT

TABLE 1

UNDEFENDED ACTIONS

PART 1

UNDEFENDED ACTIONS IN WHICH DECREE WAS GRANTED IN
ACCORDANCE WITH RULE 7.2 OR 7.3 OF THE ORDINARY CAUSE RULES 1993

	Units
1. All work up to and including obtaining extract decree—	
(a) where settlement is effected after service of a writ but before the expiry of the period of notice	15
(b) otherwise	17.5
Further charge where a court appearance is necessary because of an application for a time to pay direction	3.75

PART 2

UNDEFENDED ACTIONS OF DIVORCE OR DISSOLUTION OF CIVIL
PARTNERSIP, OR OF SEPARATION, IN WHICH THE FACTS SET OUT IN
SECTION 1(2)(a) OR (b) OF THE DIVORCE (SCOTLAND) ACT 1976 OR IN

Document Generated: 2019-04-29
Status: *This is the original version (as it was originally made). This item of legislation is currently only available in its original format.*

SECTION 117(3)(a) OF THE CIVIL PARTNERSHIP ACT 2004 WERE RELIED ON AND IN WHICH EVIDENCE WAS GIVEN BY AFFIDAVIT ALONE

	Units
All work up to and including obtaining extract decree	96.25
Further charge where decree granted in respect of a crave relating to an ancillary matter	25

PART 3

UNDEFENDED ACTIONS OF DIVORCE OR DISSOLUTION OF CIVIL PARTNERSIP, OR OF SEPARATION, IN WHICH THE FACTS SET OUT IN SECTION 1(1) (b), (2)(d) or 2(e) OF THE DIVORCE (SCOTLAND) ACT 1976 OR IN SECTION 117(2)(b), (3)(c) OR 3(d) OF THE CIVIL PARTNERSHIP ACT 2004 WERE RELIED ON AND IN WHICH EVIDENCE WAS GIVEN BY AFFIDAVIT ALONE

	Units
All work up to and including obtaining extract decree	71.5
Further charge where decree granted in respect of a crave relating to an ancillary matter	25

PART 4

UNDEFENDED ACTIONS SUBJECT TO SECTION 8(1) OF THE CIVIL EVIDENCE (SCOTLAND) ACT 1988 IN WHICH DECREEE WAS GRANTED FOLLOWING A PAROLE PROOF

	Units
All work up to and including obtaining extract decree	71.5

TABLE 2

DEFENDED ORDINARY ACTIONS (OTHER THAN THOSE TO WHICH TABLE 3 APPLIES)

	Units
1. Precognitions, reports and affidavits	
(a) Taking and drawing precognitions, per 250 words	5
(b) Where a skilled person prepares his or her own precognition or report, charge for perusing it (whether or not in the course of doing so the solicitor revises or adjusts it), per 250 words	2.5
(c) All work in connection with preparation and lodging of affidavits, per 250 words	2.5
2. Work before commencement of proceedings – other than Commercial Actions	
All work (except as otherwise specifically provided for) which the Auditor is satisfied has reasonably been undertaken in contemplation of, or preparatory to, the commencement of proceedings	40
3. Work before commencement of proceedings – Commercial Actions	

Document Generated: 2019-04-29

Status: This is the original version (as it was originally made). This item of legislation is currently only available in its original format.

All work (except as otherwise specifically provided for) which the Auditor is satisfied has reasonably been undertaken in contemplation of, or preparatory to, the commencement of proceedings in a commercial action	45
4. Instruction	
(a) All work (except as otherwise specifically provided for) from commencement to the lodging of defences	55
(b) Instructing re-service by sheriff officers where necessary	1.25
(c) Further charge where counterclaim lodged	17.5
5. Case Management Conference – Commercial Action	
(a) Preparation for first case management conference	15
(b) Preparation for each subsequent conference	7.5
(c) Time engaged at conference, per 6 minutes	1
(d) Waiting time, per 6 minutes	1
Note:	
Where case management conference takes place by way of telephone or other remote means the foregoing charges will apply.	
6. Adjustment	
(a) All work (except as otherwise specifically provided for) in connection with the adjustment of the record including making up and lodging certified copy record—	
(i) where cause settled or disposed of before expiry of adjustment period	12.5
(ii) otherwise	30
(b) Further charge to each existing party for each pursuer, defender or third party brought in before the Options Hearing	10
(c) Further charge to each existing party for each pursuer, defender or third party brought in after the Options Hearing	15
7. Note of arguments – Commercial Actions	
(a) Lodging and intimating, or considering first Note of Arguments	12.5
(b) Each Note lodged thereafter	5
8. Options Hearing or Child Welfare Hearing	
Preparation for and conduct of each Options Hearing or Child Welfare Hearing, to include noting interlocutor—	
(a) where initial hearing does not exceed half an hour	20
(b) thereafter, per 6 minutes	1
(c) where hearing continued, for each continued hearing that does not exceed half an hour	10
(d) thereafter, per 6 minutes	1
(e) lodging and intimating or considering note of basis of preliminary plea, for each note lodged	5

9. Additional Procedure	
All work subsequent to Options Hearing including preparation for and attendance at procedural hearing—	
(a) where initial hearing does not exceed half an hour	20
(b) thereafter, per 6 minutes	1
10. Procedural Hearing in actions proceeding under Chapter 36A	
Preparation for and conduct of Procedural Hearing—	
(a) where hearing does not exceed half an hour	20
(b) thereafter, per 6 minutes	1
11. Debate (other than on evidence)	
(a) Where counsel not employed—	
(i) preparation for, and all work in connection with, any hearing or debate other than on evidence	20
(ii) conduct of debate, per 6 minutes	1
(b) Where counsel employed, appearance with counsel, per 6 minutes	1
(c) Waiting time, per 6 minutes	1
12. Adjustment of issues and counter issues	
(a) All work in connection with, and incidental to, the lodging, adjustment and approval of an issue	10
(b) Further charge to pursuer for considering—	
(i) first counter-issue	2.5
(ii) each additional counter-issue	1.25
(c) Charge to defender or third party for—	
(i) all work in connection with, and incidental to, the lodging, adjustment and approval of a counter-issue	10
(ii) considering issue where no counter-issue lodged	2.5
(iii) considering each additional counter-issue	1.25
13. Incidental Procedure (not chargeable prior to allowance of proof or jury trial)	
All work in connection with noting diet of proof or jury trial and—	
(a) preparing note on line of evidence; or	22.5
(b) instructing counsel to prepare a note on line of evidence	12.5
14. Amendment of Record	
(a) Charge to proposer—	
(i) drawing, intimating and lodging minute of amendment and relative motion	10

Document Generated: 2019-04-29
*Status: This is the original version (as it was originally made). This
item of legislation is currently only available in its original format.*

(ii) perusal of answers	5
(iii) any court appearance necessary, per 6 minutes	1
(b) Charge to opponent—	
(i) perusing minute of amendment	7.5
(ii) preparation of answers	5
(iii) any court appearance necessary, per 6 minutes	1
(c) Further charge for adjustment of minute and answers, where applicable, to be allowed to each party	10
15. Productions	
(a) Lodging productions, each inventory	5
(b) Considering opponent's productions, each inventory	2.5
16. Motions and minutes	
(a) Drawing, intimating and lodging any written motion or minute, including a reponing note, and initial attendance at court (except as otherwise specifically provided for)—	
(i) where opposed	12.5
(ii) where unopposed (including for each party a joint minute other than under paragraph 26(b))	5
(b) Considering opponent's written motion, minute or reponing note, and attendance at court—	
(i) where opposed	12.5
(ii) where unopposed	5
17. Interim Interdict Hearings and other Interim Hearings	
(a) Preparation for each hearing	10
(b) Conducting hearing, per 6 minutes	1
(c) Where counsel employed, appearance with counsel, per 6 minutes	1
(d) Waiting time, per 6 minutes	1
18. Withdrawal of solicitors	
(a) All work in preparation for any diet fixed under rule 24.2(1) and attendance at first such diet	10
(b) Attendance at each additional diet, per quarter hour	1
19. Attendance not otherwise provided for	
(a) Where hearing does not exceed half an hour	5
(b) Thereafter, per 6 minutes	1
20. Specification of documents or property	
(a) Drawing, intimating and lodging specification and relative motion—	

Legislation and Protocols   299

Document Generated: 2019-04-29
***Status:** This is the original version (as it was originally made). This
item of legislation is currently only available in its original format.*

(i) where motion unopposed	10
(ii) where motion opposed, further charge for attendance at hearing of motion, per 6 minutes	1
(b) Charge to opponent—	
(i) where motion unopposed	5
(ii) where motion opposed, further charge for attendance at hearing of motion, per 6 minutes	1
(c) Arranging commission, citing havers, instructing commissioner and shorthand writer and preparing for commission	10
(d) Charge to opponent	5
(e) Attendance at execution of commission, per 6 minutes	1
(f) If optional procedure adopted, charge per person upon whom order is served	1
(g) Perusal of documents or inspection of property recovered, per 6 minutes	1
21. Commissions to take evidence	
(a) On interrogatories—	
(i) applying for commission to include drawing, intimating and lodging motion, drawing and lodging interrogatories, instructing commissioner and all incidental work (except as otherwise specifically provided for), but excluding attendance at execution of commission	27.5
(ii) charge to opponent if cross-interrogatories prepared and lodged	17.5
(iii) if no cross-interrogatories lodged	5
(b) Open commissions—	
(i) applying for commission to include all work (except as otherwise specifically provided for) up to lodging report of commission but excluding attendance at execution of commission	17.5
(ii) charge to opponent	10
(iii) attendance at execution of commission, per 6 minutes	1
22. Reports obtained under order of court	
(a) All work incidental to the report	10
(b) Further charge for perusal of report, per 6 minutes	1
23. Preparation for proof or jury trial	
(a) All work involved in preparing for proof or jury trial (except as otherwise specifically provided for)—	
(i) if action settled or abandoned not later than 14 days before the diet of proof or jury trial	31.25
(ii) in any other case	55
(b) For each day or part day after the first, including instruction of counsel	7.5

Document Generated: 2019-04-29
Status: *This is the original version (as it was originally made). This item of legislation is currently only available in its original format.*

(c) Preparing for adjourned diet and all incidental work as in (a) if diet postponed for more than 6 days, for each additional diet	12.5
24. Valuation of claim in actions proceeding under Chapter 36A	
(a) Preparation of valuation of claim—	
(i) where counsel not employed	30
(ii) where valuation of claim prepared by counsel	15
(b) Considering opponent's valuation of claim	15
25. Pre-trial meeting in actions proceeding under Chapter 36A	
(a) Arranging pre-trial meeting (each occasion)	5
(b) Preparing for pre-trial meeting—	
(i) where counsel not employed	27.5
(ii) where counsel employed	20
(c) Attending pre-trial meeting, per 6 minutes	1
(d) Joint minute of pre-trial meeting	5
Note: where pre-trial meeting takes place by way of video conference, the foregoing charges are to apply.	
26. Settlements	
(a) Judicial tender or pursuer's offer—	
(i) preparing and lodging, or considering first tender or pursuer's offer	15
(ii) preparing and lodging each further tender or pursuer's offer, subject to the Auditor being satisfied that the tender or offer was a genuine attempt to settle the proceedings	10
(iii) considering each further tender or pursuer's offer	10
(iv) if tender accepted, further charge to each accepting party to include preparation and lodging of minute of acceptance of tender and attendance at court when decree granted (not including drawing, intimating and lodging any written motion)	10
(v) if pursuer's offer accepted, further charge to offering party to include consideration of minute of acceptance and attendance at court when decree granted (not including drawing, intimating and lodging any written motion)	10
(b) Extra-judicial settlement, to include negotiations resulting in settlement, framing or revising joint minute and attendance at court when authority interponed thereto (not to include drawing, intimating and lodging any written motion)	18.75
(c) Whether or not charges are payable under (a) or (b) above, where additional work has been undertaken with a view to effecting settlement, including offering settlement, although settlement is not agreed	18.75
27. Hearing limitation fee	
All work (except as otherwise specifically provided for) undertaken with a view to limiting the scope of any hearing, and including the exchange of documents,	45

Legislation and Protocols 301

Document Generated: 2019-04-29

Status: *This is the original version (as it was originally made). This item of legislation is currently only available in its original format.*

precognitions and expert reports, agreeing any fact, statement or document not in dispute, preparing and intimating any notice to admit or notice of non-admission (and consideration thereof) and preparing and lodging any joint minute

28. Proof or jury trial	
(a) Conduct of proof or jury trial, and debate on evidence if taken at close of proof or jury trial, per 6 minutes	1
(b) If counsel employed, appearing with counsel, per 6 minutes	1
(c) Waiting time, per 6 minutes	1
29. Debate on evidence	
(a) Where debate on evidence not taken at conclusion of proof or jury trial, preparing for debate	10
(b) Conduct of debate, per 6 minutes	1
(c) If counsel employed, appearing with counsel, per 6 minutes	1
(d) Waiting time, per 6 minutes	1
30. Accounts	
(a) Preparation and lodging of judicial account, to include production of vouchers and adjustment of expenses	20
(b) Preparing for taxation, per 6 minutes	1
(c) Attendance at taxation, per 6 minutes	1
31. Final procedure	
All work to the conclusion of proceedings so far as not otherwise provided for—	
(a) if case goes to proof or jury trial, or is settled within 14 days before the diet of proof or jury trial	13.75
(b) in any other case	6.25
32. Instruction of counsel	
(a) Instructing counsel to revise pleadings	5
(b) Instructing counsel to attend court	12.5
(c) Arranging and attending consultation with counsel, including consultation held to consider tender, pursuer's offer or extra-judicial settlement, or with a view to settlement—	
(i) where total time engaged does not exceed one hour	12.5
(ii) for each additional 6 minutes	1

TABLE 3

DEFENDED PERSONAL INJURIES ACTIONS PROCEEDING UNDER
PART AI OF CHAPTER 36 OF THE ORDINARY CAUSE RULES 1993

	Units
1. Precognitions, reports and affidavits	

Document Generated: 2019-04-29
Status: *This is the original version (as it was originally made). This item of legislation is currently only available in its original format.*

(a) Taking and drawing precognitions, per 250 words	5
(b) Where a skilled person prepares his or her own precognition or report, charge for perusing it (whether or not in the course of doing so the solicitor revises or adjusts it), per 250 words	2.5
(c) All work in connection with preparation and lodging of affidavits, per 250 words	2.5
2. Work before commencement of proceedings	
(1) Where the Protocol in Appendix 4 of the Ordinary Cause Rules 1993 applied to the claim prior to the commencement of proceedings, the sum of—	
(a) £574;	
(b) 3.5% of the total amount of any damages awarded, or payable under a settlement, up to £25,000; and	
(c) such further sum, not exceeding 50% of the sum of (a) and (b), as the Auditor considers to be justified in respect of work undertaken prior to the commencement of proceedings that (i) was not required for the purposes of complying with the Protocol, (ii) involved the sharing of information with the opposing party, and (iii) is not included in any other fee in this Part.	
(2) In any other case, all work which the Auditor is satisfied has reasonably been undertaken in contemplation of, or preparatory to the commencement of proceedings.	40
Note: Where the Protocol applied and the Auditor is satisfied that the party found entitled to expenses failed to adhere to its terms in material respects, there may be substituted for the fees specified at paragraph 2(1)(a) and (b) such lesser sum as in the opinion of the Auditor is justified.	
3. Instruction	
(a) All work (except as otherwise specifically provided for) from commencement to the lodging of defences	55
(b) Instructing re-service by sheriff officers where necessary	1.25
(c) Specification of documents as per Form PI2	5
(d) Charge to opponent for considering specification of documents	5
(e) Arranging commission to recover documents, citing havers, instructing commissioner and shorthand writer and preparation for commission	10
(f) Charge to opponent where a commission arranged	5
(g) Attendance at execution of commission, per 6 minutes	1
(h) If optional procedure adopted, charge per person on whom order is served	1
(i) Perusal of documents recovered under a specification of documents (or by informal means) where not otherwise provided for, per 6 minutes	1
(j) Attendance in chambers for appointment of cause to Chapter 36A, per 6 minutes	1
(k) Further charge where separate counterclaim and answers lodged	17.5
4. Adjustment	

Document Generated: 2019-04-29

Status: *This is the original version (as it was originally made). This item of legislation is currently only available in its original format.*

(a) All work (except as otherwise specifically provided for) in connection with adjustment of the record including making up and lodging certified copy record—	
(i) where cause settled or disposed of before expiry of adjustment period	12.5
(ii) otherwise	30
(b) Further charge to each existing party for each pursuer, defender or third party brought in before the record is lodged under the timetable issued under rule 36.G1(1)(b) (to include necessary amendments)	10
(c) Further charge to each existing party for each additional pursuer, defender or third party brought in after the record is lodged under the timetable issued under rule 36.G1(1)(b)	15
5. Debate (other than on evidence)	
(a) Where counsel or solicitor advocate not employed—	
(i) preparing for debate, to include all incidental work	20
(ii) conduct of debate, per 6 minutes	1
(b) Where counsel employed—	
(i) preparing for debate, to include all incidental work	10
(ii) appearing with counsel, per 6 minutes	1
(c) Waiting time, per 6 minutes	1
(d) Lodging and intimating or considering first note of arguments	5
(e) For each note lodged thereafter	5
6. Adjustment of issues and counter issues	
(a) All work in connection with and incidental to the lodging, adjustment and approval of an issue	10
(b) Further charge to pursuer for considering—	
(i) first counter-issue	2.5
(ii) each additional counter-issue	1.25
(c) Charge to defender or third party for—	
(i) all work in connection with, and incidental to, the lodging, adjustment and approval of a counter-issue	10
(ii) considering issue where no counter-issue	2.5
(iii) considering each additional counter-issue	1.25
7. Incidental Procedure (not chargeable prior to allowance of proof or jury trial)	
All work in connection with noting diet of proof or jury trial and—	
(a) preparing note on line of evidence; or	22.5
(b) instructing counsel to prepare a note on line of evidence	12.5
8. Amendment of Record	

Document Generated: 2019-04-29

Status: *This is the original version (as it was originally made). This item of legislation is currently only available in its original format.*

(a) Charge to proposer	
(i) drawing, intimating and lodging minute of amendment and relative motion	10
(ii) perusal of answers	5
(iii) any court appearance necessary, per 6 minutes	1
(b) Charge to opponent—	
(i) perusal of minute of amendment	7.5
(ii) preparation of answers	5
(iii) any court appearance necessary, per 6 minutes	1
(c) Further charge for adjustment of minute of amendment and answers, where applicable, to be allowed to each party	10
9. Productions	
(a) Lodging productions, each inventory	5
(b) Considering opponent's productions, each inventory	2.5
10. Motions and minutes	
(a) Drawing, intimating and lodging any written motion or minute, including a reponing note, and relative attendance at court (except as otherwise specifically provided for)—	
(i) where opposed	12.5
(ii) where unopposed (including for each party a joint minute other than under paragraph 20(b))	5
(iii) attendance at continued motion, per 6 minutes	1
(b) Considering opponent's written motion, minute or reponing note and attendance at court—	
(i) where opposed	12.5
(ii) where unopposed	5
(iii) attendance at continued motion, per 6 minutes	1
11. Incidental hearings/variation of timetable order	
(a) Preparing for and attendance at hearing not exceeding half an hour	7.5
(b) Thereafter, per 6 minutes	1
(c) In event of separate advising/opinion, all work incidental thereto	7.5
12. Withdrawal of solicitors	
(a) All work in preparation for any diet fixed under rule 24.2(1) and attendance at first such diet	10
(b) Attendance at each additional diet, per 6 minutes	1
13. Attendance not otherwise provided for	
(a) Where hearing does not exceed half an hour	5

Document Generated: 2019-04-29

Status: *This is the original version (as it was originally made). This item of legislation is currently only available in its original format.*

(b) Thereafter, per 6 minutes	1
14. Valuation of claim	
(a) Preparation of statement of valuation of claim—	
(i) where counsel not employed	30
(ii) where valuation of claim prepared by counsel	15
(b) Considering opponent's valuation of claim	15
15. Specification of documents or property (if further specification deemed necessary)	
(a) Drawing, intimating and lodging specification and relative motion—	
(i) where motion unopposed	10
(ii) where motion opposed, further charge for attendance at hearing of motion, per 6 minutes	1
(b) Charge to opponent—	
(i) where motion not opposed	5
(ii) where motion opposed, further charge per 6 minutes	1
(c) Arranging commission to recover documents, citing havers, instructing commissioner and shorthand writer and preparing for commission	10
(d) Charge to opponent	5
(e) Attendance at execution of commission, per 6 minutes	1
(f) If optional procedure adopted, charge per person upon whom order is served	1
(g) Perusal of documents or inspection of property recovered under a specification (or by informal means) where not otherwise provided for in this Table, per 6 minutes	1
16. Commission to take evidence	
(a) On interrogatories—	
(i) applying for commission to include drawing, intimating and lodging interrogatories, instructing commissioner and all incidental work (except as otherwise specifically provided for) but excluding attendance at execution of commission	27.5
(ii) charge to opponent if cross-interrogatories prepared and lodged	17.5
(iii) if no cross-interrogatories lodged	5
(b) Open commission—	
(i) applying for commission to include all work (except as otherwise specifically provided for) up to lodging report of commission, but excluding attendance at execution of commission	17.5
(ii) charge to opponent	10
(iii) attendance at execution of commission, per 6 minutes	1
17. Reports obtained under order of court excluding Auditor's report	

Document Generated: 2019-04-29
*Status: This is the original version (as it was originally made). This
item of legislation is currently only available in its original format.*

(a) All work incidental to the report	10
(b) Further charge for perusal of report, per 6 minutes	1
18. Preparation for proof or jury trial	
(a) All work involved in preparing for proof or jury trial (except as otherwise specifically provided for)—	
(i) if action settled or abandoned not later than 14 days before diet of proof or jury trial	31.25
(ii) in any other case	57.5
(b) For each day or part day after the first, including instruction of counsel	7.5
(c) Preparing for adjourned diet and all incidental work as in (a) if diet postponed for more than 6 days, each additional diet	12.5
19. Pre-trial meeting	
(a) Arranging pre-trial meeting (each occasion)	5
(b) Preparing for pre-trial meeting	
(i) where counsel not employed	27.5
(ii) where counsel employed	20
(c) Attending pre-trial meeting, per 6 minutes	1
Note:	
Where pre-trial meeting takes place by way of video conference, the foregoing charges are to apply	
(d) Joint minute of pre-trial meeting	5
20. Settlements	
(a) Judicial tender or pursuer's offer—	
(i) preparing and lodging, or considering first tender or pursuer's offer	15
(ii) preparing and lodging each further tender or pursuer's offer, subject to the Auditor being satisfied that the tender or offer was a genuine attempt to settle the proceedings	10
(iii) considering each further tender or pursuer's offer	10
(iv) if tender accepted further charge to each accepting party to include preparation and lodging of minute of acceptance of tender and attendance at court when decree granted (not including drawing, intimating and lodging any written motion)	10
(v) if pursuer's offer accepted, further charge to offering party to include consideration of minute of acceptance and attendance at court when decree granted (not including drawing, intimating and lodging any written motion)	10
(b) Extra-judicial settlement, to include negotiations resulting in settlement, framing or revising joint minute and attendance at court when authority interponed thereto (not to include drawing, intimating and lodging any written motion)	18.75

Document Generated: 2019-04-29
Status: *This is the original version (as it was originally made). This item of legislation is currently only available in its original format.*

(c) Whether or not charges are payable under (a) above, where additional work has been undertaken with a view to effecting settlement, including offering settlement, although settlement is not agreed	18.75
21. Hearing limitation fee	
All work (except as otherwise specifically provided for) undertaken with a view to limiting the scope of any hearing, and including the exchange of documents, precognitions and expert reports, agreeing any fact, statement or document not in dispute, preparing and intimating any notice to admit or notice of non-admission (and consideration thereof) and preparing and lodging any joint minute	17.5
22. Conduct of proof or jury trial	
(a) Conduct of proof or jury trial, and debate on evidence if taken at close of proof or jury trial, per 6 minutes	1
(b) If counsel employed, appearing with counsel, per 6 minutes	1
(c) Waiting time, per 6 minutes	1
23. Debate on evidence	
(a) Where debate on evidence not taken at conclusion of proof or jury trial, preparing for debate	10
(b) Conduct of debate, per 6 minutes	1
(c) If counsel employed, appearing with counsel, per 6 minutes	1
(d) Waiting time, per 6 minutes	1
24. Accounts	
(a) Preparation and lodging of judicial account, to include production of vouchers and adjustment of expenses	20
(b) Preparing for taxation, per 6 minutes	1
(c) Attendance at taxation, per 6 minutes	1
25. Final procedure	
All work to the conclusion of proceedings so far as not otherwise provided for—	
(a) if case goes to proof or jury trial, or is settled within 14 days before the diet of proof or jury trial	13.75
(b) in any other case	6.25
26. Instruction of counsel	
(a) Instructing counsel to revise pleadings	5
(b) Instructing counsel to attend court	12.5
(c) Arranging and attending consultation with counsel, including consultation held to consider tender, pursuer's offer or extra-judicial settlement, or with a view to settlement—	
(i) where total time engaged does not exceed one hour	12.5
(ii) for each additional 6 minutes	1

Document Generated: 2019-04-29
*Status: This is the original version (as it was originally made). This
item of legislation is currently only available in its original format.*

SCHEDULE 5   Rule 3.3(4)

TABLES OF INCLUSIVE CHARGES FOR SIMPLE PROCEDURE CASES

TABLE 1

ADMITTED CLAIMS

	Units
All work including taking instructions, preparing Claim Form, first formal service and applying for a decision	15
Further charge for instructing formal service of a party, after first formal service of a party—	
(a) within the United Kingdom, Isle of Man, Channel Islands or Republic of Ireland	1.25
(b) elsewhere	2.5

TABLE 2

DISPUTED CLAIMS

	Units
1. Before the simple procedure case begins	
All work before the simple procedure case begins, including discussions and correspondence with the other party, exchanges of documentation, etc.	15
2. Making and responding to a claim	
(a) Taking instructions, preparing the Claim Form and considering the Response Form	15
(b) Taking instructions, considering the Claim Form and preparing a Response Form	15
(c) Where additional respondents are brought in, work incurred by an original party	10
3. Formal service	
(a) Formal service by post of a party within the United Kingdom, Isle of Man, Channel Islands or Republic of Ireland	1.25
(b) Formal service elsewhere	2.5
(c) Instructing formal service of a party by sheriff officer, including considering a confirmation of service and paying the sheriff officer	1.25
(d) Instructing service by advertisement	1.25
4. Attendance at a discussion in court, a case management discussion or an eviction case discussion	
(a) Preparing for and attendance at a case management discussion or an eviction case discussion (up to the first half hour)	15
(b) Where a case management discussion or eviction case discussion exceeds half an hour, or for any part of a continued case management discussion or eviction case discussion, per 6 minutes	1

Document Generated: 2019-04-29

(c) Any other attendance ordered by the sheriff (except as otherwise provided for), per 6 minutes	1
(d) Waiting time, per 6 minutes	1
5. Precognitions and reports	
(a) Taking and drawing precognitions, per 250 words	5
(b) Where a skilled person prepares his or her own report, charge for perusing it (whether or not in the course of doing so the solicitor revises or adjusts it), per 250 words	2.5
(c) All work relating to a report ordered to be obtained by the sheriff	10
(d) Perusing a report ordered to be obtained by the sheriff, per 6 minutes	1
(e) All work in connection with preparation and lodging of affidavits, per 250 words	2.5
6. Applications	
(a) Preparing any application (except as otherwise provided for), including sending it to the court and the other party	5
(b) Considering and returning any application (except as otherwise provided for), including sending it to the court and the other party	5
(c) Where the sheriff orders a discussion in court to consider the application, preparing for that discussion in court	2.5
7. Limiting the scope of the hearing	
All work done (except as otherwise provided for) with a view to limiting the scope of the hearing, including agreeing evidence, exchanging documents, precognitions and reports, and agreeing facts and statements not in dispute	10
8. Preparing for the hearing	
(a) Preparing for the hearing (except as otherwise provided for), where the claim is settled not later than 7 days before the hearing	27.5
(b) Preparing for the hearing (except as otherwise provided for), in any other case	32.5
(c) Preparing for the hearing continued to another day, where that continuation is for more than 6 days	10
(d) Inspecting the other party's documents, per 6 minutes	1
9. The hearing	
(a) Conducting the hearing, per 6 minutes	1
(b) Waiting time, per 6 minutes	1
10. Settlement	
(a) Negotiating a settlement, including preparing an Incidental Orders Application to give effect to that settlement and any attendance at court required	17.5
(b) Additional work done with a view to a settlement, including offering a settlement, whether or not a settlement is agreed	17.5
(c) Preparing and lodging, or considering a tender	10

Document Generated: 2019-04-29
Status: This is the original version (as it was originally made). This item of legislation is currently only available in its original format.

(d) Accepting a tender, including any attendance at court required	7.5
11. Appeals	
(a) Taking instructions, preparing the Appeal Form, considering the draft Appeal Report, preparing any notes and sending them to the sheriff	22.5
(b) Taking instructions, considering the Appeal Form, considering the draft Appeal Report, preparing any notes and sending them to the sheriff	22.5
12. The decision and expenses	
(a) Settling with witnesses and noting the Decision Form	11.25
(b) Preparing an account of expenses, considering notice of expenses as assessed, attending an expenses hearing and all connected work	10
(c) Considering the other party's account of expenses and attending an expenses hearing, per 6 minutes	1
13. Instruction of counsel	
(a) Instructing counsel to attend court	12.5
(b) Arranging and attending consultation with counsel—	
(i) for the first hour	12.5
(ii) thereafter, per 6 minutes	1

SCHEDULE 6   Rule 7.1

REIMBURSEMENT OF WITNESSES

Liability to reimburse witnesses

1.—(1) A party to proceedings at whose instance a person is cited or requested to attend a hearing or commission as a witness is liable to reimburse losses and expenses incurred by that person in accordance with paragraph 2.

(2) No person other than a person who has been cited or requested to attend a hearing or commission as a skilled witness is entitled to payment of a fee in respect of work done, time engaged or time committed in consequence of such citation or request.

Losses and expenses to be reimbursed

2. The liability is to reimburse—

    (a) financial loss reasonably incurred by the witness in consequence of being cited or requested to appear, not exceeding £400 per day;

    (b) expenses reasonably incurred by the witness in travelling between the court and the witness's residence or place of business;

    (c) the additional cost of subsistence during the witness's absence from the witness's home or place of business, in so far as reasonably incurred; and

    (d) the reasonable cost of board and lodgings, in so far as reasonably incurred.

Value Added Tax

3. Where the amount payable to the witness is consideration for a supply liable to value added tax, the amount of the value added tax payable must be added to the amount payable to the witness.

Remit to the Auditor

4.—(1) On the application of a party the court may remit to the Auditor to determine the extent to which losses and expenses were reasonably incurred for the purpose of paragraph 2.

(2) A party must apply for such a remit when requested to do so by a witness.

SCHEDULE 7   Rule 7.2

SHORTHAND WRITERS AND TRANSCRIBERS

PART 1

FEES

		£
Attendance of shorthand writer		
1.	Time engaged—	
(a)	attendance at proof, jury trial or commission, per 15 minutes	11.10
(b)	travelling to and from the court or other place where the shorthand writer is instructed to attend, per 15 minutes (not chargeable for first 30 minutes of each journey)	5.55
(c)	minimum per day (only chargeable on date of attendance)	177.60
Cancellation		
2.	Fee payable on cancellation, per day on which attendance instructed—	
(a)	cancellation more than 21 days before date of attendance – no fee	
(b)	first day – 75% of minimum daily fee where cancellation before 4 p.m. on previous day, otherwise minimum daily fee	
(c)	subsequent days	50.00
Transcription		
3.	Extending notes of evidence or transcribing recording of evidence, per 250 words—	
(a)	where prepared daily	8.85
(b)	otherwise	7.25
Copying		
4.	Provision of copy transcript, per 250 words	0.61

PART 2

EXPENSES

Document Generated: 2019-04-29
*Status: This is the original version (as it was originally made). This
item of legislation is currently only available in its original format.*

		£
Travel		
1.	Travel to and from the court or other place where the shorthand writer is instructed to attend (recoverable only where the distance exceeds 15 miles) —	
	the cost actually incurred in travelling by public transport	
	or	
	allowance per mile where the shorthand writer uses a private vehicle	0.45
Day subsistence		
2.	The additional cost of food and drink actually incurred (recoverable only where the shorthand writer is away from his or her home or normal place of business for in excess of 10 hours in consequence of the instruction to attend), up to	10.70
Overnight subsistence		
3.	Where the shorthand writer requires to stay overnight—	
(a)	the actually incurred cost of overnight accommodation and breakfast, up to	75.00
(b)	the actually incurred cost of an evening meal, up to	23.50

EXPLANATORY NOTE

(This note is not part of the Act of Sederunt)

Introduction

This Act of Sederunt makes provision regarding—

the taxation of accounts of expenses as between party and party in civil proceedings;

the reimbursement of losses and expenses incurred by witnesses cited to attend court in such proceedings;

the fees payable to shorthand writers and transcribers in relation to such proceedings; and

the sums chargeable against a debtor in respect of the work of a solicitor in instructing steps in diligence.

With the exception of rule 8.1, the Act of Sederunt applies in relation to civil proceedings in the Court of Session, Sheriff Appeal Court and sheriff court where the proceedings are commenced on or after 29th April 2019. For this purpose appeal proceedings are considered to be distinct proceedings from the proceedings in the lower court from which the appeal is taken. Taxation of accounts in proceedings commenced before 29th April 2019, and in summary causes commenced on or after that date, continue to be subject to the pre-existing rules and tables of fees.

Rule 8.1 (diligence) applies when the work involved in instructing a step in diligence is carried out on or after 29th April 2019.

Document Generated: 2019-04-29

Status: *This is the original version (as it was originally made). This item of legislation is currently only available in its original format.*

General principles

Rule 2.1 prescribes the form of an account of expenses, which must include a statement as to whether the entitled party (as defined in rule 1.2(1)(c)) will bear the ultimate burden of value added tax charged on solicitors' fees or on outlays that are sought to be recovered.

Rule 2.2 sets out the general principle governing the taxation of expenses and instances of circumstances in which the Auditor may refuse to allow expenses that have been incurred.

Charges for work by entitled party's solicitor

Chapter 3, and the tables of charges in schedules 1 to 5, apply for the purpose of calculating the charges to be allowed at taxation in respect of the work carried out by the entitled party's solicitor in the conduct of the proceedings. Where applicable, the provisions of Chapter 3 and the tables apply with equal effect where the entitled party has been represented by a member of the Association of Commercial Attorneys.

The charges prescribed in the tables of charges are expressed as multiples of a unit of monetary charge. Rule 3.2 sets the value of the unit at £16.40.

Subject to direction by the court, the provisions of rule 3.3 determine which of the tables of charges is to be applied at taxation. The entitled party may elect to have an account taxed on the basis of the table of detailed charges in schedule 1 in relation to any proceedings other than a simple procedure case, and that table must be used when there is no applicable table of inclusive charges. When there is a table of inclusive charges applicable to the proceedings in schedule 2 (Court of Session), schedule 3 (Sheriff Appeal Court), or schedule 4 (sheriff court ordinary cause), the entitled party may elect to have the account taxed either on the basis of that table, or on the basis of the table of detailed charges in schedule 1. Accounts of expenses relating to simple procedure cases in the sheriff court must be taxed on the basis of the tables of inclusive charges in schedule 5.

Rule 3.4 makes provision regarding charges for copying and scanning documents. A charge is only to be allowed where the Auditor is satisfied that it was reasonable for more than 2000 pages to be scanned or copied. In that event the applicable charge is 1 unit per 100 pages copied or scanned in excess of that number.

Rule 3.5 provides that a charge of 0.9 units per 6 minutes of travelling time may be allowed at the Auditor's discretion.

Where an account of expenses is being taxed on the basis of a table of inclusive charges, rule 3.6 allows the Auditor to increase or reduce a charge, or to apportion a charge between parties represented by different solicitors.

Where an account of expenses is being taxed by reference to the tables of charges for simple procedure cases in schedule 5, rule 3.7 provides that all charges allowed by the Auditor are to be reduced by 10%, and are to be reduced by a further 25% or 50% where the total value of the claim is less than £2500, or less than £1000, as the case may be.

Rule 3.8 makes provision regarding charges for instructing counsel (as defined in rule 1.3) in the sheriff court or Sheriff Appeal Court. Such charges may be allowed only where (1) counsel's fees have been allowed as an outlay under rule 4.3, and (2) in the case of a solicitor advocate, where he or she was instructed by another solicitor.

Rule 3.8 also provides that the Auditor may allow an attendance charge where a solicitor advocate is assisted by another solicitor. In the sheriff court or Sheriff Appeal Court the allowance of such a charge would be dependent on the solicitor advocate's fees having been allowed as an outlay under rule 4.3.

Rule 3.9 applies where, on an application under rule 5.2, the court has granted an application for an additional charge, or the Auditor of the Court of Session has determined that an increase should be allowed. The rule provides for the charges allowed under Chapter 3 to be increased by the percentage specified by the court, or in accordance with the Auditor's determination.

Document Generated: 2019-04-29
*Status: This is the original version (as it was originally made). This
item of legislation is currently only available in its original format.*

Where the entitled party was not represented by a solicitor rule 3.10 provides that the Auditor may allow a reasonable sum in respect of work done by the entitled party not exceeding two thirds of the charges that would be allowed under Chapter 3 if the same work had been done by a solicitor.

Outlays

The provisions of Chapter 4 apply for the purpose of determining the outlays incurred by, or on behalf of, an entitled party that are to be allowed at taxation. Rule 4.2 sets out a general rule that outlays reasonably incurred in order to conduct the proceedings in a proper manner are to be allowed.

Counsel's fees in the sheriff court and Sheriff Appeal Court

The circumstances in which fees incurred to counsel in relation to proceedings in the sheriff court and Sheriff Appeal Court may be allowed as an outlay is regulated by rule 4.3, and by rule 5.4 which makes provision regarding applications to the court to sanction the employment of counsel.

Fees incurred to counsel in relation to proceedings in the sheriff court or Sheriff Appeal Court may not be allowed as an outlay unless, and to the extent that, the court has sanctioned the employment of counsel on an application under rule 5.4. On such an application the court may sanction as suitable for the employment of counsel—

the proceedings;

any part of the proceedings;

particular work involved in the proceedings; or

any combination of the foregoing.

Where particular work has been sanctioned as suitable for the employment of counsel, the Auditor is to allow counsel's reasonable fees for that work. Where proceedings or parts of proceedings have been sanctioned as suitable for the employment of counsel, it is for the Auditor to determine the work for which it was reasonable for counsel to be instructed, and to allow a reasonable fee for that work.

Other than in personal injury proceedings under Chapter 36 of the Ordinary Cause Rules, simple procedure cases, and proceedings in the Sheriff Appeal Court, there are restrictions on the sanctioning of work already carried out by counsel. An interlocutor sanctioning proceedings, or parts of proceedings as suitable for the employment of counsel has no effect as regards work carried out before the date of the interlocutor, and particular work carried out before the date of the interlocutor may only be sanctioned where the court is satisfied that cause has been shown for sanction not having been sought previously.

Skilled persons

The circumstances in which charges incurred to skilled persons may be allowed as an outlay is regulated by rule 4.5, and by rule 5.3 which makes provision regarding applications to the court for certification of such persons.

Charges incurred to a person who has been engaged for the application of that person's skill may only be allowed as an outlay if that person has been certified by the court on an application under rule 5.3. The court may only grant such an application if satisfied that the person is a skilled person, and that it is, or was, reasonable and proportionate for that person to be employed. In the event of certification the Auditor is to allow such charges as the Auditor determines to be fair and reasonable for work done which was reasonably required for a purpose in connection with the proceedings, or in contemplation of the proceedings.

Other than in personal injury proceedings under Chapter 43 of the Rules of the Court of Session, personal injury proceedings under Chapter 36 of the Ordinary Cause Rules, or simple procedure cases, the Auditor may not allow charges relating to work done before the date of certification unless that court has determined in accordance with rule 5.3(4) that the certification has effect for the purposes of work already done. The court may only make such a determination if satisfied that cause has been shown for certification not having been sought previously.

Document Generated: 2019-04-29

Additional charge

Rule 5.2 makes provision for applications to the court for an increase in the charges to be allowed at taxation in respect of the work carried out by the entitled party's solicitor.

The court (or Auditor) must grant an application when satisfied that an increase is justified to reflect the responsibility undertaken by the solicitor in the conduct of the proceedings. Rule 5.2(6) prescribes factors that the court (or Auditor) must have regard to in considering both whether to grant an application, and the level of any increase.

On the making of such an application in the Court of Session the court may either determine the application itself or remit the application to the Auditor to determine if an increase should be allowed (and the level of any increase). If the Court grants the application it may either specify the percentage increase to be allowed, or remit to the Auditor to determine the level of increase.

On the making of such an application in the sheriff court or Sheriff Appeal Court it is for the court to determine the application and to specify the percentage increase to be allowed.

Value Added Tax

Rule 6.1 sets out the circumstances in which a provision for value added tax may be added to the charges allowed under Chapter 3, and in which the amount allowed in respect of an outlay under Chapter 4 may include value added tax charged on the outlay by the provider of the goods or services.

Payments to witnesses and fees of shorthand writers

Rule 7.1 and schedule 6 make provision regarding payments to witnesses. Witnesses other than skilled witnesses are not entitled to payment of a fee. A party who cites or requests the attendance of a witness is liable to reimburse—

financial loss reasonably incurred not exceeding £400 per day;

travelling expenses reasonably incurred;

the reasonable cost of subsistence; and

the reasonable cost of board and lodging.

On the application of a party the court may remit to the Auditor to determine the extent to which loses and expenses were reasonably incurred. A party must apply for such a remit when requested to do so by a witness.

Rule 7.2 and schedule 7 make provision regarding the fees and expenses of shorthand writers and persons preparing transcripts of evidence.

Diligence

Rule 8.1 prescribes the sum that may be included in the expenses chargeable against a debtor in respect of the work of a solicitor in instructing a step in diligence.

Status: *This is the original version (as it was originally made). This*
item of legislation is currently only available in its original format.

SCOTTISH STATUTORY INSTRUMENTS

2020 No. 110

COURT OF SESSION
SHERIFF APPEAL COURT
SHERIFF COURT
SCOTTISH COURTS AND TRIBUNALS SERVICE

The Civil Litigation (Expenses and Group Proceedings) (Scotland) Act 2018 (Success Fee Agreements) Regulations 2020

Made - - - -	*1st April 2020*
Coming into force - -	*27th April 2020*

The Scottish Ministers make the following Regulations in exercise of the powers conferred by section 4(1), 4(2), 5(1), 5(2) and 7(3) of the Civil Litigation (Expenses and Group Proceedings) (Scotland) Act 2018(1) and all other powers enabling them to do so.

In accordance with section 24(2) of that Act, a draft of this instrument has been laid before and approved by resolution of the Scottish Parliament.

Citation, commencement, interpretation and application

1.—(1) These Regulations may be cited as the Civil Litigation (Expenses and Group Proceedings) (Scotland) Act 2018 (Success Fee Agreements) Regulations 2020 and come into force on 27 April 2020.

(2) In these Regulations, "the 2018 Act" means the Civil Litigation (Expenses and Group Proceedings) (Scotland) Act 2018.

(3) These Regulations apply to success fee agreements entered into on or after the date on which these Regulations come into force.

Success fee cap

2.—(1) Subject to section 4 (power to cap success fees) of the 2018 Act, a success fee agreement must not require the recipient of relevant services to pay to the provider a success fee which,

---

(1)   2018 asp 10.

Document Generated: 2020-04-27

including VAT, exceeds the maximum amount provided for by these Regulations ("the success fee
cap").

(2) The success fee cap is determined by reference to the financial benefit obtained by the
recipient ("the financial benefit").

(3) In a matter that is, or could become, a claim for damages for personal injuries(**2**) or the death
of a person from personal injuries, the success fee cap is—

   (a) in respect of the first £100,000 of the financial benefit, 20%,

   (b) in respect of the amount of the financial benefit over £100,000 but not exceeding £500,000,
     10%,

   (c) in respect of the amount of the financial benefit over £500,000, 2.5%.(**3**)

(4) In a matter that is, or could become, the subject of proceedings before an employment tribunal,
the success fee cap is 35% of the financial benefit.

(5) In any other matter to which these Regulations apply, the success fee cap is 50% of the
financial benefit.

(6) Where in connection with the same matter a recipient receives relevant services from more
than one provider, whether under one or more success fee agreements, the success fee cap applies
to the total amount payable by the recipient to those providers.

Exclusion for family proceedings

3.—(1) A damages-based agreement must not be entered into in connection with a matter which
is or may become the subject of family proceedings.

(2) In paragraph (1)—

   (a) "damages-based agreement" is a success fee agreement under which the success fee is
     determined by reference to the amount of financial benefit obtained by the recipient,

   (b) "family proceedings" has the same meaning as in section 135 of the Courts Reform
     (Scotland) Act 2014(**4**).

(3) Nothing in paragraph (1) is to be construed as restricting the use of other types of success
fee agreement.

Terms of a success fee agreement

4.—(1) A success fee agreement must—

   (a) include details of the matter, claim or proceedings, or parts thereof, to which the success
     fee agreement relates,

   (b) specify the type of civil remedy which the recipient seeks,

   (c) include a description of the work to be carried out by the provider,

   (d) provide that in the event of a conflict with the provider's standard terms of engagement,
     the terms of the success fee agreement take precedence,

   (e) specify the basis on which the amount of any fee potentially payable under the success
     fee agreement is to be determined,

   (f) oblige the provider to consult with the recipient on any significant development including,
     but not limited to, the receipt of an offer of settlement,

---

(**2**)   In these Regulations, "personal injuries" has the same meaning as in section 6 (personal injury claims) of the 2018 Act.
(**3**)   Section 6 (personal injury claims) of the 2018 Act makes provision for which damages may be included in the calculation
     of the financial benefit obtained.
(**4**)   2014 asp 18.

Document Generated: 2020-04-27

(g) specify whether or not the provider intends to retain any expenses which are awarded to the recipient in civil proceedings or which it is agreed with another person that the recipient is entitled to recover(**5**),

(h) explain how to access the relevant procedure for dealing with complaints about the provider or providers,

(i) set out the circumstances in which the provider may, as a consequence of the recipient's conduct, terminate the agreement prior to the resolution of the matter to which it relates and require payment from the recipient for services provided prior to termination,

(j) provide that where the recipient terminates the success fee agreement prior to the resolution of the matter to which it relates, the recipient will normally be liable to pay for services provided prior to termination, and

(k) provide details of the fee which would be charged by the provider and any other sums which would be payable by the recipient to the provider, in the event that the provider or recipient terminates the agreement prior to the resolution of the matter to which it relates.

(2) If the success fee agreement provides that any fee potentially payable may be subject to change without further agreement, such as in the case of periodic increases to hourly rates charged by the provider, the success fee agreement must provide that changes will be notified to the recipient in writing as soon as reasonably practicable.

(3) In a matter that is, or could become, a claim for damages for personal injuries or the death of a person from personal injuries, the success fee agreement must provide that the provider is liable to pay where—

(a) a court makes an award of expenses in consequence of proceedings being conducted in the manner described in section 8(4)(a), (b) or (c) of the 2018 Act, and

(b) the court indicates that the conduct concerned was that of the provider and not the recipient.

Failure to comply with requirements

5. A success fee agreement is unenforceable to the extent that it makes provision which is materially contrary to section 7(1) or 7(2) of the 2018 Act or these Regulations.

St Andrew's House,
Edinburgh   *ASH DENHAM*
1st April 2020   Authorised to sign by the Scottish Ministers

---

(**5**) Section 3 (expenses in the event of success) of the 2018 Act makes provision for the provider's entitlement to recover expenses, in addition to the success fee.

Document Generated: 2020-04-27
Status: *This is the original version (as it was originally made). This item of legislation is currently only available in its original format.*

EXPLANATORY NOTE

(This note is not part of the Regulations)

These Regulations set out a number of requirements applying to success fee agreements.

The term "success fee agreement" is defined in section 1 of the Civil Litigation (Expenses and Group Proceedings) (Scotland) Act 2018 (the "2018 Act") and covers all types of speculative fee agreements and damages-based agreements. Both speculative fee agreements and damages-based agreements are types of "no win, no fee" agreements, entered into in connection with actual or contemplated civil proceedings. In both of these types of agreements, there is a fee to be paid in the event of success (the "success fee"), but no fee, or a lower one, if the action is lost. Success fee agreements concern "relevant services", which are defined in section 1(2) of the 2018 Act to be one of "legal services" or "claims management services". The definition of success fee agreement also includes speculative fee agreements that fall within section 61A of the Solicitors (Scotland) Act 1980 (c.46).

Regulation 2 caps the success fee which providers of relevant services can charge recipients of those services under a success fee agreement. In all cases, the cap is determined by reference to the financial benefit obtained by the recipient in respect of the matter. There are specific caps for matters which are or could become a claim for damages for personal injuries and for matters which are or could become proceedings before an employment tribunal. A single cap applies to all other matters to which these Regulations apply.

Regulation 3 prohibits the use of damage-based agreements in family proceedings.

Regulation 4 sets out a number of requirements relating to the terms of a success fee agreement, in order to ensure that agreements are offered on a relatively standard basis and can be readily compared by potential recipients of relevant services. For example, the success fee agreement must make clear the basis on which the amount of any fee potentially payable under it is to be determined. It must also set out the circumstances in which the provider may, as a consequence of the recipient's conduct, terminate the agreement prior to the resolution of the matter to which it relates and require payment from the recipient for services provided prior to termination. Examples of circumstances the success fee agreement might include are where the recipient fails to provide adequate instructions, fails to attend any medical or expert examination without reasonable excuse or rejects the provider's opinion about making a settlement with their opponent, such opinion having been arrived at objectively and in good faith.

It remains open to the provider and recipient of relevant services to agree further terms. To continue the above example, the success fee agreement may set out other circumstances in which the provider may terminate early and require payment from the recipient.

Regulation 5 provides that a success fee will be unenforceable to the extent that the requirements in these Regulations are not complied with. Non-compliance with these requirements may also have consequences for providers under the regulatory regime which is applicable to them.

SCOTTISH STATUTORY INSTRUMENTS

2020 No. 208

COURT OF SESSION

Act of Sederunt (Rules of the Court of Session 1994 Amendment) (Group Proceedings) 2020

Made - - - -	*8th July 2020*
Laid before the Scottish	
Parliament - - - -	*9th July 2020*
Coming into force - -	*31st July 2020*

In accordance with section 4 of the Scottish Civil Justice Council and Criminal Legal Assistance Act 2013(**1**), the Court of Session has approved draft rules submitted to it by the Scottish Civil Justice Council.

The Court of Session therefore makes this Act of Sederunt under the powers conferred by section 103(1) of the Courts Reform (Scotland) Act 2014(**2**), section 21(1) of the Civil Litigation (Expenses and Group Proceedings) (Scotland) Act 2018(**3**) and all other powers enabling it to do so.

Citation and commencement, etc.

1.—(1) This Act of Sederunt may be cited as the Act of Sederunt (Rules of the Court of Session 1994 Amendment) (Group Proceedings) 2020.

(2) It comes into force on 31st July 2020.

(3) A certified copy is to be inserted in the Books of Sederunt.

Amendment of the Rules of the Court of Session 1994

2.—(1) The Rules of the Court of Session 1994(**4**) are amended in accordance with this paragraph.

(2) In rule 4.2(3) (signature of documents)(**5**), after sub-paragraph (b) insert—

"(bza)   an application in Form 26A.5 or Form 26A.8 may be signed by the applicant or an agent;".

(**1**)   2013 asp 3. Section 4 was amended by the Courts Reform (Scotland) Act 2014 (asp 18), schedule 5, paragraph 31(3) and by the Inquiries into Fatal Accidents and Sudden Deaths etc. (Scotland) Act 2016 (asp 2), schedule 1, paragraph 1(4).
(**2**)   2014 asp 18.
(**3**)   2018 asp 10.
(**4**)   The Rules of the Court of Session 1994 are in schedule 2 of the Act of Sederunt (Rules of the Court of Session 1994) 1994 (S.I. 1994/1443), last amended by S.S.I. 2020/198.
(**5**)   Rule 4.2(3) was last amended by S.S.I. 2019/293.

Document Generated: 2020-08-01

(3) In rule 5.1 (orders against which caveats may be lodged)(**6**)—

    (a) in sub-paragraph (d), after "in which he has an interest;" omit "and";

    (b) in sub-paragraph (e), after "a petition for his sequestration" insert "; and"; and

    (c) after sub-paragraph (e) insert—

> "(f)   an order permitting the bringing of group proceedings (within the meaning given in Chapter 26A)".

(4) In rule 13.2 (form of summonses)(**7**), after paragraph (1) insert—

> "(1A) A summons in an action to which Chapter 26A (group procedure) applies is to be in Form 13.2-AA.".

(5) After Chapter 26 (third party procedure)(**8**), insert—

"CHAPTER 26A

GROUP PROCEDURE

PART 1

GENERAL PROVISIONS

Interpretation and application of this Chapter

26A.1.—(1) In this Chapter—

"the Act" means the Civil Litigation (Expenses and Group Proceedings) (Scotland) Act 2018(**9**);

"group" has the meaning provided in section 20(2) of the Act;

"group member" means a person who, along with one or more other persons, expressly consents to the group proceedings to be brought on his or her behalf;

"group proceedings" has the meaning provided in section 20(1) of the Act;

"group register" is a record, in Form 26A.15, of those persons who are group members;

"representative party" has the meaning provided in section 20(2) of the Act.

(2) In rules 26A.6, 26A.7, 26A.9, 26A.11 and 26A.15 "applicant" has the meaning given in rule 26A.5(1).

(3) This Chapter applies to group proceedings as provided for by Part 4 of the Act.

Disapplication of certain rules

26A.2.—(1) The requirement in rule 4.1(4) (form, size, etc., of documents forming the process) for a step in process to be folded lengthwise does not apply in proceedings to which this Chapter applies.

(2) An open record is not to be made up in, and Chapter 22 (making up and closing records)(**10**) does not apply to, proceedings to which this Chapter applies unless otherwise ordered by the Lord Ordinary.

(**6**)   Rule 5.1 was amended by S.S.I. 2001/92.

(**7**)   Rule 13.2 was last amended by S.S.I. 2008/349.

(**8**)   Chapter 26 was last amended by S.S.I. 2009/104.

(**9**)   2018 asp 10.

(**10**) Chapter 22 was last amended by S.S.I. 2007/7.

(3) The following rules do not apply to proceedings to which this Chapter applies—

    (a) rule 6.2 (fixing and allocation of diets in Outer House)(**11**);

    (b) rule 36.3 (lodging productions).

Procedure in group proceedings

26A.3.—(1) Subject to the other provisions of this Chapter, the procedure in proceedings to which this Chapter applies is to be such as the Lord Ordinary is to order or direct.

(2) All proceedings in the Outer House to which this Chapter applies are to be heard or determined on such dates and at such times as are fixed by the Lord Ordinary.

(3) The fixing of a hearing for a specified date and time in proceedings to which this Chapter applies does not affect the right of any party to apply by motion at any time under these rules.

Motions under this Chapter

26A.4.—(1) Chapter 23 (motions)(**12**) applies to motions under this Chapter.

(2) Motions under this Chapter may be intimated and enrolled in accordance with Part 2 of Chapter 23.

PART 2

REPRESENTATIVE PARTY

Application to be a representative party

26A.5.—(1) An application by a person (the "applicant") under section 20(3)(b) of the Act to be a representative party to bring group proceedings is to be made by motion, in Form 26A.5.

(2) On a motion being enrolled under paragraph (1), the application is to be brought before a Lord Ordinary on the first available day after being made, for an order for—

    (a) intimation and service of the application on the defender and such other person as the Lord Ordinary thinks fit within 7 days of the date of the order, or within such other period as the Lord Ordinary thinks fit;

    (b) such advertisement as the Lord Ordinary thinks fit to take place within 7 days of the date of the order, or within such other period as the Lord Ordinary thinks fit;

    (c) any person on whom the application has been served, to lodge answers and any relevant documents, if so advised, within 21 days after the date of service, or within such other period as the Lord Ordinary thinks fit.

(3) A person served with the application who intends to participate in the decision as to whether authorisation should be given must lodge answers within the period ordered for the lodging of answers.

(4) Where answers are lodged under paragraph (2)(c) a hearing must be fixed.

(5) The applicant and any person who has lodged answers must be given at least 7 days' notice of a hearing ordered under paragraph (4).

(6) Where application for permission to bring proceedings is being made under rule 26A.9(1) at the same time as an application is made under paragraph (1) then paragraphs (7) and (8) apply.

(**11**) Rule 6.2 was last amended by S.S.I. 2007/548.
(**12**) Chapter 23 was last amended by S.S.I. 2017/414.

Document Generated: 2020-08-01

(7) The applicant must, at the same time as making the applications under this rule and rule 26A.9(1), lodge in the General Department—

    (a) the summons by which it is proposed to institute proceedings;

    (b) a group register in Form 26A.15; and

    (c) all relevant documents in the applicant's possession which are necessary for the court to determine whether or not to give permission.

(8) The applicant must, at the same time as lodging papers in the General Department under paragraph (7), serve those papers on the defender.

(9) Evidence of service in accordance with Chapter 16 must be provided to the General Department within 14 days from the date of service.

Application by more than one person to be a representative party

26A.6.—(1) This rule applies where—

    (a) more than one application made under rule 26A.5(1) is received by the court from more than one applicant in connection with the same issues (whether of fact or law) which may be subject to group proceedings; and

    (b) the Lord Ordinary has not determined the first received application at the point a subsequent application is received.

(2) A hearing on the applications must be fixed by the court.

(3) The applicants must be given at least 7 days' notice of a hearing fixed under paragraph (2).

Determination of an application by a person to be a representative party

26A.7.—(1) An applicant may be authorised under section 20(3)(b) of the Act to be a representative party in group proceedings only where the applicant has satisfied the Lord Ordinary that the applicant is a suitable person who can act in that capacity should such authorisation be given.

(2) The matters which are to be considered by the Lord Ordinary when deciding whether or not an applicant is a suitable person under paragraph (1) include—

    (a) the special abilities and relevant expertise of the applicant;

    (b) the applicant's own interest in the proceedings;

    (c) whether there would be any potential benefit to the applicant, financial or otherwise, should the application be authorised;

    (d) confirmation that the applicant is independent from the defender;

    (e) demonstration that the applicant would act fairly and adequately in the interests of the group members as a whole, and that the applicant's own interests do not conflict with those of the group whom the applicant seeks to represent; and

    (f) the demonstration of sufficient competence by the applicant to litigate the claims properly, including financial resources to meet any expenses awards (the details of funding arrangements do not require to be disclosed).

(3) The Lord Ordinary may refuse an application made by an applicant seeking authorisation to be given under section 20(3)(b) of the Act where the applicant has not satisfied the Lord Ordinary that the applicant is a suitable person, in terms of paragraphs (1) and (2), to act in that capacity.

Document Generated: 2020-08-01

(4) Authorisation given under paragraph (1) endures until the group proceedings finish or until permission is withdrawn.

Replacement of a representative party

26A.8.—(1) A representative party may apply to the court, by motion in Form 26A.8, seeking the permission of the court to authorise, in place of that party, another person as the representative party, who may or may not be a group member.

(2) A group member may apply to the court, by motion in Form 26A.8, seeking the permission to authorise the replacement of the representative party with another person, who may or may not be a group member.

(3) On a motion being enrolled in terms of paragraph (1) or (2), the application is to be brought before a Lord Ordinary on the first available day after being made, for an order for—

   (a) intimation and service of the application on—

      (i) the defender;

      (ii) in the case of an application made under paragraph (2), the representative party;

      (iii) the group members; and

      (iv) such other person as the Lord Ordinary thinks fit,

      in a manner which the Lord Ordinary thinks most appropriate in the circumstances, within 7 days of the date of the order, or within such other period as the Lord Ordinary thinks fit;

   (b) such advertisement as the Lord Ordinary thinks fit to take place within 7 days of the date of the order, or within such other period as the Lord Ordinary thinks fit;

   (c) any person on whom the application has been served, to lodge answers and any relevant documents, if so advised, within 21 days after the date of service, or within such other period as the Lord Ordinary thinks fit.

(4) A person served with an application under this rule who intends to participate in the decision as to whether permission should be given must lodge answers within the period ordered for the lodging of answers.

(5) Subject to paragraphs (6) and (7), the Lord Ordinary may—

   (a) where satisfied it is appropriate to do so, decide to proceed without holding a hearing;

   (b) fix a date for the hearing of the application;

   (c) require further information from the representative party, the proposed replacement representative party or the group members before making any further order.

(6) Where—

   (a) in the case of an application made under paragraph (2), the representative party;

   (b) in the case of an application made under paragraph (1) or (2), a group member,

has lodged answers in opposition to the application then paragraph (7) applies.

(7) A hearing on the application and the answers lodged thereto must be fixed by the court.

(8) Where a hearing on the application is fixed by the court, it must give—

   (a) the applicant;

   (b) the defender;

   (c) the representative party;

   (d) the person who is to replace the representative party; and

Document Generated: 2020-08-01

Status: *This is the original version (as it was originally made). This item of legislation is currently only available in its original format.*

    (e) the group members,

an opportunity to be heard before considering whether to grant the application or not.

(9) Subject to paragraph (10), the Lord Ordinary may grant an application made under paragraph (2) only where it appears to the Lord Ordinary that the representative party is not able to represent the interests of the group members adequately.

(10) No application made under paragraph (1) or (2) may be granted unless the Lord Ordinary is satisfied that—

    (a) the person who is to replace the representative party is a suitable person who can act in that capacity should such authorisation be given, having regard to the matters mentioned in rule 26A.7(2); and

    (b) the best interests of the group members are met.

(11) Where the Lord Ordinary makes an order authorising a person to be a representative party under section 20(3)(b) of the Act in place of a person who had previously been so authorised, the newly authorised representative party must, as soon as practicable and no later than 14 days after the date on which the order is made, inform all other parties and the group members of the order.

(12) The Lord Ordinary may, when making an order under this rule, make any such order as the Lord Ordinary thinks fit.

PART 3
PERMISSION TO BRING GROUP PROCEEDINGS

Application for permission

26A.9.—(1) An application for permission to bring group proceedings under section 20(5) of the Act is to be made by the representative party or, as the case may be, the applicant by motion, in Form 26A.9.

(2) On a motion being enrolled in terms of paragraph (1), the application is to be brought before a Lord Ordinary on the first available day after being made, for an order for—

    (a) intimation and service of the application on the defender and such other person as the Lord Ordinary thinks fit within 7 days of the date of the order, or within such other period as the Lord Ordinary thinks fit;

    (b) such advertisement as the Lord Ordinary thinks fit to take place within 7 days of the date of the order, or within such other period as the Lord Ordinary thinks fit;

    (c) any person on whom the application has been served, to lodge answers and any relevant documents, if so advised, within 21 days after the date of service, or within such other period as the Lord Ordinary thinks fit.

(3) The representative party or, as the case may be, the applicant must lodge in the General Department—

    (a) the summons by which it is proposed to institute proceedings;

    (b) a group register in Form 26A.15; and

    (c) all relevant documents in their possession which are necessary for the court to determine whether or not to give permission,

at the same time as making an application for permission under paragraph (1).

(4) The representative party or, as the case may be, the applicant must, at the same time as lodging papers in the General Department under paragraph (3), serve those papers on the defender.

6

Document Generated: 2020-08-01

(5) Evidence of service in accordance with Chapter 16 must be provided to the General Department within 14 days from the date of service.

(6) A person served with the application who intends to participate in the decision as to whether permission should be given must lodge answers within the period ordered for the lodging of answers.

Application for permission: further provision

26A.10.—(1) If a party seeks any of the orders mentioned in paragraph (3), that party must apply by motion.

(2) The Lord Ordinary must have regard to the need for the fair and efficient determination of the action when making any such order.

(3) The orders are—

    (a) dispensing with intimation, service or advertisement;

    (b) adjusting the period for intimation, service or advertisement;

    (c) adjusting the period for the lodging of answers and any relevant documents;

    (d) an interim order; or

    (e) a sist, on cause shown.

(4) A sist must be for no longer than 28 days, but can be renewed.

(5) The representative party must, within 7 days of the date of the interlocutor, notify the Scottish Legal Aid Board of a sist for legal aid.

The permission stage

26A.11.—(1) Within 14 days of the expiry of the period within which answers may be lodged the Lord Ordinary may—

    (a) if satisfied that it is appropriate to do so, make an order giving permission for group proceedings to be brought under section 20(5) of the Act without holding a hearing;

    (b) require further information from any of the parties before making any further order; or

    (c) fix a date and time for a hearing of the application for permission and of any answers thereto.

(2) The Keeper of the Rolls must notify—

    (a) the representative party or, as the case may be, the applicant; and

    (b) any person who has lodged answers,

of the date and time of any hearing fixed under paragraph (1)(c).

(3) The parties must be given at least 7 days' notice of a hearing fixed under paragraph (1)(c).

(4) At a hearing fixed under paragraph (1)(c), the Lord Ordinary may—

    (a) grant the application (including the giving of permission subject to conditions or only on particular grounds); or

    (b) refuse the application.

(5) The circumstances in which permission to bring proceedings to which this Chapter applies may be refused by the Lord Ordinary are as follows—

Document Generated: 2020-08-01

Status: *This is the original version (as it was originally made). This item of legislation is currently only available in its original format.*

(a) the criteria set out in section 20(6)(a) or (b) (or both (a) and (b)) of the Act have not been met;

(b) it has not been demonstrated that there is a prima facie case;

(c) it has not been demonstrated that it is a more efficient administration of justice for the claims to be brought as group proceedings rather than by separate individual proceedings;

(d) it has not been demonstrated that the proposed proceedings have any real prospects of success.

(6) Where permission is refused (or permission is granted subject to conditions or only on particular grounds), the Lord Ordinary must give reasons for the decision.

Grant of permission

26A.12.—(1) Where the Lord Ordinary gives permission for group proceedings to be brought the Lord Ordinary is to make an order which—

(a) states the name and designation of the representative party;

(b) defines the group and the issues (whether of fact or law) which are the same as, or similar or related to, each other raised by the claims;

(c) requires the lodging, by the representative party, of a group register;

(d) specifies the procedure which must be followed for a person to be a group member;

(e) specifies the period of time in which claims may be brought by persons in the group proceedings;

(f) specifies that group members may withdraw their consent to being bound by the group proceedings;

(g) specifies the procedure which must be followed by a group member to withdraw their claim from the group proceedings; and

(h) requires such advertisement of the permission to bring group proceedings to take place—

(i) within 7 days of the date of the order; and

(ii) thereafter, within the period during which persons may opt-in to the proceedings,

as the Lord Ordinary thinks fit.

(2) The Lord Ordinary may, when making an order under this rule, make any such order as the Lord Ordinary thinks fit.

The permission stage: appeals

26A.13. An appeal against the granting or refusing of permission (including the granting of permission either subject to conditions or only on particular grounds) for group proceedings to be brought is made by reclaiming motion.

PART 4

OPT-IN PROCEDURE

Document Generated: 2020-08-01

Status: *This is the original version (as it was originally made). This item of legislation is currently only available in its original format.*

Opt-in proceedings – notices

26A.14.—(1) A person gives consent for their claim to be brought in group proceedings by sending notice to that effect to the representative party in Form 26A.14-A.

(2) A group member withdraws their consent for their claim to be brought in group proceedings by sending notice to that effect to the representative party in Form 26A.14-B.

(3) A notice under paragraph (1) or (2) may be sent either—

    (a) by first class post; or

    (b) where paragraph (4) applies, by email.

(4) This paragraph applies where the representative party has confirmed consent to—

    (a) a prospective group member;

    (b) a group member,

to receiving a notice under paragraph (1) or (2) by electronic means, and has provided an email address to such persons for that purpose.

(5) In this rule a "representative party" includes a person who has made or, as the case may be, is to make an application seeking the authorisation of the court under section 20(3)(b) of the Act to be a representative party in group proceedings.

Opt-in proceedings – group register

26A.15.—(1) A group register is to be in Form 26A.15.

(2) Subject to paragraph (4), paragraph (3) applies where, following the lodging in the General Department and the service upon the defender of a group register under rule 26A.5(7)(b) and (8) or, as the case may be, rule 26A.9(3)(b) and (4), the membership of the group of persons on whose behalf proceedings are to be, or have been, brought changes following either, or both—

    (a) the addition into the group of a new group member;

    (b) the withdrawal from the group of a group member.

(3) The representative party or, as the case may be, the applicant must—

    (a) lodge in the General Department; and

    (b) at the same time, serve on the defender,

a revised group register, in Form 26A.15, as soon as possible and no later than 21 days following the representative party's or, as the case may be, the applicant's receipt of any notice made under rule 26A.14.

(4) Where the Lord Ordinary grants an application made under rule 26A.16(1) or 26A.17(1) the representative party must—

    (a) lodge in the General Department; and

    (b) at the same time, serve on the defender,

a revised group register, in Form 26A.15, as soon as possible and no later than 21 days following the grant of the application by the Lord Ordinary.

(5) The representative party or, as the case may be, the applicant must, at the same time as lodging in the General Department and serving on the defender a revised group register, inform all group members of the changes to the membership of the group of persons.

(6) The lodging of a group register in the General Department and the service on a defender under rule 26A.5(8), 26A.9(4) or paragraph (3) or (4) of this rule, may be by first class post or by electronic means.

Document Generated: 2020-08-01

(7) The group register is to be considered by the court at all hearings of the proceedings.

(8) Evidence of service in accordance with Chapter 16 must be provided to the General Department within 14 days from the date of service.

Opt-in proceedings – late application

26A.16.—(1) This rules applies where, following the allowance of proof, a person sends notice under rule 26A.14(1) in Form 26A.14-A, to the representative party seeking their claim to be brought in the group proceedings.

(2) Application is to be made by the representative party by motion in Form 26A.16.

(3) On a motion being enrolled under paragraph (2), the application is to be brought before the Lord Ordinary on the first available day after being made, for an order for—

(a) intimation and service of the application on the defender and such other person as the Lord Ordinary thinks fit within 7 days of the date of the order, or within such other period as the Lord Ordinary thinks fit;

(b) such advertisement as the Lord Ordinary thinks fit to take place within 7 days of the date of the order, or within such other period as the Lord Ordinary thinks fit;

(c) any person on whom the application has been served, to lodge answers and any relevant documents, if so advised, within 14 days after the date of service, or within such other period as the Lord Ordinary thinks fit.

(3) A person served with an application made under paragraph (2) who intends to participate in the decision as to whether the application should be granted must lodge answers within the period ordered for the lodging of answers.

(4) A motion enrolled under paragraph (2) is to be granted only—

(a) after giving the defender the opportunity to be heard;

(b) on cause shown; and

(c) on such conditions, if any, as to the expenses or otherwise as the Lord Ordinary thinks fit.

Opt-in proceedings – late withdrawal of consent for a claim to be brought in the proceedings or where, following withdrawal, there would be less than two pursuers

26A.17.—(1) This rule applies where a group member sends notice under rule 26A.14(2), in Form 26A.14-B, to the representative party either (or both)—

(a) after the commencement of any proof;

(b) where there would, should that person's claim not be brought in the proceedings, be less than two persons having a claim in the proceedings.

(2) Application is to be made by the representative party by motion in Form 26A.17.

(3) On a motion being enrolled in terms of paragraph (2), the application is to be brought before the Lord Ordinary on the first available day after being made, for an order for—

(a) intimation and service of the application on the defender and such other person as the Lord Ordinary thinks fit within 7 days of the date of the order, or within such other period as the Lord Ordinary thinks fit;

(b) such advertisement as the Lord Ordinary thinks fit to take place within 7 days of the date of the order, or within such other period as the Lord Ordinary thinks fit;

Document Generated: 2020-08-01

(c) any person on whom the application has been served, to lodge answers and any relevant documents, if so advised, within 14 days after the date of service, or within such other period as the Lord Ordinary thinks fit.

(4) A motion enrolled under paragraph (2) is to be granted only—

(a) after giving the defender an opportunity to be heard; and

(b) on such conditions, if any, as to expenses or otherwise as the Lord Ordinary thinks fit.

PART 5
COMMENCEMENT OF GROUP PROCEEDINGS

Commencement of group proceedings

26A.18.—(1) The service upon a defender of a group register under either rule 26A.5(8) or rule 26A.9(4) amounts to the commencement of the proceedings in respect of those persons who are group members, and are recorded as such on the group register that is served.

(2) The lodging with the court of a group register, in revised form, under rule 26A.15(3)(a) amounts to the commencement of the proceedings in respect of any new group member who has, following the lodging and service of the group register under either rule 26A.5(7)(b) and (8) or rule 26A.9(3)(b) or (4), joined the group.

(3) Paragraph (4) applies where, following an application being made by the representative party under rule 26A.16(1), the Lord Ordinary grants the application allowing a claim for a person to which rule 26A.16(1) applies to be brought in the proceedings.

(4) The enrolment of a motion under rule 26A.16(2) in connection with an application made under rule 26A.16(1) amounts to the commencement of the proceedings in respect of a person to which rule 26A.16(1) applies.

PART 6
SUMMONSES AND DEFENCES

Summons in group proceedings actions

26A.19.—(1) A summons in proceedings to which this Chapter applies is made in Form 13.2-AA.

(2) A summons in proceedings to which this Chapter applies is to—

(a) specify, in the form of conclusions, the orders sought;

(b) identify the parties to the proceedings and the matters from which the proceedings arise;

(c) specify any special capacity in which the representative party is bringing the proceedings or any special capacity in which the proceedings are brought against the defender;

(d) summarise the circumstances out of which the proceedings arise; and

(e) set out the grounds on which the action proceeds.

(3) There is to be appended to a summons in a group proceedings action a schedule listing the documents founded on or adopted as incorporated in the summons, which is also to be lodged as an inventory of productions.

Document Generated: 2020-08-01

Defences

26A.20.—(1) Defences in proceedings to which this Chapter applies are to be in the form of answers to the summons with any additional statement of facts or legal grounds on which it is intended to rely.

(2) There is to be appended to the defences in proceedings to which this Chapter applies a schedule listing the documents founded on or adopted as incorporated in the defences, which must be lodged as an inventory of productions.

PART 7

PROCEDURE

Preliminary hearing

26A.21.—(1) An action in proceedings to which this Chapter applies is to call for a preliminary hearing within 14 days after defences have been lodged.

(2) At the preliminary hearing, the Lord Ordinary—

(a) is to determine whether and to what extent and in what manner further specification of the claims and defences must be provided;

(b) may make an order in respect of any of the following matters—

(i) detailed written pleadings to be made by a party either generally or restricted to particular claims or issues;

(ii) a statement of facts to be made by one or more parties either generally or restricted to particular claims or issues;

(iii) the allowing of an amendment by a party to their pleadings;

(iv) disclosure of the identity of witnesses and the existence and nature of documents relating to the proceedings or authority to recover documents either generally or specifically;

(v) documents constituting, evidencing or relating to the subject-matter of the proceedings or any correspondence or similar documents relating to the proceedings to be lodged in process within a specified period;

(vi) each party to lodge in process, and send to every other party, a list of witnesses;

(vii) reports of skilled persons or witness statements to be lodged in process;

(viii) affidavits concerned with any of the issues in the proceedings to be lodged in process; and

(ix) to proceed to a hearing without any further preliminary procedure either in relation to the whole, or any particular aspect or any particular claim, of the proceedings;

(c) may fix the period within which any such order is to be complied with;

(d) may continue the preliminary hearing to a date to be appointed by the Lord Ordinary;

(e) may make such other order as the Lord Ordinary thinks fit for the efficient determination of the proceedings.

(3) Where the Lord Ordinary makes an order under paragraph (2)(b)(i) or (ii) or (2)(c), the Lord Ordinary may ordain the representative party to—

(a) make up a record; and

(b) lodge that record in process within such period as the Lord Ordinary thinks fit.

Document Generated: 2020-08-01

(4) At the conclusion of the preliminary hearing, the Lord Ordinary must, unless the Lord Ordinary has made an order under paragraph (2)(b)(ix), fix a date for a case management hearing to determine further procedure.

(5) The date fixed under paragraph (4) for a case management hearing may be extended on cause shown by application to the court, by motion, not less than two days prior to the date fixed for the case management hearing.

(6) In paragraph (2)(b)(i) to (iii) "party" and "parties" may, where the Lord Ordinary so orders after being addressed on the matter, include a group member, group members or a sub-set of group members.

Case management hearing

26A.22.—(1) Not less than 14 days, or such other period as may be prescribed by the Lord Ordinary at the preliminary hearing, before the date fixed under rule 26A.21(4) for the case management hearing, each party must—

(a) lodge in process and, at the same time, send to every other party a written statement of proposals for further procedure which must state—

   (i) whether the party seeks to have the proceedings appointed to debate or to have the proceedings sent to proof on the whole or any part of it;

   (ii) what the issues are which the party considers should be sent to debate or proof; and

   (iii) the estimated duration of any debate or proof;

(b) where it is sought to have the proceedings appointed to proof, lodge a list of the witnesses the party proposes to cite or call to give evidence, identifying the matters to which each witness is to speak;

(c) where it is sought to have the proceedings appointed to proof, lodge the reports of any skilled persons;

(d) where it is sought to have the proceedings appointed to debate, lodge a note of argument consisting of concise numbered paragraphs stating the legal propositions on which it is proposed to submit that any preliminary plea should be sustained or repelled with reference to the principal authorities and statutory provisions to be founded on; and

(e) send a copy of any such written statement, lists, reports or note of argument, as the case may be, to every other party.

(2) At the case management hearing, the Lord Ordinary—

(a) must determine whether the group proceedings are to be appointed to debate or sent to proof on—

   (i) all or some of the claims;

   (ii) all or some of the issues raised by the claims,

   made in the proceedings;

(b) where the proceedings are appointed to debate or sent to proof, may order that written arguments on any question of law must be submitted;

(c) where the proceedings are sent to proof, may determine whether evidence at the proof is to be by oral evidence, the production of documents or affidavits on any issue;

(d) where the proceedings are sent to proof, may direct that parties serve on one another, and lodge in process, signed witness statements or affidavits from each witness whose evidence they intend to adduce, setting out in full the evidence which it

Document Generated: 2020-08-01

Status: *This is the original version (as it was originally made). This item of legislation is currently only available in its original format.*

is intended to take from that witness, and fix a timetable for the service (whether by exchange or otherwise) and lodging of such statements or affidavits as may be thought necessary;

(e) may direct that such witness statements or affidavits are to stand as evidence in chief of the witness concerned, subject to such further questioning in chief as the Lord Ordinary may allow;

(f) may determine, in the light of any witness statements, affidavits or reports produced, that proof is unnecessary on any issue;

(g) where the proceedings are sent to proof, may appoint parties to be heard at a pre-proof hearing under rule 26A.24;

(h) may direct that skilled persons hold a meeting with a view to reaching agreement and identifying areas of disagreement, and may order them thereafter to produce a joint note, to be lodged in process by one of the parties, identifying areas of agreement and disagreement, and the basis of any disagreement;

(i) without prejudice to Chapter 12 (assessors)(**13**), may appoint an expert to examine, on behalf of the court, any reports of skilled persons or other evidence submitted and to report to the court within such period as the Lord Ordinary may specify;

(j) where the proceedings are sent to proof, may make an order fixing the time allowed for the examination and cross-examination of witnesses;

(k) may, on the motion of a party, direct the proceedings to be determined on the basis of written submissions, or such other material, without any oral hearing;

(l) may continue the case management hearing to a date to be appointed by the Lord Ordinary;

(m) may make an order for parties to produce a joint bundle of productions arranged in chronological order or such other order as will assist in the efficient conduct of the proof;

(n) may order and fix a date for a further case management hearing or fix a date for the hearing of any debate or proof;

(o) may make such other order as the Lord Ordinary thinks fit.

Debates

26A.23.—(1) Where a party seeks to have the proceedings appointed to debate, the application must include—

(a) the legal argument on which any preliminary plea is to be sustained or repelled;

(b) the principal authorities (including statutory provisions) on which the argument is founded.

(2) Following application being made to the court under paragraph (1), before determining whether the action is to be appointed to debate the Lord Ordinary is to hear from the parties with a view to ascertaining whether agreement can be reached on the points of law in contention.

(3) The Lord Ordinary, having heard the parties, is to determine whether the action is to be appointed to debate.

(4) Where the action is appointed to debate, the Lord Ordinary may order that written arguments on any question of law are to be submitted.

(**13**) Chapter 12 was amended by S.S.I. 2007/7.

Document Generated: 2020-08-01

(5) With the exception of rule 28.1(3)(d) which is not to apply, Chapter 28 (procedure roll), applies to a debate ordered under rule 26A.22(2)(a) as it applies to a cause appointed to the Procedure Roll.

Pre-proof hearing

26A.24. Not less than 2 days prior to any hearing appointed under rule 26A.22(2)(g), parties must lodge in process an estimated timetable for the conduct of the proof together with a note of any issues which are to be addressed prior to the proof.

Lodging of productions for proof

26A.25.—(1) Unless an earlier date is specified by the Lord Ordinary, any document not previously lodged but required for any proof in proceedings to which this Chapter applies must be lodged as a production not less than 7 days before the date fixed for the proof.

(2) No document may be lodged as a production after the date referred to in paragraph (1), even by agreement of all parties, unless the court is satisfied that any document sought to be lodged could not with reasonable diligence have been lodged in time.

PART 8
WITHDRAWAL FROM GROUP PROCEEDINGS

Withdrawal of claim from group proceedings

26A.26. The lodging with the court of a group register, in revised form, under rule 26A.15(3)(a) or (4)(a), following the withdrawal from the group of a group member, amounts to the point at which the person concerned withdraws consent for their claim to be brought in the group proceedings.

PART 9
ORDERS OF THE COURT

Power to make orders

26A.27. At any time before final judgment, the Lord Ordinary may, at the Lord Ordinary's own instance or on the motion of any party, make such order as the Lord Ordinary thinks necessary to secure the fair and efficient determination of the proceedings.

Effect of interlocutor given in group proceedings

26A.28.—(1) Subject to paragraph (2), an interlocutor given in group proceedings—

(a) must describe or otherwise identify the group members who will be affected by it; and

(b) binds all such persons, other than any person who has, as at the date of the interlocutor, withdrawn their consent to their claim being brought in the proceedings.

(2) An interlocutor given in group proceedings prior to a person joining the group as a group member binds such a person, except where the Lord Ordinary, on cause shown, orders otherwise.

Document Generated: 2020-08-01

Status: *This is the original version (as it was originally made). This item of legislation is currently only available in its original format.*

Failure to comply with rule or order of Lord Ordinary

26A.29. Any failure by a party to comply timeously with a provision in these Rules or any order made by the Lord Ordinary in proceedings to which this Chapter applies entitles the Lord Ordinary, at his or her own instance—

(a) to refuse to extend any period of compliance with a provision in these Rules or an order of the court;

(b) to dismiss the action, as the case may be, in whole or in part;

(c) to grant decree in respect of all or any of the conclusions of the summons, as the case may be; or

(d) to make an award of expenses,

as the Lord Ordinary thinks fit.

PART 10

SETTLEMENT

Settlement of proceedings

26A.30. The representative party must consult with the group members on the terms of any proposed settlement before any damages in connection with the proceedings may be distributed.".

(6) For rule 38.3(3) (leave to reclaim etc. in certain cases)(**14**), substitute—

"(3) An interlocutor, other than an interlocutor—

(a) deciding whether to give permission (including the giving of permission either subject to conditions or only on particular grounds) for group proceedings to be brought under Chapter 26A (group procedure);

(b) deciding whether to grant permission for the application to proceed under section 27B(1) of the Act of 1988(**15**) or an interlocutor determining the application, pronounced under Chapter 58 (applications for judicial review)(**16**),

may be reclaimed against only with the leave of the Lord Ordinary within 14 days after the date on which the interlocutor was pronounced.".

(7) In the appendix (forms)—

(a) after Form 13.2-A (form of summons and backing)(**17**), insert Form 13.2-AA (form of summons and backing – actions subject to Chapter 26A Procedure (Group Procedure));

(b) in Form 13.7 (form of citation of defender) after "(*name of pursuer*)", on both occasions where it appears, insert "[*or (name of lead pursuer, if any, in proceedings to which Chapter 26A applies)*]";

(c) after Form 26.1-C (form of third party notice by third party), insert—

(i) Form 26A.5 (form of application under section 20(3)(b) of the Civil Litigation (Expenses and Group Proceedings) (Scotland) Act 2018 seeking authorisation to be a representative party);

---

(14) Rule 38.3 was substituted by S.S.I. 2010/30 and amended by S.S.I. 2015/228.
(15) Section 27B was inserted by the Courts Reform (Scotland) Act 2014 (asp 18), section 89 and amended by S.I. 2015/700.
(16) Chapter 58 was substituted by S.S.I. 2015/228 and amended by S.S.I. 2017/200.
(17) Form 13.2-A was last amended by S.S.I. 2008/349.

Document Generated: 2020-08-01

(ii) Form 26A.8 (form of application under 20(3)(b) of the Civil Litigation (Expenses and Group Proceedings) (Scotland) Act 2018 seeking the replacement of a representative party);

(iii) Form 26A.9 (form of application under section 20(5) of the Civil Litigation (Expenses and Group Proceedings) (Scotland) Act 2018 for permission for group proceedings to be brought);

(iv) Form 26A.14-A (group proceedings under section 20(7)(a) of the Civil Litigation (Expenses and Group Proceedings) (Scotland) Act 2018 – opt-in proceedings – form of notice of consent for a person's claim to be brought in group proceedings);

(v) Form 26A.14-B (group proceedings under section 20(7)(a) of the Civil Litigation (Expenses and Group Proceedings) (Scotland) Act 2018 – opt-in proceedings – notice withdrawing consent for a person's claim to be brought in group proceedings);

(vi) Form 26A.15 (group proceedings under section 20(7)(a) of the Civil Litigation (Expenses and Group Proceedings) (Scotland) Act 2018 – opt-in proceedings – the group register);

(vii) Form 26A.16 (group proceedings under section 20(7)(a) of the Civil Litigation (Expenses and Group Proceedings) Scotland) Act 2018 – opt-in proceedings – late application); and

(viii) Form 26A.17 (group proceedings under section 20(7)(a) of the Civil Litigation (Expenses and Group Proceedings (Scotland) Act 2018 – opt-in proceedings – withdrawal of consent for a claim to be brought in group proceedings).

CJM SUTHERLAND
Lord President

Edinburgh   I.P.D.
8th July 2020

Document Generated: 2020-08-01
Status: *This is the original version (as it was originally made). This item of legislation is currently only available in its original format.*

SCHEDULE   Paragraph 2(7)

EXPLANATORY NOTE

(This note is not part of the Act of Sederunt)

This Act of Sederunt makes provision about group procedure, as provided by Part 4 of the Civil Litigation (Expenses and Group Proceedings) (Scotland) Act 2018 ("the Act"). Group procedure is a new form of proceedings available in the Court of Session. The instrument amends the Rules of the Court of Session ("the RCS") by, among other matters, the insertion of new Chapter 26A by paragraph 2(5), and comes into force on 31st July 2020.

General Provisions

Part 1 of Chapter 26A makes general provision. The procedural framework, as provided by rule 26A.3 and Part 7 of Chapter 26A, provides the court with flexibility as to how to deal with these new proceedings efficiently.

Numerous applications are made to the court under the new procedure, by motion. Rule 26A.4 provides that Chapter 23 (motions) of the RCS applies to motions made under Chapter 26A and that they may be intimated and enrolled by email.

Representative Party

The Act provides that a person who is a representative party may bring group proceedings on behalf of a group of persons. Under section 20(3)(b) of the Act a person may be a representative party only if authorised by the court. Part 2 of Chapter 26A, and Forms 26A.5 and 26A.8, makes relevant provision for this.

Permission to bring Group Proceedings

Document Generated: 2020-08-01
    Status: *This is the original version (as it was originally made). This
    item of legislation is currently only available in its original format.*

Under section 20(5) of the Act group proceedings may be brought only with the permission of the court. The court may give permission where it is satisfied that the criteria set out in section 20(6) (a) and (b) of the Act are met and, by section 20(6)(c), in accordance with provision made in Part 3 of Chapter 26A. The applicant must, together with an application, lodge the summons by which it is proposed to institute proceedings, a record of group members and relevant supporting documentation. Applications for permission are determined in accordance with rule 26A.11(5). Where the court gives permission for group proceedings to be brought under rule 26A.12, the Lord Ordinary makes an order which sets out certain specified matters about the group. Under rule 26A.13 an appeal against a decision of the court on an application for permission is made by reclaiming motion. By virtue of paragraph 2(6) of the Act of Sederunt leave to reclaim is not required in such appeals.

Opt-in Procedure

The Act of Sederunt provides for group proceedings to be brought as opt-in proceedings under section 20(7)(a) of the Act. Part 4 of Chapter 26A, together with the accompanying Forms, make relevant provision. Under rule 26A.14, notices are sent by potential group members to the representative party (or the person who has applied, or is to apply, to be a representative party), who then records persons who are group members in a group register. Under rule 26A.15, the register must be lodged with the court and served on the defender. The representative party must be satisfied that the person may be a group member before they can record the person as a group member on the register. This includes an assessment of their claim and being satisfied that it raises issues (whether of fact or law) which are the same as, or similar or related, to each other and subject to the proceedings, and being satisfied that their claim has not prescribed before joining the register.

The membership of the group may change during the course of the group proceedings either by the joining of new group members or by the departure from the group of group members. Group members withdraw their consent to their claims being brought in group proceedings in the same way as persons join the group, by the sending of a notice in Form 26A.14-B, to the representative party.

The Act of Sederunt makes provision for the procedure that is to be followed in cases where a person seeks to join or leave a group late in the proceedings or, where their leaving results in there being less than two pursuers, by rules 26A.16 and 26A.17 respectively.

Commencement of Group Proceedings

Part 5 of Chapter 26A makes provision setting out when proceedings are deemed to have commenced by group members in a group proceeding action. It is the point at which the group register is served on the defender or, in the case of eligible persons who join the group proceedings at a later stage, the lodging with the court of a revised group register. Where application is made by a person to join the group proceedings late, and the court allows such application, then it is the point at which the application is made.

Summonses and Defences

Part 6 of Chapter 26A, and Form 13.2-AA, make provision for pleadings in group proceedings. Form 13.2-AA prescribes a new summons Form for these proceedings.

Procedural Framework

Part 7 of Chapter 26A sets out the procedural framework for group proceedings, which comprises preliminary hearings, case management hearings, debates, pre-proof hearings and the lodging of productions for proof.

Withdrawal of Group Members from Group Proceedings

Part 8 of Chapter 26A makes provision setting out the point in group proceedings at which a group member withdraws consent for their claim to be brought in the proceedings. It is the point at which the revised group register is lodged with the court.

Orders of the Court

Document Generated: 2020-08-01
Status: *This is the original version (as it was originally made). This item of legislation is currently only available in its original format.*

Part 9 of Chapter 26A makes provision concerning orders of the court in group proceedings. Rule 26A.27 permits the Lord Ordinary to make such orders as are necessary to secure the fair and efficient determination of the proceedings. Provision is made by rule 26A.28 about interlocutors given in group proceedings, and their effect. Rule 26A.29 provides powers to the Lord Ordinary in connection with a failure by a party to comply with the RCS or with any order of the Lord Ordinary in group proceedings.

Settlement

Part 10 of Chapter 26A makes provision about settlement of group proceedings. Under rule 26A.30 the representative party must consult with group members on the terms of any proposed settlement before any damages in connection with the proceedings may be distributed.

Consequential Provision

Consequential amendment of the RCS is made by paragraph 2(2) to (4) and (6) of the Act of Sederunt.

Forms

New Forms are inserted into the appendix to the RCS, and Form 13.7 is amended, by paragraph 2(7) of the Act of Sederunt.

2021 No. 226

COURT OF SESSION

SHERIFF APPEAL COURT

SHERIFF COURT

Act of Sederunt (Rules of the Court of Session 1994, Sheriff Appeal Court Rules and Sheriff Court Rules Amendment) (Qualified One-Way Costs Shifting) 2021

Made - - - -	*28th May 2021*
Laid before the Scottish Parliament	*1st June 2021*
Coming into force - -	*30th June 2021*

In accordance with section 4 of the Scottish Civil Justice Council and Criminal Legal Assistance Act 2013(**a**), the Court of Session has approved draft rules submitted to it by the Scottish Civil Justice Council.

The Court of Session therefore makes this Act of Sederunt under the powers conferred by sections 103(1) and 104(1) of the Courts Reform (Scotland) Act 2014(**b**), section 8(6) of the Civil Litigation (Expenses and Group Proceedings) (Scotland) Act 2018(**c**) and all other powers enabling it to do so.

Citation and commencement etc.

1.—(1) This Act of Sederunt may be cited as the Act of Sederunt (Rules of the Court of Session 1994, Sheriff Appeal Court Rules and Sheriff Court Rules Amendment) (Qualified One-Way Costs Shifting) 2021.

(2) It comes into force on 30th June 2021.

(3) A certified copy is to be inserted in the Books of Sederunt.

Application

2. This Act of Sederunt applies to first instance proceedings commenced on or after 30th June 2021, and to any appeals arising from first instance proceedings commenced on or after the same date.

(**a**) 2013 asp 3. Section 4 was amended by the Courts Reform (Scotland) Act 2014 (asp 18), schedule 5, paragraph 31(3) and by the Inquiries into Fatal Accidents and Sudden Deaths etc. (Scotland) Act 2016 (asp 2), schedule 1, paragraph 1(4).
(**b**) 2014 asp 18.
(**c**) 2018 asp 10.

Amendment of the Rules of the Court of Session 1994

3.—(1) The Rules of the Court of Session 1994(a) are amended in accordance with this paragraph.

(2) After Chapter 41A (appeals to the Supreme Court)(b) insert—

"CHAPTER 41B

QUALIFIED ONE-WAY COSTS SHIFTING

Application and interpretation of this Chapter

41B.1.—(1) This Chapter applies in civil proceedings, where either or both—

(a) an application for an award of expenses is made to the court;

(b) such an award is made by the court.

(2) Where this Chapter applies—

(a) rules 29.1(2) and (3) (abandonment of actions)(c), 40.15(6) (appeals deemed abandoned)(d) and 41.17(3)(b) (procedure on abandonment)(e);

(b) any common law rule entitling a pursuer to abandon an action or an appeal, to the extent that it concerns expenses,

are disapplied.

(3) In this Chapter—

"the Act" means the Civil Litigation (Expenses and Group Proceedings) (Scotland) Act 2018(f);

"the applicant" has the meaning given in rule 41B.2(1), and "applicants" is construed accordingly;

"civil proceedings" means civil proceedings to which section 8 of the Act (restriction on pursuer's liability for expenses in personal injury claims) applies.

Application for an award of expenses

41B.2.—(1) Where civil proceedings have been brought by a pursuer, another party to the action ("the applicant") may make an application to the court for an award of expenses to be made against the pursuer, on one or more of the grounds specified in either or both—

(a) section 8(4)(a) to (c) of the Act;

(b) paragraph (2) of this rule.

(2) The grounds specified in this paragraph, which are exceptions to section 8(2) of the Act, are as follows—

(a) failure by the pursuer to obtain an award of damages greater than the sum offered by way of a tender lodged in process;

(b) unreasonable delay on the part of the pursuer in accepting a sum offered by way of a tender lodged in process;

(c) abandonment of the action or the appeal by the pursuer in terms of rules 29.1(1), 40.15(1) or 41.15(1), or at common law.

(a) The Rules of the Court of Session 1994 are in schedule 2 of the Act of Sederunt (Rules of the Court of Session 1994) 1994 (S.I. 1994/1443), last amended by S.S.I. 2021/153.
(b) Chapter 41A was inserted by S.S.I. 2015/228.
(c) Rule 29.1(2) was amended by S.S.I. 2001/305.
(d) Rule 40.15 was substituted by S.S.I. 2010/30.
(e) Chapter 41 was substituted by S.S.I. 2011/303.
(f) 2018 asp 10.

Award of expenses

41B.3.—(1) Subject to paragraph (2), the determination of an application made under rule 41B.2(1) is at the discretion of the court.

(2) Where, having determined an application made under rule 41B.2(1), the court makes an award of expenses against the pursuer on the ground specified in rule 41B.2(2)(a) or (b)—

(a) the pursuer's liability is not to exceed the amount of expenses the applicant has incurred after the date of the tender;

(b) the liability of the pursuer to the applicant, or applicants, who lodged the tender is to be limited to an aggregate sum, payable to all applicants (if more than one) of 75% of the amount of damages awarded to the pursuer, and that sum is to be calculated without offsetting against those expenses any expenses due to the pursuer by the applicant, or applicants, before the date of the tender;

(c) the court must order that the pursuer's liability is not to exceed the sum referred to in sub-paragraph (b), notwithstanding that any sum assessed by the Auditor of Court as payable under the tender procedure may be greater or, if modifying the expenses in terms of rule 42.5 (modification or disallowance of expenses)**(a)** or 42.6(1) (modification of expenses awarded against assisted persons), that such modification does not exceed that referred to in sub-paragraph (b);

(d) where the award of expenses is in favour of more than one applicant the court, failing agreement between the applicants, is to apportion the award of expenses recoverable under the tender procedure between them.

(3) Where, having determined an application made under rule 41B.2(1), the court makes an award of expenses against the pursuer on the ground specified in rule 41B.2(2)(c), the court may make such orders in respect of expenses, as it considers appropriate, including—

(a) making an award of decree of dismissal dependant on payment of expenses by the pursuer within a specified period of time;

(b) provision for the consequences of failure to comply with any conditions applied by the court.

Procedure

41B.4.—(1) An application under rule 41B.2(1)—

(a) must be made by motion, in writing, and Chapter 23 (motions)**(b)** otherwise applies to motions made under this Chapter;

(b) may be made at any stage in the case prior to the pronouncing of an interlocutor disposing of the expenses of the action or, as the case may be, the appeal.

(2) Where an application under rule 41B.2(1) is made, the court may make such orders as it thinks fit for dealing with the application, including an order—

(a) requiring the applicant to intimate the application to any other person;

(b) requiring any party to lodge a written response;

(c) requiring the lodging of any document;

(d) fixing a hearing.

(a) Rule 42.5 was amended by S.S.I. 2019/74.
(b) Chapter 23 was last amended by S.S.I. 2017/414

Award against legal representatives

41B.5. Section 8(2) of the Act does not prevent the court from making an award of expenses against a pursuer's legal representative in terms of section 11 (awards of expenses against legal representatives) of the Act.".

Amendment of the Sheriff Appeal Court Rules 2015

4.—(1) The Act of Sederunt (Sheriff Appeal Court Rules) 2015(**a**) is amended in accordance with this paragraph.

(2) After Chapter 19 (expenses)(**b**) insert—

"CHAPTER 19A

QUALIFIED ONE-WAY COSTS SHIFTING

Application and interpretation of this Chapter

19A.1.—(1) This Chapter applies in civil proceedings, where either or both—

   (a) an application for an award of expenses is made to the Court;

   (b) such an award is made by the Court.

(2) Where this Chapter applies—

   (a) rules 9.1(4) and (5) (application to abandon appeal);

   (b) any common law rule entitling a pursuer to abandon an appeal, to the extent that it concerns expenses,

are disapplied.

(3) In this Chapter—

"the Act" means the Civil Litigation (Expenses and Group Proceedings) (Scotland) Act 2018(**c**);

"the applicant" has the meaning given in rule 19A.2(1), and "applicants" is construed accordingly;

"civil proceedings" means civil proceedings to which section 8 of the Act (restriction on pursuer's liability for expenses in personal injury claims) applies.

Application for an award of expenses

19A.2.—(1) Where civil proceedings have been brought by a pursuer, another party to the action ("the applicant") may make an application to the Court for an award of expenses to be made against the pursuer, on one or more of the grounds specified in either or both—

   (a) section 8(4)(a) to (c) of the Act;

   (b) paragraph (2) of this rule.

(2) The grounds specified in this paragraph, which are exceptions to section 8(2) of the Act, are as follows—

   (a) failure by the pursuer to obtain an award of damages greater than the sum offered by way of a tender lodged in process;

   (b) unreasonable delay on the part of the pursuer in accepting a sum offered by way of a tender lodged in process;

(**a**) S.S.I. 2015/356, last amended by S.S.I. 2020/28.
(**b**) Chapter 19 was amended by S.S.I. 2019/74.
(**c**) 2018 asp 10.

(c) abandonment of the appeal by the pursuer in terms of rule 9.1(1) to (3), or at common law.

Award of expenses

19A.3.—(1) Subject to paragraph (2), the determination of an application made under rule 19A.2(1) is at the discretion of the court.

(2) Where, having determined an application made under rule 19A.2(1), the Court makes an award of expenses against the pursuer on the ground specified in rule 19A.2(2)(a) or (b)—

(a) the pursuer's liability is not to exceed the amount of expenses the applicant has incurred after the date of the tender;

(b) the liability of the pursuer to the applicant, or applicants, who lodged the tender is to be limited to an aggregate sum, payable to all applicants (if more than one) of 75% of the amount of damages awarded to the pursuer and that sum is to be calculated without offsetting against those expenses any expenses due to the pursuer by the applicant, or applicants, before the date of the tender;

(c) the Court must order that the pursuer's liability is not to exceed the sum referred to in sub-paragraph (b), notwithstanding that any sum assessed by the Auditor of Court as payable under the tender procedure may be greater or, if modifying those expenses to a fixed sum in terms of rule 19.1(2) (taxation of expenses), that such sum does not exceed that referred to in sub-paragraph (b);

(d) where the award of expenses is in favour of more than one applicant the Court, failing agreement between the applicants, is to apportion the award of expenses recoverable under the tender procedure between them.

(3) In the event that the Court makes an award of expenses against the pursuer on the ground specified in rule 19A.2(2)(c), the Court may make such orders in respect of expenses, subject to such conditions if any, as it considers appropriate.

Procedure

19A.4.—(1) An application under rule 19A.2(1)—

(a) must be made by motion, in writing, and Chapters 12 (motions: general), 13 (motions lodged by email)**(a)** and 14 (motions lodged by other means) otherwise apply to motions made under this Chapter;

(b) may be made at any stage in the case prior to the granting of an order disposing of the expenses of the appeal.

(2) Where an application under rule 19A.2(1) is made, the Court may make such orders as it thinks fit for dealing with the application, including an order—

(a) requiring the applicant to intimate the application to any other person;

(b) requiring any party to lodge a written response;

(c) requiring the lodging of any document;

(d) fixing a hearing.

Award against legal representatives

19A.5. Section 8(2) of the Act does not prevent the Court from making an award of expenses against a pursuer's legal representative in terms of section 11 (awards of expenses against legal representatives) of the Act.".

(a) Chapter 13 was amended by S.S.I. 2015/419.

5

Amendment of the Ordinary Cause Rules 1993

5.—(1) The Ordinary Cause Rules 1993(**a**) are amended in accordance with this paragraph.

(2) After Chapter 31 (appeals)(**b**) insert—

"CHAPTER 31A

QUALIFIED ONE-WAY COSTS SHIFTING

Application and interpretation of this Chapter

31A.1.—(1) This Chapter applies in civil proceedings, where either or both—

    (a) an application for an award of expenses is made to the sheriff;

    (b) such an award is made by the sheriff.

(2) Where this Chapter applies—

    (a) rules 23.1(2) and (3) (abandonment of causes)(**c**);

    (b) any common law rule entitling a pursuer to abandon a cause, to the extent that it concerns expenses,

are disapplied.

(3) In this Chapter—

"the Act" means the Civil Litigation (Expenses and Group Proceedings) (Scotland) Act 2018(**d**);

"the applicant" has the meaning given in rule 31A.2(1), and "applicants" is construed accordingly;

"civil proceedings" means civil proceedings to which section 8 of the Act (restriction on pursuer's liability for expenses in personal injury claims) applies.

Application for an award of expenses

31A.2.—(1) Where civil proceedings have been brought by a pursuer, another party to the action ("the applicant") may make an application to the sheriff for an award of expenses to be made against the pursuer, on one or more of the grounds specified in either or both—

    (a) section 8(4)(a) to (c) of the Act;

    (b) paragraph (2) of this rule.

(2) The grounds specified in this paragraph, which are exceptions to section 8(2) of the Act, are as follows—

    (a) failure by the pursuer to obtain an award of damages greater than the sum offered by way of a tender lodged in process;

    (b) unreasonable delay on the part of the pursuer in accepting a sum offered by way of a tender lodged in process;

    (c) decree of absolvitor or decree of dismissal has been granted against the pursuer in terms of rule 17.2(3)(b) (applications for summary decree)(**e**);

    (d) abandonment of the cause in terms of rule 23.1(1), or at common law.

(**a**) The Ordinary Cause Rules 1993 are in schedule 1 of the Sheriff Courts (Scotland) Act 1907 (c.51). Schedule 1 was substituted by S.I. 1993/1956 and last amended by S.S.I. 2021/75.

(**b**) Chapter 31 was last amended by S.S.I. 2015/419.

(**c**) Rule 23.1 was amended by S.S.I. 2003/26.

(**d**) 2018 asp 10.

(**e**) Rule 17.2 was substituted by S.S.I. 2012/188 and amended by S.S.I. 2015/227.

Award of expenses

31A.3.—(1) Subject to paragraph (2), the determination of an application under rule 31A.2(1) is at the discretion of the sheriff.

(2) Where, having determined an application made under rules 31A.2(1), the sheriff makes an award of expenses against the pursuer on the ground specified in rule 31A.2(2)(a) or (b)—

    (a) the pursuer's liability is not to exceed the amount of expenses the applicant has incurred after the date of the tender;

    (b) the liability of the pursuer to the applicant, or applicants, lodging the tender is to be limited to an aggregate sum, payable to all applicants (if more than one) of 75% of the amount of damages awarded to the pursuer and that sum is to be calculated without offsetting against those expenses any expenses due to the pursuer by the applicant, or applicants, before the date of the tender;

    (c) the sheriff must order that the pursuer's liability is not to exceed the sum referred to in sub-paragraph (b), notwithstanding that any sum assessed by the Auditor of Court as payable under the tender procedure may be greater or, if modifying those expenses to a fixed amount in terms of rule 32.1 (taxation before decree for expenses)(**a**), that such amount does not exceed that referred to in sub-paragraph (b);

    (d) where the award of expenses is in favour of more than one applicant the sheriff, failing agreement between the applicants, is to apportion the award of expenses recoverable under the tender procedure between them.

(3) In the event that the sheriff makes an award of expenses against the pursuer on the ground specified in rule 31A.2(2)(d), the sheriff may make such orders in respect of expenses, as it considers appropriate, including—

    (a) making an award of decree of dismissal dependant on payment of expenses by the pursuer within a specified period of time;

    (b) provision for the consequences of failure to comply with any conditions applied by the court.

Procedure

31A.4.—(1) An application under rule 31A.2(1)—

    (a) must be made by written motion, and Chapters 15 (motions)(**b**) and 15A (motions intimated and lodged by email)(**c**) otherwise apply to motions made under this Chapter;

    (b) may be made at any stage in the case prior to the granting of an order disposing of the expenses of the cause.

(2) Where an application under rule 31A.2(1) is made, the sheriff may make such orders as the sheriff thinks fit for dealing with the application, including an order—

    (a) requiring the applicant to intimate the application to any other person;

    (b) requiring any party to lodge a written response;

    (c) requiring the lodging of any document;

    (d) fixing a hearing.

(**a**) Rule 32.1 was amended by S.S.I. 2019/74.
(**b**) Chapter 15 was last substituted by S.I. 1996/2445 and last amended by S.S.I. 2015/227.
(**c**) Chapter 15A was inserted by S.S.I. 2015/227 and amended by S.S.I. 2015/296.

Award against legal representatives

31A.5. Section 8(2) of the Act does not prevent the sheriff from making an award of expenses against a pursuer's legal representative in terms of section 11 (awards of expenses against legal representatives) of the Act.".

Amendment of the Summary Cause Rules 2002

6.—(1) The Summary Cause Rules 2002(**a**) are amended in accordance with this paragraph.

(2) After Chapter 23 (decrees, extracts, execution and variation)(**b**) insert—

"CHAPTER 23A

QUALIFIED ONE-WAY COSTS SHIFTING

Application and interpretation of this Chapter

23A.1.—(1) This Chapter applies in civil proceedings, where either or both—

(a) an application for an award of expenses is made to the sheriff;

(b) such an award is made by the sheriff.

(2) Where this Chapter applies—

(a) rules 21.1(2) to (4) (abandonment of action);

(b) any common law rule entitling a pursuer to abandon an action, to the extent that it concerns expenses,

are disapplied.

(3) Where the sheriff would be entitled to make an award of expenses, and before expenses are dealt with in terms of rules 23.3 (expenses)(**c**), 23.3A (taxation)(**d**) and 23.3B (objections to auditor's report), the sheriff is to have regard to rules 23A.2 and 23A.3.

(4) In this Chapter—

"the Act" means the Civil Litigation (Expenses and Group Proceedings) (Scotland) Act 2018(**e**);

"the applicant" has the meaning given in rule 23A.2(1), and "applicants" is construed accordingly;

"civil proceedings" means civil proceedings to which section 8 of the Act (restriction on pursuer's liability for expenses in personal injury claims) applies.

Application for an award of expenses

23A.2.—(1) Where proceedings have been brought by a pursuer, another party to the action ("the applicant") may make an application to the sheriff for an award of expenses to be made against the pursuer, on one or more of the grounds specified in either or both—

(a) section 8(4)(a) to (c) of the Act;

(b) paragraph (2) of this rule.

(**a**) The Summary Cause Rules are in schedule 1 of the Act of Sederunt (Summary Cause Rules) 2002 (S.S.I. 2002/132), last amended by S.S.I. 2017/186.

(**b**) Chapter 23 was last amended by S.S.I. 2015/419.

(**c**) Rule 23.3 was last amended by S.S.I. 2015/419.

(**d**) Rules 23.3A and 23.3B were inserted by S.S.I. 2002/516.

(**e**) 2018 asp 10.

(2) The grounds specified in this paragraph, which are exceptions to section 8(2) of the Act, are as follows—

  (a) failure by the pursuer to obtain an award of damages greater than the sum offered by way of a tender lodged in process;

  (b) unreasonable delay on the part of the pursuer in accepting a sum offered by way of a tender lodged in process;

  (c) abandonment of the action by the pursuer in terms of rule 21.1, or at common law.

Award of expenses

23A.3.—(1) Subject to paragraph (2), the determination of an application made under rule 23A.2(1) is at the discretion of the sheriff.

(2) Where, having determined an application made under rule 23A.2(1), the sheriff makes an award of expenses against the pursuer on the ground specified in either rule 23A.2(2)(a) or (b)—

  (a) the pursuer's liability is not to exceed the amount of expenses the applicant has incurred after the date of the tender;

  (b) the liability of the pursuer to the applicant, or applicants, lodging the tender is to be limited to an aggregate sum, payable to all applicants (if more than one) of 75% of the amount of damages awarded to the pursuer and that sum is to be calculated without offsetting against those expenses any expenses due to the pursuer by the applicant, or applicants, before the date of the tender;

  (c) the sheriff is to order that the pursuer's liability is not to exceed the sum referred to in sub-paragraph (b), notwithstanding that any sum assessed by the Sheriff Clerk, or by the Auditor of Court as payable under the tender procedure may be greater;

  (d) where the award of expenses is in favour of more than one applicant the sheriff, failing agreement between the applicants, is to apportion the award of expenses recoverable under the tender procedure between them.

(3) In the event that the sheriff makes an award of expenses against the pursuer on the ground other than that specified in rule 23A.2(2)(c), the sheriff may make such orders in respect of expenses, as it considers appropriate, including—

  (a) making an award of decree of dismissal dependant on payment of expenses by the pursuer within a specified period of time;

  (b) provision for the consequences of failure to comply with any conditions applied by the court.

Procedure

23A.4.—(1) An application under rule 23A.2(1)—

  (a) is to be made by incidental application, in writing, and Chapter 9 (incidental applications and sists) otherwise applies to incidental applications under this Chapter;

  (b) may be made at any stage in the case prior to assessment of the amount of expenses to be awarded in the cause, in terms of rule 23.3, an order for an account of expenses to be taxed in terms of rule 23.3A or a finding by the sheriff that expenses in the cause are to be awarded as not due to or by any party.

(2) Where an application under rule 23A.2(1) is made, the sheriff may make such orders as the sheriff thinks fit for dealing with the application, including an order—

  (a) requiring the applicant to intimate the application to any other person;

  (b) requiring any party to lodge a written response;

  (c) requiring the lodging of any document;

(d) fixing a hearing.

Award against legal representatives

23A.5. Section 8(2) of the Act does not prevent the sheriff from making an award of expenses against a pursuer's legal representative in terms of section 11 (awards of expenses against legal representatives) of the Act.".

CJM SUTHERLAND
Lord President
I.P.D.

Edinburgh
28th May 2021

EXPLANATORY NOTE

(This note is not part of the Act of Sederunt)

This Act of Sederunt amends the Rules of the Court of Session 1994, the Act of Sederunt (Sheriff Appeal Court Rules) 2015, the Ordinary Cause Rules 1993 and the Summary Cause Rules 2002.

Section 8 of the Civil Litigation (Expenses and Group Proceedings) (Scotland) Act 2018 ("the Act") introduces a procedure known as "Qualified One-Way Costs Shifting". Section 8 of the Act makes provision in civil proceedings for damages for personal injury or death to the effect that the court must not make an award of expenses against the person bringing the action or the appeal arising therefrom, even if the person fails in their claim, provided the person has conducted the proceedings in an appropriate manner. Section 8(4) of the Act sets out exceptions to that principle whereby such a person, or their legal representative, may be held not to have conducted proceedings in an appropriate manner. Section 8(6) of the Act provides that further exceptions may be specified by Act of Sederunt.

This instrument makes amendments to the Rules of the Court of Session, the Sheriff Appeal Court Rules, the Ordinary Cause Rules and the Summary Cause Rules to add a new Chapter to each set of rules. In each case it specifies further exceptions, in terms of section 8(6) of the Act, and establishes court procedure for assessing whether exceptions apply.

The instrument provides that where the court makes an award of expenses on the ground that the pursuer has failed to beat a tender, or unreasonably delayed in accepting it, the liability of that person to the applicant, or applicants, lodging the tender is not to exceed expenses incurred by the applicant after the date of the tender, and is limited to an aggregate sum, payable to all applicants (if more than one) of 75% of the amount of damages awarded to the pursuer.

In each case the relevant new Chapter provides that an application may refer to one or more of the exceptions set out in section 8(4) of the Act and in the instrument itself. The instrument provides that applications are to be in writing, made by way of motion procedure in the Court of Session, the Sheriff Appeal Court and in ordinary causes in the sheriff court, and by way of incidental application in summary causes; and that such an application must be made before the pronouncing of an interlocutor disposing of the expenses of the action or, as the case may be, the appeal.

Appendix 2

Success Fee Agreement and Cooling Off Notice Templates

SUCCESS FEE AGREEMENT

NOTICE OF THE RIGHT TO CANCEL

IN TERMS OF THE CONSUMER CONTRACTS (INFORMATION, CANCELLATION AND ADDITIONAL CHARGES) REGULATIONS 2013

Name :   [insert client details]

Address :   [insert client postal address]

Date :   [insert date of signature]

Right to cancel ("cooling off period")

You have the right to cancel this contract within 14 days without giving any reason. This notice was posted to you on [   ] and the cancellation period you are entitled to will expire at midnight on [insert date 14 days after deemed service   ].

To exercise the right to cancel this contract, you must inform us :-

[insert name and postal address for service of notice]
Email : [insert email address for sending notice]

of your decision to cancel this contract by a clear statement (e.g. a letter sent by tracked post or email). You may use the attached model cancellation form if that is helpful but it is not obligatory.

To meet the cancellation deadline, it is sufficient for you to send your communication concerning your exercise of the right to cancel before the cancellation period has expired. Proof of posting should be obtained by you and produced on request. An email will date itself.

Effect of agreement

By signing a Success Fee Agreement you are agreeing to a success fee being deducted from any compensation which you are awarded. It is open to you to seek independent advice from a personal injury solicitor (at your own expense) as to the terms of the Agreement. The Law Society of Scotland have a list of specialist personal injury solicitors.

Effect of cancellation

If you requested us to begin the performance of services during the cancellation period, you shall pay us an amount which is in proportion to what has been performed until you have communicated to us your cancellation from this contract, in comparison with the full coverage of the contract.

CANCELLATION FORM

To :   [insert name and address for service of cancellation notice]

        Email : [insert email address for sending notice]

I/We [*] hereby give notice that I/We [*] cancel my/our [*] contract for the supply of the following service [(insert details)   ] received on [insert dates)   ].

Name   …………………………………..

Address   …………………………………..

Signature   …………………………………..

Date   …………………………………..

[*] Delete as appropriate

SUCCESS FEE CHARGING AGREEMENT
(Applicable to claims for damages arising from Personal Injury or Death from Personal Injury)

between

X Solicitors (the "Provider")

and

Y Client (the "Recipient")

In this Agreement the term the "Provider" shall mean the solicitor or firm of solicitors advising the Recipient and the "Recipient" shall mean the client or, where appropriate, the client's attorney, executor or other formally appointed party representing the client's interests.

1) WHAT IS COVERED BY THE AGREEMENT:

All work carried out by the Provider on behalf of the Recipient relating to the Recipient's personal injury claim for compensation arising from an accident/ clinical negligence on [insert date if applicable]/*insert details of disease/condition/ insert details of fatality leading to claim by family members.*

2) THE RECIPIENT'S OBLIGATIONS:

You should:
    (a)   Give instructions that allow the Provider to do their work properly.
    (b)   Not ask the Provider to work in an improper or unreasonable way.
    (c)   Not deliberately mislead the Provider.
    (d)   Co-operate with the Provider when asked.
    (e)   Go to any medical or expert examination when asked to do so by the Provider or the opponents.
    (f)   Subject to clause 3(a), accept the Provider's professional opinion given in good faith if they believe objectively that you are unlikely to win.

    (g) Subject to clause 3(a), accept the Provider's professional opinion given in good faith about making a settlement with the opponents.

3) THE PROVIDER'S OBLIGATIONS

    (a) The Provider undertakes to perform all necessary legal work on behalf of the Recipient in pursuing the compensation claim arising out of the accident/clinical negligence/condition/disease mentioned above. At all times the Provider will take all reasonable steps to carry out the necessary legal work in accordance with current professional standards applicable to the legal profession in Scotland and shall use their best endeavours to achieve the best outcome for the Recipient.

    (b) The Provider undertakes to consult with the Recipient on any significant developments, including, but not limited to the receipt of an offer of settlement.

    (c) Assuming the Recipient complies with their obligations under Clause 2) the Provider will not charge the Recipient any amount, whether relating to fees, VAT, outlays or otherwise (except any insurance premium for "After the Event Legal Expenses Insurance") which the Provider incurs in performing the work which is undertaken for the Recipient should the Recipient lose.

    (d) If the Recipient wins, the Provider will be entitled to, and in the normal course of events will, retain expenses which are awarded to the Recipient in the proceedings or which it is agreed with another person that the Recipient is entitled to recover. The only charges which the Recipient shall be liable for are a) any insurance premium payable in respect of "After the Event Legal Expenses Insurance" and b) a success fee calculated as a percentage of the financial benefit which the Recipient obtains, directly or indirectly, as a result of the Provider's services as follows:

Financial Benefit up to £100,000	[X]%(maximum 20%)
On the excess over £100,000 up to £500,000	[X]% (maximum 10%)
On the excess over £500,000	[X]% (maximum 2 ½%)

These success fees are inclusive of VAT and unrecovered outlays.

4) [DRAFTING NOTE – this clause only applies in situations where there is a possibility that future loss for the Recipient will be in excess of £1m]

In calculating the success fee under paragraph 3 above, any damages for future loss which form part of the Recipient's financial benefit will be included in the calculation but only if the future element is:

    (a) to be paid as a lump sum and does not exceed £1,000,000 or

    (b) to be paid as a lump sum and exceeds £1,000,000 and the Provider has not advised the Recipient to accept that the future element be paid in periodical instalments and the conditions in the following paragraph are met.

    (c) the conditions referred to in para 4. b) above are:

(i) in a case where the damages are awarded by a court or tribunal, that the court or tribunal in awarding the future element has stated that it is satisfied that it is in the Recipient's best interests that the future element be paid partly or wholly as a lump sum rather than wholly in periodical instalments;

(ii) in a case where the damages are obtained by agreement, that an independent actuary has, after having consulted the Recipient personally in the absence of the Provider, certified that in the actuary's view it is in the Recipient's best interests that the future element be paid either wholly or partly as a lump sum rather than wholly as periodical instalments.

(iii) in either case, if the damages are paid partly as a lump sum and partly as periodical instalments only that part of the damages paid as a lump sum shall be included in the amount of damages used to calculate the success fee.

(5) **(1)** The Recipient can end the Agreement at any time. If the Recipient ends the Agreement prior to the final resolution of the claim, whether litigated or not or prior to the Provider receiving payment of judicial or extra judicial fees, vat and outlays from the opponent or their insurers on settlement of the Recipient's claim, the Provider has the right to charge for all work done on the Recipient's behalf up to that date. The charge out rates as at [insert date] are:

Partner	£A per hour
Associate Solicitor	£B per hour
Assistant Solicitor	£C per hour
Administrative Assistant	£D per hour

The Provider is entitled to add VAT to the foregoing rates at the prevailing rates from time to time in force and be paid for any outlays incurred or which the Provider has committed to incur on the Recipient's behalf.

These rates are reviewed on [*specify*] each year and are available from the Provider on request. These charges will be notified by the Provider to the Recipient in writing as soon as reasonably practicable after they take effect.

(2) The Provider can end the Agreement at any time:

(a) if the Recipient does not fulfil their responsibilities as outlined in Clauses 2(a), (b), (c), (d) or (e) above. The Provider then has the right to decide whether the Recipient must pay fees, VAT and any outlays incurred for the work done on their behalf up to that date. If the Provider decides to charge said fees vat and outlays, the Provider will charge for the work using the rates mentioned in 5(1) above. The Provider shall be entitled to exercise a lien over all documents/ files relating to the Recipient's claim pending payment of said fees, VAT and outlays.

(b) if they form the opinion acting objectively and in good faith that the Recipient is unlikely to win and the Recipient rejects that advice. Provided the Recipient has complied with all of their other obligations under Clause 2, the Recipient will only be responsible to the Provider for payment of expenses recovered, relative to the period up to the date this agreement is terminated. Further, the Provider may only claim a share of expenses, if the Recipient goes on to derive a financial benefit from the claim. The Provider will be entitled to a share of expenses (including VAT and outlays) recovered on behalf of the Recipient, to be determined on an equitable basis having regard to the relevant services provided by the Provider and any new Provider who is subsequently instructed. In the event of disagreement with any new Provider or other person as to relative share or shares, the matter will be referred at the expense of the Providers to the Auditor at Edinburgh Sheriff Court, who will determine an equitable apportionment of expenses on the basis of the relevant services provided by each Provider in relation to the whole expenses recovered. In these circumstances no success fee shall be chargeable by the Provider first instructed.

(c) if the Recipient rejects the Provider's opinion, arrived at objectively and in good faith about making a settlement with their opponent.

1. In the event the recipient goes on to derive a financial benefit, the Provider is entitled to charge for the expenses (consisting of the fees, VAT and outlays) which have been incurred on the Recipient's behalf up to the date this agreement is terminated. The expenses payable by the Recipient to the Provider under this subclause are confined to those recoverable judicially from the opponent(s), and are recoverable by the Provider in addition to the success fee mentioned above. The amount of the success fee payable shall be calculated by reference to the financial benefit actually obtained but shall not exceed the level of the success fee which would have been chargeable if the Provider's advice had been accepted by the Recipient. The success fee under this agreement becomes payable as soon as the financial benefit is obtained, whether as a result of extra judicial agreement or judicial determination.

Where expenses have been recovered in the claim, a share of the recovered expenses is payable to the Provider on the receipt of those expenses from the opponent. The Provider's share of expenses shall be determined on the same basis and in the same manner as set out in clause 5(2)(b). The Recipient hereby undertakes to:

a. Notify the Provider of the identity of any new Provider who is instructed to provide relevant services in connection with the claim and

b. Instruct the new Provider to account to the Provider under this agreement for all sums due under this clause.

If the Recipient does not instruct a new provider but represents him or herself and derives a financial benefit, the Recipient shall make payment to the Provider under this agreement in accordance with the same timescales as if a new Provider had been instructed.

2. In the event that the Recipient does not go on to derive a financial benefit, having rejected the Provider's advice to settle, the Recipient shall be liable to pay to the Provider all outlays which the Provider incurred or is liable to incur on the Recipient's behalf.

(3) In any scenario in clause 5 where the Recipient pays the Provider a fee charged at the hourly rates referred to clause 5(1) above, the total paid by the Recipient to the Provider shall be fair and reasonable in the circumstances.

(4) In the event that the Recipient dies or becomes incapax prior to the final resolution of the claim, whether litigated or not, or prior to the Provider receiving payment of judicial or extra judicial fees, vat and outlays from the opponent or their insurers on settlement of the Recipient's claim, and the Recipient's executor, guardian or other representative, as the case may be, do not choose to continue instructing the Provider to provide ongoing advice with the claim, the Provider has the right to charge for all work done on the Recipient's behalf up to the date when the Provider becomes aware of the death or incapacity. The applicable charge out rates are those set out in clause 5(1) above, as amended by any annual increases.

6) In the event of a conflict with the Provider's standard terms of engagement, the terms of this Success Fee Agreement take precedence.

7) For the avoidance of doubt this Agreement is effective from [*specify*], being the date that the Recipient first instructs the Provider in the case, not the date of signing the Agreement. Where this Agreement is entered into by a parent on behalf of his or her child, the parent accepts responsibility for all of the foregoing clauses as if the agreement applied directly to said parent.

8) In the event that a Court makes an award of expenses against the Recipient specifically stating that the award is as a result of the conduct of the Provider which amounts to:

   a) the Provider making a fraudulent representation or otherwise acting fraudulently in connection with the claim or proceedings or
   b) the Provider behaving in a manner which is manifestly unreasonable in the claim or proceedings or
   c) the Provider conducting the proceedings in a manner which is tantamount to an abuse of process

the Provider shall be liable to pay the expenses awarded by the Court for that conduct.

9) In the event of the recipient being dissatisfied with the conduct of the claim or any aspect of the Provider's services, the Recipient may raise their concerns by writing to the Provider's Client Relations Partner [name] in the first instance. The Recipient shall allow the Client Relations Partner 28 days to fully respond. In the event that the Recipient remains dissatisfied, they can then proceed with a complaint to the Scottish Legal Complaints Commission based at 10–14 Waterloo Place, Edinburgh, EH1 3EG. Further details, including the time limits within which a complaint can be raised with the SLCC can be found on the SLCC's website, https://www.scottishlegalcomplaints.org.uk/

....

Signature of Provider   **Date**

....

Signature of Recipient/Recipients Representative/Executor   Date

Appendix 3

Faculty of Advocates Fees Scheme

FACULTY OF ADVOCATES

Scheme for the Accounting for and Recovery Of Counsel's Fees August 2020

1. Status and scope of the Scheme

1.1. The Scheme sets out the basis upon which any counsel to whom the Scheme applies accepts instructions.

1.2. Advocates hold a public office to which they are admitted by the Court of Session. Nothing in the Scheme affects the professional status or obligations of counsel and, in the event of any conflict between the terms of this Scheme and the professional status or obligations of counsel, the latter shall prevail.

1.3. The Scheme applies to any counsel who is a subscriber to Faculty Services Limited.

1.4. Counsel who is not a subscriber to Faculty Services Limited may (subject to compliance at all times with the professional status and obligations of counsel) accept instructions on the basis of his or her own terms and conditions. Counsel who has not adopted such terms and conditions shall be assumed to have adopted the Scheme.

1.5. An instructing person who instructs counsel to whom the Scheme applies accepts the provisions of the Scheme and accepts a professional obligation to pay counsel's fees in accordance with the Scheme.

1.6. The Scheme does not apply to work undertaken or services provided by counsel otherwise than as a practising advocate.

2. Definitions

2.1. In the Scheme, unless the context otherwise requires:-

"counsel" means a practising advocate;

"Fees Committee" is the committee appointed by the Dean of Faculty under paragraph 9 of the Scheme;

"instructing person" means the instructing solicitor, commercial attorney, or person approved under the Faculty of Advocates Direct Access Scheme who instructs counsel. In the case of a solicitor or a commercial attorney, where a correspondent firm is referred to in the letter of instruction, instructing person means that correspondent firm;

"List of Defaulting Solicitors and other Instructing Persons" means a list of solicitors and instructing persons whose name has been placed on the list by authority of the Dean by reason of failure to pay counsel's fee;

"subscriber" means a subscriber to Faculty Services Limited; and

"the Scheme" means this Scheme.

2.2. In the Scheme, unless the context otherwise requires, the masculine includes the feminine and references to the singular include the plural, and vice versa in each case.

3. Letter of instruction

3.1. Subject to clause 3.4, the instructing person shall send counsel a letter of instruction providing counsel with all the information and documents reasonably required and in reasonably sufficient time for counsel to provide the services requested.

3.2. Where the services are required within a specific timescale, the letter of instruction shall clearly specify that timescale.

3.3. The letter of instruction may state the amount of the fee which the instructing person offers in respect of the services covered by the letter of instruction.

3.4. Counsel is not bound to accept instructions unless he has received a letter of instruction in accordance with clause 3.1 of the Scheme; but is entitled to accept instructions which are given orally by an instructing person or which are the subject of oral arrangement between an instructing person and counsel's clerk.

4. Acceptance of instructions

4.1. Upon receipt of a letter of instructions, counsel shall within a reasonable time decide whether or not to accept the instructions and counsel or counsel's clerk shall intimate counsel's decision to the instructing person. What is a reasonable time for these purposes will depend on the circumstances.

4.2. In deciding whether or not to accept or decline instructions counsel shall act in accordance with the Faculty of Advocates Guide to Professional Conduct.

4.3. Counsel will be deemed to have accepted instructions if counsel has failed to take any action within a reasonable time.

4.4. In accepting instructions in fulfillment of the public office of advocate, counsel does not enter into any contractual relationship with the instructing person or the lay client.

4.5. Acknowledgment of receipt of instructions by counsel or counsel's clerk does not constitute the acceptance of instructions. An entry in counsel's diary does not constitute the giving or acceptance of instructions.

4.6. Counsel may return instructions previously accepted in the circumstances required or permitted under the Faculty of Advocates Guide to Professional Conduct.

4.7. Acceptance of instructions on any particular basis whether it be speculative or deferred will be a matter for that individual counsel and that individual case and will not bind any subsequent or other counsel in the case to accept instructions on the same basis, nor will it be binding on any subsequent proceedings such as an appeal in that case.

5. Amount of fee

5.1. Except in legal aid cases or where the amount of the fee is otherwise prescribed by law, the instructing person may, in advance of acceptance of the instruction, agree with counsel the amount or basis of the fee to be paid for the services provided by counsel.

5.2. Except in legal aid cases or where the amount of the fee is otherwise prescribed by law, if the amount or basis of counsel's fee has not been agreed in advance, counsel shall be entitled to be paid a reasonable fee for the services provided. If the instructing person wishes to question the fee proposed by counsel they should inform Faculty Services Limited in writing as soon as possible and in any event within 4 weeks of date of issue of the feenote.

5.3. In cases falling within paragraph 5.2 hereof, in default of agreement as to the amount of a reasonable fee, the instructing person or counsel may require counsel's fee to be taxed by the Auditor of the Court of Session or, in the case of proceedings in the sheriff court, the Auditor of the relevant sheriff court, on an agent and client, client paying basis.

5.4. In the event of late payment of fees, counsel has the right to request interest in line with current legislation.

5.5. Unless otherwise stipulated, counsel's fees cover all expenses incurred by counsel in the conduct of the case.

5.6. Where counsel has a clerk, all communications in relation to the amount of counsel's fee shall be between the instructing person and counsel's clerk.

6. Speculative fees

6.1. Counsel may accept instructions on a speculative basis but is not bound to do so. An instructing person may only instruct counsel to act on a speculative basis in any case where the instructing person is acting on such a basis.

6.2. If an instructing person wishes to instruct counsel on a speculative basis, this must be stated explicitly in every letter of instruction in the case. In the absence of an explicit statement to that effect counsel shall be entitled to be paid a reasonable fee regardless of whether or not any fee has been recovered from the other party to the litigation. Every letter of instruction on a speculative basis must also specify whether or not the client has entered into a success fee agreement within the meaning of sec. 1 of the Civil Litigation (Expenses and Group Proceedings) (Scotland) Act 2018 (asp. 10) with any provider relevant to the instruction (whether or not the provider is the instructing person or another person).

6.3. Subject to para 6.5 below, counsel may accept instructions on the basis that counsel will receive only such fees as are recovered by way of judicial expenses from another party to the litigation (the judicial recovery basis) but is not bound to do so.

6.4. If an instructing person wishes to instruct counsel on the basis set out in paragraph 6.3 this must be stated explicitly in every letter of instruction in the case. In the absence of an explicit statement to that effect counsel shall be entitled to be paid a fee regardless of whether or not any fee has been recovered by way of expenses from another party to the litigation where successful.

6.5. Counsel may not accept instructions on the basis specified in paragraph 6.3 where the client has entered into a success fee agreement within the meaning of sec. 1 of the Civil Litigation (Expenses and Group Proceedings) (Scotland) Act 2018 (asp. 10) with any provider relevant to the instruction (whether or not the provider is the instructing person or another person). In any such case, counsel shall be entitled to be paid a fee, on success, regardless of whether or not any fee has been recovered by way of expenses from another party to the litigation where successful.

6.6. Subject to para 6.5 in Sheriff Court proceedings, it is permissible in cases instructed on a speculative or speculative/judicial recovery basis, for counsel to agree with the instructing person that in the event of success, where sanction for counsel is not granted by the court, a separate fee will be payable.

6.7. In judicial recovery only cases, before the judicial expenses are agreed or determined, the instructing person (or their representative) shall confer with counsel's clerk in order to agree (i) what part or amount of any proposed agreed global sum for judicial expenses is to be attributed to counsels fees; and (ii) the sums for counsel's fees to be included in any account of judicial expenses to be submitted to the auditor for taxation. In the absence of agreement in advance between counsel and the instructing person regarding the part attributable to counsel's fees, the instructing person shall not agree any abatement of counsel's fee or a global agreement which assumes such abatement. If an instructing person does so in the absence of counsel's prior consent, counsel shall not be obliged to abate their fee to the level agreed by the instructing person or implied in the global agreement, the instructing person will be obliged to pay counsel such fees as counsel would otherwise be entitled to recover.

7. Payment of fee

7.1. The instructing person may tender the fee with the instruction to counsel. In such an event, counsel shall issue a feenote for that amount on acceptance of the instruction.

7.2. Where the instructing person has not tendered the fee with the instruction to counsel and counsel has not agreed to deferment of payment under paragraph 7.3 hereof, counsel may render a feenote upon completion of a specific item or items of work encompassed within the instruction or upon completion of all the items of work encompassed within the instruction.

7.3. Counsel may accept instructions on the basis that payment will be deferred but is not bound to do so. Where the instructing person wishes to instruct counsel on the basis that payment will be deferred, agreement to that effect must be reached before the instruction is accepted. Where counsel has agreed to deferral of payment, all subsequent payments to that counsel in relation to the same case or matter will, in the absence of contrary agreement, be deferred on the same basis provided that each letter of instruction states the basis of deferral.

7.4. Where counsel has accepted instructions on the basis that payment will be deferred counsel shall issue a feenote in accordance with the agreement as to deferment of payment.

7.5. If counsel has not issued a feenote within 30 days of completion of an item of work encompassed within the instruction or within 30 days after any period of deferment agreed under paragraph 7.3, the instructing person may make a request in writing to the counsel for the issue of a feenote.

7.6. Unless otherwise agreed, if counsel fails without good reason to issue a feenote within 6 weeks of a request made under paragraph 7.5, the instructing person shall have no obligation to ensure payment thereof.

7.7. Any dispute arising in relation to paragraphs 7.5 and 7.6 shall be referred to the Fees Committee.

7.8. Unless otherwise agreed, counsel's fee will be due for payment from the date of issue of the feenote. The instructing person shall pay counsel's fee whether or not the instructing person has been put in funds by the lay client and without any set-off, deduction or withholding.

7.9. In the event that counsel's fee has not been received within 40 days of the feenote issue date or, if a date for payment has been agreed, within 40 days of that agreed date, and the instructing person has not intimated a reason acceptable to counsel for delayed payment or non-payment, intimation shall be given on behalf of counsel, to the instructing person that, if the instructing person does not pay the full amount within a further 30 days, the matter may be referred to the Fees Committee.

7.10. If the instructing person has a reason for non-payment of counsel's fee, he shall, within 21 days after receipt of intimation of counsel's intention to refer the matter to the Fees Committee, provide a report explaining that reason and a proposed timescale for payment or an explanation as to why the instructing person believes the proposed fee should be withdrawn.

7.11. If the instructing person provides a report in accordance with paragraph 7.10 the Fees Committee shall consider the report along with any representations from counsel.

7.12. If the instructing person does not pay the amount due or provide a report within the periods of notice mentioned in clauses 7.9 and 7.10, intimation will be made to the instructing person on behalf of counsel that the matter has been passed direct to the Dean of Faculty.

7.13. Where counsel has a clerk all communications in relation to payment of counsel's fees shall be with counsel's clerk or (where counsel is a subscriber) with Faculty Services Limited.

7.14. In the case of a subscriber, payment of counsel's fee shall be made to Faculty Services Limited. In the case of counsel who is not a subscriber, payment of counsel's fee shall be made to counsel's clerk or, if counsel does not have a clerk, to counsel.

8. Legal aid

8.1. Where counsel is instructed under the legal aid legislation, the instructing person shall comply with any requirements of the Scottish Legal Aid Board which fall to be met in order that counsel may be paid the appropriate fee.

8.2. In civil legal aid cases where an instructing person proposes to accept judicial expenses in lieu of a claim against the legal aid fund, before those judicial expenses are agreed or determined the instructing person shall confer with counsel's clerk in order to agree (i) what part of any proposed agreed global sum for judicial expenses represents counsel's fees; (ii) the sums for counsel's fees to be included in any account of judicial expenses to be submitted to the Auditor for taxation. In the event of non-agreement regarding the part attributable to counsel's fees, the instructing person shall not agree any abatement of counsel's fee or a global agreement which assumes such abatement. If an instructing person does so in the absence of counsel's prior consent, counsel shall not be obliged to abate their fees to the level agreed by the instructing person or implied in the global agreement and the instructing person will be obliged to pay to counsel such fees as the counsel would otherwise be entitled to recover.

8.3. In legal aid cases, the instructing person shall furnish counsel or counsel's clerk with such documentation as may be required to enable counsel to submit counsel's fee.

8.4. In criminal legal aid cases the instructing person and counsel shall each submit his account to the Scottish Legal Aid Board within Board within four calendar months of conclusion of the relevant hearing. Where the instructing person's account cannot be submitted within this timescale, the instructing person shall advise counsel or counsel's clerk of the delay and the reasons for it in writing within the four month period.

8.5. In civil legal aid cases the instructing person will submit his account, including counsel's fees to the Scottish Legal Aid Board within four calendar months of conclusion of the relevant hearing. Where the instructing person's account cannot be submitted within this timescale, the instructing person shall advise counsel or counsel's clerk of the delay and the reasons for it in writing within the four month period.

9. Dispute resolution

9.1. The Dean of Faculty shall appoint three members of the Faculty of Advocates to be the Fees Committee.

9.2. The Fees Committee shall consider any matter referred to it under paragraph 7.7, 7.9, 7.10, and 7.11 and shall make a recommendation as to the disposal of that matter to the Dean of Faculty.

9.3. Upon receipt of a recommendation from the Fees Committee under paragraph 9.2 or referral of a matter under paragraph 7.12 the Dean of Faculty shall determine the matter. The Dean's determination shall be final and conclusive.

9.4. Upon determining the matter, the Dean shall intimate his determination to counsel and to the instructing person.

9.5. In the event that the Dean determines that the instructing person is obliged to make payment to counsel but has failed to do so, the Dean shall take such further steps as he considers appropriate. Such steps may include (with or without such further warning as the Dean may consider appropriate): (i) a complaint to the Scottish Legal Complaints Commission or any other professional body to which the instructing person belongs; and

(ii) inclusion of the instructing person and the instructing person's firm on the List of Defaulting Solicitors and other Instructing Persons.

9.6. The powers of the Dean under the Scheme are without prejudice to the freedom of counsel to complain to the Scottish Legal Complaints Commission in respect of the failure of a solicitor to pay or to take reasonable steps to ensure payment of counsel's fee or to take equivalent steps in the case of any instructing person who is not a solicitor who has failed to pay counsel's fee.

9.7. Any dispute as to the meaning or effect of the Scheme will be determined by the Dean of Faculty whose decision shall be final.

Appendix 4

Styles Relating to Pursuers' Offers and Tenders

PURSUER'S OFFER GROSS OF BENEFITS COURT OF SESSION

IN THE COURT OF SESSION	
	Court Ref: [COURT REF]
MINUTE OF PURSUER'S OFFER	
in the cause	
[NAME OF PURSUER], [(Company Number [NUMBER]), whose registered office is [ADDRESS] **OR** residing at [ADDRESS]]	
	Pursuer
against	
[NAME OF DEFENDER], [(Company Number [NUMBER]), whose registered office is [ADDRESS] **OR** residing at [ADDRESS]]	
	Defender

[SURNAME OF PERSON SIGNING] for the pursuer states to the court, without prejudice to, and under reservation of their whole rights and pleas, under and in terms of Chapter 34A.4 of the Rules of the Court of Session 1994 (as amended) the pursuer offered and hereby offers to accept from the [defender **OR** defenders jointly and severally] the sum of **[AMOUNT IN WORDS] (£[AMOUNT IN FIGURES]) STERLING** inclusive of interest to the date of this offer, of which £[AMOUNT OF BENEFITS ATTRIBUTABLE TO LOST EARNINGS] represents compensation for earnings lost during the relevant period, £[AMOUNT OF BENEFITS ATTRIBUTABLE TO CARE] represents compensation for the cost of care during the relevant period and £[AMOUNT OF BENEFITS ATTRIBUTABLE TO LOSS OF MOBILITY] represents compensation for loss of mobility during the relevant period, in terms of the Social Security (Recovery of Benefits) Act 1997, together with the expenses of process to date as taxed [in full satisfaction of the conclusions **OR** in satisfaction of the [CONCLUSIONS SATISFIED BY OFFER]] of the summons.

IN RESPECT WHEREOF

IN THE COURT OF SESSION
Court Ref: [COURT REFERENCE]
MINUTE OF PURSUER'S OFFER
in the cause
[NAME OF PURSUER], PURSUER
And
[NAME OF DEFENDER], DEFENDER

[YEAR]

[FIRM NAME]
[FIRM REFERENCE]

PURSUER'S OFFER GROSS OF BENEFITS SHERIFF COURT

SHERIFFDOM OF [SHERIFFDOM] AT [COURT]	
[IN THE ALL SCOTLAND PERSONAL INJURY COURT]	
	Court Ref: [COURT REF]
MINUTE OF PURSUER'S OFFER	
in the cause	
[NAME OF PURSUER], [(Company Number [NUMBER]), whose registered office is [ADDRESS] **OR** residing at [ADDRESS]]	
	Pursuer
against	
[NAME OF DEFENDER], [(Company Number [NUMBER]), whose registered office is [ADDRESS] **OR** residing at [ADDRESS]]	
	Defender

[SURNAME OF PERSON SIGNING] for the pursuer states to the court, without prejudice to, and under reservation of their whole rights and pleas, under and in terms of Chapter 27A.4 of the Ordinary Cause Rules 1993 (as amended) the pursuer offered and hereby offers to accept from the [defender OR defenders jointly and severally] the sum of **[AMOUNT IN WORDS] (£[AMOUNT IN FIGURES]) STERLING**, inclusive of interest to the date of this offer, of which £[AMOUNT OF BENEFITS ATTRIBUTABLE TO LOST EARNINGS] represents compensation for earnings lost during the relevant period, £[AMOUNT OF BENEFITS ATTRIBUTABLE TO CARE] represents compensation for cost of care during the relevant period and £[AMOUNT OF BENEFITS ATTRIBUTABLE TO LOSS OF MOBILITY] represents compensation for loss of mobility during the relevant period, in terms of the Social Security (Recovery of Benefits) Act 1997, together with the expenses of process to date as taxed [in full satisfaction of the craves **OR** in satisfaction of the [CRAVES SATISFIED BY OFFER]] of the initial writ.

IN RESPECT WHEREOF

....

[FIRM NAME]

[FIRM ADDRESS]

[Solicitor for the pursuer **OR**

Solicitor for the [PURSUER NUMBER] pursuer]

PURSUER'S OFFER MINUTE OF ACCEPTANCE COURT OF SESSION

IN THE COURT OF SESSION	
	Court Ref: [COURT REF]
MINUTE OF ACCEPTANCE OF PURSUER'S OFFER	
in the cause	
[NAME OF PURSUER], [(Company Number [NUMBER]), whose registered office is [ADDRESS] **OR** residing at [ADDRESS]]	
	Pursuer
against	
[NAME OF DEFENDER], [(Company Number [NUMBER]), whose registered office is [ADDRESS] **OR** residing at [ADDRESS]]	
	Defender

[SURNAME OF PERSON SIGNING] for the [NUMBER OF DEFENDER] defender states to the court that the [NUMBER OF DEFENDER] defender hereby accepts the pursuer's offer contained in the minute of pursuer's offer number [PROCESS NUMBER] of process [in full settlement of the conclusions **OR** in satisfaction of the [CONCLUSIONS SATISFIED BY THE PURSUER'S OFFER]] of the summons.

IN RESPECT WHEREOF

IN THE COURT OF SESSION
Court Ref: [COURT REFERENCE]

MINUTE OF ACCEPTANCE OF PURSUER'S OFFER
in the cause
[NAME OF PURSUER], PURSUER
And
[NAME OF DEFENDER], DEFENDER

[YEAR]

[FIRM NAME]
[FIRM REFERENCE]

PURSUER'S OFFER MINUTE OF ACCEPTANCE SHERIFF COURT

SHERIFFDOM OF [SHERIFFDOM] AT [COURT]	
[IN THE ALL SCOTLAND PERSONAL INJURY COURT]	
	Court Ref: [COURT REF]
MINUTE OF ACCEPTANCE OF PURSUER'S OFFER	
in the cause	
[NAME OF PURSUER], [(Company Number [NUMBER]), whose registered office is [ADDRESS] **OR** residing at [ADDRESS]]	
	Pursuer
against	
[NAME OF DEFENDER], [(Company Number [NUMBER]), whose registered office is [ADDRESS] **OR** residing at [ADDRESS]]	
	Defender

[SURNAME OF PERSON SIGNING] for the [NUMBER OF DEFENDER] defender states to the court that the [NUMBER OF DEFENDER] defender hereby accepts the pursuer's offer contained in the minute of pursuer's offer number [PROCESS NUMBER] of process [in full settlement of the craves **OR** in satisfaction of the [CRAVES SATISFIED BY THE PURSUER'S OFFER]] of the initial writ.

IN RESPECT WHEREOF

....

[FIRM NAME]

[FIRM ADDRESS]

[Solicitor for the defender **OR**

Solicitor for the [DEFENDER NUMBER] defender]

PURSUER'S OFFER MINUTE OF ACCEPTANCE SUBJECT TO CONTRIBUTION FROM CO-DEFENDER COURT OF SESSION

IN THE COURT OF SESSION	
	Court Ref: [COURT REF]
MINUTE OF ACCEPTANCE OF PURSUER'S OFFER	
in the cause	
[NAME OF PURSUER], [(Company Number [NUMBER]), whose registered office is [ADDRESS] **OR** residing at [ADDRESS]]	
	Pursuer
against	
(FIRST) [NAME OF FIRST DEFENDER], [(Company Number [NUMBER]), whose registered office is [ADDRESS] **OR** residing at [ADDRESS]]; (SECOND) [NAME OF SECOND DEFENDER], [(Company Number [NUMBER]), whose registered office is [ADDRESS] **OR** residing at [ADDRESS]]	
	Defender

[SURNAME OF PERSON SIGNING] for the [NUMBER OF DEFENDER] defender states to the court[, without prejudice to their whole rights and pleas,] that the [NUMBER OF DEFENDER] defender, on the condition that the [NUMBER OF OTHER DEFENDER] defender contributes [CONTRIBUTION SOUGHT FROM CO-DEFENDER], hereby accepts the pursuer's offer contained in the minute of pursuer's offer number [PROCESS NUMBER] of process [in full settlement of the conclusions **OR** in satisfaction of the [CONCLUSIONS SATISFIED BY THE PURSUER'S OFFER]] of the summons.

IN RESPECT WHEREOF

IN THE COURT OF SESSION
Court Ref: [COURT REFERENCE]

MINUTE OF ACCEPTANCE OF PURSUER'S OFFER
in the cause
[NAME OF PURSUER], PURSUER
And
[NAME OF DEFENDER], DEFENDER

[YEAR]

[FIRM NAME]
[FIRM REFERENCE]

PURSUER'S OFFER MINUTE OF ACCEPTANCE SUBJECT TO CONTRIBUTION FROM CO-DEFENDER SHERIFF COURT

SHERIFFDOM OF [SHERIFFDOM] AT [COURT]	
[IN THE ALL SCOTLAND PERSONAL INJURY COURT]	
	Court Ref: [COURT REF]
MINUTE OF ACCEPTANCE OF PURSUER'S OFFER	
in the cause	
[NAME OF PURSUER], [(Company Number [NUMBER]), whose registered office is [ADDRESS] **OR** residing at [ADDRESS]]	
	Pursuer
against	
(FIRST) [NAME OF FIRST DEFENDER], [(Company Number [NUMBER]), whose registered office is [ADDRESS] **OR** residing at [ADDRESS]]; (SECOND) [NAME OF SECOND DEFENDER], [(Company Number [NUMBER]), whose registered office is [ADDRESS] **OR** residing at [ADDRESS]]	
	Defender

[SURNAME OF PERSON SIGNING] for the [NUMBER OF DEFENDER] defender states to the court[, without prejudice to their whole rights and pleas,] that the [NUMBER OF DEFENDER] defender, on the condition that the [NUMBER OF OTHER DEFENDER] defender contributes [CONTRIBUTION SOUGHT FROM CO-DEFENDER], hereby accepts the pursuer's offer contained in the minute of pursuer's offer number [PROCESS NUMBER] of process [in full settlement of the craves of the initial writ **OR** in satisfaction of the [CRAVES SATISFIED BY THE PURSUER'S OFFER] of the initial writ].

IN RESPECT WHEREOF

....
[FIRM NAME]
[FIRM ADDRESS]
Solicitor for the [DEFENDER NUMBER] defender

PURSUER'S OFFER MINUTE OF WITHDRAWAL COURT OF SESSION

IN THE COURT OF SESSION	
	Court Ref: [COURT REF]
MINUTE OF WITHDRAWAL OF PURSUER'S OFFER	
in the cause	
[NAME OF PURSUER], [(Company Number [NUMBER]), whose registered office is [ADDRESS] **OR** residing at [ADDRESS]]	
	Pursuer
against	
[NAME OF DEFENDER], [(Company Number [NUMBER]), whose registered office is [ADDRESS] **OR** residing at [ADDRESS]]	
	Defender

[SURNAME OF PERSON SIGNING] for the pursuer states to the court that the pursuer withdraws the pursuer's offer contained in the minute of pursuer's offer number [NUMBER] of process.

IN RESPECT WHEREOF

IN THE COURT OF SESSION
Court Ref: [COURT REFERENCE]

MINUTE OF WITHDRAWAL OF PURSUER'S OFFER
in the cause
[NAME OF PURSUER], PURSUER
And
[NAME OF DEFENDER], DEFENDER

[YEAR]

[FIRM NAME]
[FIRM REFERENCE]

PURSUER'S OFFER MINUTE OF WITHDRAWAL SHERIFF COURT

SHERIFFDOM OF [SHERIFFDOM] AT [COURT]	
[IN THE ALL SCOTLAND PERSONAL INJURY COURT]	
	Court Ref: [COURT REF]
MINUTE OF WITHDRAWAL OF PURSUER'S OFFER	
in the cause	
[NAME OF PURSUER], [(Company Number [NUMBER]), whose registered office is [ADDRESS] **OR** residing at [ADDRESS]]	
	Pursuer
against	
[NAME OF DEFENDER], [(Company Number [NUMBER]), whose registered office is [ADDRESS] **OR** residing at [ADDRESS]]	
	Defender

[SURNAME OF PERSON SIGNING] for the pursuer states to the court that the pursuer withdraws the pursuer's offer contained in the minute of pursuer's offer number [NUMBER] of process.

IN RESPECT WHEREOF

....

[FIRM NAME]
[FIRM ADDRESS]
Solicitor for the pursuer

PURSUER'S OFFER NET OF BENEFITS COURT OF SESSION

IN THE COURT OF SESSION	
	Court Ref: [COURT REF]
MINUTE OF PURSUER'S OFFER	
in the cause	
[NAME OF PURSUER], [(Company Number [NUMBER]), whose registered office is [ADDRESS] **OR** residing at [ADDRESS]]	
	Pursuer
against	
[NAME OF DEFENDER], [(Company Number [NUMBER]), whose registered office is [ADDRESS] **OR** residing at [ADDRESS]]	
	Defender

[SURNAME OF PERSON SIGNING] for the pursuer states to the court, without prejudice to, and under reservation of their whole rights and pleas, under and in terms of Chapter Rule 34A.4 of the Rules of the Court of Session (as amended) the pursuer offered and hereby offers to accept from the [defender OR defenders jointly and severally] the sum of **[AMOUNT IN WORDS]** (£**[AMOUNT IN FIGURES]**) **STERLING**, free and net of any recoupment in terms of the Social Security (Recovery of Benefits) Act 1997, and inclusive of interest to the date of this offer, together with the expenses of process to date as taxed [in full satisfaction of the conclusions **OR** in satisfaction of the [CONCLUSIONS SATISFIED BY OFFER]] of the summons.

IN RESPECT WHEREOF

....

[FIRM NAME]

[FIRM ADDRESS]

[Solicitor for pursuer **OR**

Solicitor for [PURSUER NUMBER] pursuer]

in the cause

[NAME OF PURSUER], PURSUER

And
[NAME OF DEFENDER], DEFENDER

[YEAR]

[FIRM NAME]
[FIRM REFERENCE]

PURSUER'S OFFER NET OF BENEFITS SHERIFF COURT

SHERIFFDOM OF [SHERIFFDOM] AT [COURT]	
[IN THE ALL SCOTLAND PERSONAL INJURY COURT]	
	Court Ref: [COURT REF]
MINUTE OF PURSUER'S OFFER	
in the cause	
[NAME OF PURSUER], [(Company Number [NUMBER]), whose registered office is [ADDRESS] **OR** residing at [ADDRESS]]	
	Pursuer
against	
[NAME OF DEFENDER], [(Company Number [NUMBER]), whose registered office is [ADDRESS] **OR** residing at [ADDRESS]]	
	Defender

[SURNAME OF PERSON SIGNING] for the pursuer states to the court, without prejudice to, and under reservation of their whole rights and pleas, under and in terms of Chapter 27A.4 of the Ordinary Cause Rules 1993 (as amended) the pursuer offered and hereby offers to accept from the [defender OR defenders jointly and severally] the sum of **[AMOUNT IN WORDS] (£[AMOUNT IN FIGURES]) STERLING,** free and net of any recoupment in terms of the Social Security (Recovery of Benefits) Act 1997, and inclusive of interest to the date of this offer, together with the expenses of process to date as taxed [in full satisfaction of the craves **OR** in satisfaction of the [CRAVES SATISFIED BY OFFER]] of the initial writ.

IN RESPECT WHEREOF

....

[FIRM NAME]
[FIRM ADDRESS]
[Solicitor for pursuer **OR**
Solicitor for [PURSUER NUMBER] pursuer]

PURSUER'S OFFER STANDARD OFFER WITH NO BENEFITS
COURT OF SESSION

IN THE COURT OF SESSION	
	Court Ref: [COURT REF]
MINUTE OF PURSUER'S OFFER	
in the cause	
[NAME OF PURSUER], [(Company Number [NUMBER]), whose registered office is [ADDRESS] **OR** residing at [ADDRESS]]	
	Pursuer
against	
[NAME OF DEFENDER], [(Company Number [NUMBER]), whose registered office is [ADDRESS] **OR** residing at [ADDRESS]]	
	Defender

[SURNAME OF PERSON SIGNING] for the pursuer states to the court, without prejudice to, and under reservation of their whole rights and pleas, under and in terms of Chapter 34A.4 of the Rules of the Court of Session 1994 (as amended) the pursuer offered and hereby offers to accept from the [defender **OR** defenders jointly and severally] the sum of **[AMOUNT IN WORDS]** (£**[AMOUNT IN FIGURES]**) **STERLING** inclusive of interest to the date of this offer, together with the expenses of process to date as taxed [in full satisfaction of the conclusions **OR** in satisfaction of the [CONCLUSIONS SATISFIED BY OFFER]] of the summons.

IN RESPECT WHEREOF

IN THE COURT OF SESSION
Court Ref: [COURT REFERENCE]

MINUTE OF PURSUER'S OFFER
in the cause
[NAME OF PURSUER], PURSUER
And

[NAME OF DEFENDER], DEFENDER

[YEAR]

[FIRM NAME]
[FIRM REFERENCE]

PURSUER'S OFFER STANDARD OFFER WITH NO BENEFITS SHERIFF COURT

SHERIFFDOM OF [SHERIFFDOM] AT [COURT]	
[IN THE ALL SCOTLAND PERSONAL INJURY COURT]	
	Court Ref: [COURT REF]
MINUTE OF PURSUER'S OFFER	
in the cause	
[NAME OF PURSUER], [(Company Number [NUMBER]), whose registered office is [ADDRESS] **OR** residing at [ADDRESS]]	
	Pursuer
against	
[NAME OF DEFENDER], [(Company Number [NUMBER]), whose registered office is [ADDRESS] **OR** residing at [ADDRESS]]	
	Defender

[SURNAME OF PERSON SIGNING] for the pursuer states to the court, without prejudice to, and under reservation of his whole rights and pleas, under and in terms of Chapter 27A.4 of the Ordinary Cause Rules 1993 (as amended) the pursuer offered and hereby offers to accept from the [defender OR defenders jointly and severally] the sum of **[AMOUNT IN WORDS] (£[AMOUNT IN FIGURES]) STERLING** inclusive of interest to the date of this offer, together with the expenses of process to date as taxed [in full satisfaction of the craves **OR** in satisfaction of the [CRAVES SATISFIED BY OFFER]] of the initial writ.

IN RESPECT WHEREOF

....

[FIRM NAME]
[FIRM ADDRESS]
[Solicitor for the pursuer **OR**
Solicitor for the [PURSUER NUMBER] pursuer]

TENDER GROSS OF BENEFITS COURT OF SESSION

IN THE COURT OF SESSION	
	Court Ref: [COURT REF]
MINUTE OF TENDER FOR THE DEFENDER	
in the cause	
[NAME OF PURSUER], [(Company Number [NUMBER]), whose registered office is [ADDRESS] **OR** residing at [ADDRESS]]	
	Pursuer
against	
[NAME OF DEFENDER], [(Company Number [NUMBER]), whose registered office is [ADDRESS] **OR** residing at [ADDRESS]]	
	Defender

[SURNAME OF PERSON SIGNING FOR FIRST DEFENDER] for the [[NUMBER OF DEFENDER]] defender [and [SURNAME OF PERSON SIGNING FOR SECOND DEFENDER] for the [NUMBER OF DEFENDER] defender] [states **OR** hereby concur in stating] to the court that, without admitting liability and under reservation of their whole rights and pleas, the defender[s] hereby

[tender[s] to the [[NUMBER OF PURSUER]] pursuer the sum of **[AMOUNT IN WORDS] (£[AMOUNT IN FIGURES]) STERLING** [([inclusive **OR** exclusive] of the amount of £[AMOUNT IN FIGURES] paid by way of an interim payment)] of which £[AMOUNT OF BENEFITS ATTRIBUTABLE TO LOST EARNINGS] represents compensation for earnings lost during the relevant period, £[AMOUNT OF BENEFITS ATTRIBUTABLE TO CARE] represents compensation for the cost of care during the relevant period and £[AMOUNT OF BENEFITS ATTRIBUTABLE TO LOSS OF MOBILITY] represents compensation for loss of mobility during the relevant period, in terms of the Social Security (Recovery of Benefits) Act 1997, together with the expenses of process to date as taxed [in full satisfaction of the conclusions **OR** in satisfaction of the [CONCLUSIONS SATISFIED BY TENDER]] of the summons [so far as directed against this defender].]
OR

[I. tender[s] to the [[NUMBER OF PURSUER]] pursuer the sum of **[AMOUNT IN WORDS] (£[AMOUNT IN FIGURES]) STERLING** [([inclusive **OR** exclusive] of the amount of £[AMOUNT IN FIGURES] paid by way of an interim payment)] [so far as directed against this defender] with the expenses of process to the date hereof [in full satisfaction of the conclusions OR in satisfaction of the [CONCLUSIONS SATISFIED BY TENDER]] of the summons; and

II. states that, of the sum tendered to the [[NUMBER OF PURSUER]] of **[AMOUNT IN WORDS] (£[AMOUNT IN FIGURES]) STERLING,** the following sums shall be attributable to the heads of compensation in Schedule 2 to the Social Security (Recovery of Benefits) Act 1997:

(a) Compensation for earnings lost during the relevant period: £[AMOUNT ATTRIBUTABLE TO LOST EARNINGS].

(b) Compensation for cost of care during the relevant period: £[AMOUNT ATTRIBUTABLE TO CARE COSTS].

(c) Compensation for loss of mobility during the relevant period: £[AMOUNT ATTRIBUTABLE TO LOSS OF MOBILITY].]

IN RESPECT WHEREOF

IN THE COURT OF SESSION
Court Ref: [COURT REFERENCE]

MINUTE OF TENDER FOR THE DEFENDER
in the cause
[NAME OF PURSUER], PURSUER
And
[NAME OF DEFENDER], DEFENDER

[YEAR]

[FIRM NAME]
[FIRM REFERENCE]

TENDER GROSS OF BENEFITS SHERIFF COURT

	Court Ref: [COURT REF]
MINUTE OF TENDER	
in the cause	
[NAME OF PURSUER], [(Company Number [NUMBER]), whose registered office is [ADDRESS] **OR** residing at [ADDRESS]]	
	Pursuer
against	
[NAME OF DEFENDER], [(Company Number [NUMBER]), whose registered office is [ADDRESS] **OR** residing at [ADDRESS]]	
	Defender

[SURNAME OF PERSON SIGNING FOR FIRST DEFENDER] for the [[NUMBER OF DEFENDER]] defender [and [SURNAME OF PERSON SIGNING FOR SECOND DEFENDER] for the [NUMBER OF DEFENDER] defender] [states **OR** hereby concur in stating] to the court that, without admitting liability and under reservation of their whole rights and pleas, the defender[s] hereby
[tender[s] to the [[NUMBER OF PURSUER]] pursuer the sum of **[AMOUNT IN WORDS] (£[AMOUNT IN FIGURES]) STERLING** [([inclusive **OR** exclusive] of the amount of £[AMOUNT IN FIGURES] paid by way of an interim payment)] of which £[AMOUNT OF BENEFITS ATTRIBUTABLE TO LOST EARNINGS] represents compensation for earnings lost during the relevant period, £[AMOUNT OF BENEFITS ATTRIBUTABLE TO CARE] represents compensation for the cost of care during the relevant period and £[AMOUNT OF BENEFITS ATTRIBUTABLE TO LOSS OF MOBILITY] represents compensation for loss of mobility during the relevant period, in terms of the Social Security (Recovery of Benefits) Act 1997, together with the expenses of process to date as taxed [in full satisfaction of the craves **OR** in satisfaction of the [CRAVES SATISFIED BY TENDER]] of the initial writ [so far as directed against this defender].]
OR
[I. tender[s] to the [[NUMBER OF PURSUER]] pursuer the sum of

[AMOUNT IN WORDS] (£[AMOUNT IN FIGURES]) STERLING [([inclusive **OR** exclusive] of the amount of £[AMOUNT IN FIGURES] paid by way of an interim payment)] [so far as directed against this defender] with the expenses of process to the date hereof [in full satisfaction of the craves **OR** in satisfaction of the [CRAVES SATISFIED BY TENDER]] of the initial writ; and

II. states that, of the sum tendered to the [[NUMBER OF PURSUER]] of [AMOUNT IN WORDS] (£[AMOUNT IN FIGURES]) STERLING, the following sums shall be attributable to the heads of compensation in Schedule 2 to the Social Security (Recovery of Benefits) Act 1997:

(a) Compensation for earnings lost during the relevant period: £[AMOUNT ATTRIBUTABLE TO LOST EARNINGS].
(b) Compensation for cost of care during the relevant period: £[AMOUNT ATTRIBUTABLE TO CARE COSTS].
(c) Compensation for loss of mobility during the relevant period: £[AMOUNT ATTRIBUTABLE TO LOSS OF MOBILITY].]

IN RESPECT WHEREOF

....

[FIRM NAME]
[FIRM ADDRESS]
[Solicitor for the defender **OR**
Solicitor for the [DEFENDER NUMBER] defender]

TENDER HOUSTON TENDER GROSS OF BENEFITS COURT OF SESSION

IN THE COURT OF SESSION	
	Court Ref: [COURT REF]
MINUTE OF TENDER FOR THE DEFENDER	
in the cause	
[NAME OF PURSUER], [(Company Number [NUMBER]), whose registered office is [ADDRESS] **OR** residing at [ADDRESS]]	
	Pursuer
against	
[NAME OF DEFENDER], [(Company Number [NUMBER]), whose registered office is [ADDRESS] **OR** residing at [ADDRESS]]	
	Defender

[SURNAME OF PERSON SIGNING FOR DEFENDER] for the [NUMBER OF DEFENDER] defender states to the court that, without prejudice to and under reservation of their whole rights and pleas, the [NUMBER OF DEFENDER] defender hereby offers to accept a contribution from the [NUMBER OF OTHER DEFENDER] defender of [PROPORTION SOUGHT FROM OTHER DEFENDER] defender of any [damages **OR** sums] and expenses which the [[NUMBER OF PURSUER]] pursuer may be awarded in any joint and several decree against the defenders and that the [[NUMBER OF PURSUER]] pursuer shall be entitled to decree against the defenders jointly and severally for the sum of **[AMOUNT IN WORDS] (£[AMOUNT IN FIGURES]) STERLING,**
[of which £[AMOUNT OF BENEFITS ATTRIBUTABLE TO LOST EARNINGS] represents compensation for earnings lost during the relevant period, £[AMOUNT OF BENEFITS ATTRIBUTABLE TO CARE] represents compensation for the cost of care during the relevant period and £[AMOUNT OF BENEFITS ATTRIBUTABLE TO LOSS OF MOBILITY] represents compensation for loss of mobility during the relevant period, in terms of the Social Security (Recovery of Benefits) Act 1997, together with the expenses of process to date as taxed [in full satisfaction of

the conclusions **OR** in satisfaction of the [CONCLUSIONS SATISFIED BY TENDER]] of the summons.]

OR

[with the expenses of process to the date hereof in [in full satisfaction of the conclusions **OR** in satisfaction of the [CONCLUSIONS SATISFIED BY TENDER]] of the summons; and the [NUMBER OF DEFENDER] defender hereby states that, of the sum tendered to the [[NUMBER OF PURSUER]] of [AMOUNT IN WORDS] (£[AMOUNT IN FIGURES]) STERLING, the following sums shall be attributable to the heads of compensation in Schedule 2 to the Social Security (Recovery of Benefits) Act 1997:

(a) Compensation for earnings lost during the relevant period: £[AMOUNT ATTRIBUTABLE TO LOST EARNINGS].

(b) Compensation for cost of care during the relevant period: £[AMOUNT ATTRIBUTABLE TO CARE COSTS].

(c) Compensation for loss of mobility during the relevant period: £[AMOUNT ATTRIBUTABLE TO LOSS OF MOBILITY].]

IN RESPECT WHEREOF

IN THE COURT OF SESSION
Court Ref: [COURT REFERENCE]

MINUTE OF TENDER FOR THE DEFENDER
in the cause
[NAME OF PURSUER], PURSUER
And
[NAME OF DEFENDER], DEFENDER

[YEAR]

[FIRM NAME]
[FIRM REFERENCE]

TENDER HOUSTON TENDER GROSS OF BENEFITS SHERIFF COURT

SHERIFFDOM OF [SHERIFFDOM] AT [COURT]	
[IN THE ALL SCOTLAND PERSONAL INJURY COURT]	
	Court Ref: [COURT REF]
MINUTE OF TENDER	
in the cause	
[NAME OF PURSUER], [(Company Number [NUMBER]), whose registered office is [ADDRESS] **OR** residing at [ADDRESS]]	
	Pursuer
against	
[NAME OF DEFENDER], [(Company Number [NUMBER]), whose registered office is [ADDRESS] **OR** residing at [ADDRESS]]	
	Defender

[SURNAME OF PERSON SIGNING FOR DEFENDER] for the [NUMBER OF DEFENDER] defender states to the court that, without prejudice to and under reservation of their whole rights and pleas, the [NUMBER OF DEFENDER] defender hereby offers to accept a contribution from the [NUMBER OF OTHER DEFENDER] defender of [PROPORTION SOUGHT FROM OTHER DEFENDER] defender of any [damages **OR** sums] and expenses which the [[NUMBER OF PURSUER]] pursuer maybe awarded in any joint and several decree against the defenders and that the [[NUMBER OF PURSUER]] pursuer shall be entitled to decree against the defenders jointly and severally for the sum of **[AMOUNT IN WORDS] (£[AMOUNT IN FIGURES]) STERLING,**
[of which £[AMOUNT OF BENEFITS ATTRIBUTABLE TO LOST EARNINGS] represents compensation for earnings lost during the relevant period, £[AMOUNT OF BENEFITS ATTRIBUTABLE TO CARE] represents compensation for the cost of care during the relevant period and £[AMOUNT OF BENEFITS ATTRIBUTABLE TO LOSS OF MOBILITY]

represents compensation for loss of mobility during the relevant period, in terms of the Social Security (Recovery of Benefits) Act 1997, together with the expenses of process to date as taxed [in full satisfaction of the craves **OR** in satisfaction of the [CRAVES SATISFIED BY TENDER]] of the initial writ.] **OR**
[with the expenses of process to the date hereof in [in full satisfaction of the craves **OR** in satisfaction of the [CRAVES SATISFIED BY TENDER]] of the initial writ; and the [NUMBER OF DEFENDER] defender hereby states that, of the sum tendered to the [[NUMBER OF PURSUER]] pursuer of [AMOUNT IN WORDS] (£[AMOUNT IN FIGURES]) STERLING, the following sums shall be attributable to the heads of compensation in Schedule 2 to the Social Security (Recovery of Benefits) Act 1997:

(a) Compensation for earnings lost during the relevant period: £[AMOUNT ATTRIBUTABLE TO LOST EARNINGS].
(b) Compensation for cost of care during the relevant period: £[AMOUNT ATTRIBUTABLE TO CARE COSTS].
(c) Compensation for loss of mobility during the relevant period: £[AMOUNT ATTRIBUTABLE TO LOSS OF MOBILITY].]

IN RESPECT WHEREOF

....

[FIRM NAME]
[FIRM ADDRESS]
[Solicitor for the defender **OR**
Solicitor for the [DEFENDER NUMBER] defender]

TENDER HOUSTON TENDER NET OF BENEFITS COURT OF SESSION

IN THE COURT OF SESSION	
	Court Ref: [COURT REF]
MINUTE OF TENDER FOR THE DEFENDER	
in the cause	
[NAME OF PURSUER], [(Company Number [NUMBER]), whose registered office is [ADDRESS] **OR** residing at [ADDRESS]]	
	Pursuer
against	
[NAME OF DEFENDER], [(Company Number [NUMBER]), whose registered office is [ADDRESS] **OR** residing at [ADDRESS]]	
	Defender

[SURNAME OF PERSON SIGNING FOR DEFENDER] for the [NUMBER OF DEFENDER] defender states to the court that, without prejudice to and under reservation of their whole rights and pleas, the [NUMBER OF DEFENDER] defender hereby offers to accept a contribution from the [NUMBER OF OTHER DEFENDER] defender of [PROPORTION SOUGHT FROM OTHER DEFENDER] defender of any [damages **OR** sums] and expenses which the [[NUMBER OF PURSUER]] pursuer may be awarded in any joint and several decree against the defenders and that the [[NUMBER OF PURSUER]] pursuer shall be entitled to decree against the defenders jointly and severally for the sum of **[AMOUNT IN WORDS] (£[AMOUNT IN FIGURES]) STERLING,** [net of any liability that the defenders may have in terms of section 6 of the Social Security (Recovery of Benefits) Act 1997] together with the expenses of process to date as taxed [in full satisfaction of the conclusions **OR** in satisfaction of the [CONCLUSIONS SATISFIED BY TENDER]] of the summons.

IN RESPECT WHEREOF

IN THE COURT OF SESSION

Court Ref: [COURT REFERENCE]

MINUTE OF TENDER FOR THE DEFENDER
in the cause
[NAME OF PURSUER], PURSUER
And
[NAME OF DEFENDER], DEFENDER

[YEAR]

[FIRM NAME]
[FIRM REFERENCE]

TENDER HOUSTON TENDER NET OF BENEFITS SHERIFF COURT

SHERIFFDOM OF [SHERIFFDOM] AT [COURT]	
[IN THE ALL SCOTLAND PERSONAL INJURY COURT]	
	Court Ref: [COURT REF]
MINUTE OF TENDER	
in the cause	
[NAME OF PURSUER], [(Company Number [NUMBER]), whose registered office is [ADDRESS] **OR** residing at [ADDRESS]]	
	Pursuer
against	
[NAME OF DEFENDER], [(Company Number [NUMBER]), whose registered office is [ADDRESS] **OR** residing at [ADDRESS]]	
	Defender

[SURNAME OF PERSON SIGNING FOR DEFENDER] for the [NUMBER OF DEFENDER] defender states to the court that, without prejudice to and under reservation of their whole rights and pleas, the [NUMBER OF DEFENDER] defender hereby offers to accept a contribution from the [NUMBER OF OTHER DEFENDER] defender of [PROPORTION SOUGHT FROM OTHER DEFENDER] defender of any [damages **OR** sums] and expenses which the [[NUMBER OF PURSUER]] pursuer maybe awarded in any joint and several decree against the defenders and that the [[NUMBER OF PURSUER]] pursuer shall be entitled to decree against the defenders jointly and severally for the sum of **[AMOUNT IN WORDS] (£[AMOUNT IN FIGURES]) STERLING,** [net of any liability that the defenders may have in terms of section 6 of the Social Security (Recovery of Benefits) Act 1997] together with the expenses of process to date as taxed [in full satisfaction of the craves **OR** in satisfaction of the [CRAVES SATISFIED BY TENDER]] of the initial writ.

IN RESPECT WHEREOF

....

[FIRM NAME]
[FIRM ADDRESS]
[Solicitor for the defender **OR**
Solicitor for the [DEFENDER NUMBER] defender]

TENDER MINUTE OF ACCEPTANCE COURT OF SESSION

IN THE COURT OF SESSION	
	Court Ref: [COURT REF]
MINUTE OF ACCEPTANCE OF TENDER	
in the cause	
[NAME OF PURSUER], [(Company Number [NUMBER]), whose registered office is [ADDRESS] **OR** residing at [ADDRESS]]	
	Pursuer
against	
[NAME OF DEFENDER], [(Company Number [NUMBER]), whose registered office is [ADDRESS] **OR** residing at [ADDRESS]]	
	Defender

[SURNAME OF PERSON SIGNING] for the [[NUMBER OF PURSUER]] pursuer states to the court that the [[NUMBER OF PURSUER]] pursuer hereby accepts the tender contained in the minute of tender number [PROCESS NUMBER] of process [in full settlement of the conclusions **OR** in satisfaction of the [CONCLUSIONS SATISFIED BY THE TENDER]] of the summons.

IN RESPECT WHEREOF

IN THE COURT OF SESSION
Court Ref: [COURT REFERENCE]

MINUTE OF ACCEPTANCE OF TENDER
in the cause
[NAME OF PURSUER], PURSUER
And
[NAME OF DEFENDER], DEFENDER

[YEAR]

[FIRM NAME]
[FIRM REFERENCE]

TENDER MINUTE OF ACCEPTANCE SHERIFF COURT

SHERIFFDOM OF [SHERIFFDOM] AT [COURT]	
[IN THE ALL SCOTLAND PERSONAL INJURY COURT]	
	Court Ref: [COURT REF]
MINUTE OF ACCEPTANCE OF TENDER	
in the cause	
[NAME OF PURSUER], [(Company Number [NUMBER]), whose registered office is [ADDRESS] **OR** residing at [ADDRESS]]	
	Pursuer
against	
[NAME OF DEFENDER], [(Company Number [NUMBER]), whose registered office is [ADDRESS] **OR** residing at [ADDRESS]]	
	Defender

[SURNAME OF PERSON SIGNING] for the [[NUMBER OF PURSUER]] pursuer states to the court that the [[NUMBER OF PURSUER]] pursuer hereby accepts the tender contained in the minute of tender number [PROCESS NUMBER] of process [in full settlement of the craves **OR** in satisfaction of the [CRAVES SATISFIED BY THE TENDER]] of the initial writ.

IN RESPECT WHEREOF

································

[FIRM NAME]

[FIRM ADDRESS]

[Solicitor for the pursuer **OR**

Solicitor for the [PURSUER NUMBER] pursuer]

TENDER MINUTE OF WITHDRAWAL COURT OF SESSION

IN THE COURT OF SESSION	
	Court Ref: [COURT REF]
MINUTE OF WITHDRAWAL OF TENDER	
in the cause	
[NAME OF PURSUER], [(Company Number [NUMBER]), whose registered office is [ADDRESS] **OR** residing at [ADDRESS]]	
	Pursuer
against	
[NAME OF DEFENDER], [(Company Number [NUMBER]), whose registered office is [ADDRESS] **OR** residing at [ADDRESS]]	
	Defender

[SURNAME OF PERSON SIGNING] for the [[NUMBER OF DEFENDER]] defender states to the court that the [[NUMBER OF DEFENDER]] defender hereby withdraws the tender contained in the minute of tender number [PROCESS NUMBER] of process.

IN RESPECT WHEREOF

IN THE COURT OF SESSION
Court Ref: [COURT REFERENCE]

MINUTE OF WITHDRAWAL OF TENDER
in the cause
[NAME OF PURSUER], PURSUER
And
[NAME OF DEFENDER], DEFENDER

[YEAR]

[FIRM NAME]
[FIRM REFERENCE]

TENDER MINUTE OF WITHDRAWAL SHERIFF COURT

SHERIFFDOM OF [SHERIFFDOM] AT [COURT]	
[IN THE ALL SCOTLAND PERSONAL INJURY COURT]	
	Court Ref: [COURT REF]
MINUTE OF WITHDRAWAL OF TENDER	
in the cause	
[NAME OF PURSUER], [(Company Number [NUMBER]), whose registered office is [ADDRESS] **OR** residing at [ADDRESS]]	
	Pursuer
against	
[NAME OF DEFENDER], [(Company Number [NUMBER]), whose registered office is [ADDRESS] **OR** residing at [ADDRESS]]	
	Defender

[SURNAME OF PERSON SIGNING] for the [[NUMBER OF DEFENDER]] defender states to the court that the [[NUMBER OF DEFENDER]] defender hereby withdraws the tender contained in the minute of tender number [PROCESS NUMBER] of process.

IN RESPECT WHEREOF

....

[FIRM NAME]
[FIRM ADDRESS]
[Solicitor for the defender **OR**
Solicitor for the [DEFENDER NUMBER] defender]

TENDER NET OF BENEFITS COURT OF SESSION

IN THE COURT OF SESSION	
	Court Ref: [COURT REF]
MINUTE OF TENDER FOR THE DEFENDER	
in the cause	
[NAME OF PURSUER], [(Company Number [NUMBER]), whose registered office is [ADDRESS] **OR** residing at [ADDRESS]]	
	Pursuer
against	
[NAME OF DEFENDER], [(Company Number [NUMBER]), whose registered office is [ADDRESS] **OR** residing at [ADDRESS]]	
	Defender

[SURNAME OF PERSON SIGNING FOR FIRST DEFENDER] for the [[NUMBER OF DEFENDER]] defender [and [SURNAME OF PERSON SIGNING FOR SECOND DEFENDER] for the [NUMBER OF DEFENDER] defender] [states **OR** hereby concur in stating] to the court that, without admitting liability and under reservation of their whole rights and pleas, the defender[s] hereby tender[s] to the [[NUMBER OF PURSUER]] pursuer the sum of **[AMOUNT IN WORDS] (£[AMOUNT IN FIGURES]) STERLING** [[inclusive **OR** exclusive] of the amount of £[AMOUNT IN FIGURES] paid by way of an interim payment and] free and net of any recoupment in terms of section 6 of the Social Security (Recovery of Benefits) Act 1997, together with the expenses of process to date as taxed [in full satisfaction of the conclusions **OR** in satisfaction of the [CONCLUSIONS SATISFIED BY TENDER]] of the summons [so far as directed against this defender].

IN RESPECT WHEREOF

IN THE COURT OF SESSION
Court Ref: [COURT REFERENCE]

MINUTE OF TENDER FOR THE DEFENDER
in the cause
[NAME OF PURSUER], PURSUER
And
[NAME OF DEFENDER], DEFENDER

[YEAR]

[FIRM NAME]
[FIRM REFERENCE]

TENDER NET OF BENEFITS SHERIFF COURT

SHERIFFDOM OF [SHERIFFDOM] AT [COURT]	
[IN THE ALL SCOTLAND PERSONAL INJURY COURT]	
	Court Ref: [COURT REF]
MINUTE OF TENDER	
in the cause	
[NAME OF PURSUER], [(Company Number [NUMBER]), whose registered office is [ADDRESS] **OR** residing at [ADDRESS]]	
	Pursuer
against	
[NAME OF DEFENDER], [(Company Number [NUMBER]), whose registered office is [ADDRESS] **OR** residing at [ADDRESS]]	
	Defender

[SURNAME OF PERSON SIGNING FOR FIRST DEFENDER] for the [[NUMBER OF DEFENDER]] defender [and [SURNAME OF PERSON SIGNING FOR SECOND DEFENDER] for the [NUMBER OF DEFENDER] defender] [states **OR** hereby concur in stating] to the court that, without admitting liability and under reservation of their whole rights and pleas, the defender[s] hereby tender[s] to the [[NUMBER OF PURSUER]] pursuer the sum of **[AMOUNT IN WORDS] (£[AMOUNT IN FIGURES]) STERLING** [[inclusive **OR** exclusive] of the amount of £[AMOUNT IN FIGURES] paid by way of an interim payment and] free and net of any recoupment in terms of section 6 of the Social Security (Recovery of Benefits) Act 1997, together with the expenses of process to date as taxed [in full satisfaction of the craves **OR** in satisfaction of the [CRAVES SATISFIED BY TENDER]] of the initial writ [so far as directed against this defender].

IN RESPECT WHEREOF

....

[FIRM NAME]

[FIRM ADDRESS]
[Solicitor for the defender **OR**
Solicitor for the [DEFENDER NUMBER] defender]

TENDER STANDARD TENDER WITH NO BENEFITS COURT OF SESSION

IN THE COURT OF SESSION	
	Court Ref: [COURT REF]
MINUTE OF TENDER FOR THE DEFENDER	
in the cause	
[NAME OF PURSUER], [(Company Number [NUMBER]), whose registered office is [ADDRESS] **OR** residing at [ADDRESS]]	
	Pursuer
against	
[NAME OF DEFENDER], [(Company Number [NUMBER]), whose registered office is [ADDRESS] **OR** residing at [ADDRESS]]	
	Defender

[SURNAME OF PERSON SIGNING FOR FIRST DEFENDER] for the [[NUMBER OF DEFENDER]] defender [and [SURNAME OF PERSON SIGNING FOR SECOND DEFENDER] for the [NUMBER OF DEFENDER] defender] [states **OR** hereby concur in stating] to the court that, without admitting liability and under reservation of their whole rights and pleas, the defender[s] hereby tender[s] to the [[NUMBER OF PURSUER]] pursuer the sum of **[AMOUNT IN WORDS] (£[AMOUNT IN FIGURES]) STERLING** [[inclusive **OR** exclusive] of the amount of £[AMOUNT IN FIGURES] paid by way of an interim payment], together with the expenses of process to date as taxed [in full satisfaction of the conclusions **OR** in satisfaction of the [CONCLUSIONS SATISFIED BY TENDER]] of the summons [so far as directed against this defender].

IN RESPECT WHEREOF

IN THE COURT OF SESSION
Court Ref: [COURT REFERENCE]

MINUTE OF TENDER FOR THE DEFENDER

in the cause
[NAME OF PURSUER], PURSUER
And
[NAME OF DEFENDER], DEFENDER

[YEAR]

[FIRM NAME]
[FIRM REFERENCE]

TENDER STANDARD TENDER WITH NO BENEFITS SHERIFF COURT

SHERIFFDOM OF [SHERIFFDOM] AT [COURT]	
[IN THE ALL SCOTLAND PERSONAL INJURY COURT]	
	Court Ref: [COURT REF]
MINUTE OF TENDER	
in the cause	
[NAME OF PURSUER], [(Company Number [NUMBER]), whose registered office is [ADDRESS] **OR** residing at [ADDRESS]]	
	Pursuer
against	
[NAME OF DEFENDER], [(Company Number [NUMBER]), whose registered office is [ADDRESS] **OR** residing at [ADDRESS]]	
	Defender

[SURNAME OF PERSON SIGNING FOR FIRST DEFENDER] for the [[NUMBER OF DEFENDER]] defender [and [SURNAME OF PERSON SIGNING FOR SECOND DEFENDER] for the [NUMBER OF DEFENDER] defender] [states OR hereby concur in stating] to the court that, without admitting liability and under reservation of their whole rights and pleas, the defender[s] hereby tender[s] to the [[NUMBER OF PURSUER]] pursuer the sum of [AMOUNT IN WORDS] (£[AMOUNT IN FIGURES]) STERLING [[inclusive OR exclusive] of the amount of £[AMOUNT IN FIGURES] paid by way of an interim payment], together with the expenses of process to date as taxed [in full satisfaction of the craves OR in satisfaction of the [CRAVES SATISFIED BY TENDER]] of the initial writ [so far as directed against this defender].

IN RESPECT WHEREOF

....

[FIRM NAME]

[FIRM ADDRESS]
[Solicitor for the defender **OR**
Solicitor for the [DEFENDER NUMBER] defender]

TENDER WILLIAMSON TENDER COURT OF SESSION

IN THE COURT OF SESSION	
	Court Ref: [COURT REF]
MINUTE OF TENDER FOR THE DEFENDER	
in the cause	
[NAME OF PURSUER], [(Company Number [NUMBER]), whose registered office is [ADDRESS] **OR** residing at [ADDRESS]]	
	Pursuer
against	
[NAME OF DEFENDER], [(Company Number [NUMBER]), whose registered office is [ADDRESS] **OR** residing at [ADDRESS]]	
	Defender

[SURNAME OF PERSON SIGNING FOR DEFENDER] for the [NUMBER OF DEFENDER] defender states to the court that, without prejudice to and under reservation of their whole rights and pleas, the [NUMBER OF DEFENDER] defender hereby offers to the [NUMBER OF OTHER DEFENDER] defender to admit liability to make [reparation **OR** payment] to the pursuer jointly and severally but only on the basis that the defenders will be liable *inter se* to contribute to towards any [damages **OR** sums] and expenses awarded to the pursuer[s] in the proportions of [PROPORTION OFFERED BY DEFENDER] by the [NUMBER OF DEFENDER] defender and [PROPORTION SOUGHT FROM OTHER DEFENDER] by the [NUMBER OF OTHER DEFENDER].

IN RESPECT WHEREOF

IN THE COURT OF SESSION
Court Ref: [COURT REFERENCE]

MINUTE OF TENDER FOR THE DEFENDER
in the cause
[NAME OF PURSUER], PURSUER

And
[NAME OF DEFENDER], DEFENDER

[YEAR]

[FIRM NAME]
[FIRM REFERENCE]

TENDER WILLIAMSON TENDER SHERIFF COURT

SHERIFFDOM OF [SHERIFFDOM] AT [COURT]	
[IN THE ALL SCOTLAND PERSONAL INJURY COURT]	
	Court Ref: [COURT REF]
MINUTE OF TENDER	
in the cause	
[NAME OF PURSUER], [(Company Number [NUMBER]), whose registered office is [ADDRESS] **OR** residing at [ADDRESS]]	
	Pursuer
against	
[NAME OF DEFENDER], [(Company Number [NUMBER]), whose registered office is [ADDRESS] **OR** residing at [ADDRESS]]	
	Defender

[SURNAME OF PERSON SIGNING FOR DEFENDER] for the [NUMBER OF DEFENDER] defender states to the court that, without prejudice to and under reservation of their whole rights and pleas, the [NUMBER OF DEFENDER] defender hereby offers to the [NUMBER OF OTHER DEFENDER] defender to admit liability to make [reparation **OR** payment] to the pursuer jointly and severally but only on the basis that the defenders will be liable *inter se* to contribute to towards any [damages **OR** sums] and expenses awarded to the pursuer[s] in the proportions of [PROPORTION OFFERED BY DEFENDER] by the [NUMBER OF DEFENDER] defender and [PROPORTION SOUGHT FROM OTHER DEFENDER] by the [NUMBER OF OTHER DEFENDER].

IN RESPECT WHEREOF

....

[FIRM NAME]
[FIRM ADDRESS]
[Solicitor for the defender **OR**
Solicitor for the [DEFENDER NUMBER] defender]

Index

Index entries relating to the text are given by paragraph number; those relating to appendices have the prefix 'App' followed by page number.